This Is Grime

Words Hattie Collins / Images Olivia Rose

HODDER &
STOUGHTON

This

is Grime

First published in Great Britain in 2016
by Hodder & Stoughton
An Hachette UK company

1

Text Copyright © Hattie Collins, 2016
Images © Olivia Rose, 2016

Design by Laura Liggins

The right of Hattie Collins to be identified as the Author of the Work has been asserted by her in accordance with the Copyright, Designs and Patents Act 1988.

All rights reserved. No part of this publication may be reproduced, stored in a retrieval system, or transmitted, in any form or by any means without the prior written permission of the publisher, nor be otherwise circulated in any form of binding or cover other than that in which it is published and without a similar condition being imposed on the subsequent purchaser.

A CIP catalogue record for this title is available from the British Library

Trade Paperback ISBN 9781473639270
eBook ISBN 9781473639294

All films processed and hand printed by Robin Bell

Printed and bound by Firmengruppe APPL, aprinta druck, Wemding, Germany

Hodder & Stoughton policy is to use papers that are natural, renewable and recyclable products and made from wood grown in sustainable forests. The logging and manufacturing processes are expected to conform to the environmental regulations of the country of origin.

Hodder & Stoughton Ltd
Carmelite House
50 Victoria Embankment
London EC4Y 0DZ

www.hodder.co.uk

Dedicated to...

My mum (for her love of writing), my dad (for his love of photography),
Jill, Jake, Alice, Jason, Ruben, Issie, Jez, Jennie, Sonny, Scout.
– Hattie Collins

My granny (for her unconditional support of even my wildest ideas)
and to Mum, Dad, Nick, Georgia, Joe, Jack, Richard and Fruity Polo 506k
(the *Thriller* to my *Dangerous* and the best trouble I almost got myself into).
– Olivia Rose

R.I.P. Richard Antwi, Esco, N.E., Skyjuice, TNT AKA Trend, Slinga,
Bianca Foster, Mark Duggan.

#BlackLivesMatter

contents

010 GRIMELINE: The Beginning
022 Lethal Bizzle on 'Pow!'
044 Pay As U Go
048 Danny & Target on Style
052 Roll Deep
064 N.A.S.T.Y. Crew
074 Terror Danjah
076 Wot Do U Call It?
080 Wiley
096 Dizzee
112 Kano
122 Jammer
132 Mizz Beats on Depression
134 Chantelle Fiddy
138 Documenting Grime
152 Channel U
154 Pirate Radio
160 Plastician on Dubstep
162 Eskimo Dance & Sidewinder
166 Visualising Grime
172 Forums
174 Rhythm Division
176 Durrty Goodz
180 Crazy Titch
186 Titch on Religion
188 Clashing and Beef

196 The Adenugas
207 Skepta
212 JME
214 Sian & Julie on Sian & Julie
216 JME & MSM Engineer on Fruity Loops
226 GRIMELINE: The Middle
236 Ironik on Violence
242 Ghetts on Religion
248 NoLay
250 Form 696
252 This Is Not Grime
258 Eskimo Dance UK Tour 2016

266 GRIMELINE: Today and Tomorrow
272 Go On, Go On Then, Draw For The Tool
280 Bonkaz & Stormzy on Rap V. MCing
284 Lioness, Nolay, NY & Shystie on Inequality
288 Grime and the US
296 Blakie on Ambition
300 Novelist on Pirate
304 Stormzy
310 Stormzy on Religion
314 The Future

14 years ago, from the bowels of Bow E3, the voice of a generation emerged, blinking furiously under the glare of Canary Wharf's aggressively gleaming paean to financial power.

It was dark, it was angry, it was loud, it was unapologetic.

It was innately provocative, it was fiercely independent.

It was the brittle sound of disillusionment, resentment and despair, but also the voice of hope...

It was Grime. This Is Grime.

Punk. Reggae. Dancehall. Jungle. Garage. Crack-cocaine. Thatcher's Britain. 9/11. The Internet. The Analogue. DIY. Major labels. Minor labels. Synths. Rinse. Target. Triton. Club EQ. Deja Vu. Mystic FM. Kool FM. Palace Pavilion. Sidewinder. Slimzee. Geeneus. Genius. The Godafather. Donaeo. God's Gift. Bow. Creeper. Eskimo. Crazy Titch. Terror Danjah. Durrty Goodz. E3. E14. Plaistow. Wilehouse. Newham. Bow. N.A.S.T.Y. The Basement. Lord of the Mics. Lord of the Decks. Risky Roadz. MSN. MSM. JME. BBK. Fruity Loops. Music House. Channel U. 1Xtra. Pay As U Go. Waltham Forest College. Bow School. Three Flats. Limewire. Qubase. Skibadee. *Functions On The Low.* Wiley. Will. Bill. Dizzee. Diz. Raskit. Devons Road. Ruff Sqwad. Youth Club. *Destruction VIP.* Risky Roadz. Run The Roads. *Wot Do U Call It. Boy In The Corner. Treddin' On Thin Ice.* Rhythm Division. DJ Cameo. Commander B. East Connection. *Cop Back. Ice Rink. Terrible.* Tape packs. Dubplates. Pulse X. A 16. An 8. A 32. 138. Step 140. Major Ace. Mac 10. Maxwell D. Youngster. Raw Mission. Double O. Nicki Slim Ting. Trim. Trimble. Taliban Trim. An 8. A 16. A 32. 138 Step. 140. Major Ace. Mac 10. Maxwell D. Musical Mob. Youth Clubs. Youngster. Kylea. Wiley. Will. Bill.

Told by the people who created it, for the people who live it...

This. Is. Grime.

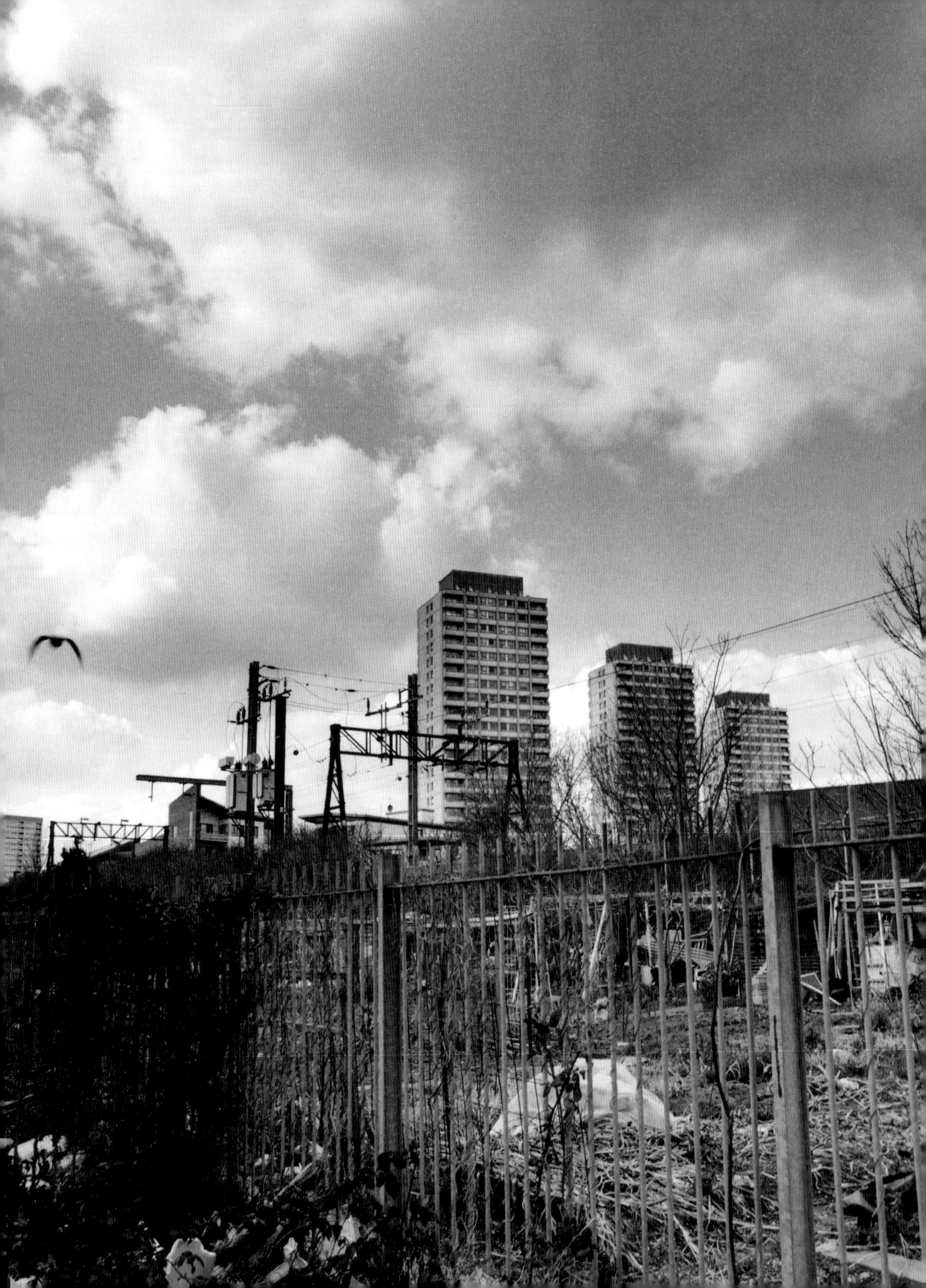

I'm From A Place

Richard Cowie (Wiley's dad) This all came from a bad place: people stabbing, robbing, guns, young people hustling drugs, bad parents. You name it. This whole thing, it came from these kids rising out of the ashes.

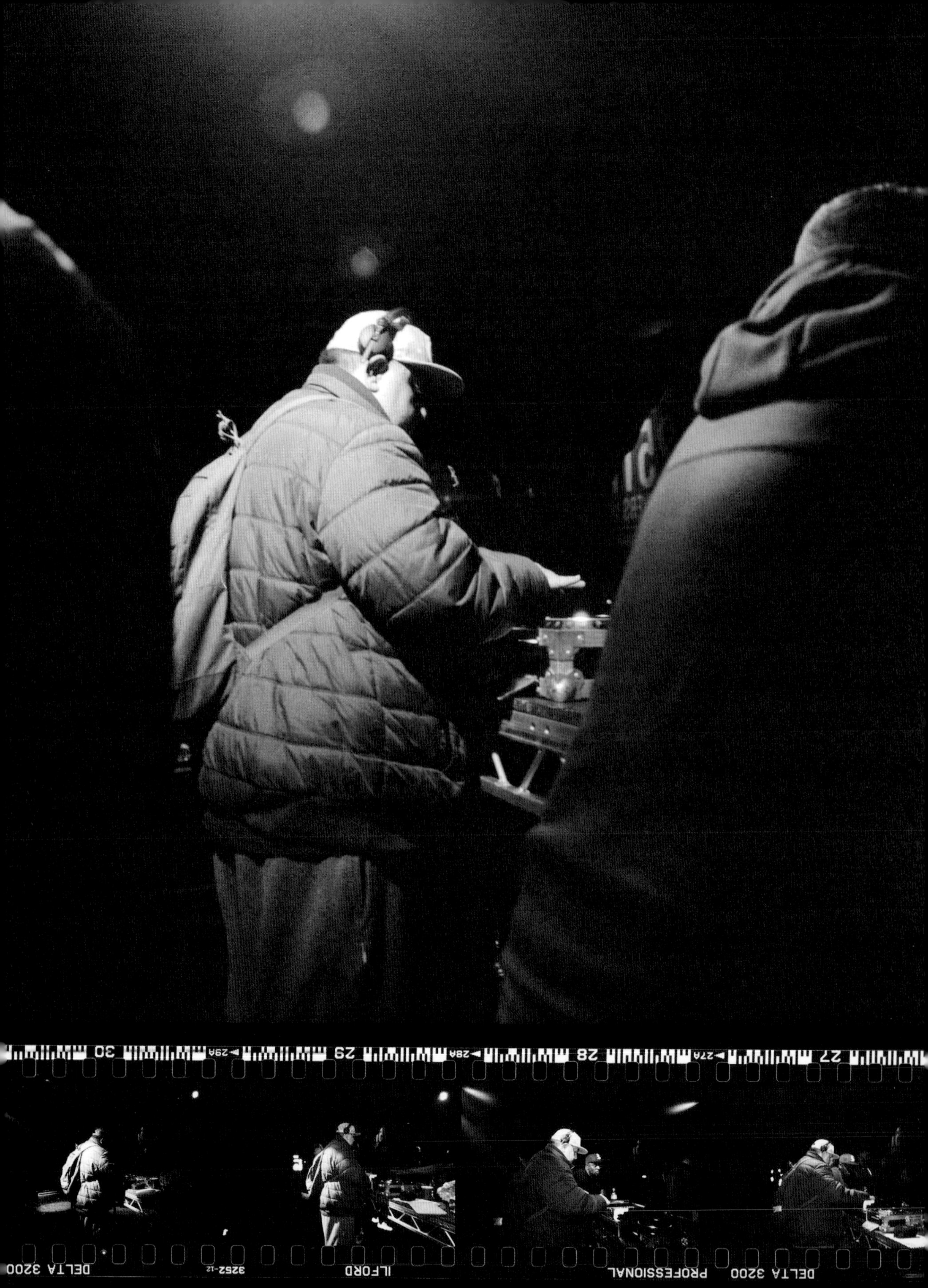
DELTA 3200
ILFORD
PROFESSIONAL
DELTA 3200

Queenie (Jammer's mum) He's always loved music. The first music he ever heard, the day after he was born, was his dad's first release with his band. I had this cassette player in the hospital with my headphones, and the day after Jahmek was born, I put the headphones on the pillow next to him and turned the music on. He was one day old.

Richard Cowie Jammer's dad I know. Footsie's dad I know. Footsie's dad, well, I was in a band with Footsie's dad. That's how it all started with Kylea [Wiley, Richard's son] as well; his bedroom was our rehearsal room, before he was born. There's a video somewhere of me and my band performing in Tunbridge Wells, and Kylea's at the front, tapping the tambourine. He was about two or three years old, tapping along to this reggae.

Queenie Even in his cot, he had a radio.

Richard Cowie I had a lot of instruments in my place: drums – Footsie's dad's drums – bass guitar, a piano. One day I was standing by the door and I watched him climb out of the cot, get down to the floor and get to the instruments to bang on the drums. He wasn't much more than a baby at that point.

Footsie I told my dad who his [Wiley's] dad was and he said, 'Yeah man, me tek you there nuff time.' 'I was there, yeah.' So I was there with Will, running around as kids, I just don't really remember it. Do you know how many kids, before they grew up to do anything, that I knew through my dad knowing their parents? Jammer and my dad, they went to Sunday school together as kids. So yeah, man, we've known each other *before* before. It's so deep. Sometimes I think I'm not doing nothing special, other than carrying on what was already done. That's what's important, to carry it on.

Jammer The other day I came home and my dad was sitting down with D Double's dad in the front room. My dad went to school with Double's dad. They were friends.

Footsie My dad taught Wiley how to play the drums. The legacies are so... it's even out of our hands, in fact. We're just trying to take something and carry it on. I can't tell you anything my dad doesn't know – he's done it all, he's travelled, it just wasn't so documented in his day. But if you had blogs, or if my dad had Snapchat back in the day, he would have been banging. He understands what we do, so to have that support really helped.

Wiley They was in a band, they did exactly the same thing as us, but they did it on a smaller scale – no, not a smaller scale 'cause they was sick musicians, they just didn't get the same recognition. My dad used to work with Footsie's dad and a few other people that influenced me. They had a little band and they would play at one or two little hippy festivals near Tunbridge Wells. All this just came from wanting to do what him and his mates were doing.

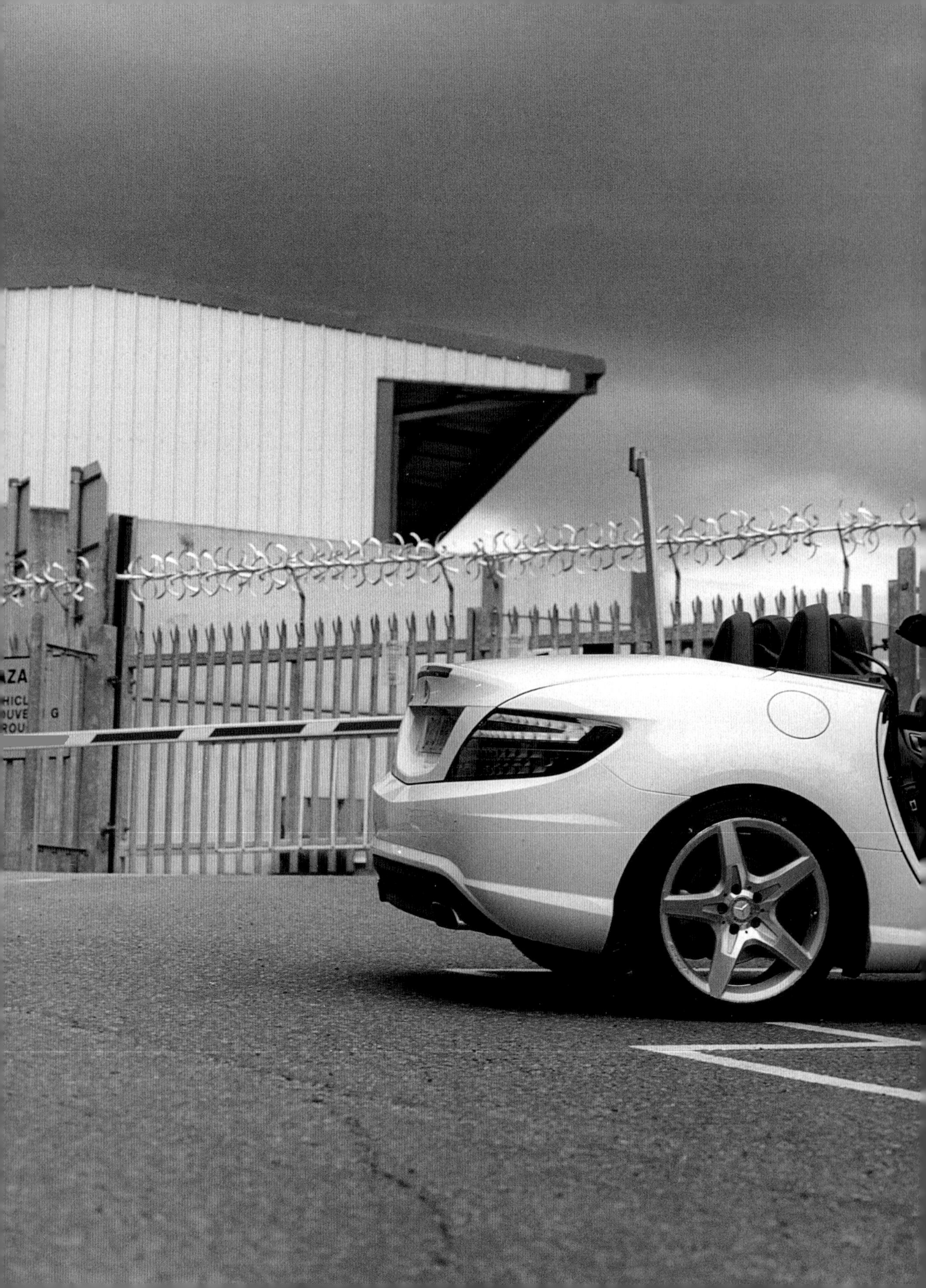

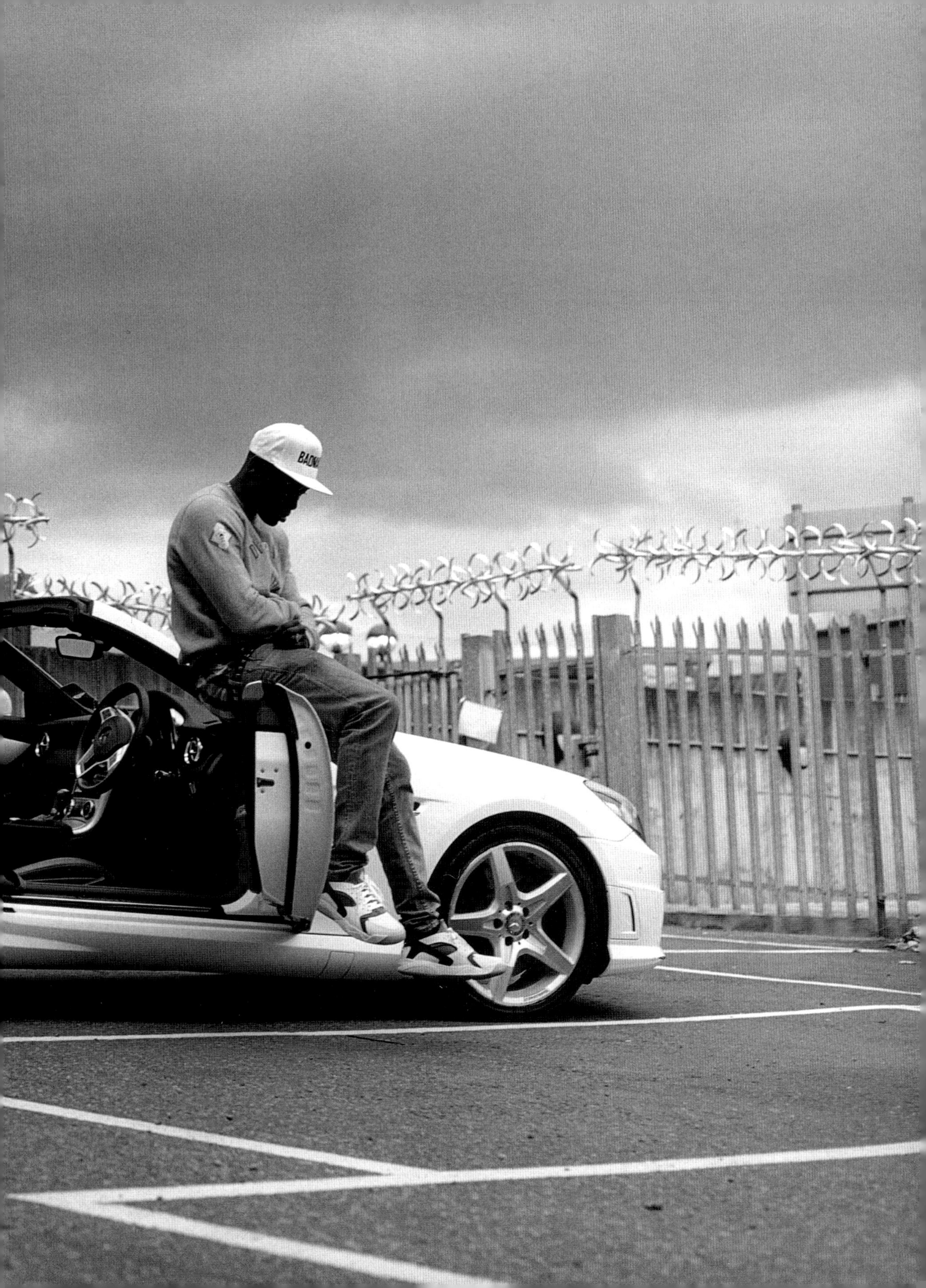

Jammer I started out in East London, playing music from seven years old, but I didn't take it seriously. At school, I was unsettled. The only thing I did like was the music class. That was evident throughout my whole school journey. I liked poems and I liked writing poems. I've actually got a picture of one of my poems I wrote in school. Someone found it and sent it to me the other day; it was about when Dunblane happened and I wrote a poem about it. They put it up all around the school and gave it to parents and my mum framed it. That was my first thing that I knew I had a skill to put words together.

Kano I think music was always there, and also a talent for reciting lyrics. My uncles always said that when I was small I'd hear a song and I'd be able to sing it straight away. Going to Jamaica was when I fell in love with music. I remember writing songs with my cousin Karis in one little place in Runaway Bay. Music was always around. My uncles used to play music in the house; they were really into their soundsystems.

DJ Target When we were about ten, we made a rap group. That's what we wanted to do. Wiley's dad was a musician and had connections, we thought he would hook us up. I used to rap, my name was Lil D! Then that turned into DJing, and into producing, for me. For others, it became about MCing.

Tinchy Stryder Before there was Ruff Sqwad, there was me, Dirty, Words and Charms. We had a crew called All 4 One. We got the name from one of one of my sister's Soul 4 Real posters. We thought 'All 4 One' sounded cool. We used to do loads of tapes in my room, that's why I still thank my mum so much, 'cause in that small house in Bow, in my small room that I shared with my brother, that's how we got started on the scene.

Mikey J (producer) It was the youth clubs. We used to meet up and spit.

Tinchy Stryder We was always in youth club, Link Centre, just off Devons Road. Me, Dizzee, a lot of us that would end up in Ruff Sqwad. We were just kids, mucking about.

Lethal B I never thought it was gonna be a career, it was just fun, just something else to do. Me and Ozzie B went to school with another guy called Jonathan who DJ'd and we would just go round to his and do tapes of us spitting lyrics. Then we'd go and listen to ourselves and pass the tapes around school. That's all it was. It was more about fun and something to do. It was never something I thought I'd end up doing, but all that time we spent practicing, writing, spitting, doing tapes was enhancing and perfecting our skills without us even realising.

D Double E I used to do a bit of dancing, but more sort of body-popping, jump up in the air and come down, go back up. All of that. I was that guy. In primary school we had to do a play or something and I was Michael Jackson. I done a performance

Footsie and Footsie's Dad, King Original – Ace Hotel, Shoreditch, E1

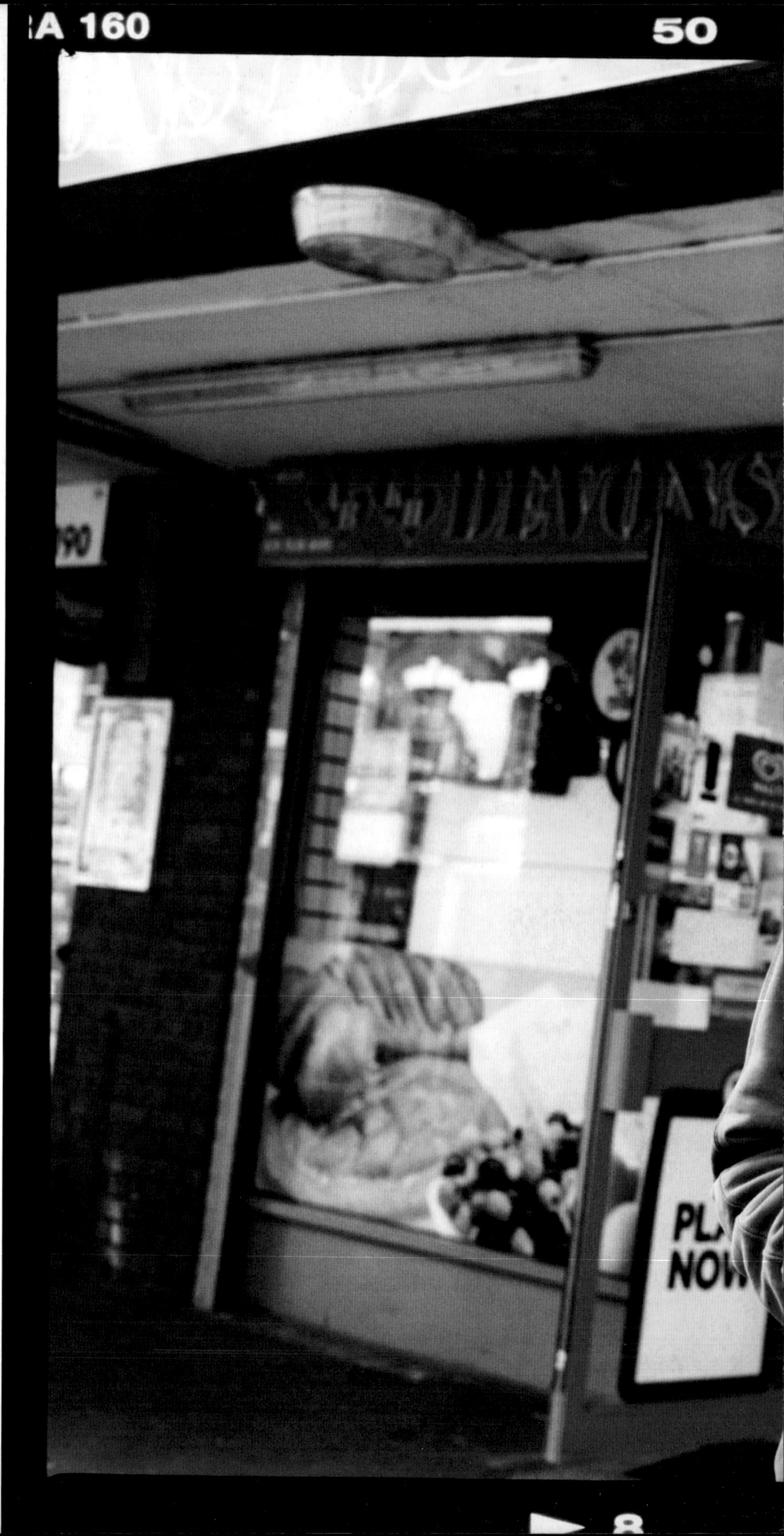
50
8

KODAK PORTRA 160
STAR IN THE
OFF LICENCE
GAS
CABLE
WATER
RENT

and I done the Moonwalk and I just smashed it, man. I was a mover! All of that technique has gone into my bars. It's in the riddim, it's there [points to chest]. You can tell by the way some people bop their head. If you meet a drummer, the way the man is drumming the ting, the beat is going through them different. Without playing nothing, they're listening to the beat on a next tek. You know them ones? I do bust moves now and again still [laughs].

Footsie I came into the music through Esco. In the early years, he bought Mac 10 to my house. Esco and Double, they was the first two people that heard my music and said, 'Yo, you're on some next shit.' They had heard me just local, just on the block. I knew Double from kids, he lived around the corner from me. Double was like a local youth centre legend, he was getting reloads *before*, before, before. The first time I met Dubz was in a house rave maybe. I'd seen him about for years and then one day we must have started speaking.

Terror Danjah Me and Double, I remember the first day I saw him in school, around 1992 times. I must have been the year above him at school so he must have been in the first year. He had a pony tail and the same box [cut] that he has now. You can never forget him as a character, never. The first thing he said to me was some weird noise he was doing at the time. From that, I've always been cool with Dee.

Tinchy Stryder I first started MCing in the six weeks' holidays when I went into Year Seven and we started making music together probably around thirteen, fourteen. My mum and dad all of these people into my tiny bedroom. We'd push the bunkbeds to the side, there would be so many of us in there. Dizzee used to come, loads of us, just making tapes. To get upstairs, you had to walk through the front room. My mum could have said, 'No, this ain't the place.' I'll always thank her for letting us make music at home.

Double O Lethal B, I remember him coming to my aunt and uncle's [Walton Jay] house, St Mary's Road in Leyton. That yard there was legendary. You had everyone coming there; Shabba, Skibadee, Heartless Crew, Lethal B, Tinie, later on. Waltham Road. It was like a youth centre, everyone passed through, you could gossip, you could mix, bump into people. Anyone will tell you that.

Kano Me and Dean [Demon] were proper mates before music, from playscheme and football. That field over there [points]. We used to play football together every week for our district team. His house was right next to 69 Manor Road; I was Plaistow, he was Stratford, Corporation Street. We were proper tight, innit.

Double O Everyone grew up in the same area, it's all mates. Me and Flow Dan, we went to school together – Holy Family – it was one of the worst schools around. He used to knock for me in the morning and we would go to school together. He's been there since day one. We went to Ayia Napa in 2001, just after he joined Pay As U Go and he was so hype. He wasn't even a known member then, so he was getting fed scraps but he was happy. A lot of people have come a long way.

Crazy Titch I knew Mac 10 as a kid 'cause there was like three black families in Plaistow when I was growing up, and their's was one of them. So our parents knew each other, the kids knew each other. I used to hang out with Mac 10's brother Marcus [Nasty], when I was about ten, around '93, '94.

Kano I bought D Double E to one of my mate's houses, just up there, Ginger's place. We used to make tapes in there all the time. Back then, D Double E was the biggest thing to me. The biggest. I remember MCing a lot, at every opportunity I could get. And writing lyrics. Something I don't really do anymore is just write lyrics for no reason. It's always for a song or a verse or a feature. I miss that.

Stormin I knew Sharky through my mate, Jamie, and Sharky was friends with Marcus and Demon. So that's how we all met. Armour was mates with Dizzee and Armour was my friend, but I also knew Dizzee, we was good friends from young, he lived near my sister's family and whatnot. So I introduced Dizzee to Sharky and they got to know each other, they got on well.

Kano Sharky used to come to my house to write. Come round, sit in the bedroom, he's got his book, I've got my book. No BlackBerries, no phones, just pad and pen. I used to love it.

Ruff Sqwad reformed, L to R: Slix, Prince Rapid, Tinchy Stryder, Dirty Danger, Fuda Guy

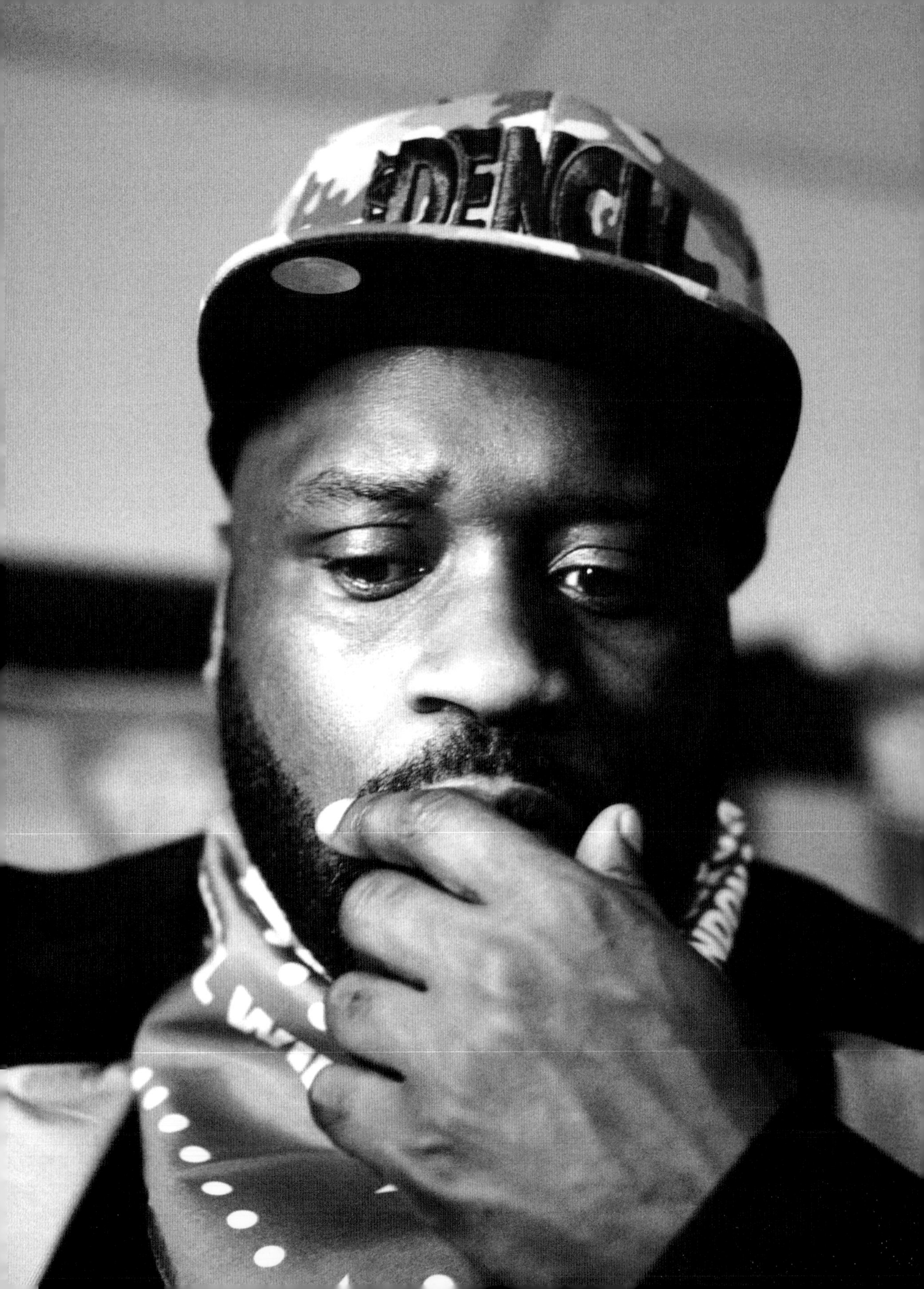

Lethal Bizzle on Pow!

Lethal Bizzle 'Pow!' was made out of pure frustration. It was around 2003. After More Fire Crew, I had to swallow my pride. I went back on pirate radio, writing bars everyday, going to any station I could, and my name started building. Wiley called my name out, and I realised I was causing some heat. We had the clash and off the back of that I knew I needed to get a big record ready. I met Dexplicit in Tottenham, Heat FM, he gave me a CD of 20 beats. The 'Pow!' beat was on there and I knew I had to get all the man dem to do their hottest 8 bars on it. I kept procrastinating about who to put on it until it got to February 2004. Dizzee had won the Mercury and we all thought, 'Yes they're all coming to sign us now, we're gone again.' But nothing happened. Grime got this terrible press, we were all gangstas, no one wanted to work with us. I thought 'Fuck this' and I set up Lethal Bizzle Records, did the tune, paid the man dem to get them to Commander B's studio in Walthamstow. No one liked the beat – the irony. Everyone was mocking it, even D Double. The majority of people did it out of love and respect for me. So we did it and Commander B played it on his Choice show, the hub of grime then and it went off. Channel U had just come in, so I got Mo Ali to do a video. When the video came on U, that's when it went nuts around the country. Bookings were going mad, we got reports saying the song was causing fights and riots [laughs]. Richard Antwi (RIP) got hold of me and he got a deal for it. Within ten months it was signed and at number eleven. Another reason I did 'Pow!' was that I wanted to do another big song that didn't involve Wiley. He had so much power, everything then was either a Wiley beat or Wiley co-signed. He gave me the co-sign; by clashing me, he put me back on, especially after More Fire. He knew I was on his toes. So I wanted to make a song and not put the bait MCs on there – Kano, Wiley, Doogz. I got members from all the major crews on there – N.A.S.T.Y., East Connection, Roll Deep, Flow Dan and Jamakabi. I think that caused a bit of conflict in their team, 'cause it was proper war with me and Wiley then. But yeah, 'Pow!', it was all chess moves [laughs]. It was sick, I wish I could relive that time – most of it.

Opposite: A pensive Lethal B backstage with Eskimo Dance – Red Bull Culture Clash 2016, o2 Arena, SE10

It Ain't Safe

Wretch 32 We're writing to escape. If you listen deep into the lyrics, there's probably a lot of cries for help in there.

Crazy Titch Sometimes I think I was born in the wrong time, in the wrong place. I just endorsed violence. I could have cowered away from violence, instead I embraced it and I think that's not a great thing. It ain't. Sometimes, when it's what you know and when you think there's not a lot of things you're good at, violence is an easy, accessible thing to be good at. You don't even have to be that good, you just do it enough, people talk about you. If you're smart enough you can work that out as a child, and I worked that out. The more violent you are, the more people hold you in higher regard. It was a key, I guess, to getting people to respect you and speak about you and make you famous.

Danny Weed We were from a place where that shit happens. We didn't go to private schools and we didn't all have perfect happy family lives, so if the MCs didn't cover it in some way they'd be lying. We lived in the poorest borough in England, but we all went to school and got brought up properly. We weren't just some moody hood-rats who didn't want to speak; we had something to say.

Bruza We didn't have a platform, a means, a mic to shout to the world to say what was going on in our lives. We was hearing about champagne dances, but I couldn't relate to that. That wasn't what we was going through. We was in the council estates, spitting to each other, beatboxing, spraying lyrics. But no one could hear us, 'cause we were trapped on this block, on this estate. No dad about, no guidance to show us that you could do something with your life. This was a platform for people to hear us, what we were going through. That's how these tunes come about, so we could vent.

Lethal B One thing about grime, the majority of the MCs spoke about their surroundings, their areas. Our heroes were the shotters – they had the clothes, the cars, the girls, the money. They was hood stars. We wanted to be them without having to sell drugs. A lot of my friends from school were involved in certain things, I was involved in certain things and so music was a release. I saw a lot of things, so a lot of what we spoke about came from true things – everyday life in East London, there was always something going on. It did help define the dream in terms of where you wanted to be, financially, without the trouble they went through. I was around real guys making real money. I wanted to buy a Stone Island jacket so bad, and the first one I saw was on a shotter from the ends. I wanted a Golf GTI, I sat in one that belonged to one of the local shotters. As soon as I got my first cheque, the first thing I bought was a Golf GTI. 100%, a lot of stories and the energy we used to tell them came from seeing what we saw growing up.

Opposite: Ghetts – Dalston, N16

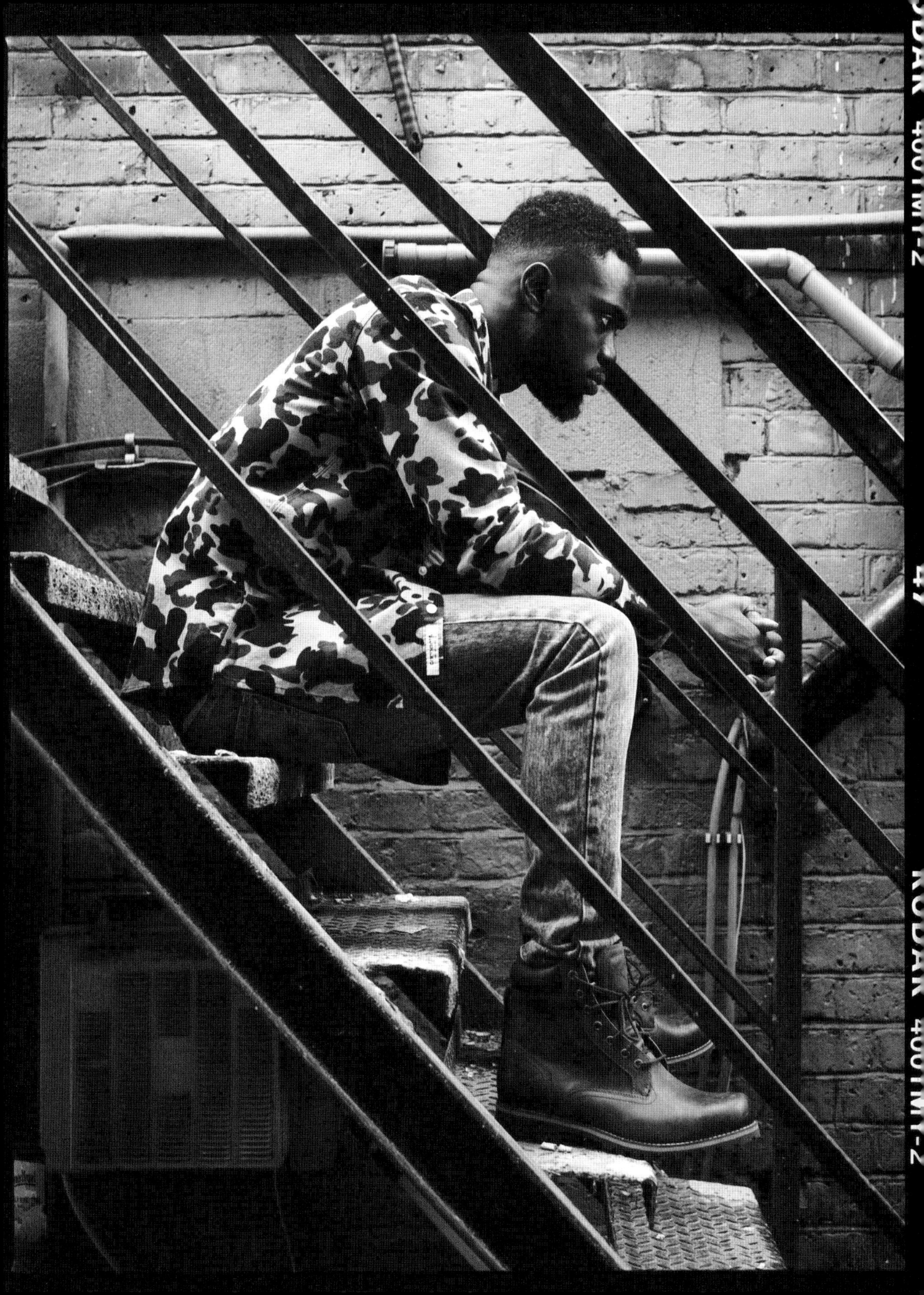
KODAK 400TMY-2
47
KODAK 400TMY-2

Maxwell D My mum had me very young, at the age of fifteen, so the age gap was very close. You got to see things that an ordinary ten-fifteen year old shouldn't see 'cause your mum is young. I saw my mum getting beaten. It's nothing to be ashamed of. I saw a lot of things; it was just all there... I didn't know about therapy in those days. Go and see someone? That was the last thing you would do. You'd go to school and take it out on the pupils, being a bully or fighting. You bring the home into school, and even later on down the line, maybe your choices and decisions in life are affected by what you've grown up with.

Ghetts At primary school, I was mischievous. In secondary, I was completely off the rails. I got stabbed in my first year so I learnt to protect myself at all times. I had a normal fist-fight with someone and I won and they turned around and stabbed me. That changed my perspective on everything. Even though I was troublesome and mischievous, I wasn't bad then. From that experience, I learnt the world is quite cruel and you have to be aware of your surroundings and that these people exist. I didn't really want to become a victim again so I started rolling with my borer everyday. And that's where all that started.

Lethal B 'Pow (Forward)!' was weird for me 'cause the song was arguably one of the biggest grime records ever, and I was still in the ends, still at my mums. That was detrimental to a point, when shit happened. I got into a lot of trouble 'cause I was so bait, so popular. I had people coming to my house with weapons and shit. I could have maybe gone out and rented somewhere for six months, but I thought I'd only have to move out when the money ran out. I had to stay at my mum's for a good two years, I had to be in the ends, keeping a low profile, rolling with certain people carrying certain things. That was a very tricky time, one of the hardest I've had – being successful and still being your local surroundings. That's the beauty of now; I can make my music, come home, it's calm. It was a tough two or three years for me – I was a Ninja them times. I'd circle the block three times, I was wearing a bulletproof vest for a year. Everywhere. Shows. Everywhere. Because the content of the record, a lot of people wanted to test me. I had to be on my toes. It was peak and the fucked up thing is that I knew the guys who did it. They think you've got a million pounds under your bed and you can help everyone. I didn't have Ps like that. As successful as that song was, there's eleven people on that track.

Wiley See, when you get stabbed, you can't even feel it until it is healing in the hospital, which is when you are in pain. Getting stabbed is not funny and too many kids stab people. So many kids are on the stabbing thing these days. The ones who are like, 'I'll stab you,' they ain't been stabbed or they have and that's why they're doing it. But I think that if you're a stabber, the day will come when your one comes. And when your one comes, that's when you will learn. Get past it, 'cause otherwise you'll be on revenge for ages. You have to just get out of it.

Maxwell D I think for all of us that came from this harsh reality, it helped us with our passion, it helped us with the music. We turned it into an art form instead of continuing to be a criminal. Yes, I've been to prison, I've done bad things, but for me the love for music changed everything, it changed the pain. We put a lot of pain, a lot of the horrible things that happened to us in our lives, we poured that into the music and we turned it into an art form. And that's how we got to where we are today.

Wiley I was always aware of black on black [crime]. I don't like to say that, but it's true. It was a lot of mates falling out, a lot of robbing, kidnapping, shooting, stabbing. And I'm not surprised at stabbing 'cause years ago it was sword and shields and beheadings and it was worse. So I'm not surprised at the knife crime 'cause that's been there through history. But the shooting was crazy 'cause how can people get hold of guns in London? Who controls the underworld? Not none of these black boys, they didn't control the underworld that created the drug dealing, the stealing of each other's women, looking at each other wrong, stepping on each other's feet. Getting shot. Getting chucked off a balcony. Kidnapping. Diamond snatching. All of that stuff. I witnessed all of it. Mad bruv. Mad. As a person, all this violence around you can fuck you up, but as a musician it can help you. It gives you a raw energy. If you're smart you can channel it in a good way and it will lead you on a good path.

Ghetts I was very curious as a kid. At eight years old I'd be gone for a week and half – and not with friends. I used to travel and I was doing road. It got to the point where my mum couldn't even phone the police and say I'd run away, because once she'd say my name they'd just know – they wouldn't even look for me anymore because I'd do it so often. It's only now yeah I think, 'Fuck, what did I put my mum through?' I was very street savvy in that I could sense danger, so even though I was out in the world doing God knows what, I still never smoked weed until I was twenty-two. Smoking weed came from me being on tag for so fucking long and having nothing to do and my bredrin living next door to me. I never drunk or smoked till I was like twenty-two. Imagine that, I could have been JME but in another form.

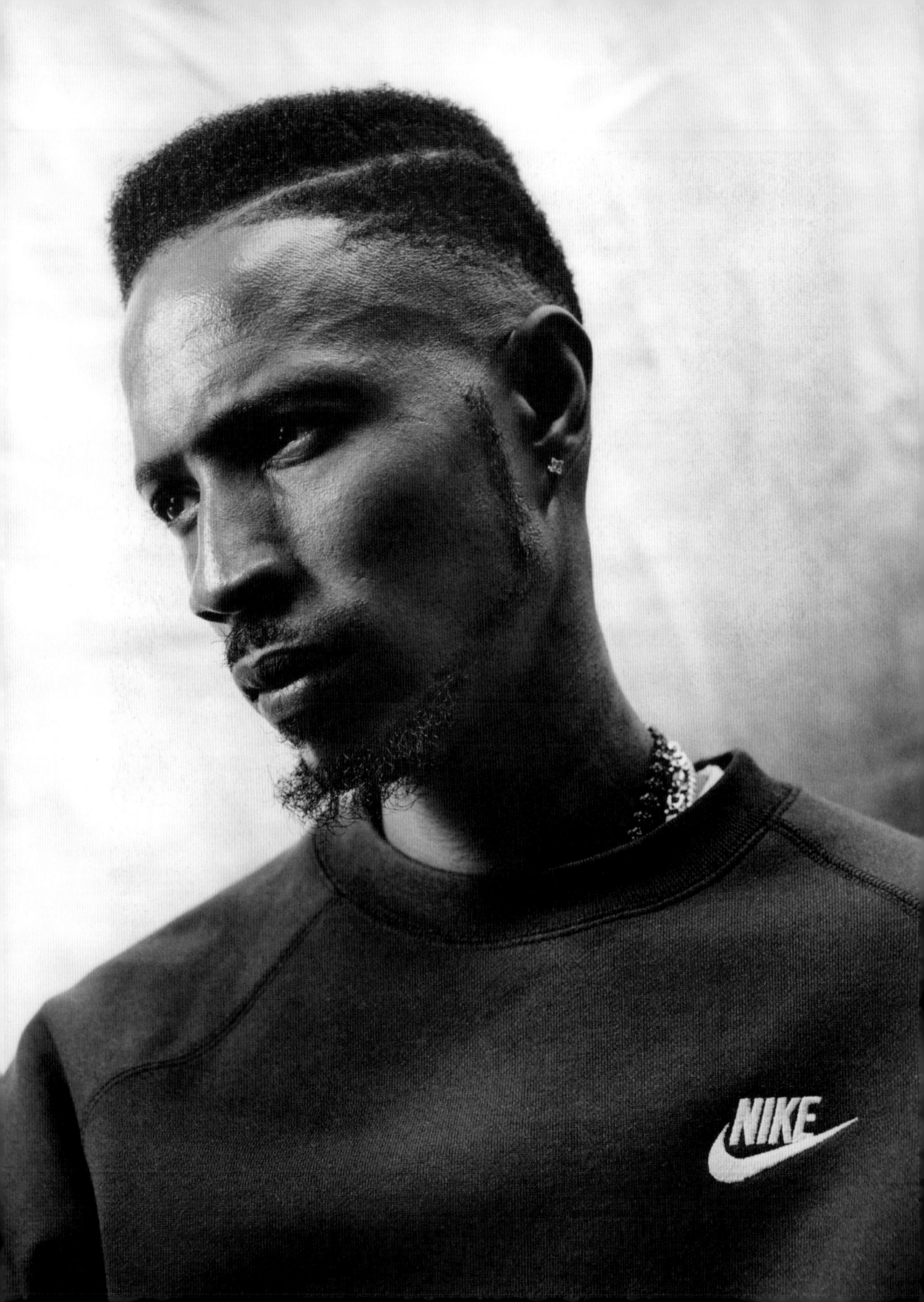
NIKE

NEVER FORGET WHERE YOU COME FROM
D.Double.E

Opposite: Photogenic D Double E – Dalston, N16
The legendary D Double E takes a spliff break – Romford, Essex, RM1

Original Nuttahs

Crazy Titch The first time I MC'd publicly, I was ten, eleven years old, way before grime. The first time I MC'd was to jungle. I'm from that era. I was still MC'ing to jungle when I was fifteen, I loved it. I thought jungle was going to last the distance.

D Double E I was onto the jungle a bit, [Leviticus'] 'Big, Bad & Heavy'. I was into the scene as a little kid. And then I saw General Levy 'Incredible' on The Box, when we first got cable in the early days and I was like, 'Oh, he's doing drum & bass like I am.' And he murked it. The way he did that rolling tongue, I used to try and do that too and I got it on lock.

Footsie Double was getting reloads from the smallest house rave on jungle, Double was duppying back then, I swear, it's nuts [laughs]. I've watched him duppy for so long, it's insane. He was the Forest Gate ledge' on jungle from back then on our little circuit, from school days in his blazer. Dubz ain't changed much.

Breeze I started out MCing for Wiley. This is when he used to be called DJ Wildchild, before Rinse even started, around '94, '95. Wiley's first name was Wildchild and then he had to change it because there was a girl on Kool FM who came out calling herself Wildchild and she was bigger than him straight away. So he went as Wiley, or Wiley Kat, sometimes.

Wiley I didn't get my name from her, I just watched *Thundercats*, I don't know if she did. God bless her though, Emma, I love any female who's got the drive to go in the game against men. She was a very sick DJ and she burst Skibadee, did she not?

Terror Danjah I had a pair of decks around my house and what happens is [Double] comes round with a few guys from school and we just used to mix. Sometimes he used to mix, he was DJ Dan then – this is around '96. Me and Double and DJ Tempo were in this crew called Bass Inject for a second and that's how we all got tied in with Footsie, because Footsie's from the ends anyway. So we're all in Bass Inject together and one time Tempo tells us to come radio, Future FM and that's how I got on radio, 9-11 prime-time, straight away. That was me and D Double's first break on radio, playing jungle. Future was basically in the same building as Deja [Vu]. It was run by Laura, who was running Deja as well and it was in the same place; Corporation St in Stratford.

D Double When I started MCing on jungle, it was proper hardcore. Them houses they used to have the stations in... doors not locked, just push it and go in and it's an empty flat. Nothing was official. It was all mad beat-down houses. They're my days of going on stations. I remember going to meet my mate who lived in a block of flats. One day he was like, 'There's music coming out of the block.' There was a

Opposite: Footsie wearing Newham Generals cap – Dalston, N16

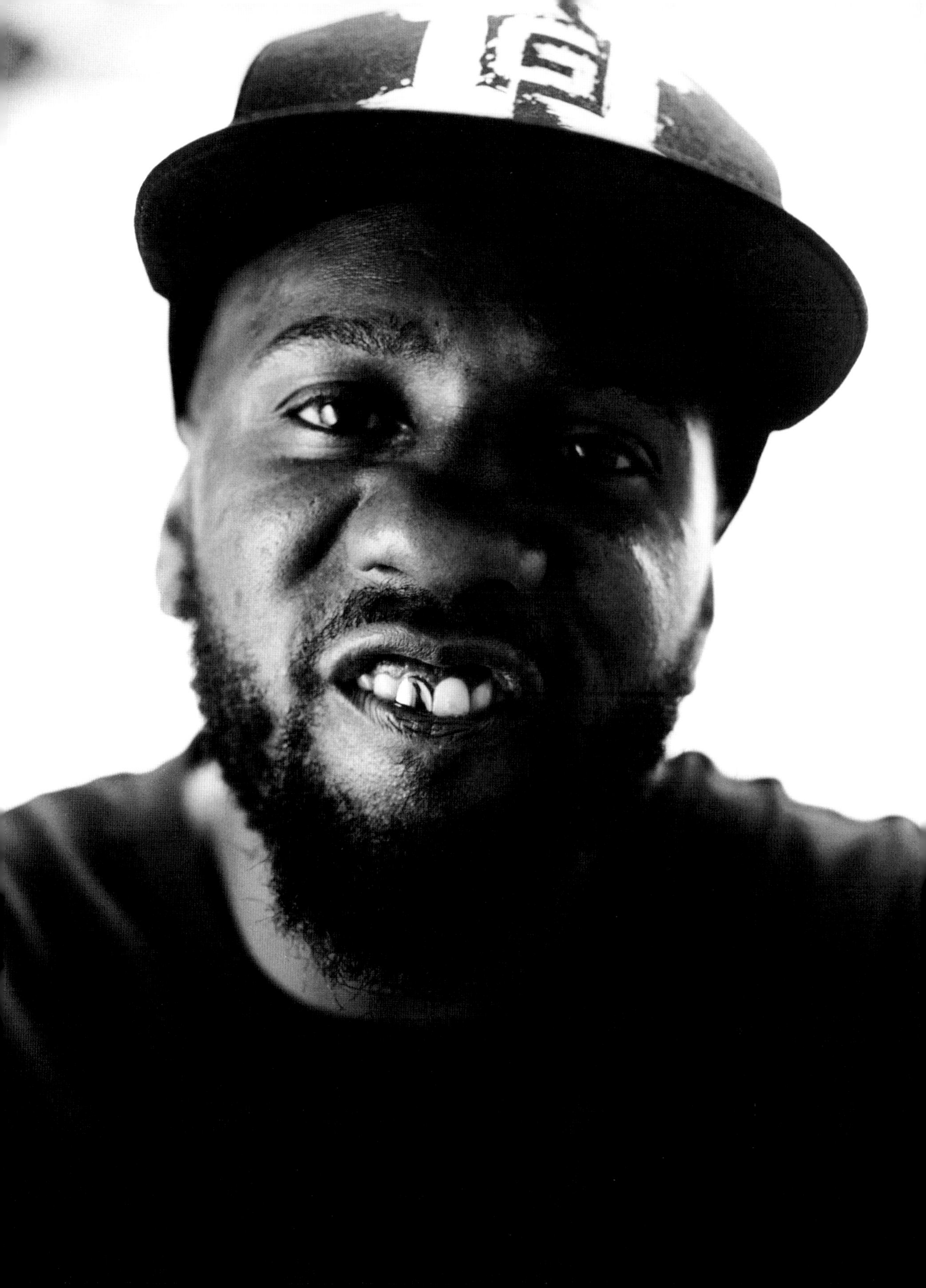

radio station just on his block and so we went outside the door. We pushed it and the door was open and we went in and there was a DJ there and he didn't even say nothing to us. So we just stayed there and we watched him and then we left. Then we found out the frequency and we used to listen. One day I wanted to MC and so we went to the station and I asked the DJ if I could MC and he said 'yeah.' So that's how I started MCing. I started going there everyday until someone said, 'Who are you, mate?' Then that station just left and I didn't go there anymore. I don't know what it's called. It was in Leyton in a block called Thatch House. That block is knocked down now, it's gone.

Maxwell D Jungle for me, we're talking, '95, '96 and everyone's in the house parties. The reason I had a direct connect with jungle was because of Nicky Slim Ting. Nicky used to live round the corner from my mum's house, so as a little kid he used to go to the same park as me. As we got older, he'd say 'I like jungle' and I'd say, 'Yeah, I want to MC', and so I used to go to his house after school and practise MCing jungle 'cause he had his little decks. Nicky's uncle was Noah who ran Living Dream and Orange, one of the biggest jungle raves back in the day. They used to have it at the Hippodrome Leicester Square, 4am to 12pm on a Sunday. It was crazy. Being so young, we couldn't have got in, but because of Nicky's uncle, we got the pass. So I used to go raving with him and that's when I saw Stevie Hyper D. My love for MCing started right there.

Double O Growing up I was just around music all the time, through my uncles. Myself and [Nicky] Slim [Ting] – his cousin is my cousin – so we're family basically. Our uncle did Orange and nights like that, so we got in through there. Slim then did an event called Rumble, which was an under-21's jungle rave and I started an under-eighteens rival to that called Stampede. This is the times when Tinchy was entering the MC competitions. A lot of the grime artists will refer back to that event. Me and Nicky then joined up and they became iconic events for everyone. The first reload that Lethal got was at Rumble in Temple. He came round my uncle's and begged for the tape – he's still got it, the little git. This was between 1997 to 2000, it was Stampede and Rumble. I remember doing Stampede and seeing Dizzee in Stratford. He said, 'I'm gonna be at your next event, Double O'. He was a cocky bastard [laughs]. I didn't take him serious. I was the main man in East London for events, so I had my ego. At a young age, I was making money, doing events and I had everyone asking to be on Stampede. Marcus was my mate, he was DJing, Sharky, all the N.A.S.T.Y crew lot. This is before grime was called grime.

Bruza Me and Terror went to the same college. My cousin, Triple Threat, him and Terror had met in youth clubs, but I met him a bit later at Waltham Forest College. He was DJing jungle and Triple – who was known as MC Lethal at that point – he was quite good in the jungle scene. I started MCing later on, really. I'd mess about in my bedroom, but I would never go radio; D Double, Terror, Lethal, all that lot, they'd be at radio or raves, and I'd be there, but I'd just spit for a minute or two. I was alright, but I wasn't really that confident. Triple would kill it in a rave. That was a learning curve for me though; getting the mic technique, spraying 16s. I didn't know about bars back then, I'd just come in anywhere and stop anywhere, so it was more learning the trade. Slowly, I started MCing more with D Double, Wiley, Riko, all that lot. But to be honest, us lot was just young and having fun with it.

Maxwell D Me and Wiley, we used to go to the same college, plus I went out with a girl from their area who knew them lot in Bow, so I was always in Bow after college. That's how we bonded, they were my college friends, that's how I found out about Rinse and how I used to go radio and all that. I used to make jokes with them lot 'cause they used to wear their raving clothes to college; it used to be like a fashion show, Versace, Moschino… I'd see them at Jungle Fever or whatever and then see them in college in the same clothes the next week.

Crazy Titch I knew Wiley from jungle days, Riko Dan from jungle days. I got to meet Wiley, it was just Wiley innit, just Will then. No one special. They had a Cool School, an MC competition that used to run every year. That first one, Doogz said he won it but he didn't, neither of us won it. The next one, someone else won. The third one, I won. Oh yeah, God's Gift – he was Pepsi at the time – was onstage as well trying to compete but he couldn't. This is jungle days. One day I was in Bow to see my cousin. I was in the chippy and Wiley came in and asked who won the competition. I was fourteen years old, all cocky: 'I did! Me! Titch! Plaistow!' Then my cousin walked in: they're all scared of him and from there everyone wants to be your friend. But yeah, Wiley was doing stuff then but their biggest MC then, I shit you not, was Riko. He was that guy for jungle.

Jammer Wiley was introduced to me by Flow Dan. One of my best friends from school was family with him. He said to Flow Dan, 'My bredrin from Leytonstone, Jammer, he's a DJ but he makes beats, you should let Wiley hear his beats.' This is when Wiley was still doing garage, before 'Know We', this is when he made 'Nicole's Groove'. So when I got my studio, Flow Dan got Wiley to come down, I met him and we made a tune together on that day. And that was it from there. It sounded like 'Terrible', the same beat, with some strings. But he was like, 'Nah, you're the next one, you've got the strings.' And we never left each other from then. He had a lot of heat around him at that time too, so him being around me, that gave me that step up.

Wiley Don't get me wrong donny, I love garage equally, but without jungle there would be no grime.

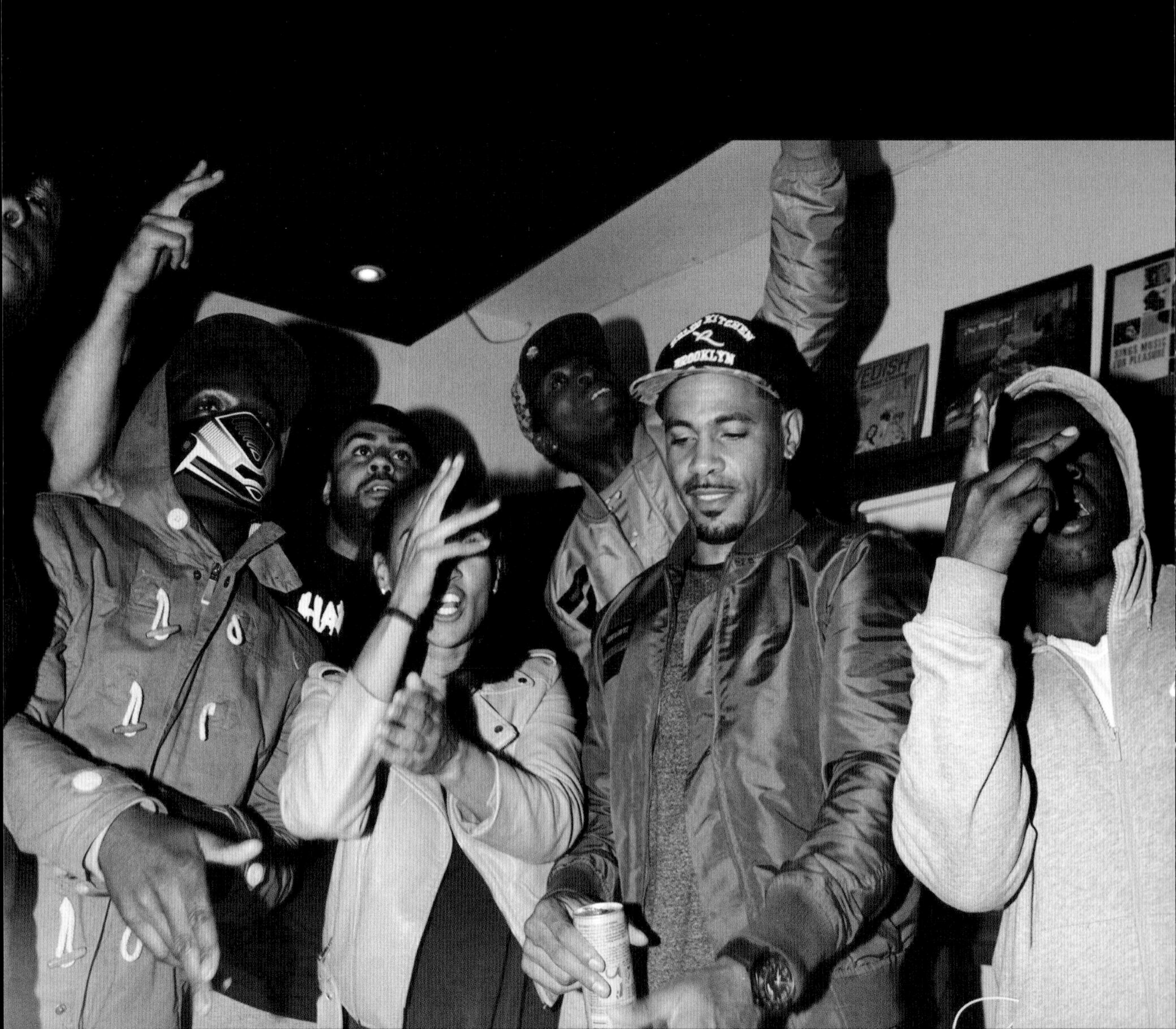
BROOKLYN

Playtime Is Over

Chantelle Fiddy I was into jungle, garage, then of course the So Solid movement. You could tell it was a moment and something was happening. It wasn't so much sonically though if I'm honest, it was more this idea that it was 30 black guys mobbing the music industry that was exciting.

Harvey I probably understand So Solid a lot more now to be honest, but to us, even back then, it was a movement. So Solid wasn't about each individual being a star, it was about bringing through our community. When we won a Brit Award or a MOBO, we celebrated like that because we were celebrating for our communities, South London, Brixton, anywhere that we grew up 'cause we came from the struggle. We'd all grown up in youth clubs, which is why So Solid had that community feel. So for me it was a celebration and kids could relate to people that they actually see, daily, on the street. No disrespect, but they couldn't relate to Kylie Minogue in London 'cause that's not their upbringing. So Solid gave people hope. We know what we done and how we influenced it.

Donaeo I think So Solid was the start of grime, to a certain extent, because grime was like a youth thing, our version of rap and that's what So Solid were making – our version of rap music. Then me, Wiley, Youngsta from Musical Mob, Dizzee Rascal – we were all making beats, but it wasn't called anything. Before then, we were all kinda making the same thing, we were all mentally in the same place. I think what we know today is that the initial seeds were planted by So Solid, then by us lot, and then Wiley watered it and made it grow.

Harvey You've got to look at the history of music. It started to get darker when it got to us, Pay As U Go, that's when the sound started to get darker. You've got to understand, Wiley came from a garage crew initially and then obviously he continued that sound. So yeah, we're definitely a contribution to that art form. They went and did their East London thing, the Dizzees and the Wileys and it became its own genre.

Crazy Titch I was sick to death of So Solid saying they're the only ones to go to Number One. Fuck off. They pissed me off with that shit. They deserve some homage? Fuck off, you done garage. Craig David might as well say that. Fucking Daniel Bedingfield might as well say that. Victoria Beckham might as well say that! I'm serious. Pink had a fucking garage remix. Don't go down that route; it's a whole different genre. Your MCs are talking about champagne splashing and flossing and shit. Grime is not about showing off. Grime is about aggression and anger and pain. When kids are saying they've got AKs and they've not even seen an AK! Fucking garage. I did like garage as well, but [it was separate]. Garage was gay. Lets just be honest, garage was gay. I couldn't get on radio because the stuff

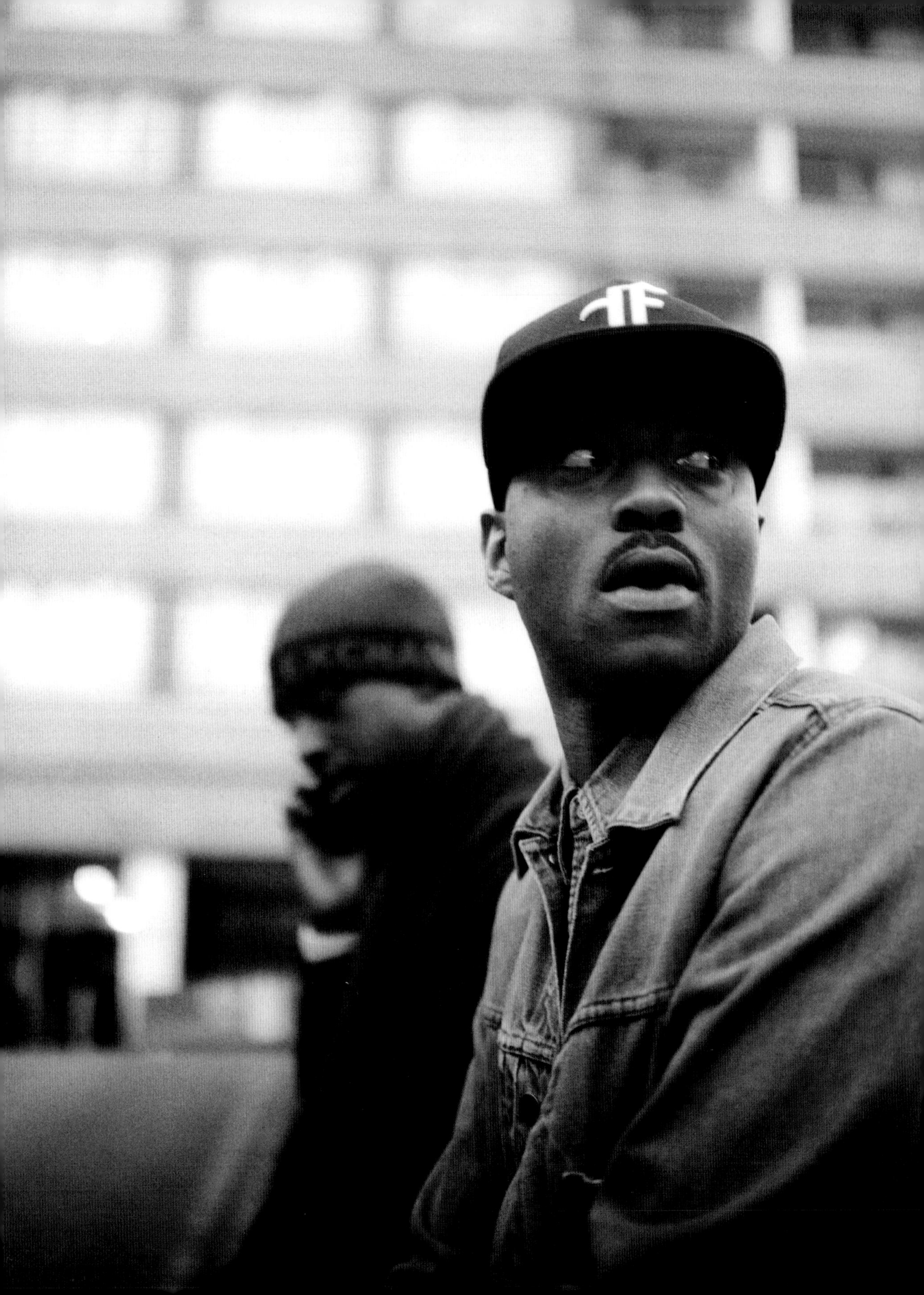

I was saying wasn't, 'I go raving and pop champagne'. I was saying about robbing you, I might burgle your house [laughs]. I have to laugh because I was doing grime on garage. I was spitting that on garage. I had some fucked up lyrics, so they wouldn't let me on radio, they blocked me. But in a house rave, everyone knew my lyrics, it was crazy.

Harvey UKG never went away. We're booked constantly. The younger generation look at the Internet to define success, but we've been doing this a long time.

Terror Danjah When Ms. Dynamite and Sticky came out with 'Booo!' I think that opened up everything. More Fire Crew came out in 2001 as well and from that time, it was on. Sticky came with the artistry thing. What Sticky done was give me the blueprint to go and do Aftershock. I wanted Aftershock to be like Sticky's Social Circles and Bryan G's label, V Recordings, so when you see the label on the record in the shop you know what you're getting, you're not even listening. When that did eventually happen for me, I was in the eye of the storm, so it's only with hindsight I saw now that it happened.

Matt Mason (Editor-In-Chief, RWD, 2001 – 2005) I was DJing on Mac FM and Ice FM when I first noticed grime was becoming something different to garage. At first I didn't like that garage was splintering. There were so many names and subgenres happening – this was early 2000 – and my feeling was this would make the garage scene weaker. I had the same reservations about dubstep. I was wrong on both counts. When I saw grime start to take on a different personality from garage – when artists emerged that weren't inspired by garage as much as they saw grime as a separate sound – it became clear to me that this was Britain's first credible response to hip-hop. It was a vitally important addition to British culture. I was DJing and producing for grime artists by the summer of 2001.

Plastician For me, personally, hearing 'Pulse X' [by Youngstar of Musical Mob] around 2000 opened a lot of doors. I think a lot of people like me were playing with Fruity Loops, trying to make garage but the level of production back then was so high and a lot of the DJs just wouldn't have played something that sounded so simple, until that track blew up. The fact you could download a cracked copy of the program on Kazaa or LimeWire meant that for the first time ever, becoming a bedroom producer was really possible for an entire generation. The fact that Fruity Loops' default tempo setting was 140BPM may also have a lot to answer for. Chuck MSN Messenger into the mix and suddenly it's possible to share tracks with people, get dubs off of producers without actually meeting them in a cutting house or a record shop. Hearing 'Pulse X' made me want to be a part of that, whatever 'that' was. It definitely kicked the doors down for young people to have a go. You could actually have a big song made out of the bedroom.

John McDonnell (Prancehall) To start with, a lot of the early grime was actually quite bad, the production. I liked that. That's what got me into it, it was just so weird and there was just nothing else like it at the time. I loved it.

Maxwell D The beats were getting darker and that's where it started changing. The beats started coming in from Jon E Cash, they started coming in from Agent X, Slimzee started slowing down certain tunes to make them sound dubstep-py... we had a different sound. We started chopping up the best 8 bars from every garage track there was and the place would just erupt. To me, that was definitely the start.

Bashy Most of the scene was from East, but Jammer would invite me down. That was during a very embryonic stage of the scene, there was no money, really. If you was there at that time and doing music, you was doing it for the love of it because people wouldn't even know your face. It was just for the love.

Manga A lot of it was East. The biggest people in West was Flirta, SLK and Musical Mob. I wanted to be in SLK but they wouldn't let me in. They said I was shit.

Bashy Everyone started going to Freeze FM, which was another contributor to the scene, that was in West London. West London never had as tight of a grip on the scene as East London, it will forever be East London. It was the nucleus, but then it spread out. We had Musical Mob, 'Pulse X' is a very classic tune, and Dynamic; before me, they was the guys and yeah Donaeo of course.

Manga I was in Musical Mob for two days but I got kicked out.

Martin Clark (Journalist and Producer) You're talking about 2001, 2002 where the garage scene is fragmenting and the power base is shifting. In garage, it's DJs and it's producers as the primary complimentary powerbrokers and MCs are secondary hosts. Then the power balance shifts as Musical Mob's 'Pulse X' wipes the slate clean and creates a space in which an MC can exist. So Solid, Pay As U Go, Heartless, all that stuff. The balance is shifting, it's redistributing that power relationship. Producers and DJs made massive contributions but the reality is that it's a power shift compared to garage, where it came from. Late '90S is definitely garage with darker edges; Groove Chronicles's '1999', US Alliance... But by the time and it's 2001, 2002, it's Sidewinder, Eskimo Dance, Rinse, Deja, it's now something completely different. It doesn't sound like anything that's come before.

Sharky Major UK rappers back then, they was talking American and what grime was trying to do was not be anything to do with America. We was trying to be English. So we decided to make our tempo a bit quicker. We're wearing tracksuit bottoms, we're going to a place to be on radio where you're going to be locked in 'cause you might get your records taken from you. Garage didn't want us to come in, they used to turn up their noses at us. Well, now who's got the last laugh?

Jammer It happened naturally because there was a garage scene going on but they didn't want us on the garage sets. So Wiley said, 'Look, we're just gonna mob

Opposite: Donaeo – Dalston, N16

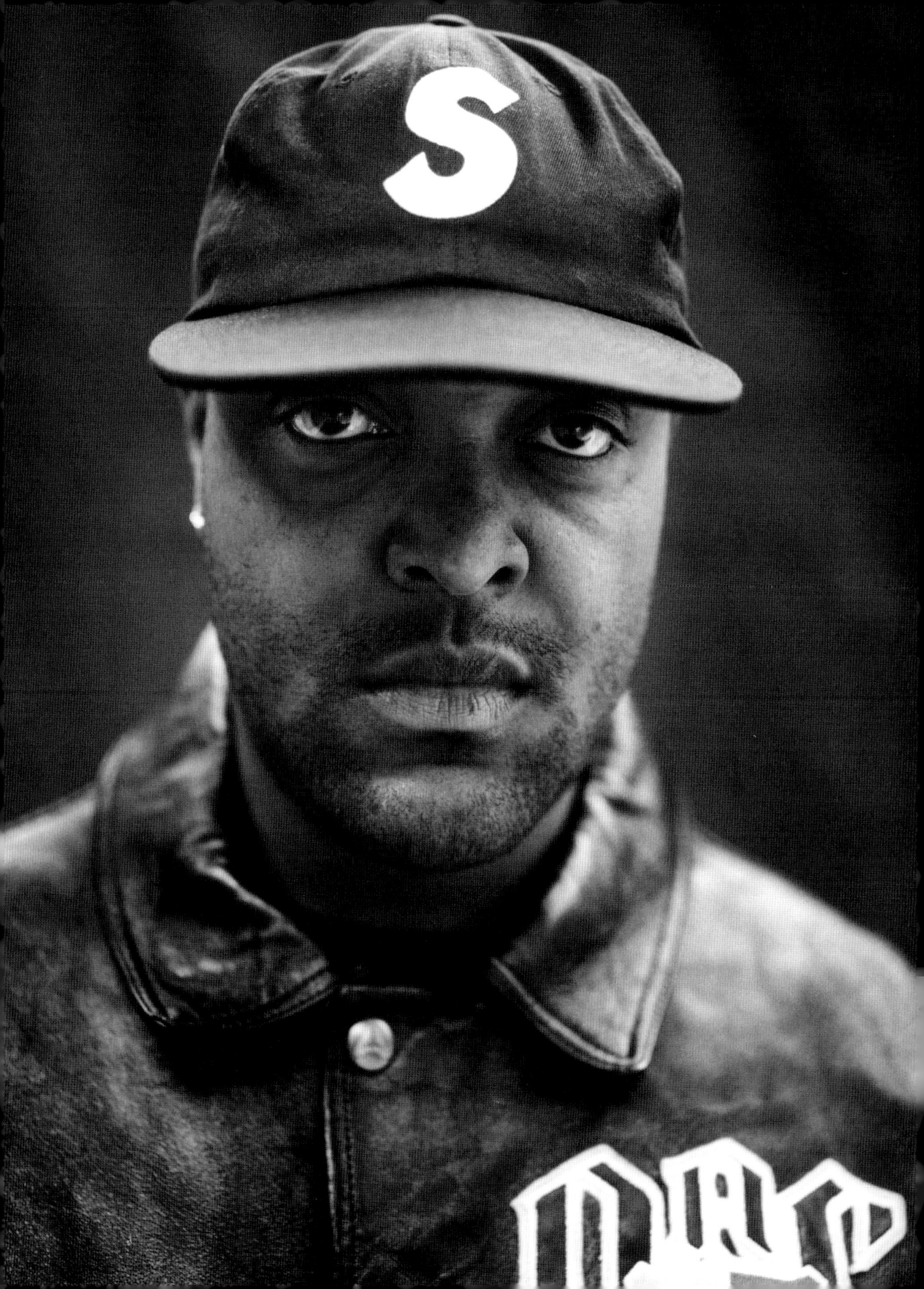

the end of these sets.' They used to get Wiley to spit 'cause he was in the garage thing, he always knew everyone. Because of that, he could get one or two man on the stage. And then that was it, he used to slow the jungle instrumentals down, mix them into the garage tunes, then man used to spit over them – Dizzee Rascal, D Double, me, Sharky, he started bringing everyone through. So that was the start of the birth. That was when the sound was coming through and all the garage people started to hear us. Dizzee Rascal came over and that was it.

Chantelle Fiddy The UK garage committee formed and tried to stop the MC records being played on radio and at shows and the garage scene shot itself in the foot. Garage didn't want anything to do with grime, they wanted it to fuck off into its own corner. If you think about it, grime was the middle finger to garage. Garage – champagne, money, nice. Grime – Playstation, cheap beats, Fruity Loops, fuck your fee I'm not paying to get into your shit club. That was the attitude.

Matt Mason I was at those meetings. They started at The Met Bar. A lot of the garage promoters, DJs and MCs were shouting at each other about stopping grime somehow because they were worried it would get the clubs shut down. But no one knew how to stop it because they couldn't. In my experience, garage handled grime's rise pretty badly, at least behind closed doors. But you can't blame garage for that, that's just people. Machiavelli wrote about it. New power structures always threaten the old ones. Luckily there's room for everyone now.

Oxide If there had been more unity then it definitely would have been a lot stronger. But this time around it's a bit different; there's more of a unity now. You've got to learn from the mistakes.

MC Neat I've always looked at drum & bass as the blueprint. Someone like Andy C, who's the godfather, runs an incredible label and brought through talent like Chase & Status and Sub Focus and was never worried about what they'd do. If there was more of that in the early years of garage, these guys might not have run away and done their thing. Now, we've learnt so many things that we're trying to bring through. There's new, young talent in garage coming through, which is nice to see. It's a different time now.

Martin Clark It felt like the DNA of the whole genre was being rearranged. That felt like the most amazing thing. So yeah, I watched that happen.

Wiley Garage, all the girls used to go and rave to it so that's why I went there. Expose at Vauxhall, bare girls would be in there, otherwise I wouldn't have gone [laughs]. Heartless, So Solid, Pay As U Go was doing stuff; Major Ace, Scratchy and Biggie Pitbull, Stormin, Sharky Major... Precious MC gave me the inspiration to know I could do it 'cause he was the Prince of garage at one point. No lie.

DJ Logan Sama backstage at Eskimo Dance – Building Six, o2 Arena, SE10

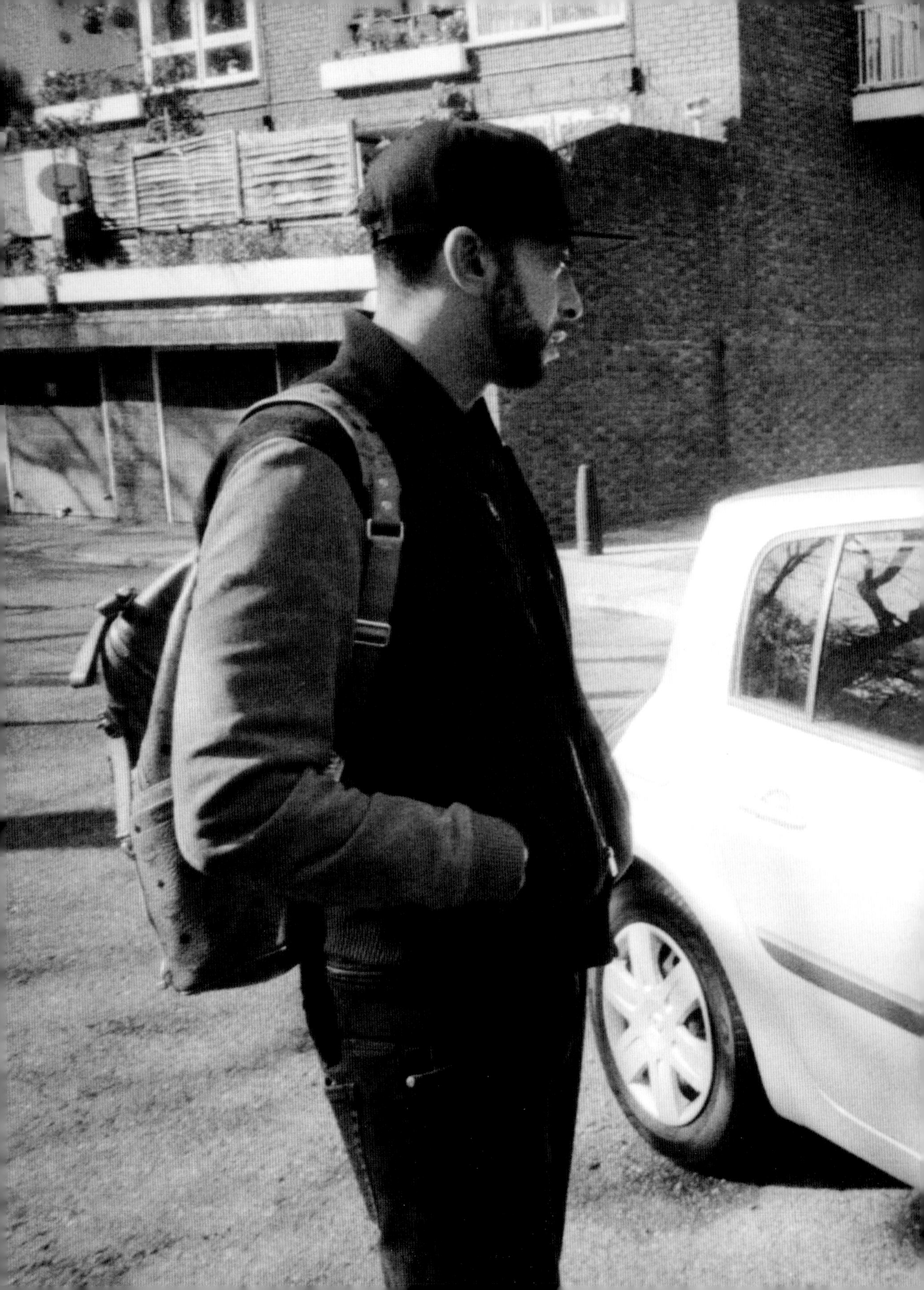

02. 3.29

Pay As U Go – League Of Their Own

Chantelle Fiddy Pay As U Go clearly marked a new time in the bars; So Solid's music was far more garage-based and if you listen to the bars now, they still very much had that garage MC element and flow. *I'll hit you like a four-leaf clooo-ver...* There was some cleverness but they weren't as deep as the bars that were about to come from Wiley and Dizzee.

Maxwell D Stevie Hyper D. That's where I got the hooks from. Not ripping off his hooks, but that's where I saw how to structure hooks in the dance. When I used to see Wiley and them, I'd say, 'Look man, you can't keep going raves and spraying out these 16, 32 bars. You need 8 bars, hooks, let the crowd sing your hooks.' They used to see me doing it and say, 'Ah that's why you're getting all the reloads.' Then everyone started doing it. Wiley, bang, ah you get it now. That's why we were so strong.

DJ Target Pay As U Go started from Rinse FM. We all had sets on Rinse; Me, Wiley and Maxwell (D) had a show and we were called Ladies Hit Squad, at the time. Major Ace, Plague, Slimzee, Geeneus – who started Rinse – and God's Gift, they had a show on a Sunday afternoon.

Wiley To be fair, Maxwell D was the leader really 'cause he had a record deal first. God's Gift had his ting as well. He was probably around fourteen, fifteen when his tune blew up, imagine that.

Maxwell D I had a song called 'Serious' that blew up for me which meant I was doing loads of things different to them, but I kind of dragged my crew with me. At this time, we was in Ladies Hit Squad – me, Wiley and Target. Wiley wanted to DJ, I was the host and the MC, but him and Trend – Rest In Peace, God rest his soul – they'd always been on making their little beats on their computers, with their floppy discs. So he had this beat and he said, 'I want Gift to sing.' Gift was always known as Pepsi from Bow to me. At the time [2000], Pepsi, God's Gift, had 'Mic Tribute', him doing all the noises of all the MCs and it was doing really well in the garage scene. God's Gift's contribution was massive. He was the first one. 'Mic Tribute' was doing really well but then he went prison. When he come out, we was in the hype of it, performing everywhere, so he come out, jumped straight into Pay As U Go. Wiley wanted him to do the hook and everyone else to do the verses. So Wiley did the first verse, Major Ace the second, I was the third... but we still weren't Pay As U Go, we was Ladies Hit Squad. The tune started growing and I remember we all met one day in a record shop and we decided we might as well become one. We had the tune, we had the heat and for me, I thought it would have more impact if I joined them lot and so we just done it. That was the birth of Pay As U Go.

Polaroid screenshot: Maxwell D on Skype from his pool house – Just outside Miami, Florida

DJ Target For some reason, every Sunday afternoon when their show was on, the pay as you go network used to go down, and everyone could call into the studio for free. It kept happening so after the fourth week they was calling it the 'pay as you go show.' That's how the name started. Then it turned into the group or crew or whatever. Their show was doing really well, our show was doing really well, so we said, 'Why don't we team up and call ourselves Pay As U Go crew or Pay As U Go Cartel?' That's how Pay As U Go was born.

Maxwell D One thing we had in common: we all loved the music. We were young, but when you take away all the egos, and attitude, we were nice underneath it all, we were all decent. It was like a sport. Everyone was competitive, everyone wanted to get better at what they was doing. I had the biggest ego, I had the latest clothes, I carried the street with me a lot. It was like my gift and curse. People don't always like arrogance and I was way too confident. I was fresh out of jail, fresh off the street; I had a whole different aura to me when I was younger. I had an attitude, I was still hanging around with like-minded beings, I was hanging around with criminals, people who were still robbing, I weren't really out of the streets, even though I'd 'made it', I was still in it. People would be like, 'Oh my God, I was in jail with him last year, now look he's on TV.'

DJ Target We did that for a few years, making garage. 'Champagne Dance' – I did that with Geeneus. That was our first hit. I still get PRS (royalties) for it [laughs]. But that whole time, Danny and all the crew from Limehouse, they were all my original friends. I met a lot of Pay As U Go through music, through Rinse. They were my friends. They're still are my friends, but Danny, Wiley, Dominic, Scratchy, Breeze and them, they were my bredrins. So when Pay As U Go started to come apart and Roll Deep was already formed, it just made sense for me to join them officially and be in Roll Deep with my friends.

Danny Weed When we were making the first Roll Deep album, Darren [Target] was in the studio anyway, that was at the end of Pay As U Go.

Jammer It was all one scene at that time, but then there was a whole generation of underground MCs who grew up on Wiley and So Solid and they hadn't broke through yet. They could only get their hands on garage instrumentals, so they was on radio spitting greazy bars over garage instrumentals. Then obviously we saw we needed beats. So Wiley made 'Know We', I made 'Take U Out', 'Destruction [VIP]', 'Army'. 'Igloo' and 'Eskimo' came through. You had D Double doing his thing on grimy instrumentals. Street kids that was doing their little bits of badness, but going radio like it was youth club in the evenings. I feel like that was the birth of the culture. The birth of grime was Roll Deep and N.A.S.T.Y. Crew, Deja and Rinse. Everything formed around that. Anything before that was a bit misty. This was reloads, murking, street stuff. Grime came raw in the beginning. Grime was murking. It was spontaneous. That's why grime raves in the beginning was very dangerous, because everybody was coming out hearing real road man lyrics. Yeah

Double and Hyper were there rhyming over jungle beats or whatever, but when the music changed, and when it's fifteen man in one room trying to get on the mic to spit, that's grime. That's grime.

Maxwell D It was a lot of things going on behind the scenes. We had a deal on the table with Universal, they wanted me and Wiley to sign the deal, but then Wiley would go in there and say he wasn't Pay As U Go, he was Roll Deep. His manager, Nick [Denton], Dizzee's manager, he was managing us but we didn't want him to be our manager no more so we went to another manager who used to manage me before – Trenton – and then Wiley double-backed on us… It was all messy behind the scenes. I think him and Dizzee were getting a lot of attention and I think he realised that he didn't really need Pay As U Go no more. That time was over. We didn't get on, all of us. There was no leader. We all had our own egos and we all thought we was as big as each other. My ego was out of this world. Also, to be fair, Roll Deep, they was Wiley's actual original friends. We were his college friends, but these was actually his boys from school, from growing up. With Pay As U Go, Ace weren't someone he hung around with, Plague weren't someone he hangs around with, other than college, I wasn't someone he hung around with. Darren [DJ Target], Breeze, these people, he's actually grown up with from school. So bringing them in was natural for him. It was Wiley, Dizzee and Flow Dan at the forefront, those were the three big swingers in Roll Deep. Then he bought the rest of them, the Jamakabi's, he started recruiting like a football coach to have the best team. There would be this little kid, Tinchy Stryder, half your size, up to your kneecaps saying *tings in boots,* like, what the hell, so he's getting bare forwards. That's why Roll Deep was so big, 'cause Wiley handpicked them properly. He had Syer B, the white boy, then Scratchy, another white boy, *warrior charge*, all that hype. That crew was constructed perfectly for grime music, definitely.

Wiley Pay As U Go was a learning curve. Everyone was their own person, their own character. Without those years none of us would be here. The arguments, the deals, the turning left, the turning right. I was gonna do Roll Deep anyway. Paco and Plague – the ones who started Pay As U Go with Slimzee – I think they was stepping stones. I hate to look at it as a stepping stone 'cause it led me to meet Dizzee Rascal, Danny S, Nick Denton and other people who made music as well. There was arguments between members, not just about money, but everyone's got different personalities and different views. To agree to one thing with ten people isn't always ideal. Most humans, if they're in a group and they get paid a small cut, if someone pops around the corner and tells you that you can get more money on your own, you're gonna walk away. Not just Zayn Malik, anyone would do that.

Danny & Target on Style

DJ Target Clothes were always important, since jungle. Moschino and that, we were always into it, we'd get hold of it however we could.

Danny Weed There was always someone on the estate who was older that would look smart and we wanted to look like that.

DJ Target My house got burgled when I was 18 and all my Mosh, all my sick stuff got taken in the burglary. I caught a guy wearing my jeans walking down the street a year later. He had to take them off. I feel like we was way ahead. We were wearing Bathing Ape way before anyone else. Dan had that Maharishi jacket that glowed in the dark too.

Danny Weed That Bathing Ape jacket was on Wiley's first album.

DJ Target The first grime uniform, though, was Akademik's tracksuits and Custom Air Force 1s that you got sprayed at this place in West London, Global. They'd have Looney Tunes or E3 or your name or whatever graffitied on there. 'Cause it was West, Shepherd's Bush, no one in East knew about it. We've always been the travel-for-trainers type people and we knew they had some Huaraches there. I'd go to the one Foot Locker in Lakeside and there was one in Clapham Junction too, but no one in East knew where they were. You'd come back with your trainers and people would be like, 'Oh my god, you've been America'. Nowadays you can buy it all online, easy. But the first ever images of grime artists in magazines, the first thing you'd see was these guys in Akademiks and it spread quick. Then it was fake Akademik tracksuits…!

Danny Weed I had DragonballZ on my Huaraches. I used to love those trainers. I remember the statement of that. I remember the first day I wore those trainers down the Roman Road. Remember, going down the Roman Road was like a catwalk.

DJ Target You had to save all your best clothes for Saturday.

Danny Weed When we was starting, we was going to garage raves with MC Creed and that, which is where it stemmed from. They was in different outfits, it was a bit more smarter. They wasn't in Akademiks; it was shirts and loafers and Patrick Cox shoes. The tracksuit thing started because we was obsessed with Dipset and people like that; that's where we got Akademiks from. That's what they was wearing, so we started wearing it. That was at the same time as grime was emerging, but it wasn't a big planned thing. At the same time, it was tracksuits in the day – for Wiley it was always tracksuits – we'd always dress up if we were going to DJ at a rave. Iceberg jeans, Iceberg jumpers, Moschino, Versace. We'd like to wear a bit more smart stuff too. I remember when Wiley first got his album deal; he went and spent £15,000 in some shop on Iceberg.

DJ Target It was a shop in Soho. They [Danny and Wiley] came back with massive boxes.

Danny Weed Just me and him. 'Cause we were so obsessed with clothes, Wiley was like, 'This is the day we're going to get everything. We're going to this shop and we're not holding back. We're going to spend every penny.' £14,000 or £15,000. He got a massive discount, obviously. Logan was there that day too. He wasn't a DJ then, he was like Wiley's financial advisor or something. Anyway, we got so much stuff that day. The jumpers were £450 each. Iceberg History jumpers that were shit, terrible, but on the day we were so happy. It started with Wiley saying, 'OK, we'll get something each. Get something Dan, get something'. He's always been super generous. After we picked a few items, he was like, 'Seriously, we're getting everything, we're going all out'. I'd never seen £14,000 in my life.

That massive box turned into 'the box'. It was in my house and anyone that came round that didn't have nothing to wear, it would be like, 'Get the box, Danny, get the box.' I'll see old pictures of people now and they're wearing things that came from that box. There was that period later in the 00s, the Louis Vuitton times, but it's gone back again to the tracksuit. That's the culture, that's the street thing, that's where they get their energy. It needed to come back to that.

DJ Target It needed to go back to basics. That's why grime is having such a good time now. We're starting to see that original energy.

Danny Weed The maddest thing with dark clothing now is that it's to be seen. We used to wear dark clothing, tracksuits, to *not* be seen. Little did we know, you stand out like sore thumbs when you all turn up in tracksuits. I was watching an interview with Wiley the other day. It was when grime was really shit and they caught him at a time when he was in a funny mood. They said, 'Everyone's saying grime's dead, is that true?' and he says 'Good! It's true. It needs to be dead. That's what everyone needs to think so we can clear out all the shit and then be reborn. Grime is dead but it's not really dead.' I think that might be the only time in the interview that he said something he really meant.

02. 3.29

YOUTH CLUBS TO ARENA'S

WILEHOUSE E14 DISCARDA

Roll Deep is the Name and We Will Show You...

Scratchy It was the start, the plant pot, the original tree that everything stems from. We was doing it blind, not knowing what it could do for us. We was doing it as a hobby, we didn't care about money, nothing, we was just doing it for fun. It's like how collecting stamps is for some people; we just liked what we were doing.

Previous page: Views of Canary Wharf from Wilehouse – Limehouse, E14
Opposite: DJ Target, Discarda and Danny Weed at Wilehouse – Limehouse, E14

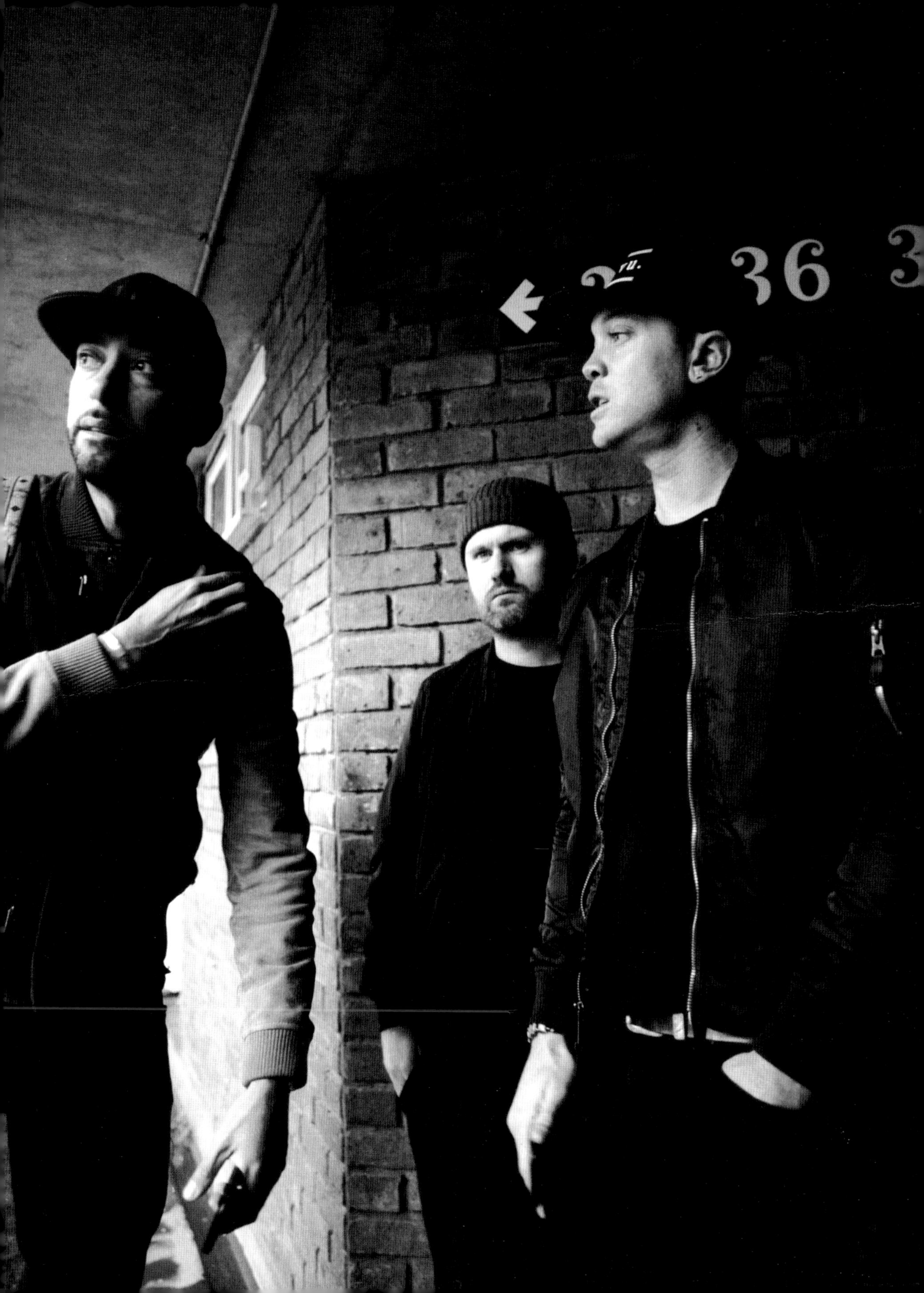
36

Danny Weed We all grew up together. Darren [DJ Target] is friends with my older brother, Dominic [Dom P].

DJ Target Me and Dominic were born two days apart in the same hospital. I lived on the same road as Dizzee and Tinchy. Diz used to come and buy records off me, he was a DJ originally.

Dizzee Rascal I started as a drum & bass DJ. If it wasn't for Target giving me his records and selling me his records and then eventually hearing his records, I dunno where I'd be. By the time I started DJing, drum & bass had kind of died out. If you weren't in that hierarchy, that was that, innit. I couldn't keep up; I couldn't afford to keep up with buying garage records. I gave up on that and then I started making beats. So that's how it started for me.

Danny Weed Our nan's knew each other, our mums knew each other and that relationship is the same with all of us; Scratchy, Breeze, we all knew each other's brothers sisters, nans, mums. Breeze used to live a few doors down, Scratchy lived on the same landing. Even when people came in later, like Trim, we still knew them.

Breeze My mum used to be a teacher at Trim's school.

Trim I sprung up from the Raw Mission days. I kept on going radio sets on Raw Mission, then I decided that I knew Geeneus and that he shouldn't have a problem with me coming on radio and so I forced my way on there a few times [laughs]. We had a few barneys. Then Wiley invited me to come to Deja and I wasn't sure if was a set up [laughs] or if he actually really liked me. When I got there, at the end of the set, him and Marcus Nasty was asking me to join each of their crews and I chose Roll Deep 'cause I grew up with Scratchy.

Flow Dan Even if you weren't good mates, it's just someone you recognise from the area and because you recognise people, you can gladly work with them.

DJ Target We grew up right in the shadow of Canary Wharf, in Limehouse, or Wilehouse we liked to say. It pushed me on. That's why I put it on the cover of my DVD [*Aim High*] 'cause we could see it. It was like, all the money is over there and that's the inspiration.

Breeze It's so close to Canary Wharf that when that bomb went off there [in 1996] my whole bedroom shook.

Danny Weed Me and Darren, our first job was in Wiley's dad's patty factory.

DJ Target Wiley's dad had a patty business, making and delivering patties to Caribbean restaurants. He employed us all.

Janaya Cowie (Wiley's sister) Everyone worked there. Jet Li. Danny, Target, Wiley, me and my cousin. It was on an industrial estate in Poplar and it was pretty successful; my dad even got the patties into Selfridges at one point.

Danny Weed We got free patties and shit money.

Janaya Cowie I worked there with my three girl cousins and we saw on the news that the minimum wage had gone up to £3 per hour and we were on £2.50 per hour, so we all got together and decided to boycott working until Dad paid us more. It worked though; he got fed up and agreed to raise our wages.

DJ Target One day, we got caught having a food fight. He sacked us all.

Richard Cowie Oh, I sacked all of them all the time, but only until the next day 'cause I needed my staff [laughs].

Janaya Cowie Wiley used to come in, stamp his time card in the morning and then sneak out and be off all day. He'd come back about an hour before the shift finished and then would clock out with the rest of us. One day, my dad caught on and pulled him up on it. He said to my dad, 'I can't do anymore, it's not me. I can't.' That day was when he really started to take the music seriously and not long after was when he started to make a bit of money here and there from selling the vinyls.

DJ Target Later on, Wiley's dad helped us out here and there, 'cause he was a musician. He engineered a track or two on the first album, he knows a lot.

Danny Weed Mark [Flow Dan] thought up the name, Roll Deep.

Flow Dan It was the main hook of a bashment song I used to listen to. Wiley came to me when we were making 'Terrible', he said we needed a collective name. He said, 'You always say you roll deep, so shall we just use that?' I said, 'Go on then,' and that's how it happened. It means to be together, to share everything you do.

Breeze When we first came onto the scene people were definitely like, 'It's another bunch of black boys.' But we are very different with our music and we were not on a bad boy thing. Yes, we were from road but we were trying to do our own thing and go in a different direction.

Danny Weed I was a DJ at first, before Roll Deep had formed properly. We were all in little bunches; I was doing a set on Rinse FM at that time with Breeze and Scratchy. Wiley would come and do my show sometimes but he was normally doing Pay As U Go. It started like that and then we had the idea of coming together as a collective – even though we were all together anyway – as Roll Deep.

DJ Target So yeah, Roll Deep started and we were all making tunes that are

ILFORD DELTA 3200 PRO

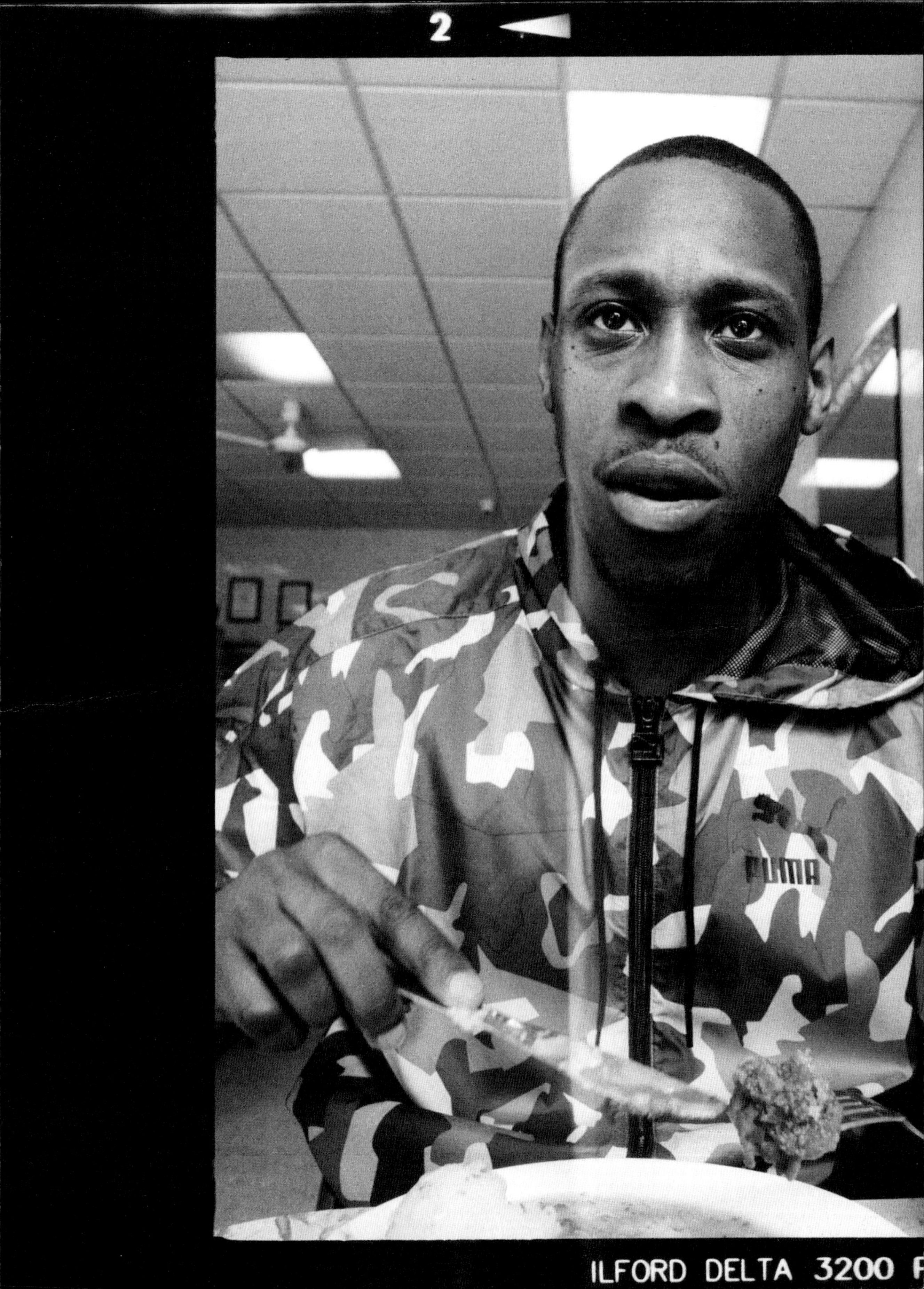
2
PUMA
ILFORD DELTA 3200

now known as grime, like 'Creeper', 'Igloo'. I had a track called 'Earth Warrior' that Wiley says inspired him to make 'Eskimo'. No one knew what the music was called then. We were just making instrumentals for the MCs, as opposed to garage where you were making vocal tunes for the girls to dance to. With early grime instrumentals, it was for the MCs – music that we thought MCs would sound sick on.

Danny Weed Danny C, everyone used to use his studio, they still use it now. They made 'Bounce' there, that was one of the first tunes Wiley recorded there. This one time, Danny went away for a week and Nick [Denton, Dizzee's manager and Wiley's former manager] was there. Nick was a scratch DJ, but he had a few industry links, I dunno how. So when Danny was away this one week, we used to go and use his studio and get this geezer to scratch on some tunes. Nick had scratched on one of the Pay As U Go tracks, that's how they met him. So Danny went away, we went down there and Nick got straight onto Wiley, like, 'I know a few people'. Nick became the person who had the links and from there he managed Wiley, Dizzee, and Roll Deep.

Scratchy I was in a crew called Flying Squad, we was on radio and Wiley heard me on radio with his cousin, Biggie Pitbull. He basically told me to come to Rinse and I joined Roll Deep then. Couple of my friends didn't get the call, which was awkward [laughs] so… yeah.

Danny Weed I got into production off the back of Wiley. He was like, 'Look, I've got a remix today for two grand. We're gonna do it. Don't worry, you can do it, trust me, this is all you have to do. Start with the drums.' Classic Wiley. I'd seen Darren and my brother and Wiley making beats in the studio this whole time anyway, so it wasn't totally new. I gave it a go and he gave me half the money – a grand or whatever it was at the time – and I was like, 'Ok, I can produce now, thanks for that, Will!' 'Creeper' come about when Wiley and Dizzee and everyone was doing a session. That was when they were all managed by the same manager, Nick [Denton] – Diz is still managed by him. When they all went to sleep I was like, 'Right, this is my opportunity to practice again.' I got onto Nick about making a beat, and we actually made that beat, 'Creeper', together.

Lewi White When 'Eskimo' landed that was really the birth of grime, I think. That was when I think Wiley did however-many-thousand out the boot of his car. That was the stamp, that was the song that said, 'This is grime, this is what it is.'

Scratchy The 'Warrior Charge', that come from back in the day. It was the olders. There was a crew called SS Crew and this guy called Jermaine that was in it had an argument or beef with someone and they chased him down the road, all doing that noise. I just put it in a lyric one day. Flow Dan used to do it as well. It came from beef, basically and I just put it in a lyric and then it became my ad-lib, or signature or whatever.

Trim I don't know what people perceive of me but I always try and correct them by the work that I do. Whatever they think of me, or think I'm doing, I always try to prove them wrong by always doing the work that they think I'm not doing. A lot of people may perceive me as a tearaway when I was young, always robbing, always doing mad shit, doing bad things. Other people see me as a man 'cause they've seen me with my son, trying to get through life and work at all kinds of jobs. Some people who know me from music probably perceive me as a mad man 'cause they always see me cussing MCs and clashing. But you can't get better at your game if you don't touch on other subjects, or other levels, whether it be higher or lower than yours. You've always got to be trying to touch on other subjects. I don't know how people perceive me, but I would like them to think of me as a guy that works hard, 'cause that's all I ever do. That's all I'm ever doing. If they have me down as anything else, it's out of order. Three years ago, I had done 14 mixtapes – I don't think anyone apart from JME and Wiley has done 14 mixtapes. They say all kinds of stuff about me, but my discography should say a lot more. That's why I work so hard because people have got me up as all kinds of things and I'm always trying to prove them wrong. I want to be thought of as the guy that works and does the job.

Danny Weed When we was making the first Roll Deep album, we were at this studio that Wiley found in Hoxton; it was non-stop vibes for two months. You'd go and never know what would happen. You'd wake up excited like 'Yes, studio today.' It would get to 7pm and it would be time for brandy, so someone would get sent to the shop to buy 12 bottles of Courvoisier. Everyone just having fun. When the Roll Deep album were done, Ruff Sqwad came in and done *Guns & Roses Volumes 1* and *2*, we done *Creeper 1* and *2* in there. That two or three months, a lot of classic songs were made during that period. The bill wasn't nice though. But Wiley got it all back in the end. It was about £35k for the studio. We spent about £15k just on cabs.

DJ Target This was pre any record deal, but he'd made money on all of his white labels. He fronted the money. The plan was like, 'We'll do it, I'll pay it, you get a deal and pay the money back.' And it worked like he said. We done the album, got an album deal, he took his money out, everyone got paid. He still supports people now, Wiley.

Manga When I joined Roll Deep, bare people hated me on my estate. 'When I'm Ere' came out, I was getting beef everyday 'cause my face was so bait and I had no idea. I'd go to the shop and I'd get beef. I didn't know how big 'When I'm Ere' was.

Danny Weed When you've got nothing, I suppose it did inspire us, we were around that energy, we were from council estates, and that's what naturally came out. So when things do start to go well, and life's a little bit more glossy, you don't naturally make that music I suppose.

Previous page: Trim eats pie, mash and liquor at Eastenders Pie 'n' Mash – Poplar, E14

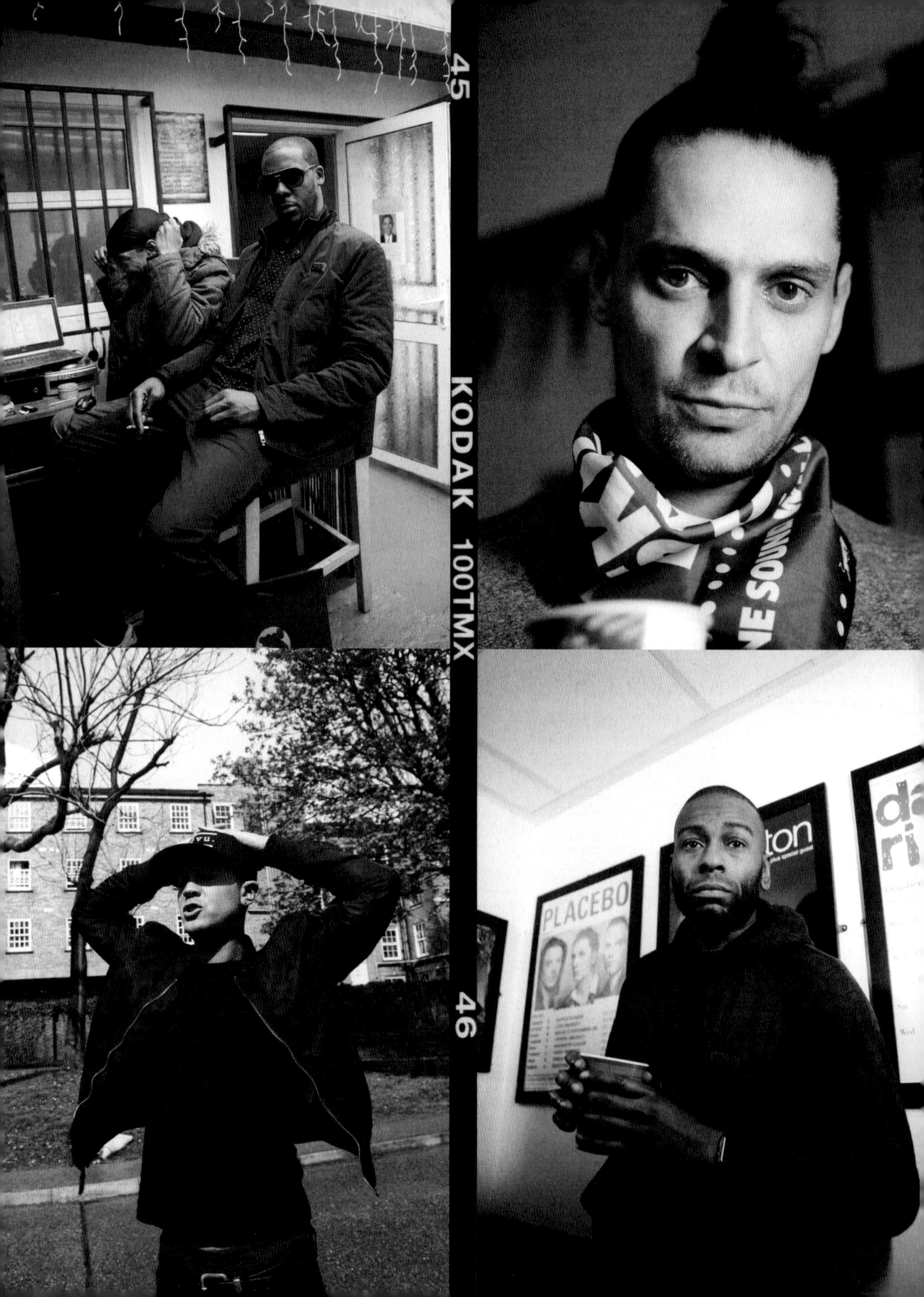
45
KODAK 100TMX
46
PLACEBO

I TOLD YOU IN '03
ITS SWITCHED UP
NOW LOOK

WE'RE THE FUCKING BEST.

DJ Target It felt like a lot of grime artists – including Roll Deep – as time progressed and you had the chance of being in the charts and selling loads of albums, the music did get less gritty.

Danny Weed What have you got to talk about when you're not stuck on the estate with nothing?

DJ Target We're still on the estate sometimes now. But in those early days, we weren't trying to make it in the music industry, it was our outlet to make music and talk about where we grew up and our friends, what we know, inner-city London streets. Without even knowing it, that was what came out.

Danny Weed I don't think *In At The Deep End* [Roll Deep's debut album] was a million miles off really. We tried to get the balance right. We always had Wiley and that's what separated us from everyone else, because he's good at making commercial music, naturally. He's a genius at it I always try and advise the younger guys coming through our label [Pitched Up]; if you've got a sound, run with that. We love making the more commercial ones too – 'Shake A Leg' was fun to make. I didn't plan to make a 'commercial track'.

DJ Target It wasn't as calculated as people over the last few years trying to get a song on Radio 1. We didn't even know who [former head of Radio 1] George Ergatoudis was. 1Xtra wasn't even around then really. It was irrelevant then. Pirate and Sidewinder was our things. 1Xtra and the charts wasn't our thing.

Trim I wasn't willing to do the same things that others were doing. I wanted people to respect me; I didn't want to be a fucking dickhead. I didn't want people to talk to me or deal with me the way they dealt with other people around me. Me and Wiley fell out. We stopped talking, over women and stuff, but for me it was that I wanted to build my own brand. To be my own thing, I knew I had to go away and develop it myself and keep working. That's why I've got so many mixtapes 'cause I had to keep working, I had to work harder than others. I knew it was a sacrifice but I was willing to do it. I didn't come into music to make more friends. I've got five sisters, a hundred million cousins. For me, it wasn't about making new friends; it was more about trying to make money for the family that I have got.

Manga I don't think Roll Deep gets enough credit and that's not me saying that 'cause I was in it, it's 'cause I was Roll Deep's biggest fan before I even met them. The era before me was incredible; God's Gift, Wiley, Dizzee, Breeze, Karnage, Target, Danny Weed, Tinchy was basically in Roll Deep, Riko, Scratchy, Flow Dan, Then my era, me, Trim, Roachee, JME, Syer Barz, Skepta. *You see the four best crews in the game, I'm in them.* All these man come from Roll Deep but no one shouts out Roll Deep and that bare gets on my nerves. We were the best grime crew in history; look who has come from Roll Deep and tell me we're not the best.

Previous page: Former members of Roll Deep, L to R: Jamakabi, Scratchy, Roachee, Manga, Danny Weed, Flow Dan, DJ Karnage, J2K
Opposite: Riko Dan – Dalston, N16

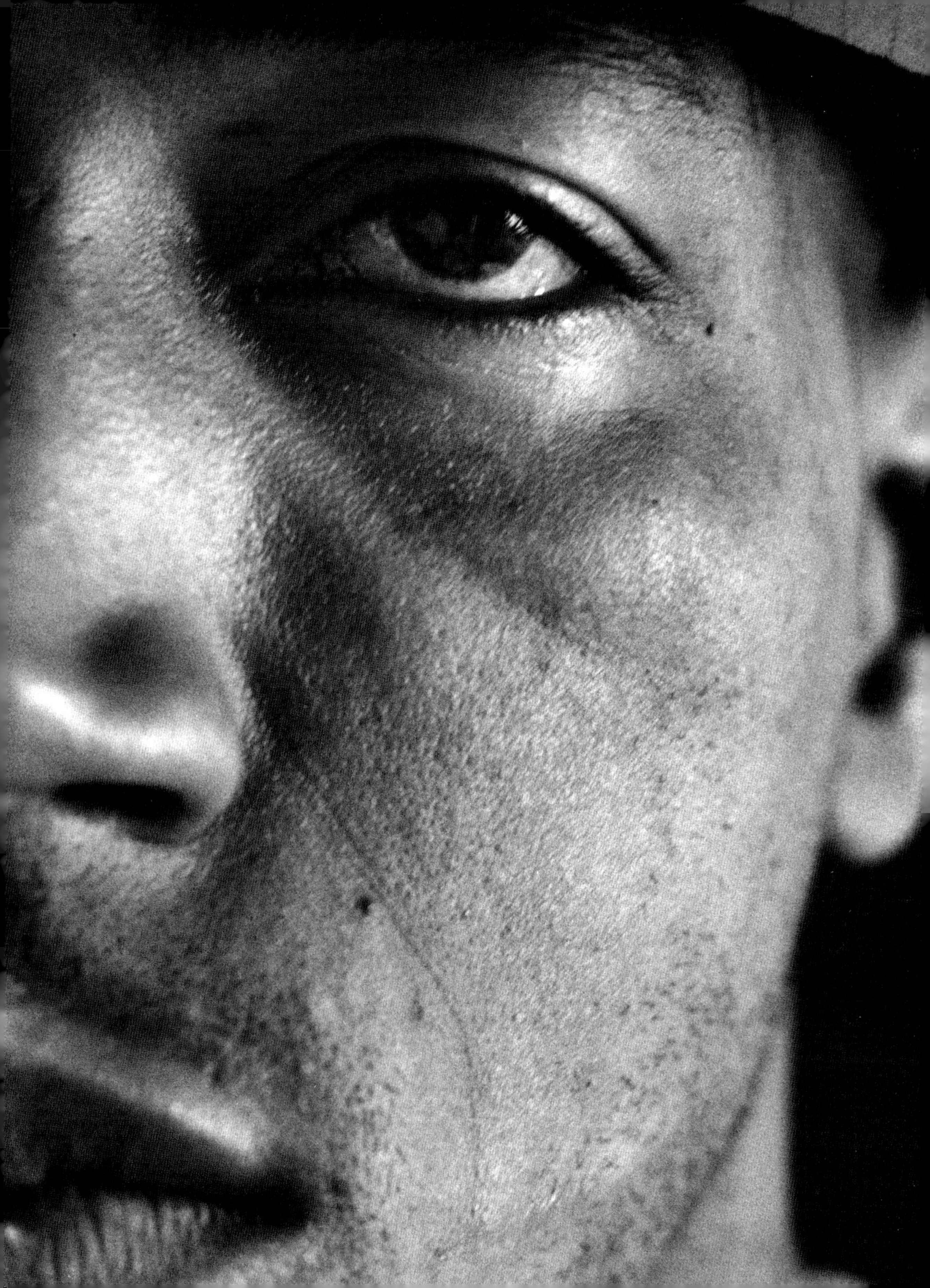

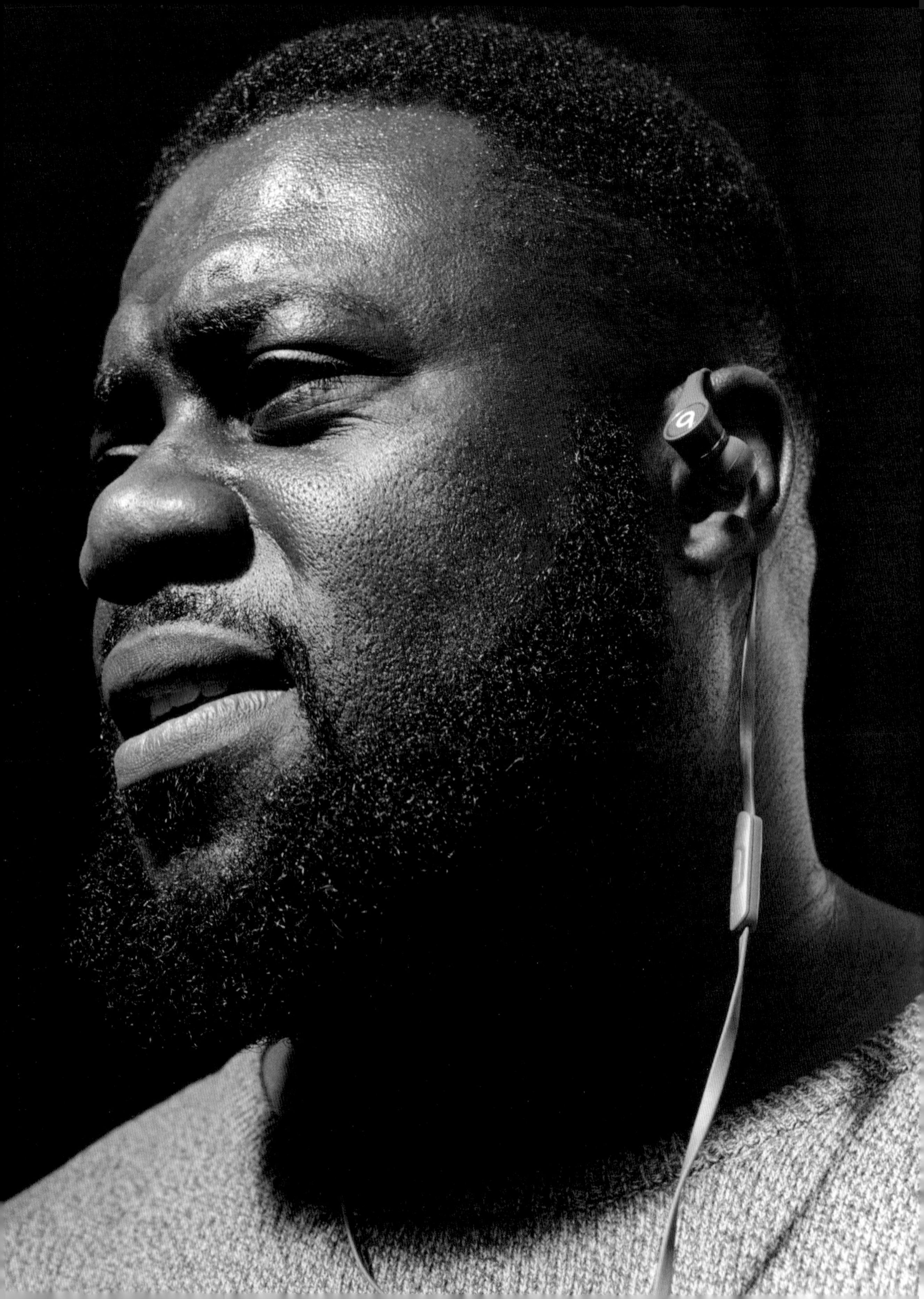

Natural. Artistic. Sounds. Touching. You.

Double O N.A.S.T.Y. Crew was the best team. They had all of the talent. But the problem with them is that there was no team players, they was all individuals. They were so far gone with the individuals they had, but I wasn't going to tell them that, being in a rival crew and Wiley wasn't going to tell them that either. They had five or six very, very strong players. Roll Deep and East Connection, honestly no, we didn't have the same talent. We didn't touch N.A.S.T.Y.

Sharky Major One day, Marcus [Nasty] said to me, 'Do you want to come radio?' Everyone knew who Marcus was in the area, and now he's a DJ, he's got this radio show, and he's asking me if I want to do it. I used to MC with Demon, so I rung him first and he was like, 'Ah, I just come back from football. I can't be bothered, I'm gonna have a bath.' He weren't on it. So I rung my friend Jamie, who was mates with Stormin, rung Stormin and he said, 'Yeah!' We went radio with Marcus, smashed it. Me, Marcus Nasty and Stormin started on Flava FM, that's how N.A.S.T.Y. started.

Stormin At the end of the show, the man said, 'Yes, that was the sound of the Nasty Boys.' and we said, 'Nah, we're not no boys, bruv, don't call us boys!' Don't get me wrong, we're kids, fifteen, sisteen years old [laughs] but you know, don't call us boys. He said, 'OK, Nasty *Crew*,' and we said, 'Yeah we'll take that.' We started creating mad waves and it got to a point where a lot of people knew us, in East London. It was me, Marcus and Sharky on Flava, then Armour joined and Dizzee came with him, 'cause Dizzee and Armour had been mates for years. I also knew Dizzee, we was good friends from young, he lived near my sister's family and whatnot. So I introduced Dizzee to Sharky, they got to know each other, they got on well. So then Dizzee must have took us to make a dubplate called 'Ready for War'. I think that must have been the first ever grime record, it must have been, 'cause there was nothing else that sounded like it. We had to go cut it in the dubplate place and everything else was garage. From there we linked up with Double and Hyper and then Kano came later on.

Sharky Major D Double E, I knew from the manor, Hyper I knew from the manor. They had their own click, 187 Crew with Jammer as the DJ. We was on different stations, but they were friends still.

Jammer I met D Double just around. At the age of about sixteen, we started playing records together, it wasn't really tunes yet, but everybody knew each other and used to play jungle. Double started to go on radio, so I did that too. Then I got a job at Essential Direct and started getting some studio equipment and building a studio. We started a crew called 187 Crew; me, Ebony JD, Double D and Hyper. We were on Flava or Mission or one of those weird stations. We were doing our thing, we were popping for a bit.

Stormin Marcus was the founder, the main guy, and he was the DJ. But then Marcus departed for a little while and his brother came in, Mac 10, another DJ who was banging. So we kept the bond going from then. Something happened and the radio's changed and we moved to Deja – and that's where everything started changing. Jammer said. 'Lets start making tracks.' Sharky made 'Chinaman,' I made 'Good Ya Know.' We went over 'Destruction', Hyper went on 'Take U Out'. That's when we really got into our stride, if you like.

Jammer Double was like, 'There's this guy named Marcus Nasty and everyone's into this crew and we should join.' I was like, 'We just started 187 Crew, I don't wanna join'. Double was like, 'Nah man, I think this would be a really good move.' Marcus came up to the radio and I thought he was gonna steal my records, 'cause that's what he was known for. But he was pretty cool, he was just looking at my records and then he left and didn't take my records and I was pretty happy. Double decided to join but I just wanted to carry on doing my own thing, so I started making beats in my basement. This went on for about two or three months. Then Double came to me: 'This crew thing's going really well, we're on the radio, it's popping off. We need a producer, we need you'. I kinda gave in to what he was saying. To cut a long story short, Sharky and Stormin come over, I started playing them some of my beats and putting some stuff down and that was it, from that day we never parted. Sharky, Stormin, Double were at my house every day, building, building, building until we came out with 'Birds in the Sky', 'Destruction', 'Army', all of my early instrumentals where you'd just hear everyone spitting on. I became, I suppose you could say, number one producer, on the street. It was me and Wiley really; it was Roll Deep and it was N.A.S.T.Y. Crew. I was the producer for them and he was the producer for Roll Deep. We kind of just took over the scene.

Crazy Titch I didn't hear too much of them when I was in prison around 2011, 2012, but I heard about them when they got good. Once they got Monkey and D Double in, that's when they got good. Someone sent me a tape. It had N.A.S.T.Y., Doogz and Dizzee Rascal on it – sickest set ever, sickest. It was ape. Ape shit. It was probably from Deja. They was hammering the life out of it, going absolutely crazy. I was like, 'Yes, this is the truth.'

Terror Danjah Dizzee was in N.A.S.T.Y. Crew – that's another part of the history that gets wiped. They say he started from Roll Deep, but it wasn't. He used to roll with Sharky, so he was rolling with N.A.S.T.Y. Crew originally, he's from the same bits as those guys. I don't even think Dizzee knew Wiley and them lot then. I've heard Dizzee tell the story from his perspective; he went studio with Roll Deep, recorded 'Bounce' and that was it, but he was in N.A.S.T.Y. before that. I think he did a few tunes with Sharky and them lot, but he didn't really do anything with N.A.S.T.Y. as such. Them times they weren't really recording, it was more sets, innit.

Footsie I came into N.A.S.T.Y. through Marcus. He come out of jail and he was like, 'Nah, you've been putting the work in, you're a member now.'

Hitman Hyper The person who put me on, I have to say, is Terror Danjah. I can't remember how I first met Terror, it was in the ends, around Forest Gate. This was when we were on the drum & bass, jungle thing. Terror was starting up a crew, Reckless Crew – he was the DJ – and he introduced me to D Double. We had me, Double, Lethal – not Lethal B, this was Lethal before he changed his name to Triple Threat – Bruza was in the camp, Jammer came along at one point, Jammer was our DJ as well. We were doing well, we were doing OK. From there we got to the point where we started making a little name for ourselves on radio. At that

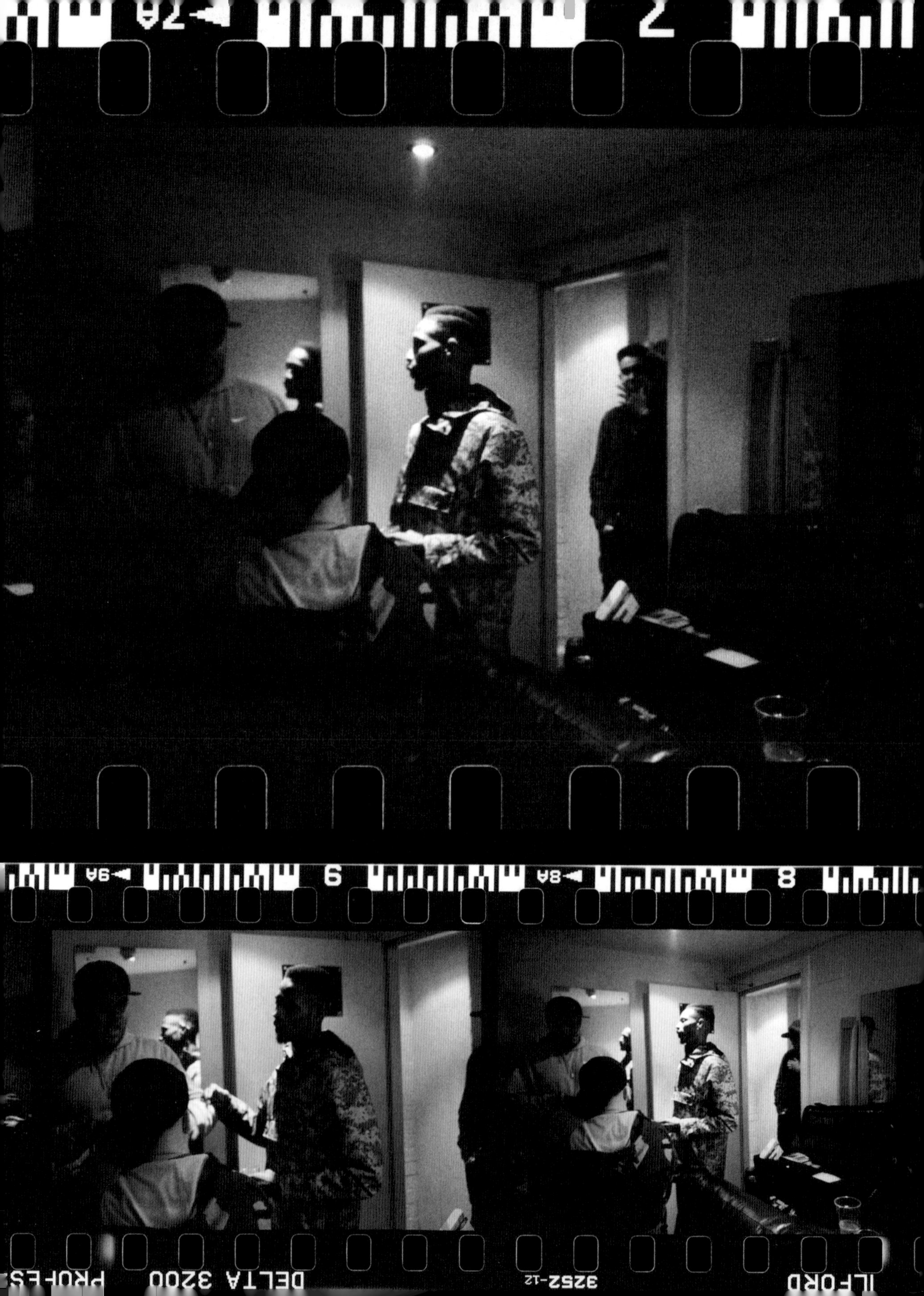

8
8A
9
9A
ILFORD
3252-12
DELTA 3200
PROFES

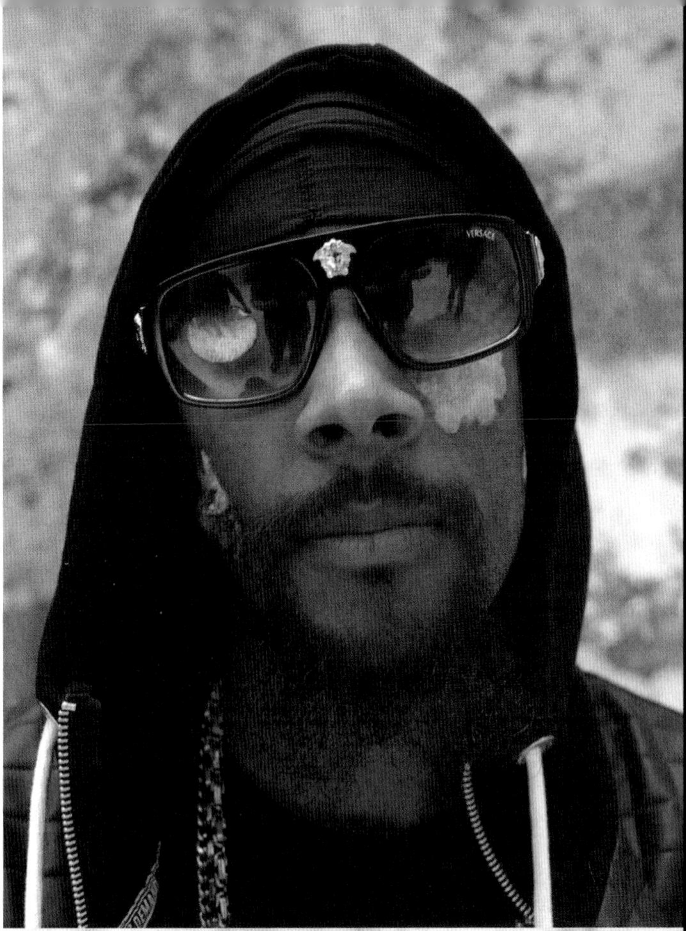
VERSACE

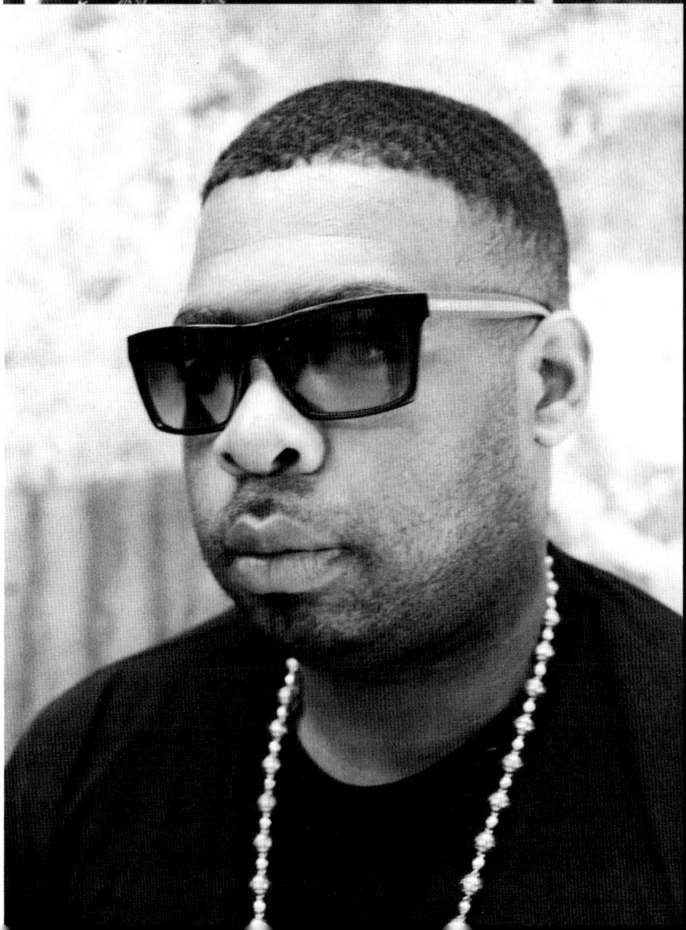

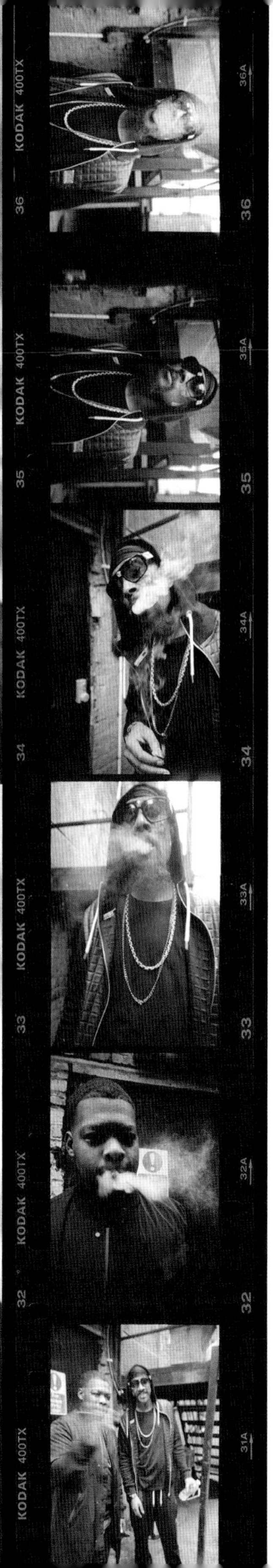
KODAK 400TX
36
36A
35
35A
34
34A
33
33A
32
32A
31A

70 This Is Grime

time, N.A.S.T.Y. Crew were on there as well. N.A.S.T.Y. Crew was only Marcus Nasty, Sharky Major and Stormin then. Things got better and we decided to join them and you know, the rest is history really. But if it weren't for Terror, saying, 'You know what, I think you can do this thing, you're alright.' I don't think I would have been involved.

Sharky Major Kano, we acknowledged his talent from early. D Double wanted to bring in Monkey, I wanted to bring in Kano. So we brought both of them to Jammer's Basement, made them go back to back on Jammer's beats. We was all looking at each other like, 'Oh, they're fucked, lets bring them both in!' That's how it was. It wasn't a clash, but it was to see what they was both about.

Ghetts I've always loved music and I tried my hand in spitting with the Sharky Majors and the Stormins and I was shit, as the man dem were quick to tell me [laughs]. I was nowhere near their level of MCing. Then something strange happened in jail. I was reading loads of books and what happened was I found the ability to paint pictures. From the books, I got the beginning, middle and end format, which is still the structure to my lyrics now. While I was in [jail], I was speaking to Sharky on the phone and asking him what I should do when I come home. I was speaking to Stormin too. On occasion, I spoke to Dizzee and I got some advice from the man dem. They was telling me that one liners is a big thing at the moment and when you come home make sure you got a few one liners there because they're doing well in the rave. I came out of jail 4 August 2003 and from that day onwards I was doing work. A guy that I was in jail with, he's out now doing his thing on the rap scene, he's called Stanaman – big up Stana – he had a relationship with Jammer, they're from the same area. It was either Stormin or Stana who took me to Jammer's first. At the time Jammer was doing the *Lord of the Decks* CD and I done my tunes on there; one was called 'My Mind Worx' and so that was my first bit of work. Then from there obviously with N.A.S.T.Y. Crew being from my area and me being childhood friends with Sharky and Stormin, it just made sense that I went in that direction, at the time.

Kano Grime was… a rebellion. I came into it around 2002, before it was 'grime', but there was this sense of kids reacting against something; garage, the system, school, life. It was so exciting, man, so exciting. It was just about energy. We used to go Deja, stations in other ends, shows, we just went everywhere, places we probably shouldn't have been going. It was Palace Pavilion every weekend. Club EQ in Stratford, Young Man Standing, Oceans, Rex, It was always something. Anywhere you could touch mic, it was just about being there.

Ghetts Being naïve, making music from a naïve point of view is an amazing thing. You don't have the stress of thinking how long a tune is, or needs to be, whether radio would play us. It didn't matter, it just felt right and it felt right because of my naïvety. It was culture. Akademiks tracksuits, the trainers with your name on and cartoon character. Pirate radio, being in that environment. The level of competition was so high.

Opposite: Former members of N.A.S.T.Y. Crew L to R: Ghetts, Monkstar, Kano, Jammer

Kano I think with us it was that we covered all angles in terms of what an MC brought to the table. We had Hyper that was the aggressive one, D Double E bought the mad originality, there was me that bought the flows and a little bit of the girl thing, Ghetto come in later on with that energy, Stormin who was the more bubbly fun side and Armour who had the Yardie vibe. We was more of a Wu-Tang Clan, than anything else [laughs]. We was proper into the lyrics and everyone was powerful in their own way. Everyone brought their thing and collectively we were…good. N.A.S.T.Y. was also a bit more underground than Roll Deep really, and, yeah, we did our thing. It was cool.

Dizzee Rascal Stormin, Ozzie B… there was so many, so much personalities… Flirta D. So much. There was nuff. You had the guys who got the most reloads, but it wasn't… Like I wouldn't even say necessarily that I was the best MC. I don't think I was the best, technically or lyrically, that's not something I should say, but the levels of how people put their bars together. Like especially with someone like Doogz or a Sharky Major, there was a lot of really technical guys. This is even before Ghetts came out, one of the most technical guys. But there was plenty of that on the come up, as well as there were people that are a bit more bouncy, for the party-type MCs too.

Ghetts Stormin's one of the stage show dons. I'm talking like, if they say grime comes from Tower Hamlets and Newham, if you wanna talk about house party circuits, then Wiley, Stormin, Crazy Titch and another guy called Spooky, they were the house party circuit guys in Tower Hamlets and Newham. Wiley was a DJ at this time too, so Stormin is like one of the earliest sound men and clash men from grime, realistically.

Bashy D Double E was my all-time hero. I don't care what anyone says, no-one was touching D Double E. It was just the style, it was so unique, you had to pay attention to it. What's crazy is people spitting his lyrics back now, but I remember when it was a brand-new lyric and it had never been heard. *When I saw your gash I was like oooer oooer, it's dirtee-tee, that's meee meee.* I remember when that was a new lyric because gash wasn't a word before and everyone started using gash and D put that in there. Oh my God, he was the best. I don't give a fuck.

Footsie N.A.S.T.Y. disbanded. It was just at that point and so we started Newham Generals. I remember that day trying to think what to call ourselves – me, Dubz and Monkey. It was Double and Monk, nah, I think it was Monkey who picked Double's lyrics; he was like, 'Come on man, we're all Newham Generals, we all live in Newham.' It was all-time classic D Double bars. It just made sense.

Stormin I'm a dibbler and dabbler. I've taken another path, although my roots is there. Maybe we can get some tracks together from other N.A.S.T.Y. members. There's talks about a N.A.S.T.Y. reunion, we'll see. It'll be hard to get Armour. No one knows where that guy is, no one can find him. He's disappeared.

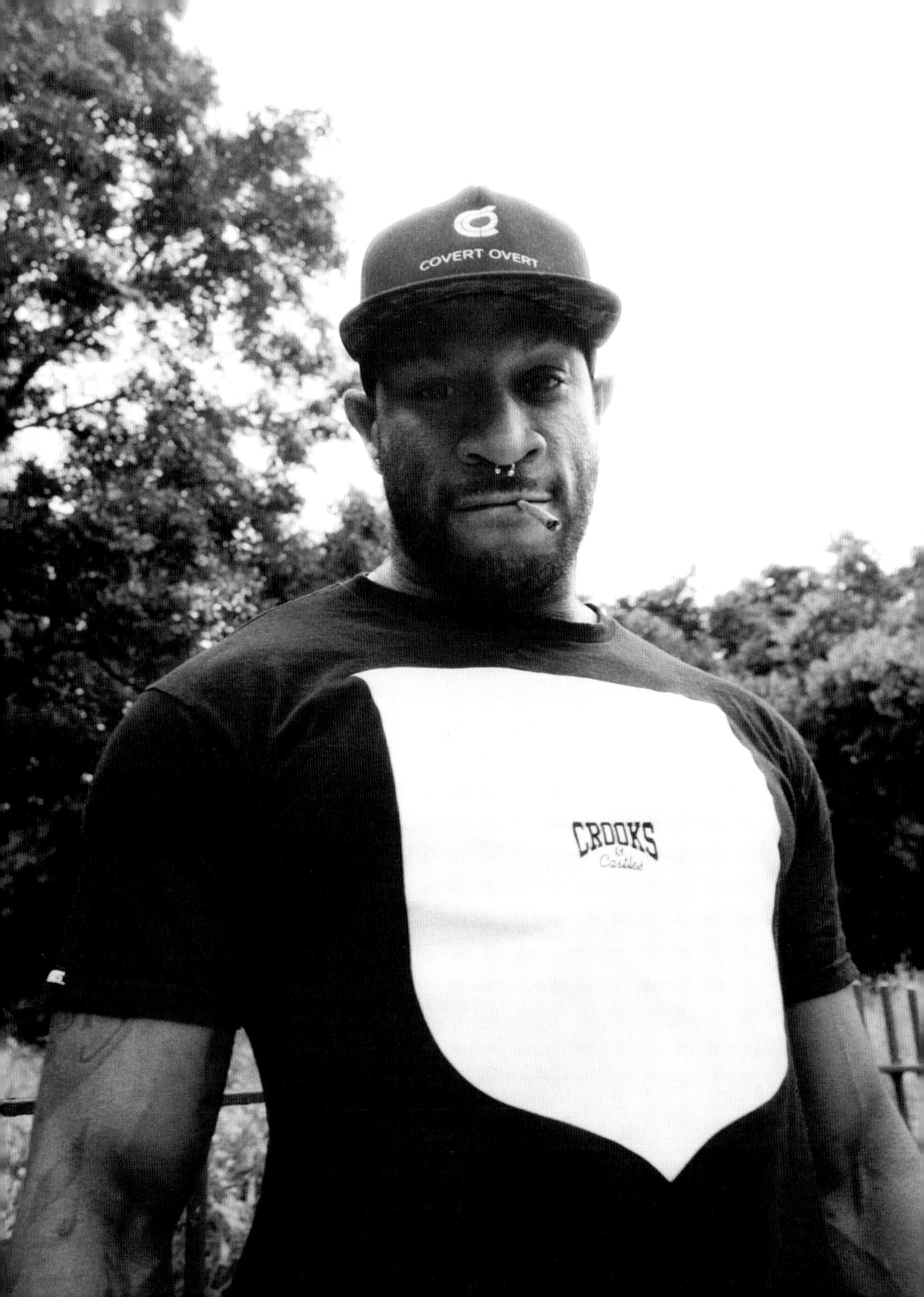
COVERT OVERT
CROOKS

Terror Danjah – So Sure

Bruza Ah, Terror is, ah mate... Terror to grime is, like a right foot or a hand. You need him. Without him, there ain't no grime. He brings a different element to it, he's got a different style, like me. When I MC, there's no one that sounds like me, but that's good, I don't want you to sound like me. You might have influences, but I'm Bruz and that person who sounds like me, he's just a bit whoever. And that's the way that Terror is. When you hear the Gremlin giggle, that's his unique style. A lot of producers try to put a signature in their tunes, Terror started all that. He started that, from day one. The amount of producers I reckon he's influenced and I don't think he gets the recognition. He's underrated, but if you know, you know. Terror is needed in this thing. The amount of people that he's influenced, it's crazy. Grime might not be about forever, but the way Terror is and the way he has brought through his own character in his music – he speaks through his beats – that will see him outlast most of us, I reckon.

Brutal and British: Bruza – Snaresbrook, E18.
Opposite: Terror Danjah in his basement studio – Pitfield Street, N1

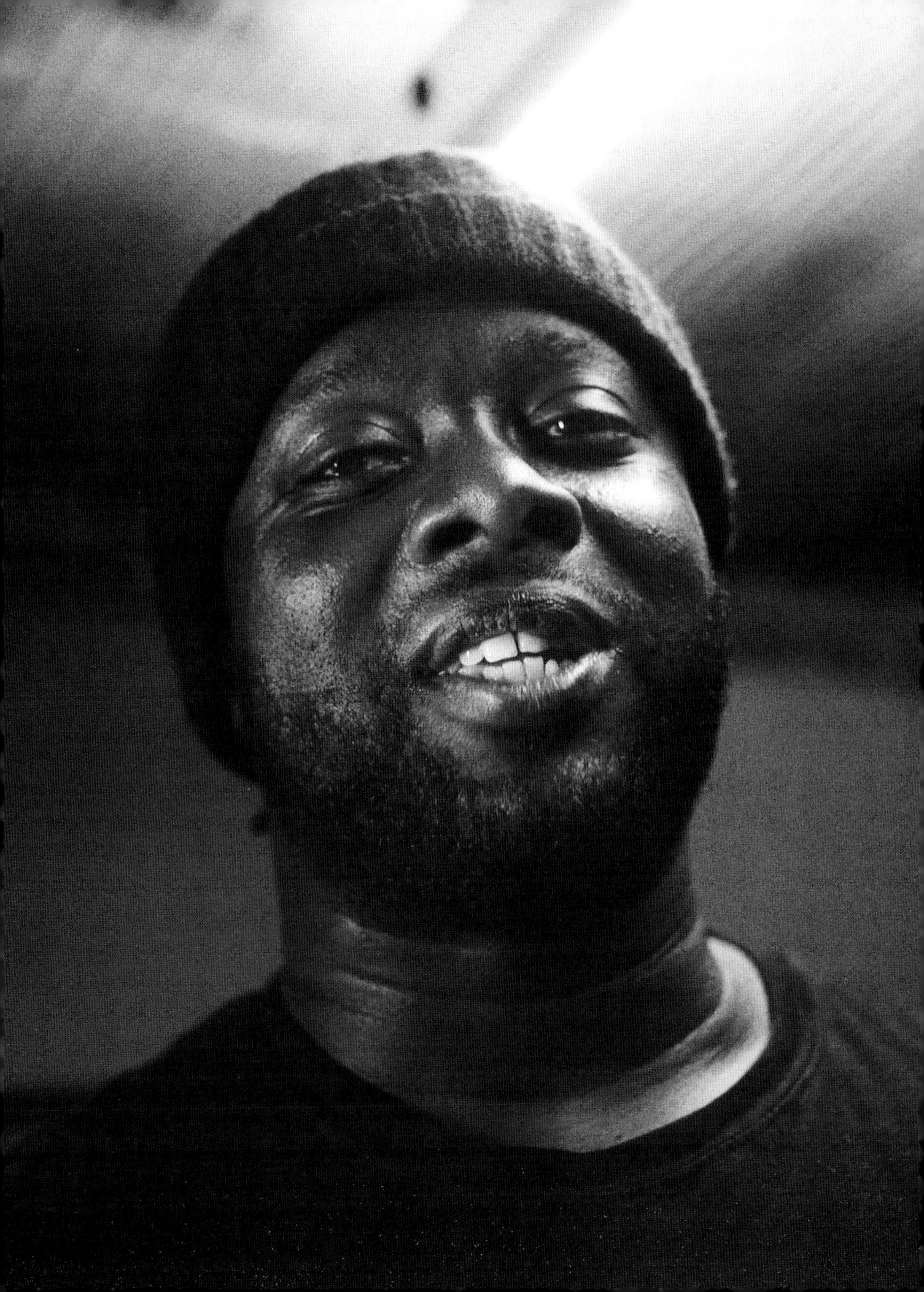

Wot Do U Call It?

Text WILEY to 85080

Wot Do U Call It?

Tinchy Stryder We didn't call it grime, I don't know who named it.

Chantelle Fiddy Someone said EZ was the first to use 'grimy garage' on his radio show on Kiss. I don't know. Saskilla tweeted me recently to say, 'Big up EZ for using the word first, Chantelle Fiddy for using it first in print'. I don't know where he got that from 'cause I ain't ever said I used it first in print.

Bashy It's a murky time, it's very vague. For a while grime didn't even have a name. I could swear it was Chantelle Fiddy. People were saying, 'Ah it's this grimy garage music from East London,' and then it got shortened to grime. For a while when Wiley was doing Eskimo Dance – when they used to be in Watford [at Area] and N.A.S.T.Y. Crew were there, me, Roll Deep – at that moment it wasn't called grime. There was no name for it, but everyone was there and so it existed. I remember everyone searching for a name – later Wiley did *Wot Do U Call It?* – but then Wiley had 'Eskibeat' and Jon E Cash had 'Sublow'. Everyone was trying to find a name but I guess grime stuck.

Crazy Titch At first I wasn't too sure about it, because we couldn't claim our own identity, but now I'm not too phased. If anything, the producers should have named it, because they was making the beats.

Bashy At first I thought, 'Why are they calling it grime?' Especially because it was mainly young black boys. I didn't really see many white boys for the first few years, there might have been the odd DJ or the producer, but from my world, it was all black boys. So I felt like, 'We're just young black boys expressing ourselves and they've found the name to call the music that we're making *grime*?' Do you know what I mean? I was young so it didn't stop me from writing lyrics but if you read the dictionary definition, it's like dirt. What happened though was we took ownership of it as a culture, so now it's cool, it's positive.

Chantelle Fiddy That would never have even crossed my mind, even once. That actually makes me sad to hear that people took it as a racial slur. If you go back to old radio sets, you'd hear the DJs going, 'This ones griiiiimy'. It was the word the DJs and MCs were using.

Matt Mason The word came long after the sound. Finding the right name for this new thing was something we talked about non-stop at *RWD*. It took the scene a while to agree on a label. I wish people still took time to label things – labelling a culture too early can hurt it. Slimzee was the first person I spoke to who defined the sound by the 8-bar arrangements. We called it '8-bar' for a few issues of *RWD* at least. Some people started calling it UK filth. I think EZ was the first person I heard say 'grimy' and later just 'grime'. There were other things happening that clouded all this too – 4/4, breakbeat garage, dubstep of course. There was so much fragmentation happening in the early 2000s. There was almost this race to brand grime. Jon E Cash was calling his stuff sublow, Wiley with the eski sound. There were at least twenty other names. It was exhausting. Everyone had their vision for what was next. At some point it just all fell together as grime.

Chantelle Fiddy It was a descriptor that stuck. The word 'grime' epitomised everything. What else could you have called it?

Alex Donne-Johnson (Online Director, RWD, 2001-2005) I just loved the chaotic time when sounds were being developed but nobody knew what to name them. It has formed the foundations of today's best mainstream music on a global level and goes to show the power of disrupting conventions. It feels like it's not really possible to do that again 'cause the internet now allows for things to be picked up and exploited by major labels before they are properly nurtured and ready to grow. In essence it was the perfect storm of just enough technology to help promote it, but not wide enough for it to be inevitably manipulated. I'd love to see that happen again but that would be much much harder now.

Chantelle Fiddy You know what I'm jealous of? Don't get me wrong, I don't want to be an MC, but I'm envious of the release that they get when they go onstage. As a fan, you get a partial release in the audience. You can achieve release through other types of music, but the difference with grime, to me, is that grime is the only 'real' genre primarily still coming from a point of honesty. Most other music is done on email, anonymous sessions, writing camps, business, business, business. With grime it feels often that business comes last. That works in its favour and against it. It's catch 22; it's why grime has suffered, because it's so hard to make money, but it's also the most important aspect of it.

Twin B (Alec Boateng) and Twin B (Alex Boateng) – High Street Kensington, W8
Next page: Wiley t-shirt, 2007

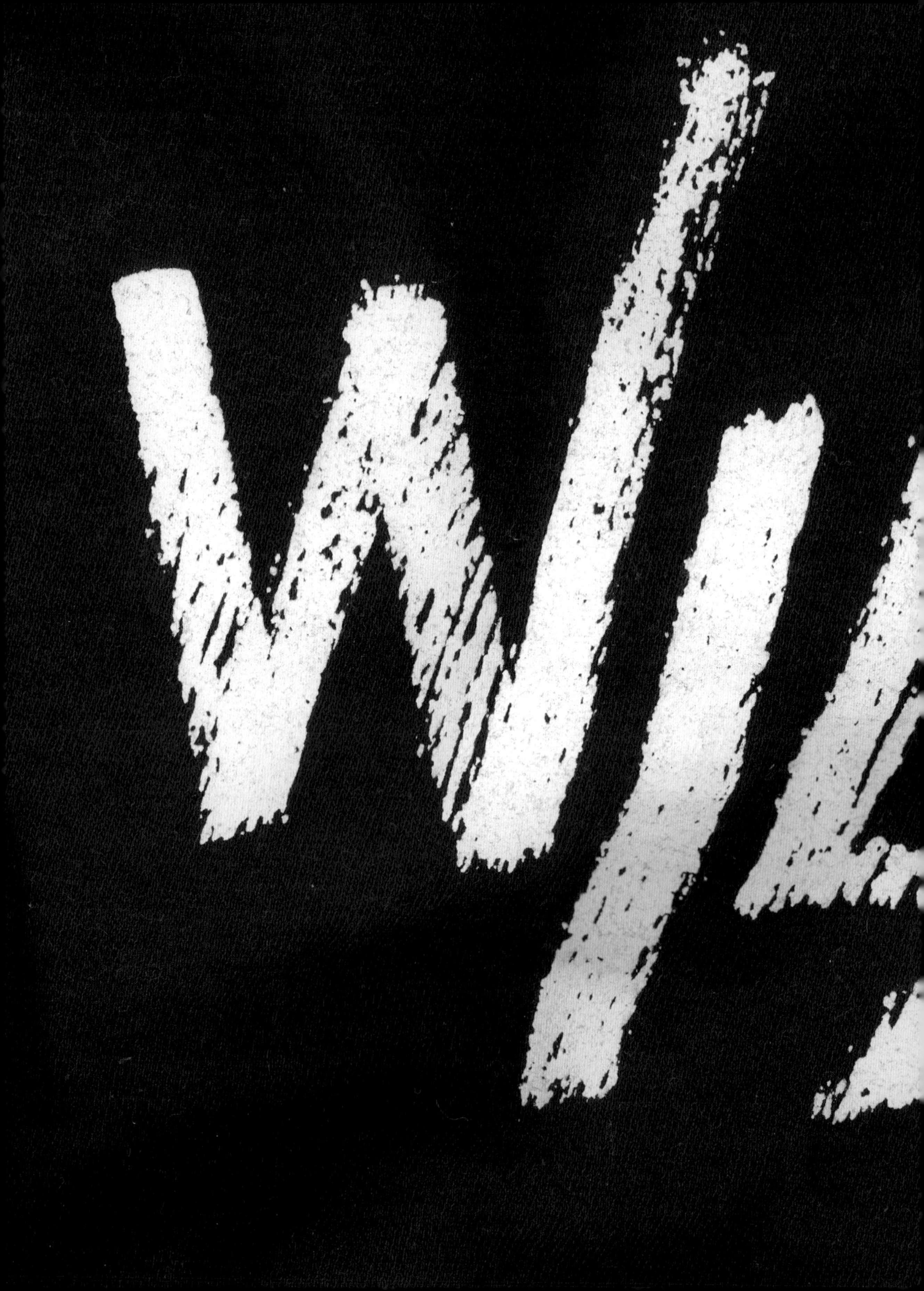

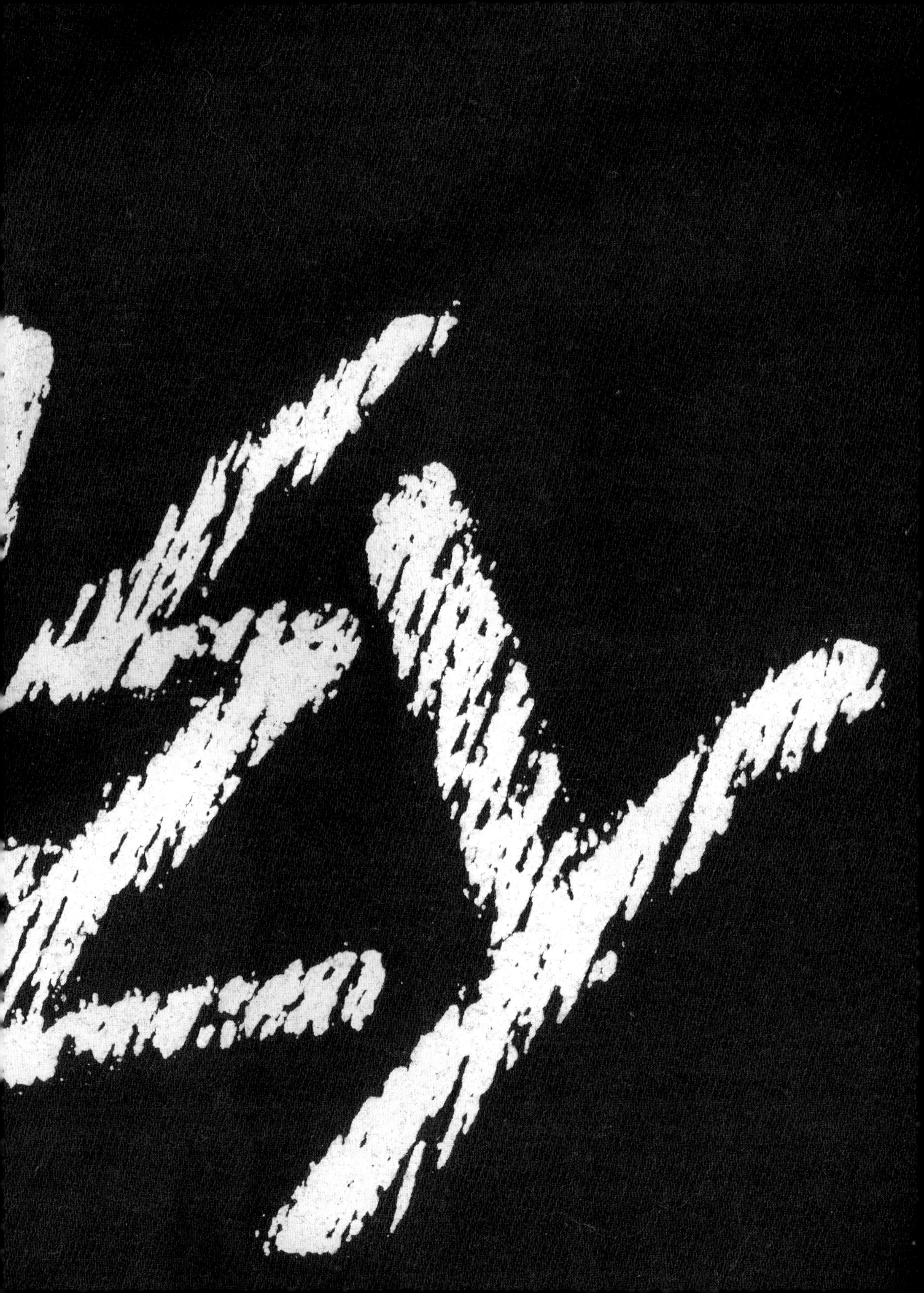

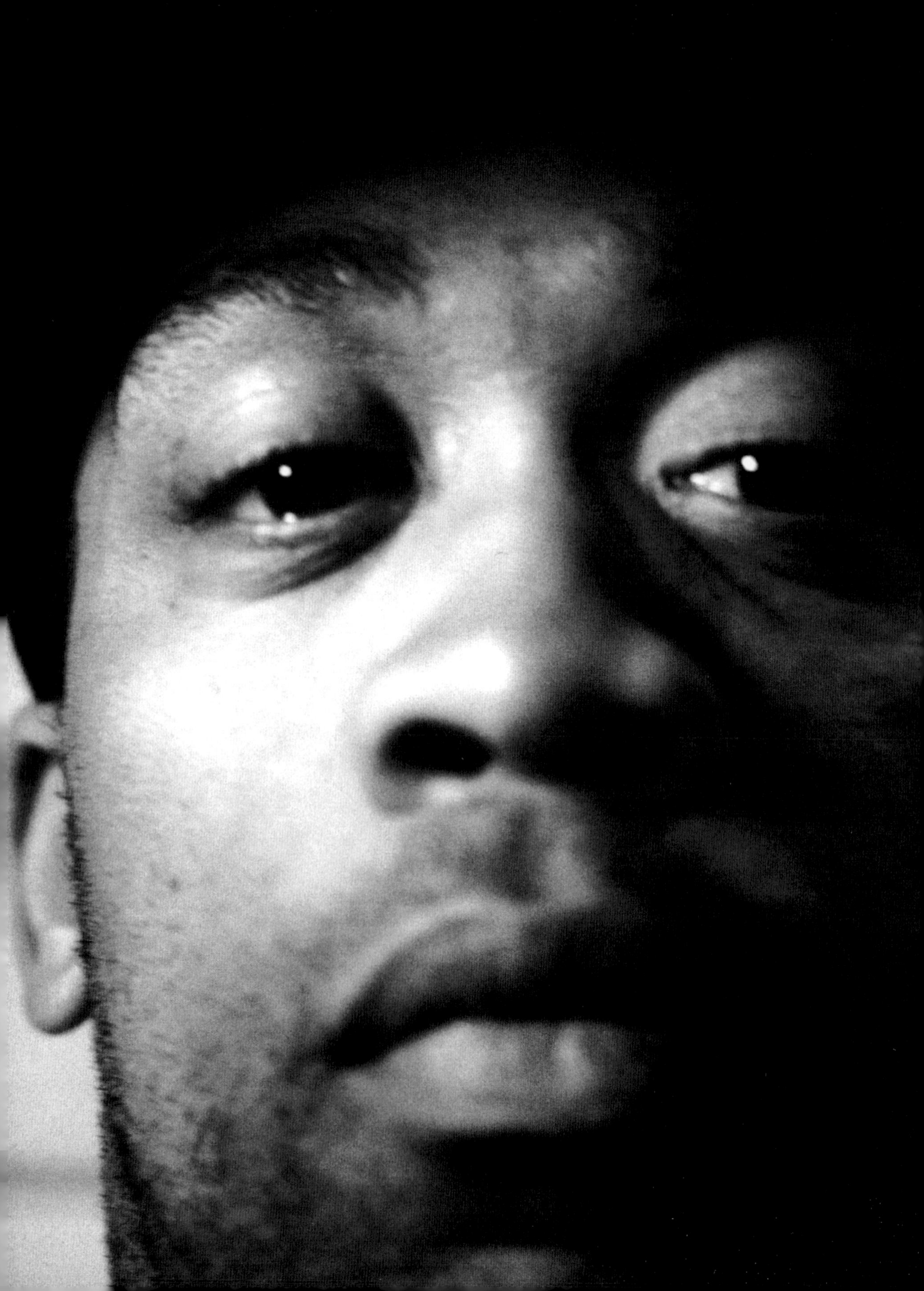

Eskiboy's the Reason Why Everybody's Here

Chantelle Fiddy Wiley does things with words that nobody else does. I've seen Wiley put bars together and I've seen how quickly he can construct a tune. His brain is not human. Well, it is, but he's wired so differently to us. A few years ago, I rang him and said, 'Dazed & Confused [magazine] have asked me to ask you to describe the last ten years of your life in ten words'. Two hours later he sent me a track called 'The Last Ten Years of My Life.' A whole song. And that's how Wiley works. I've never met anyone who works like that and whose brain works like that. As a writer, I look at what he does with words and it just blows my mind. Blows my mind. He was the first MC that I knew who religiously carried a dictionary in his backpack. And it wasn't there for show. We would be sat in my yard smoking a spliff and he would have it out, looking up words. He was very quick to study and learn new words.

Elf Kid Phenomenal. That's it. Phenomenal.
Blakie Outstanding. That's all.
Elf Kid How many generations? Five or ten? Ten. Still here. How old is he? Forty? He's a legend! Four decades.
Blakie Still here today.
Elf Kid Still here. Eski Boy!
Blakie Still watching us. Da 2nd Phaze.

Elf Kid *Treddin' on Thin Ice.*
Blakie For music.
Elf Kid New generation.
Blakie It's us.
Elf Kid Wiley Kat. Blakie and Elf Kid.
Blakie Eski Boy.
Elf Kid Square Gang.
Blakie William!
Both Bill! Bill! Bill!

Scratchy It's the reason why everyone's here, fam. It's the reason. It is.

Chip The first time I spoke to Wiley, he rang me during my maths class. I thought it was someone playing a prank. But it was him, and we worked together that same day. I would have been around fourteen, fifteen years old.

Manga Wiley found me on an estate in North West London. I was in Harlesden, randomly, walking down the road. Them times there, there wasn't cameras and that so he could walk the roads and no one knew his face, but I was a proper fan, so I knew what everyone looked like. I went up to him, I knew who he was. I said, 'I spit.' I spit to him on the roadside. He said, 'Sick, I want to help you.' The first time I ever went studio and recorded was when I met Wiley.

Doctor Wiley is the one that bought me in. When I was spitting on a little radio station in my ends, I think he heard me and he called me up and booked me for Eskimo. Wiley bought me in, 100%.

Kano Wiley, it's mad. He is clearly a visionary. For me, in terms of my career and loads of other people that I've seen, he likes to help others, he likes to see people in a position that he believes they could be in. He likes to encourage people, to see them fly. He's always been around. Since my early days, he's been there to encourage me and help me and direct me. Something he doesn't do for himself! He's a mad character, but he's got some genius about him. He could mostly be credited for this whole thing that they call grime now. He's been a big influence on my career and probably anyone from East London and anyone into grime now. Would I do a *Lord of the Mics* rematch? [laughs]. Nah, I doubt it, I doubt it. I wouldn't want to revisit that again, I'd just want it to be what it is. And I think I won that one, so…!

Sian Anderson Wiley is an anomaly, that's what Wiley is. I've decided that there's no other explanation for him than that. I mean, I sit there and I think, 'What must it feel like to have the weight of the whole industry and scene on your back?' Wiley is responsible for all of our careers in some way or another. I'm able to exist as Sian Anderson because Wiley existed as Wiley and if you go back to everyone's stories, from Twin B and his *Split Mics* compilation, to me doing marketing managing for

DELTA 3200 PRO

4329

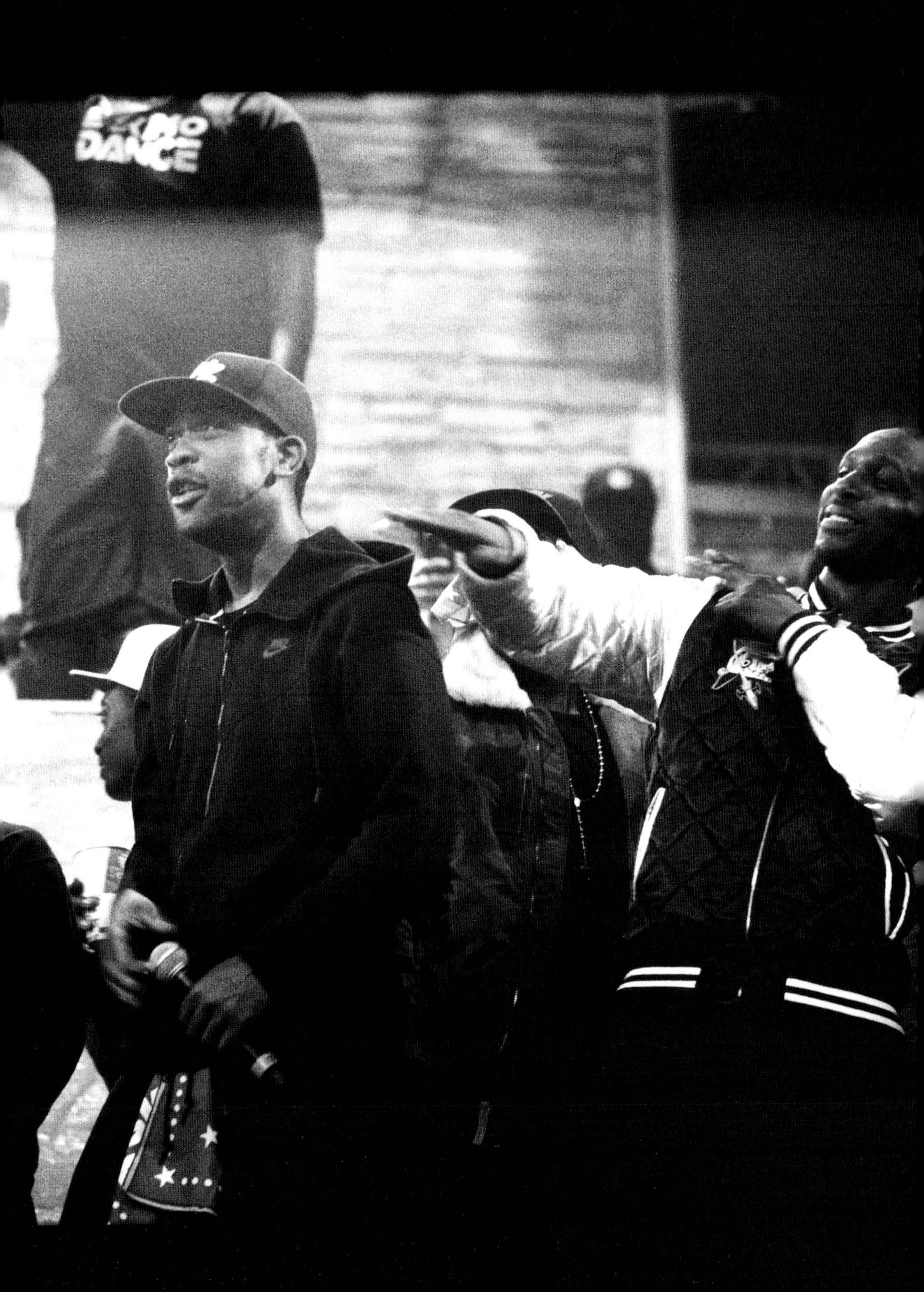
DANCE

Wiley at Atlantic. It's not just producers and MCs and DJs; everyone's career can go back to Wiley. He's always only ever been for the people and about pushing grime forward and being progressive, but he's just an anomaly, man. His mind is incredible.

Mikey J Wiley epitomises the scene. Even when I'd go down to get tracks off him, when we were working on [Kano's album] *140 Grime Street*, he was like, 'Just go down to the studio and get what you need'. He didn't think about me stealing something or being dodgy. He was like that all the time. And obviously he brought two of the biggest MCs that we have, Kane and Dizzee.

MSM Engineer JME didn't tell me Wiley was coming here. One day we were upstairs watching *Risky Roadz* or something and there's a knock on my door. I went downstairs and opened the door and I'm like, 'Wiley!' 'Yeah, Jamie told me to come here'. He's just standing there. He'd walked from Tottenham or some shit like that, I can't remember. There was times when he used to walk from Tottenham, up the A10, to here. I'd say, 'You've got money for a cab, what are you doing?' He never had an answer for that. Wiley saw who was talented, who was trying to get on, and he'd say, 'Right, I'm going to put them in the slipstream, watch them swim and away they go.'

JME Wiley, he loved music. He loves music still, so much that he always wanted to be the best, 100%, so to do that he always positioned himself with the best, in his opinion. Any artist he thinks is good, he's bringing them through with him on his journey, whether it's Dizzee Rascal, whether it's Trim, whether it's Scratchy, Manga from West London, me and Skepta from North London. If he thought they were talented, he brought them with him. The things that he did by accident, or just organically, like helping create and mould the scene, like helping to create and mould crews, giving people a work ethic, giving somebody his ideas that he has naturally, that inspires a lot of people. One thing that everyone needs to say is that Wiley inspired them.

DJ Target If you're talking the most important, the most significant, the best – hands down best of all time – then it's impossible to not say Wiley. I don't know anyone on that level. He's the most consistent.

Danny Weed He's all-round and good at everything. My thing with him is, even if he was as big as Dizzee was, he'd still be underrated. I don't think anyone gets to see how good he is. Plus think about everybody he brought through. He's the Stephen Gerrard of grime.

Riko Dan I don't think any of us would be here if it weren't for him. Everyone's got their own talent, born with their own talent – but I'm talking about this genre, this grime ting. If it weren't for him, well there would be no 'Eskimo' full stop, there would be no Eskimo Dance. There wouldn't be half the MCs out of Bow that are superstars now. I think Wiley is the most important person in grime.

Donaeo If you look at every artist that has been influential in moving grime forward, they've all come from Wiley. Tinchy Stryder. Dizzee Rascal. Chipmunk. Roll Deep. Bless Beats. Wiley was the nucleus that all talent came through. He was like the dam that he let everyone run through. Wiley is quite selfless in his own way.

Lethal B You know what people don't realise about me and Wiley and I wish camera phones were out back in 2002: me, Wiley, Dizzee, More Fire, various producers, we used to all roll. We all used to be in the studio together, we was cool as fuck. When we was making the More Fire album, Dizzee would come around and hear what we were making, Wiley would come around. I remember when he first made 'Eskimo', 2003. He made it for Maxwell D. He played it in the studio and I remember thinking, 'Oh my god, this beat is about to change the game.' Wiley was like, 'Yeah I can't give this to Maxwell, nah!'

Maxwell D Wiley made 'Eskimo' for me. I used to play it on Pay As U Go school tours, we'd get the kids to freestyle to it. I kept putting off writing to it, then one day I told Flow Dan I was gonna vocal it and he was like, 'Us man have already done it.' I was young then, so, you know, pride, ego, so I never said anything.

Lethal B Everyone told Wiley he had to keep it, but I don't think even he knew what to do with it. It was such a gamechanger. They done a dubplate for Commander B, Dizzee and Wiley and I think Taz. There's a version somewhere. But yeah, me and him never really fell out. It was more our associates, our gangs, our people, they took it somewhere else. Me and Wiley were doing it 'cause we wanted to be the best. For me and him it was strictly business. But it did get out of hand. When you mention certain areas like Boundary or Leyton or Walthamstow, people are gonna get offended. That's where it got out of control and it got mad. It was a good couple of years, Bow E3 and Leyton were a no-go zone – if you got caught slippin' in that area, it was a problem. We never really fell out, I think as time went on, we grew older, our paths went different ways. I went down the *NME* route, he did the big singles. We were doing different things and then we'd buck at certain events. You get older, you mature. Wiley always understood that this whole thing needed to be more than him being successful for it to work. I didn't get it at the time, but when I did 'Pow!', I saw it was the way forward. It's the only way it's gonna work.

Nick Huggett (A&R who signed Dizzee Rascal) I tried to get him to vocal 'Eskimo' but he couldn't. It was weird, he had a mental block on that tune. All anyone wanted was 'Eskimo' with a vocal, but he just couldn't do it. So that's why we ended up with those interludes; 'Eskimo', 'Ice Rink', 'Igloo'. That was my idea to put a minute interlude on to weave it all together with things like *Pies* and *Wot Do U Call It*. Looking back on that record, it's a really good record. It was very distinctly different to *Boy in da Corner* 'cause Wiley produced all of it, I think.

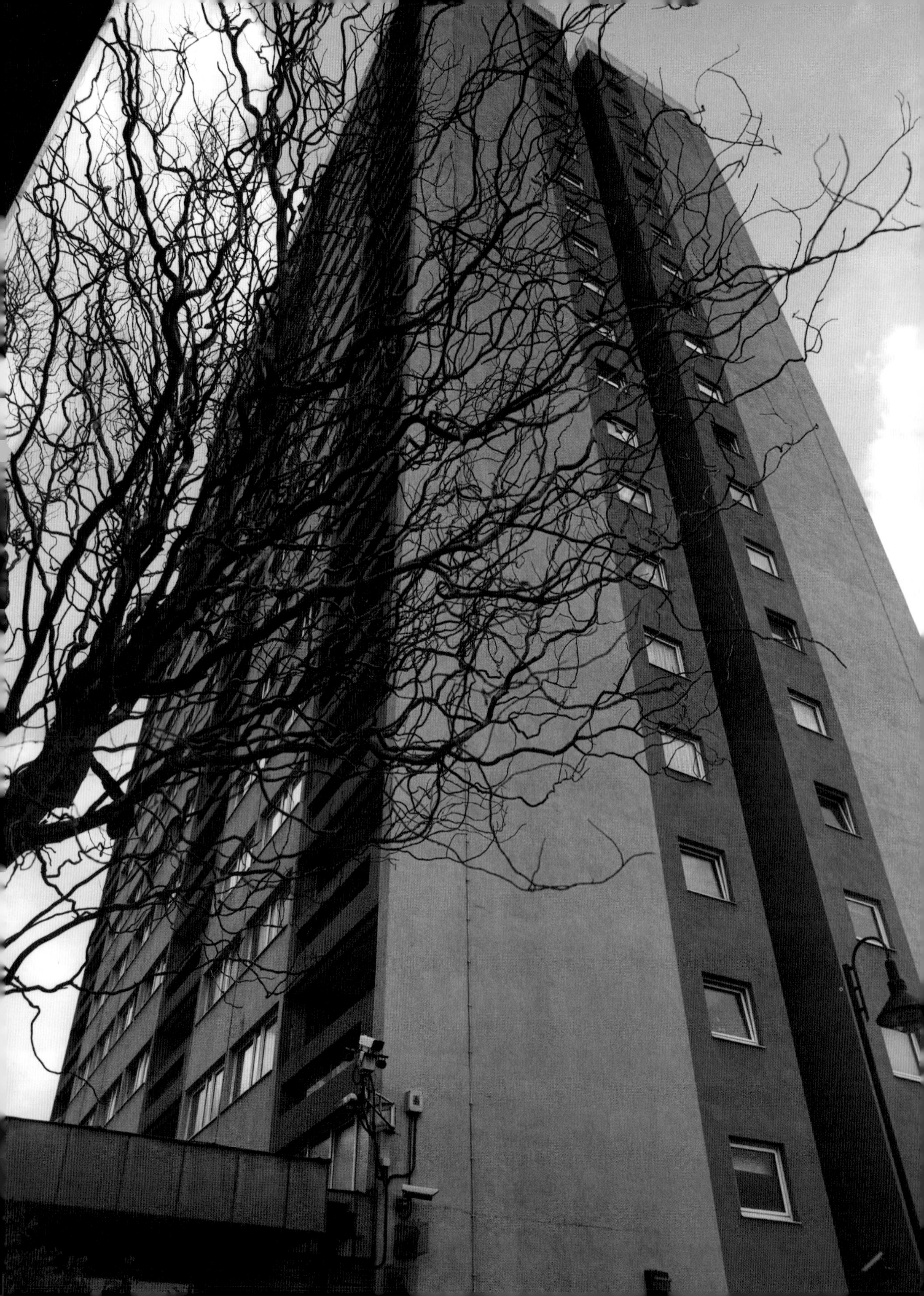

Simon Wheatley (Photographer) Wiley deserves respect on a number of levels. He's put in so much work and always tried to bring people through from day. And rather than plug the whole 'nostalgia' element, now he's happy to step aside and let the younger generation of MCs take the stage. A true godfather, in the deeper sense. I also feel that with grime having a tough image, it's easy to overlook the raw and vulnerable place it has come from and the sensitivity of some of the MCs. The title of Wiley's debut album, *Treddin' on Thin Ice*, is a subtle and beautifully apt reminder of the fragility of things.

Ghetts A lot of words get thrown around, 'legend' is one of them. Even if someone's been around a long time, they will call you a legend or a genius; I'd say Wiley is a legend in the real meaning of a legend.

John McDonnell (Prancehall) He's a weird one. I love him but he's a bit mad isn't he? He's quite hit and miss, the hits are incredible and the misses are quite embarrassing. He's prolific, whatever he makes he puts out, it seems. He's just chucking out as much as possible, seeing what sticks, that's the impression I get. A lot of it's great; he's an amazing producer, amazing MC. It's kind of a shame that he never really got proper recognition for what he's done. He basically discovered Dizzee; without Wiley there would be no Dizzee. I think maybe if Wiley had someone like [Dizzee's manager] Cage for longer in his career, he would have made it. Maybe he wasn't manageable, maybe he was too crazy to be managed. It is a shame; he should be as big as Dizzee, he's as talented.

Double O Wiley played a massive part in the genre, but one man don't make a genre. There's so many unsung heroes in this genre. You always have someone at the forefront and yes he's helped people, but there's so many others; Jon E Cash, Musical Mob, Essentials, N.A.S.T.Y., East Connection, Slew Dem… These are the collectives that was there, doing it and pushing the sound out of London and making it spread. It wasn't just one person.

MSM Engineer He's going to be one of the best people I've ever met and when I'm on my deathbed, I'm going to look back and go, 'That guy there came to my studio and gave me a direction.' I don't know if he knew he was doing it, if he's aware of what he's doing, I don't know, but he made me think bigger than hanging around in my bedroom. Back then, you didn't know anything further than the day that you were at, you had these rules and regulations of what you thought life was supposed to be and is, not what it's going to be. All of a sudden, Wiley turns up at your house and you see life in a very, very different way.

Nigel Wells (MD, RWD) Wiley. He doesn't give a fuck. We had a great time in Ibiza one night. A really great time.

Cheeky (Eskimo Dance) Man like Will. Wiley, he's a legend. I respect him to the maximum, he's my friend. We've done so much bits of business, I've DJd for him, done the vinyl, did Avalanche, Eskimo Dance. We've made a lot of money together. We've been through so much together, I've got a love of love for him, a lot of respect. I got him a booking for my Malia Live show and he missed the first flight. I said, 'Fine, get on the next one.' He's missed that one and then he's got on another flight. He gets on the plane, the plane doors close. Wiley being Wiley has gone and decided he wants to get off the plane. They let him off, but then he had to go and have a four-hour interview as to why he got off the plane [laughs]. Some people will argue and never speak to him again. But his friends understand who he is, and sometimes you have to accept him for what he is. It is what it is. Some things it's not in him to do. You can't get mad at him.

Janaya Cowie He's got kids, he's got responsibilities, and he's worked so hard for a long time now. He will only do what he wants to do, simple. He's tired; there hasn't been anyone doing this as long as him. I think he takes on too much and this is the thing, I always say to him, 'You've got to learn to say no'. But he doesn't like to say no. Neither does my nan. He gets that from my nan.

JME I think that's what I spent most of my time doing with Wiley; trying to understand him. I remember he gave me his laptop, a whole Apple Mac laptop with Logic on it, everything. Who gives someone a laptop, how are you giving me a laptop, bruv? I've still got the laptop now. I used to think, 'OK, he doesn't care about a laptop,' so what I wanted to know is, what does he care about? Then he'll fall out with somebody. Wiley's fell out with so many people, I've never fell out with him once, never, ever. People fell out with him before and they tell me why they fell out with him and 'cause I'm trying to understand him, I kind of reason with why, even though he might have been in the wrong. I remember one time I had a video shoot, it was for 'Sidetracked', and we arranged the shoot and he was paying half of it and it was all organised. The day comes, I'm ringing and ringing, he's not answering the phone. The director is like, 'How are we going to pay for the thing?' I was like, 'Oh yeah, shit.' So I borrowed the money, shot the video and I rang him after and he picked up the phone. I know in his heart, he's thinking, 'Jamie doesn't like me, 'cause this is what I do and everyone falls out with me,' but in my heart, I thought, 'No, I don't care, bruv. The amount of shit you've done for me, you can never do something to me that makes me fall out with you, bruv, nothing. No girl, no nothing's going to make me and you fall out, nothing.' Even when Skepta and Wiley had a little thing, had a little clash or whatever, Skepta's my brother, but I'm still Wiley's friend. I'm still going to speak to Wiley. He always wanted to help everybody, sometimes at his own loss, [but if] he can't do it, he physically can't do it. He's tried to help but he's got another thing planned then they fall out with him. I made it a point that I'm never going to fall out with him ever and I never have and never will. I don't think I ever will.

Opposite: Wilehouse, Roll Deep's East London estate – Limehouse, E14
Next page: Wiley tattoo, backstage at Eskimo Dance – Building Six, o2 Arena, SE10

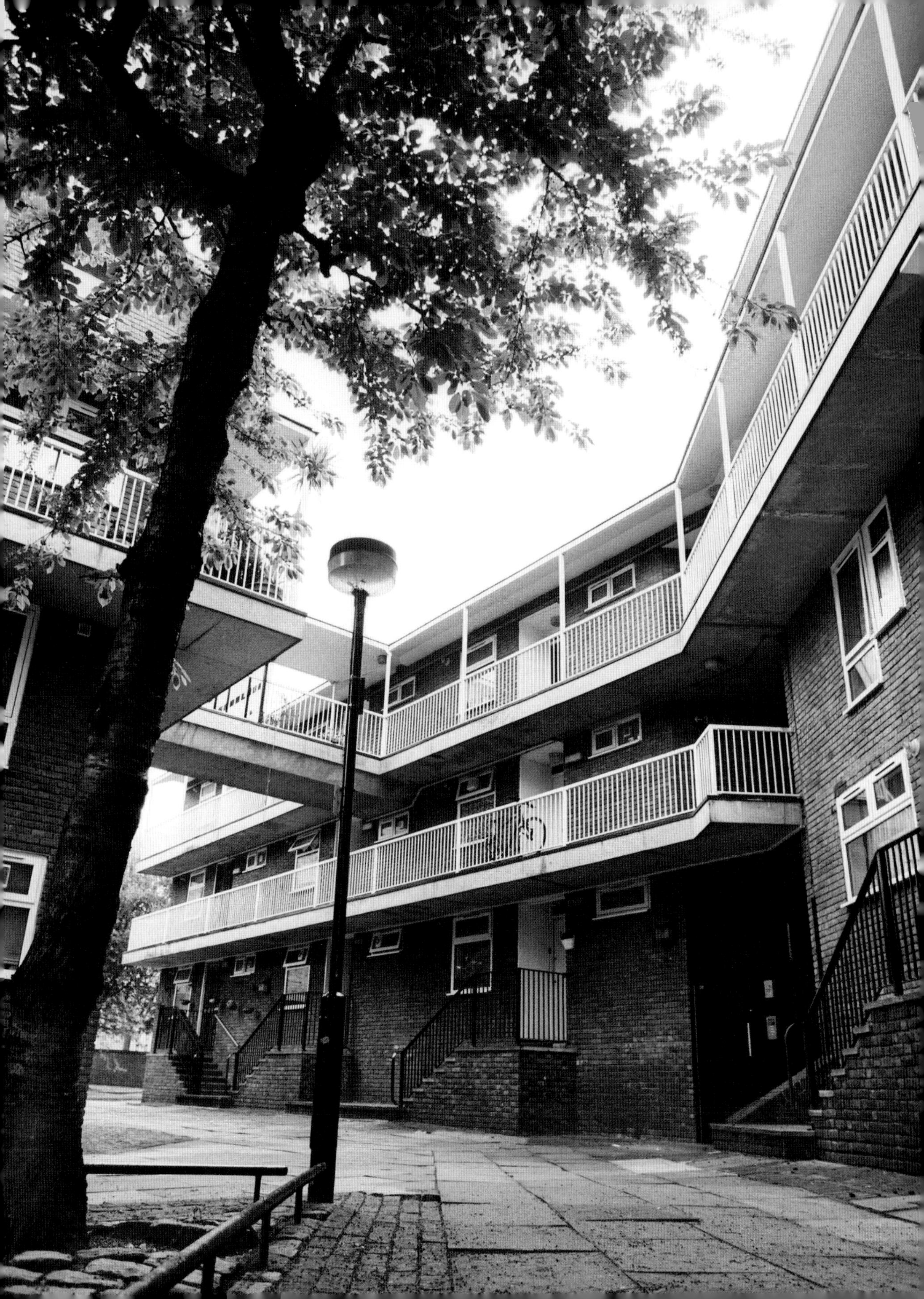

Danny Weed

THANK WILEY FOR GRIME MUSIC

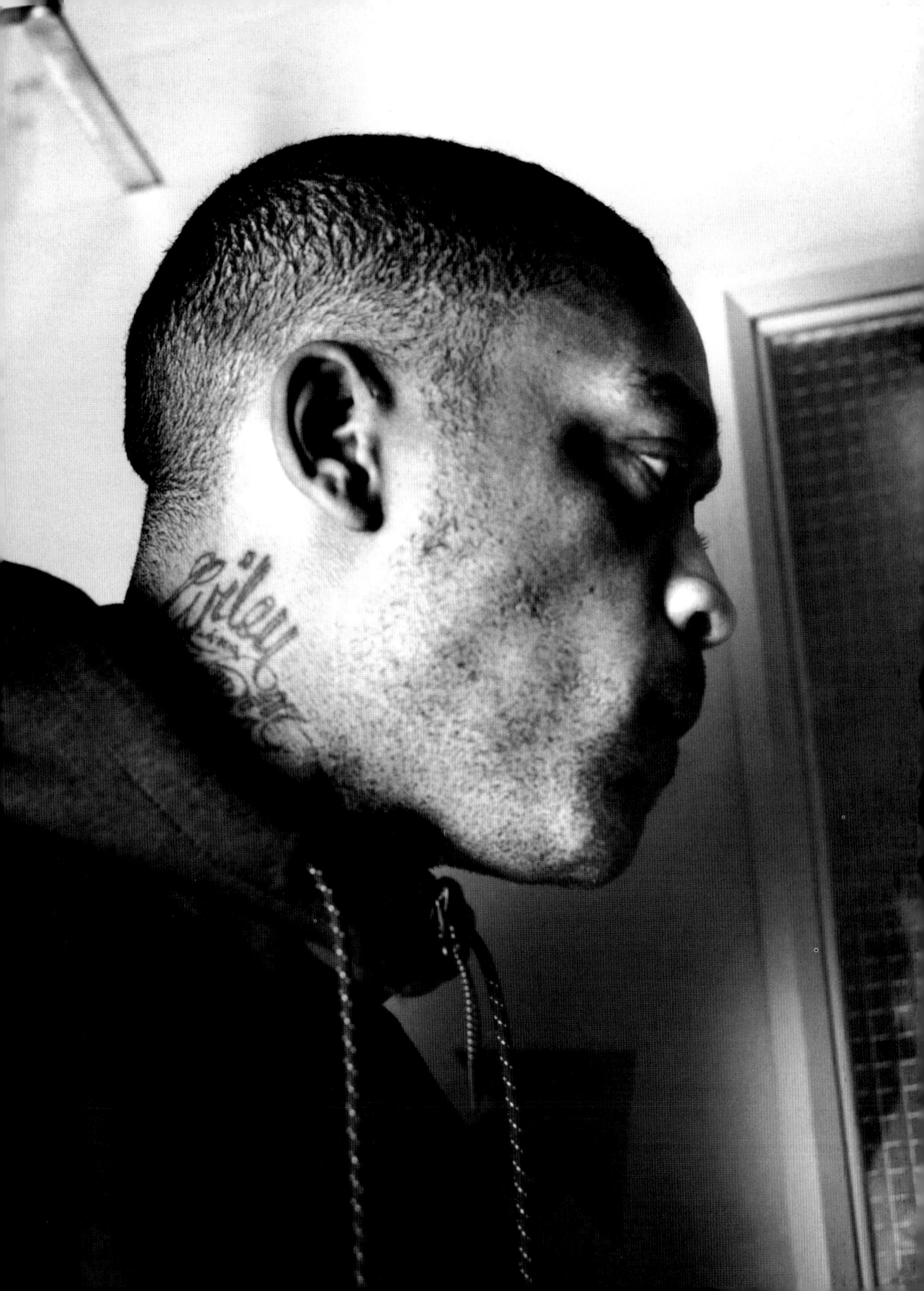

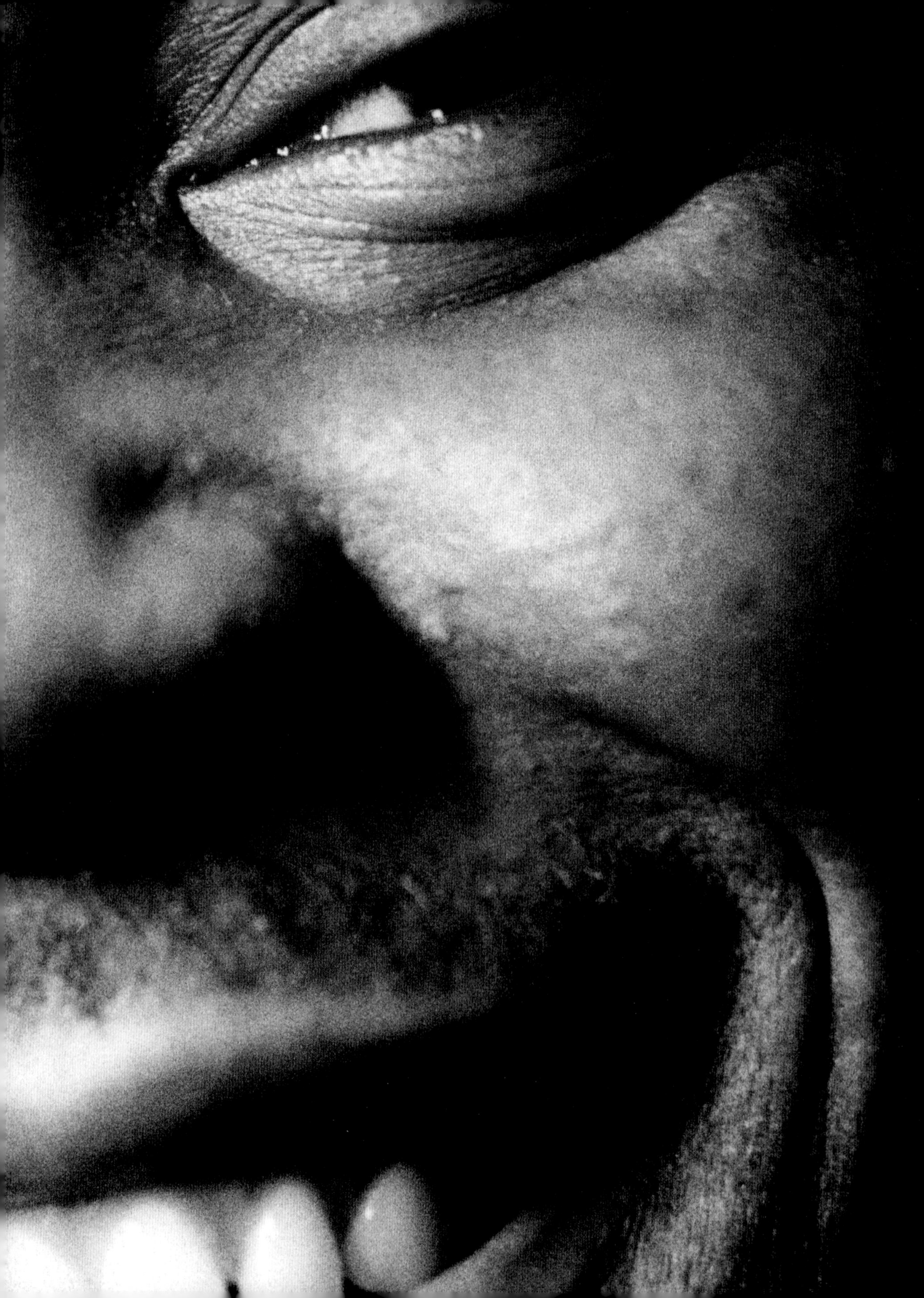

Evolve Or Be Extinct

Dizzee Rascal What happened to that boy in the corner? He's thirty-one! I went around the world. I did the US in 2004, from then I travelled. Festivals, shows, supporting Justin Timberlake, whatever. I made some really good pop tunes and I went through the roof. Fucking, I'm one away from the headliner at Glastonbury. Fucking, hundred-something thousand people laid out in front of you. Fucking, I'm in front of the Queen in my E3 jacket. That's what happened to that boy. All sorts of stuff. All sorts of stuff.

adidas
4305
3
ILFORD DELTA 3200 PRO
4
4305
5
ILFORD DELTA 3200 PRO

Tinchy Stryder I couldn't tell you the first time I met Dizzee. We were just friends from since I can remember. To explain how he was is really, *really* hard, but the only word I can use – pun not intended – is rascal. He really, really was a rascal. He was so cool, but when he knew or believed in something, he stuck to it. Not like he had a chip on his shoulder, but he just didn't really care. He was rebellious. And also talented. There are some people who have special gifts and he always knew what he wanted to do with his music, his sound, and everything he was going for. Nothing distracted him. He was focused. So focused.

Wiley I met Dizzee through Target, Dizzee was buying records off him prior to that. Target bought the tape round, I listened to it and I was like, 'Rah, this is sick, this kid is so sick'. I went down Devons Road to meet him. The thing is with Diz, when I met Dizzee, I was not Wiley. When I done *Step 1 to 20* I was Wiley. You know, I've done some freestyles and I've sprayed my heart out to the high heavens. I've killed it as much as I could. After that, I've said, 'Yeah I know I'm Wiley'. But when I met Dizzee, I wasn't Wiley yet, I wasn't good yet. I was coming out of garage MCing and adapting to MCing like, how you speak in an East London accent. 'Cause garage is slyly American bruv, it is slyly, but they're not gonna admit that [laughs]. But when I met Diz, I was Wiley, but I wasn't *Wiley*. Not yet.

Maxwell D I was at an under-eighteens in Oxford. Me and Wiley were tearing this place down and I remember afterwards this guy coming up to me saying, 'Yo bruv, you're sick,' I was like, 'Yeah, cool, thanks'. I didn't know this guy Dylan [Dizzee] from Adam. Wiley's always got new kids around him, so I didn't pay him no mind like that. He started coming more and more places with us. The first time I heard Dizzee spit, I was like, 'Ah that's baby lyrics.' With us, it was always about lyrical content, and concepts and all that and 'cause he was young I couldn't relate to *Take that Nokia, get that, stop that, what.* I'm thinking, 'I'm not taking no one's Nokia, I'm a big man, I will buy that, I've got money.' I wouldn't rate lyrics about that. It was like a flash new wave that he came with. When I first heard the 'I Luv U' track though, I thought, 'Oh shit.' That's when I knew, yeah, this was the new wave. When I used to go clubs with him and I saw the way they sung back his lyrics, I got it. His bars were actually like hooks, here was an MC who actually spits in hooks. His lyrics, word for word, were getting chanted. He actually wrote for grime. When all the beats would come out, his bars would sit on top of every single grime beat. Us man had to adapt, we'd be like, 'When's the drop coming, we don't really know this tune, we're not too sure about this tune,' whereas Dizzee, his lyrics were made for the drum pattern.

Dizzee Rascal I set up Dirtee Stank just before 'I Luv U'. We were putting out 'Ho' and 'Go' and all those instrumentals out on Dirtee Stank, so I was about eighteen, around 2001. It's just what we did at the time, I was in the zone where people did that. Wiley did it, so I did it. I thought, 'Yeah, I'd like a record label'. He did Wiley Kat and I did Dirtee Stank.

DJ Semtex I met Dizzee through Wiley. I met Wiley because obviously, he was popping and he was doing his thing. I used to see Pay As U Go posters all over London. These garage raves, I never went to them, that's really not my thing, but I was working at Universal and Def Jam in the UK and they wanted to break all these US artists. I was like, 'You've gotta start working with the UK artists,' so I reached out to Wiley to remix 'Roll Out', the Ludacris record. It's really weird because I don't really know what I was asking for; I don't think I was asking for a garage remix and I don't think I was asking for a grime remix, 'cause it wasn't grime then, it was still emerging – I just knew I needed a Wiley remix. So I hooked up with Wiley, went to the studio, did the remix with [Dizzee and Wiley's then-manager] Cage. Wiley spat on it and it was sick. I was like, 'By the way, can I get a dubplate for myself?' and he said, 'Yeah and I'll put this other kid on it.' He put this kid on the dubplate, I was like, 'Yeah, look at Wiley putting his bredrins on,' [laughs] and it was Dizzee Rascal. It's probably the rawest I've ever heard him spit. The style was just crazy, like, totally unorthodox, totally raw, totally abrasive and it was sick. That's how I got introduced to Cage and Dizzee and that's how I got into to the grime thing because it was all new, it was all emerging. Then, a couple of months later, 'I Luv U' was popping off and it really started to come into effect. It's crazy to see how it all unfolded and it was crazy to see how some people were stumbling into it all. You've got people like Diz and Wiley, they pioneered the sound. They turned nothing into something.

Wiley Dizzee was young, he was energetic, he listened to a lot of Dirty South music, which is why his first album was probably a reflection of that – his take on it. He was very determined to win, to get there. Know why? 'Cause he knew how good he was already. He knew why he was going radio; everyone else would go to spray on radio and have fun; he knew he would go and spray and everyone would be talking about him after. He didn't say it, but he knew it because he wouldn't have been such a confident MC if he didn't. He knew how much better he was than anyone else. He was the first one to be sick in grime and Kano would be next. I'm talking kids – not Wiley, Hyper MC, D Double, we're olders, I'm talking about a kid coming along and he's nang. He was a very good yute. He is cleverer than people think. He's a very, very clever kid. And he went through some shit when he was growing up, but he made it out. So I can only have respect for him.

Terror Danjah Can I swear? Dizzee didn't give a fuck. He could come across arrogant and rude but I liked him because he was real. I'd ring him to see what he was on and he's be like, 'I'm at my house, I'm broke, I need some money.' This was just before he blew. Everytime I see this boy, his arm is in a cast 'cause he was always in some madness. But I see the way he hustled. And his tunes, just listening to his tunes made me not care. I think even Wiley took inspiration from Dizzee. Dizzee created this collage of noises but it somehow worked. I took some influence, no doubt. I remember everyone hearing them cutting Wonder's 'What' in 'Music House'. Everyone's going mad. I was like, 'This tune ain't all that.' Guess what I made the next day? I came back to 'Music House' with 'Creepy Crawler'.

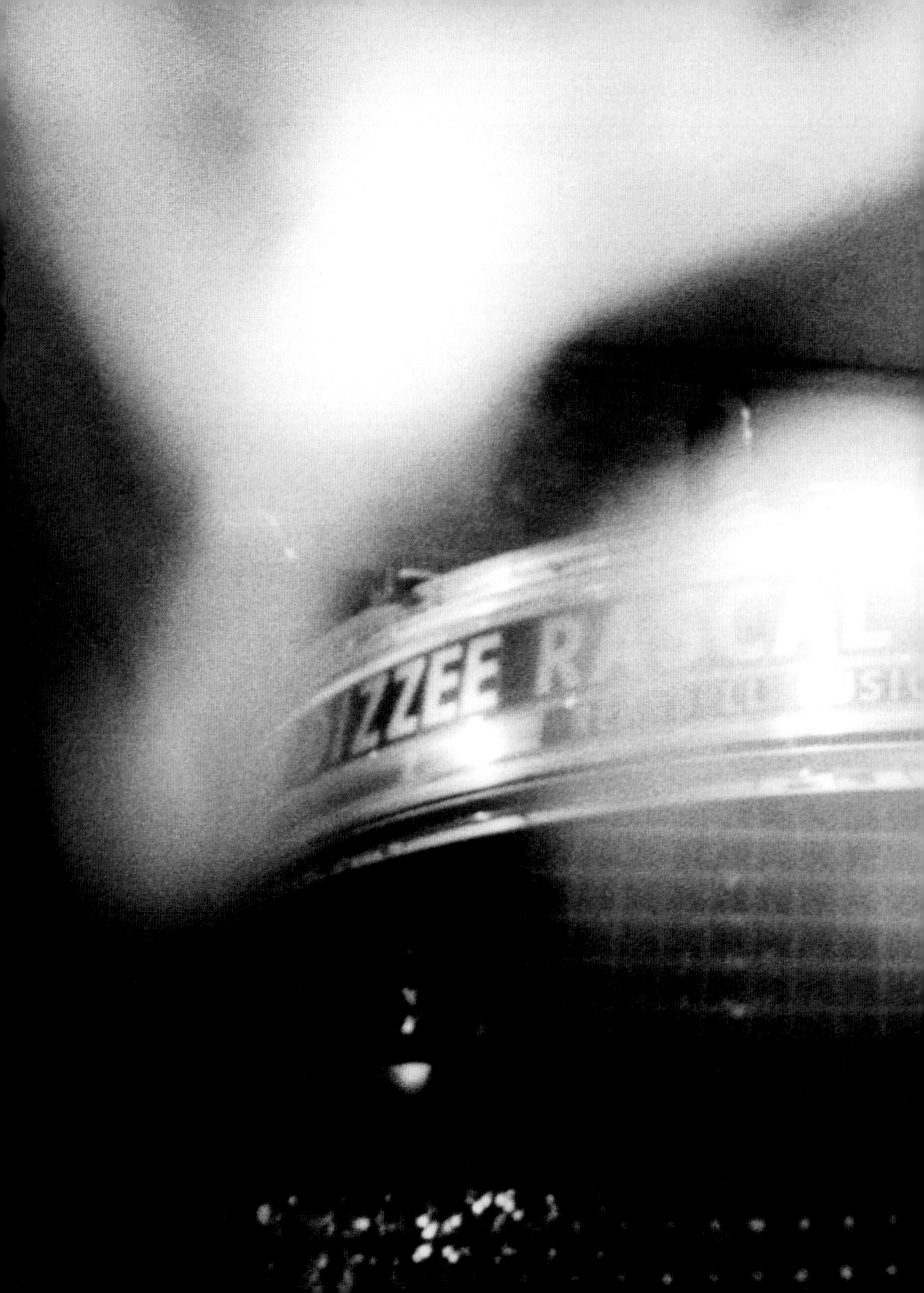

02. 4 6

Dizzee Rascal Everything changed when I came around. That includes everything Wiley and all that were doing as well. Because that went from 'Nicole's Groove' to 'Terrible' to when I came around, that's how 'Eskimo' and all them things come about. If you listen to them, you listen to my stuff, just the spaces in the beats, that's how the sound came about. Go and listen to 'Terrible' and 'I Will Not Lose', and 'Nicole's Groove' and that. Then go and listen to 'Eskimo' or 'Ice Rink 'or one of them tunes. That's when I came around. I always knew Wiley and Target and all that, but when [Wiley] bought me into the 'Bounce' session with Nick [Cage], from then, I was just in Roll Deep by default. But then I started making beats in Cage's studio, and the way I made beats, that's when everyone's started changing the way they did it. Everything Wiley was doing, to *Creeper* with Danny Weed. The way they started making the rhythm, the sounds they were using, the rhythm of the beats, all changed. I was always into those kind of sounds, I always liked Kung Fu films, all those outrageous, *Crouching Tiger*-type films. I was always into that tinkly, Chinese-y type music. And my bars and my flow, sorry, but that too influenced a lot of people. I still hear my flow today and people don't know. From the top, from whoever everyone thinks is the don today, I hear my flow in them, the way they spit, the flow [grins]. People are recycling the bars. I see kids saying, 'Oh he's doing Lethal's bars.' I see shit like that, it just goes to show you either how full cycle it is, or how far gone I am in some of them bars.

Double O Around 2003, 2004, he did [my night] Stampede at [Stratford] Rex and that's really how he got his deal. I've never seen anyone capture an audience like the way that kid did that night. It was like Jay Z or something. It was a magical experience. It got filmed and that footage helped him get his deal. They went behind my back, Wiley and Dizzee, they got the footage from Moonlight's stepdad who was filming, and that helped clinch their deal. They got signed off the back of that footage, and it's not surprising. Dizzee had everyone – 3000 kids – mesmerised, singing word for word. Not the last two words at the end of the bar, I mean, every single word. I've never seen anything like it.

Nick Huggett It was the sound as much as it was the London accent. I grew up through British hip-hop and it was fucking miserable. It was a fucking embarrassment. It was a weak imitation of US hip-hop and when it wasn't, it was just moaning. This was the first time there was something really British in sound and accent and content. It was a very British experience and it kind of blew me away. The first time I met Dizzee and Nick [Cage] was at the studio in Bermondsey. That was a really nice, big place, that was the hub, they all went there. It was like a grime factory. The whole scene had a weird youth club vibe. But Nick seemed to harness that – he was like a youth leader [laughs]. We (XL) tapped into that, with Nick as our entry point – alongside Big Apple in Croydon – and it was really exciting. I think I met Dizzee first and it became apparent that I wanted to sign both him and Wiley. People said Dizzee sold out when to signed to XL. That's bullshit. The grime scene has always been shit at supporting itself. The scene are the first people to shun you for any bit of success. Jealousy or haters, whatever you want to call it.

Trim Seeing the attention that people from the manor, people like Dizzee was getting, that made me want to do music. He went to the school across the road from my house, I know him, I actually do know him, even though he pretends not to know me today. I don't know why. We grew up together, he used to hang around with my best mate, Michael Grant. We was all one little syndicate at one stage.

Double O Grime was all about crews then. If you go back to garage, it was all crews. Everyone had a clique, we was all young, it was about your friends and everyone looked at the model and tried to follow that. But Kano and Dizzee knew what they wanted to do. Kano came with a plan of his album. No one else was thinking like that, no one was thinking in terms of albums. But Dizzee and Kano knew, they did what they did with their crews and then they cut out. *Boy in da Corner* is brilliant. I was listening to it a few months ago. Listen to what he's talking about. I appreciate it even more now. This kid was on a different planet, it was different.

Dizzee Rascal My main memories of recording *Boy in da Corner* was studio. I was always in the studio in Bermondsey, I remember how I used to make the beats. I remember having the samples laid across the keyboard, feeling them out. I remember bringing in MC Armour. Armour's in the background of 'Stop Dat' making loads of noises in the background. I remember when I made 'I Luv U'. I remember thinking, 'Ah, I want a girl to do this, but I don't know who.' I had a couple of young girls that I was fucking around with and they were a bit rougher, some rude girls – I didn't trust them in the studio, I didn't know if they could perform. That's when I thought about Jeanine. I knew her from the area. She was a singer; she thought she was a good R&B singer, so I had to lie to her. I told her I had this tune I wanted her to come and sing on. I bought her in the studio, and she heard it and was like, 'What is this?'. But she did it, she nailed it. She kinda helped make that tune what it was, man. I thought it was nice to have something for the ladies. I wanted that call and response. It's like Jay Z's 'Is That Yo Chick' and [Ludacris's] 'What's Your Fantasy', both of those tunes. I remember writing 'I Luv U' to 'Is That Yo Chick' and I wrote 'Jezebel' to Foxy Brown [and Blackstreet]'s 'Get Me Home'. Remember, I didn't have no instrumentals to none of these tunes, I just wrote it on top [of them spitting], just writing in my bedroom.

Nick Huggett Nick and Dizzee would say I did fuck all [laughs] but I was around, I was involved in the process of having the conversations about what the album would be. And I definitely made some wrong decisions. There was a song with D Double E that ended up as a B-side on a single, which should have been on the record. 'Fix Up [Look Sharp]' was an interesting one. Dizzee heard Memphis Bleek's 'One Two Y'all' and Nick played him the sample – ESG's 'UFO'. Dizzee went, 'Oh I didn't know you could just take a record, loop it and rap over it', 'cause that's what that Memphis Bleek record was. Nick was like, 'Yeah, of course you can, that's hip-hop'. And so he played him Billy Squier's 'Big Beat' sample, looped it, and that became 'Fix Up'. I think they did it as a dubplate for Semtex; they didn't necessarily see that as a single. These are the things that A&R people do, that

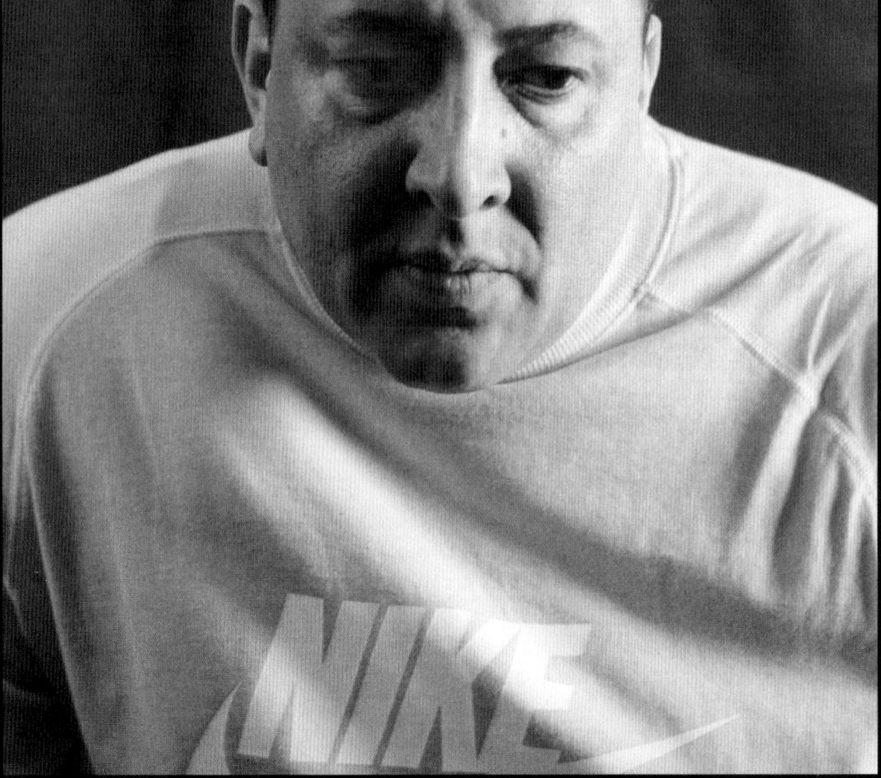
NIKE

record companies do. With 'Jus' A Rascal', Nick said, 'Oh, we've got this heavy metal track, but it can't go on the first record, it's maybe second or third album.' He played it to us and we were like, 'No, that's really good it's got to go on.' So those were the things. Look, Dizzee and Nick made the record but I think it was a valid thing that we did. We weren't trying to claim we were the geniuses behind it, they were, but there was a conversation. I feel very privileged to have been around it all, going to Germany and France, I learnt a lot from that. Back then, it was all hands on deck.

Martin Clark My favourite grime track is 'Brand New Day' by Dizzee. In a cultural way, while everyone was proving how hard they were, Dizzee was able to be weak and show his fragileness. I think that shows the breadth of the genre. And the fact that he was using sounds that sounded like he was coming from China, when he was coming from east London, it felt like he had this visionary world view from people who, I found, often had a very close geographical world view. So when Dizzee is doing stuff like 'Brand New Day', which is optimistic in a very difficult surrounding, sure it's not 'Pow!', it's not 'Eskimo', it's not 'Ice Rink', which are all incredible things, but I'd pick that track as my favourite, that's the one that touched me more than most. I can't tell you how many albums I've heard, but *Boy in da Corner* is still in my top three.

Dizzee Rascal Yeah, I liked 2Pac, innit, so I always understood why people loved him, because he had the hard stuff and then he had 'Shed So Many Tears' and all that. So I wanted to do that. Those times there, I'd already been through and seen a lot and I knew people around me had been through worse, so I wanted to make stuff that made people… I dunno. I remember playing 'Brand New Day', to [Ruff Sqwad's] Slix. I'll never forget that, I remember playing it to him before the album came out and he cried. That's the first time I saw music could be so powerful, man. Yeah, there was all sorts of lunatics around me who heard the album before it came out and it meant a lot to them. They were on the roads, differently. Listening to it now, it makes me feel a way, yeah, it does. Because of what it means to everybody else and because of, again, whatever I was feeling, I captured the spirit of it in the music. Sometimes I think the music is as important as the lyrics. Because I hear some of that music and I don't even know how I would do that again.

DJ Semtex *Boy in da Corner* is an evolutionary Rosetta Stone of lyricism in the UK. It is the true voice of the UK inner-city experience, everything prior to Dizzee's debut album was either a by-product of US hip-hop culture or Jamaican dancehall, whilst Dizzee Rascal was unapologetically British with his distinct abrasive approach to barring. Whether it's the flow, tone, audacity or slang, you can hear the DNA of Raskit in every UK MC today. Since 2002 'Stop Dat' has been the genetic primer for most grime tracks. I think for what he did with *Boy in da Corner*, he laid the blueprint and the DNA for what you should do as a grime artist. As a full body of work, it captures a moment in time for when that scene started to pop off. I'd say he's the most significant person in grime. But then again, I would say that [laughs].

Jammer The thing why you've got to respect Dizzee is, where everyone said, 'I'm a pop star,' and then when it wasn't working for them tried to jump back onto grime, Dizzee said, 'I'm a pop star, this is my lane, I'm not jumping anywhere.' Some people might say he should have done grime, or worked with this person, he's just always done what he's wanted to do. You have to respect that.

Dizzee Rascal I'm not in the field like that. When I made *Boy in da Corner*, my life revolved around pirate radio sets and raves, and that album catapulted me to the beginnings of my festival career. I'm even less in the mix than I was, so the urgency to make that type of music isn't there. I'm just not in that environment. But then, I dunno, man. I feel like rapping again, but just because I like rapping. I can't hear enough rapping in general. Everyone's singing, even on the hard shit. So that inspires me to want to spit again.

Nick Huggett Dizzee and Wiley are both very different characters and both great in their own ways. Wiley was a lively character. With both of them, it was always a struggle trying to get them to meetings on time, but Wiley was always five minutes around the corner. He was completely uncontrollable – not that we were trying to control him. We signed him, he'd made a record, they'd fallen out. He didn't have a manager and so it got difficult. He just wouldn't turn up. He was making his record with Roll Deep. In the end, he thought we cared more about Dizzee than we cared about him, which was bollocks because we wanted them both to be successful. Why would you sign someone to not be successful? I don't think he believed that but maybe that was the excuse to, in a sense, sabotage everything. I felt like Wiley liked being a big fish in a small pond. He was, still is, the lynchpin in that scene, and so respected, and maybe that was a way to explain why his career didn't go the same way as Dizzee's. I love the idea of them doing something together. As fans of grime, that's what people want. It would be amazing.

Flirta D Dizzee and Wiley. I don't know what that is. It's either egos or money innit. That's all it is. They should do a tune together, that would be a wrap.

Jammer If tomorrow, Dizzee and Wiley said they were going to make an album, people would go sick. I've been about both of them, it's just to do with no one shifting. Him and Wiley came the closest to each other when Dizzee took me to Eskimo Dance in 2012. It was the first time in, like, ten years that they was both in the same place with all the man dem. Everyone was telling Wiley to go talk to Dizzee. But Wiley didn't want to go to the car. I was in the car with Dizzee, Dizzee's in his Ferrari. Everyone should just get past it. As a fan it's always something you want to see, those two. But it might be something they don't want to do. I feel like I might be the closest person that could make them talk. But maybe it's gone past the point. As a fan, it's something I'd like to see; him and Wiley onstage going back to back, murking. But it's left to God now. Everyone was telling Wiley that

L to R: Devons Road Tube Station – London, E3 / Views of 'Three Flats' Crossways Estate – Bow, E3

day – Flow Dan, Tinchy – go and talk to him. But if grime didn't have no myths like that, it wouldn't be so interesting.

Cheeky Nah, that won't happen. Them two collaborating or whatever. I think Dizzee doesn't like Wiley like that and he's a bit stubborn so he feels like he doesn't have to. Wiley would, in a heartbeat.

Tinie Tempah Dizzee pretty much wrote the manual of how to do it. To make that transition into mainstream music in the UK and then to take it international, that's Dizzee. If there was no Dizzee, there would be no Tinie. If I hadn't seen what Dizzee was doing, I wouldn't have been able to see what I wanted to do. Seeing Dizzee supporting Justin Timberlake and the Red Hot Chili Peppers opened my mind to so much when I was a kid. Yeah, there's *I'll crack your skull* but because I could see the other side of it, my head was always there. I didn't want to be standing in a rave with fifteen guys scrambling for £15. I wanted to support the Red Hot Chili Peppers.

Nick Huggett Dizzee's never not done grime. If you listen to every record, there's grime on it. They've always made that a part of what he does. But he's ambitious and driven and wants to succeed. You can't knock it, it's the right thing for him. He'd done three critically acclaimed, worthy records. He'd done that, he didn't have anything left to prove in credibility stakes. He went and did the Calvin records and all that and they're not my favourite Dizzee records, but I wouldn't knock him for that because they're his most successful records. The most successful record he's done was one that he did on his own independently. Brilliant. Fourth record. He had three gold records and then a platinum one and millions of singles sold. If anyone can come back, it's him. He's, weirdly like, a national treasure, he's a part of British culture.

Crazy Titch I think he's done well. He's made me proud. I'm proud of him. Going number one? Sick. So sick. Credit where it's due.

Wiley It is what it is, bruv. I don't even want to keep talking about it. He pinched Lisa Maffia's bum, we got rushed by two crews. Two crews – about sixty-five man. And I don't mean Jimmy, John and Jake, normal dons. I mean name brands. The next day now, Dizzee got stabbed. But it's happened, it's done, it needs closure. But you can't make Ja Rule speak to 50 Cent. It's not even about friendship now, it just needs closure.

I'M NOT A MOOT!

Dizzee

Opposite: Dizzee Rascal recreates the *Boy in da Corner* album cover on stage – Brooklyn Music Hall, NYC

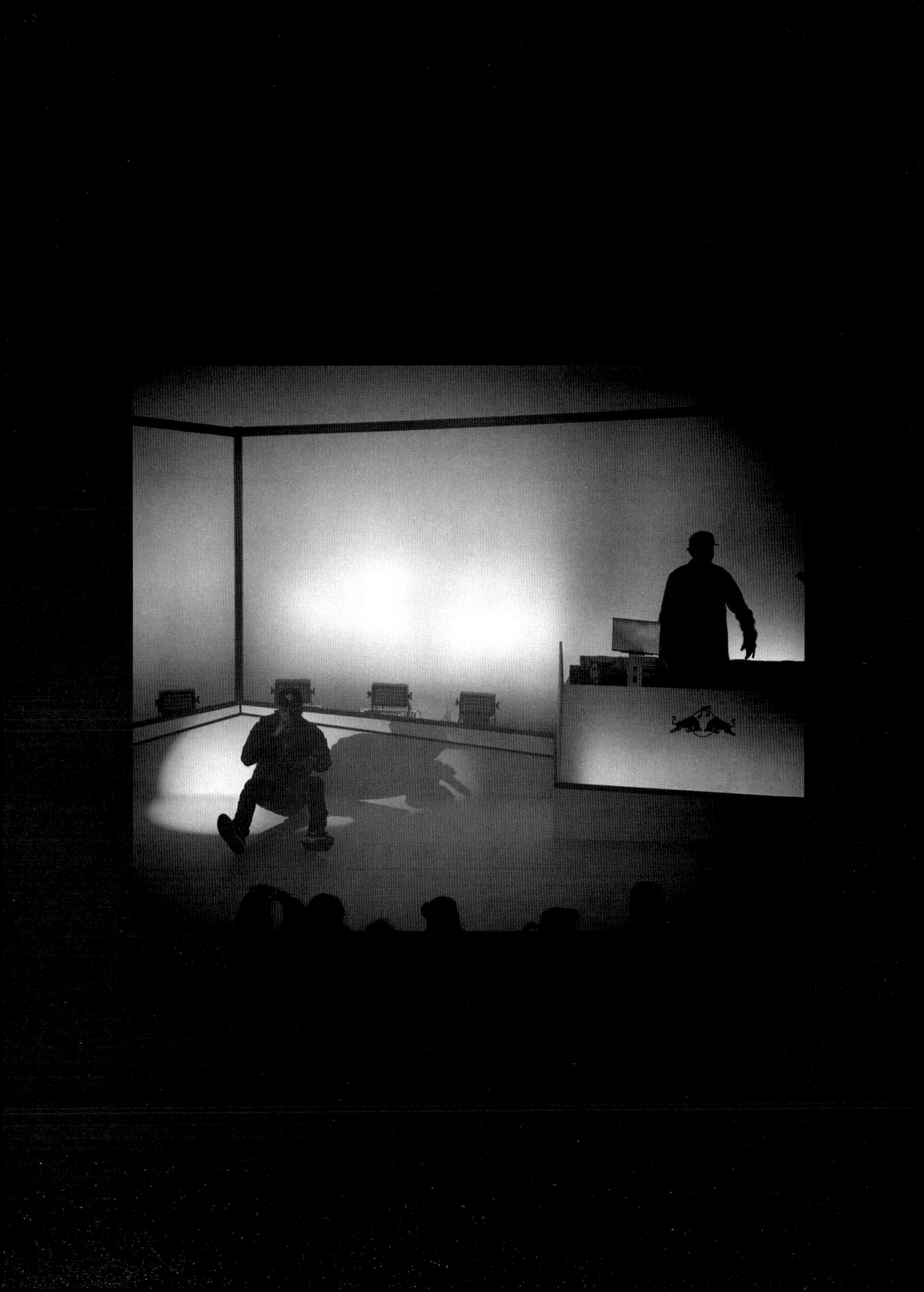

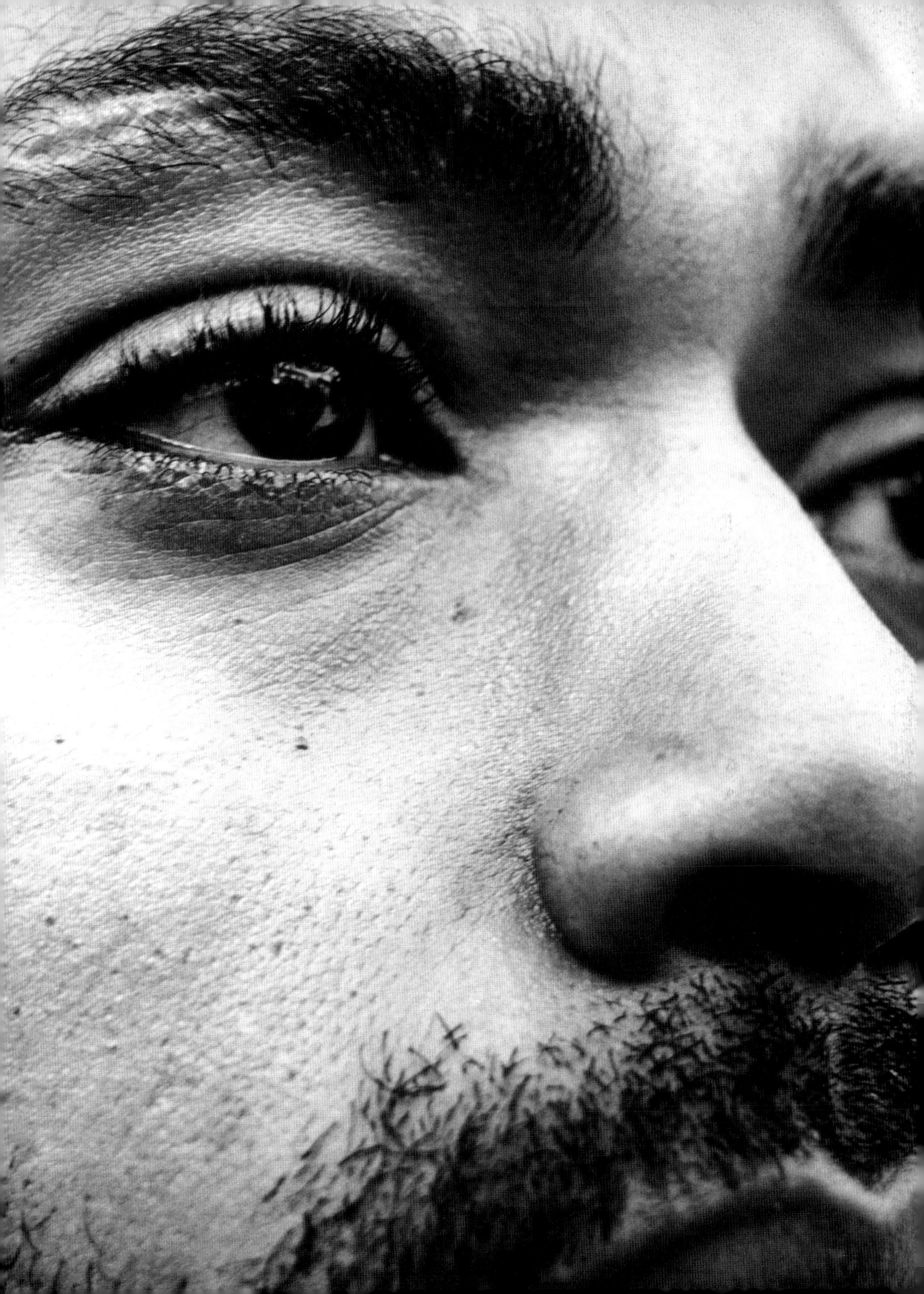

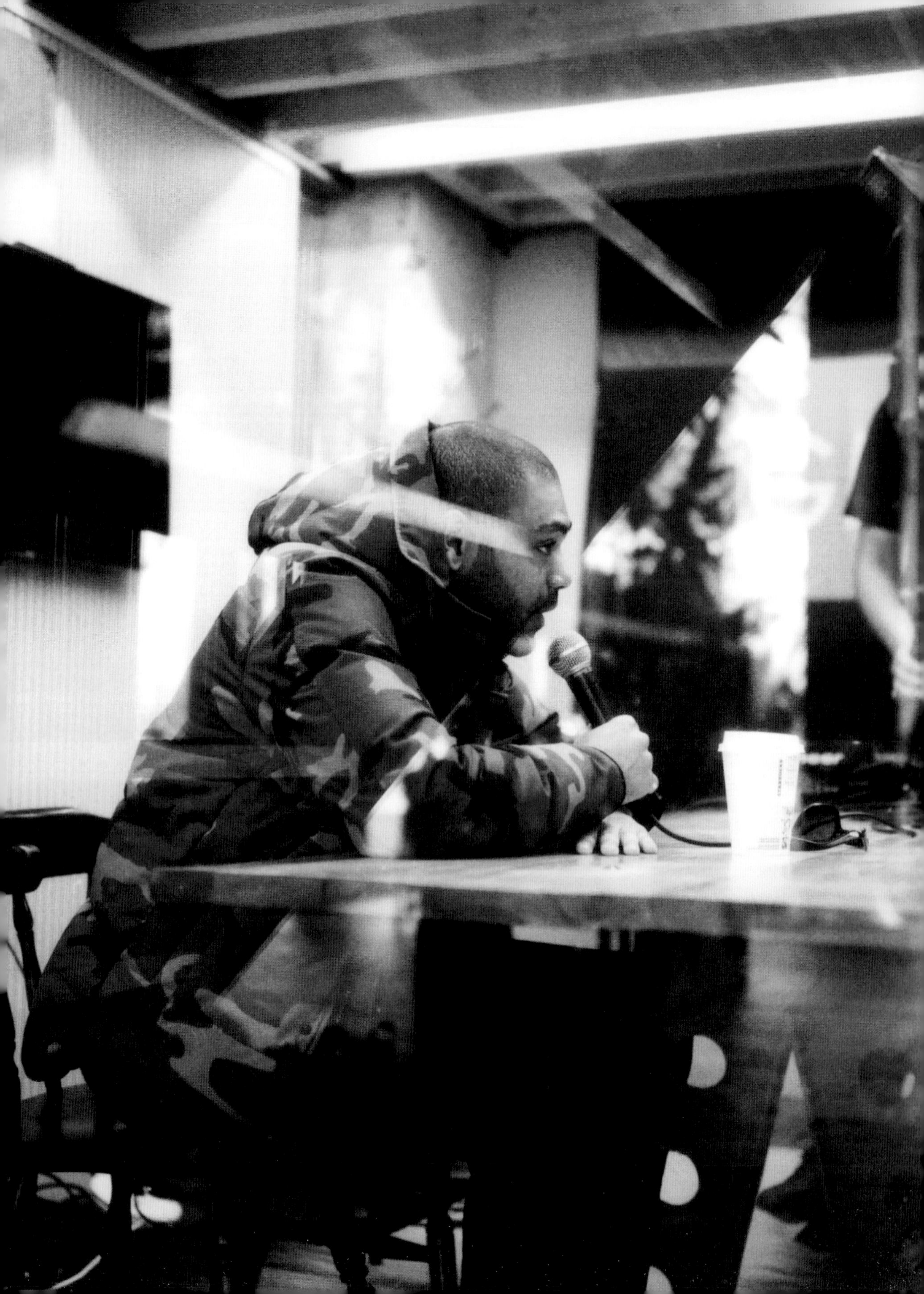

K-A. He Don't Play. N-O.

Chip My favourite MC as a yute, from that era, was Kano. Girls digged him, but he could slay, man. That's hard to do, you know.

Kano I was fifteen I think, when I made 'Boys Luv Girls', or 'Vice Versa' as it was called then. It was maybe the second or third song I made. I'd made one beat and put lyrics on it and then I went to get it cut on dubplate for my brother, Choppa, to play on radio, Flava FM in Canning Town, or Rathbone Market maybe. That was the first tune I made. The second or third one I made was 'Boys Luv Girls'. I made it and then went to the studio to vocal it. Actually, Dizzee took me to the studio, in Greenwich.

Dizzee Rascal Fucking hell, I forgot about that. Fucking hell. 'Cause I've known him ever since we was fourteen as well, I've known him a long time. I was involved, yeah? Fucking hell, I can't remember that, it's so way back. I know I was a busy cunt, but still. Wow. If I'd known, that I would have spoken up a bit more about that, still [laughs].

Kano Yeah, I think Demon knew [Dizzee] and I just kind of knew him a bit, one of my other cousin's knew him a bit as well. I don't know exactly how we met. I was just MCing on radio – but not Deja yet – and he maybe got hold of me somehow. This was before N.A.S.T.Y. It would be me and Demon on Flava, doing tapes in the house.

Dizzee Rascal We might have met through Demon because when I used to go on that station there, Flava, I think I knew Demon… I can't remember. I was all around Newham them days, as well as Bow. I forgot that, though. I took him to Greenwich, yeah? Fucking hell. I didn't know that.

Kano Dizzee phoned me one day, or I phoned him and it was one of those, 'What's going on, I've heard about you.' Touching base type of ones. I told him I had a tune or whatever and he said, 'OK, I'll take you to the studio.' He phoned me one day and said, 'Come, meet me.' I met him at the train station, we got on the DLR and we went to the studio in Greenwich. I vocalled it and I remember giving it to Jammer and him listening to it on his headphones, on Deja, and then Mac 10 played it later on in that show. I was probably about sixteen by that point. Back then, no one really had tunes. So when Mac played that, we got a bit of love on the radio, people calling up and whatever. It was more slow build though. I didn't really know it was popular until I went to Palace Pavilion with N.A.S.T.Y. I stepped on the stage, Mac dropped it and the crowd just went mad. Shortly after we decided to put it out on white label and sell some. Me and Jammer done that. We put out some white labels and we ended up doing a good few thousand of them. That's the first time I ever earned any money like that.

Ghetts Kano didn't like me, imagine that. It's weird to think that. He might say different, but actually I don't know, because you see, Kane, he is a very difficult person to read when you don't know him. We had a mutual friend called Dangermouse; we're all from Newham, so he's just down the road. Before I went to prison, Dangermouse had me to his house and was like, 'Yeah this is my friend and he does music.' Kane showed me songs with a 16-bar and a chorus. You have to understand what I'm saying: this is in the garage era when man are saying, 'Oli Oli Oli.' He showed me songs with choruses and 16-bars – weird. Kane being Kane, he's just in the yard showing man the tunes, drinking tea, just reserved and me being me at that time – little rude boy – was not trying to tell him he's good. I'm just like, 'Yeah it's alright man, it's OK still.' I left the house like, 'Oi! Your boy is fucked! He's sick!' Then Kane joined N.A.S.T.Y. Crew while I was away and when I come home, we just clicked, like a house on fire. The chemistry was just instant. I rate him highly and he rates me highly. He thinks he's the best, and I think I'm the best.

Kano Yeah, I was mainly more just a quiet person, I still am. I think that made it more impactful or shocking when I jumped on the mic and went mad. I completely changed on the mic. I kept myself to myself, spoke to who I knew. I'm not too much dissimilar now. I kinda mind my own business really.

Richard Thomas Stupidly for some stupid reason, I bought three copies of 'Boys Luv Girls' on vinyl and obviously there was something drawing me to this person. I introduced myself to Kane. The first time we met was in Canning Town McDonald's.

Kano See how he was moving back then [laughs]. Yeah, he really went out of his way to impress me.

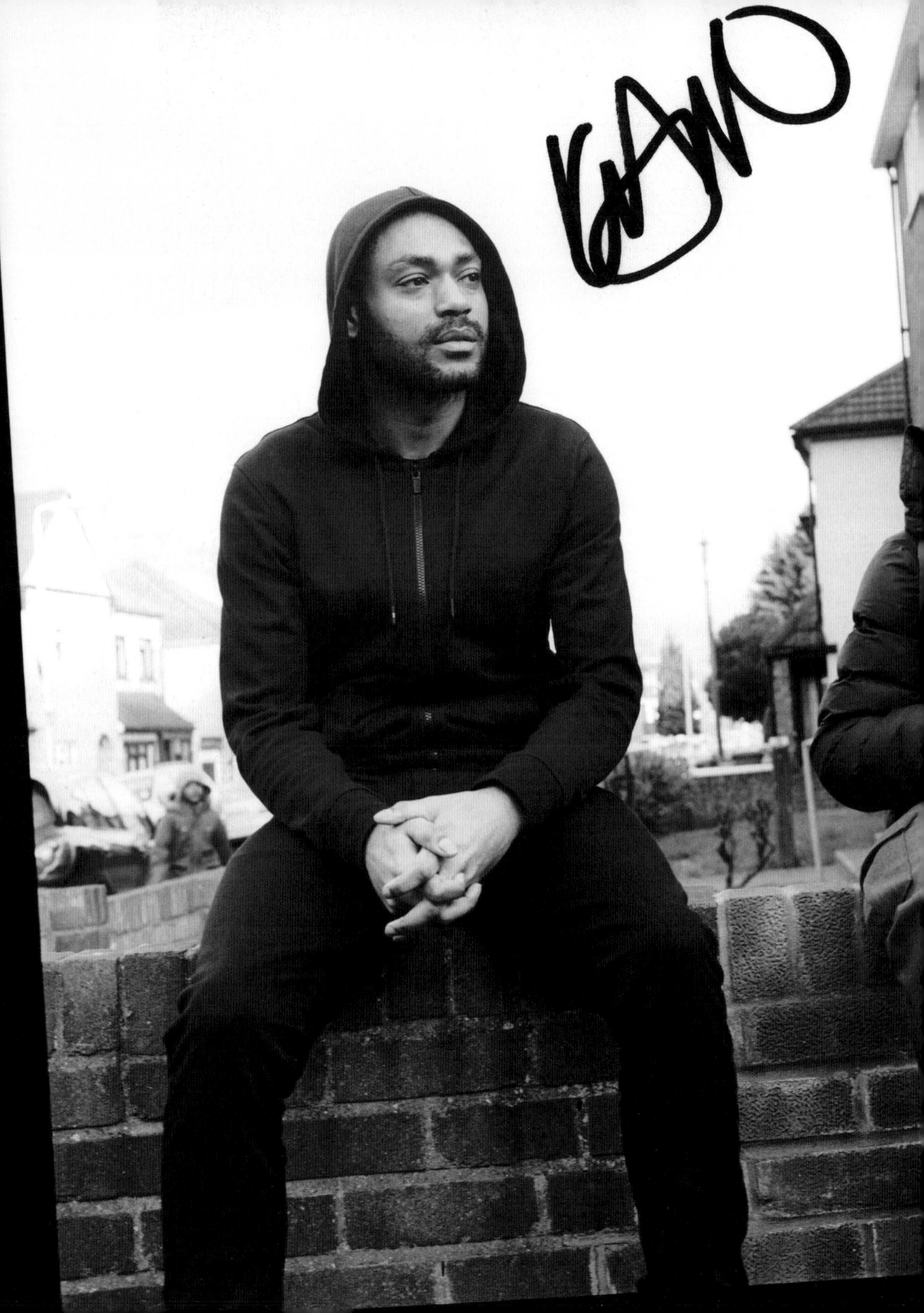

CHANGE IS GOOD!

3

Richard Thomas Do you know how many meetings have been done in there! The thing that sealed it for me and him was actually Wiley. Wiley turned round to Kane and said, 'Richard's good 'cause me and Diz are with Nick [Cage], you can be with Richard – he's cool and we all know each other and it can be all good.' On that level, I have a lot to thank Wiley for in terms of that confirmation – not to say he made the introduction, but he made it official.

Kano *Home Sweet Home*. It's hard for me. I didn't listen to it until I done the gig in 2015, and I had to learn it. When I did listen to it, I actually enjoyed it. There's some tunes on there [laughs]. It was ambitious, it was young, I was already in that mindset of creating a cohesive body of work, making an album, when at the time it wasn't really about that. Asides from Dizzee, he'd had one a couple of years before, but yeah, I'm glad that it means so much to people and it's considered an important CD really. Dan [Stacey from 679 Recordings] brought me 'Reload It'. You had Diplo before the Grammy, Paul Epworth before Adele, Fraser T Smith before Adele. Fuckin' 'ell, I've worked with so many people who have won Grammys and I ain't won shit!

Wiley I met Kano when he was really young. It was obvious he was good. He's a humble guy, laidback, very talented. Very, very talented.

Kano If *Home Sweet Home* had been bigger, maybe that would have changed me. Maybe some things wouldn't be so classic if they sold millions of records; *Reasonable Doubt* by Jay Z. Nas' *Illmatic*. The way people talk about those records – *Home Sweet Home*, *Boy in da Corner*, you would think they sold a million records, but they just didn't. I'm not in the business to not sell records, but you know, there's many other things to call success. And at the moment, just being relevant and important to people and being an inspiration to young MCs – I can clearly hear the influence of what we've done on this newer generation.

Double O Skepta's my bredrin, but listen to *Konnichiwa* and listen to Kano's *Made in the Manor* – it's different levels. Kano's album could go international. I'm not trying to put Skepta down, he's flown the flag, but I'm not gonna bumlick – *Konnichiwa* is not on the levels of Kano's last album. Listen to the album, nah, sorry. It's good but only to a certain level. Kano, that's an album. That's the album that should be representing the UK.

Kano A lot has changed, especially where I've grown up. It's probably harder in some aspects, but in terms of young creative people, hopefully it's becoming easier. The more that we can kick doors and break ground and inspire the next generation – well, we're already seeing the next generation that we've inspired. Maybe that will be our legacy. Hopefully we've encouraged a generation to be creative and live through our mistakes and triumphs. Long may that continue.

Previous page: Kano near his old school, Langdon Academy – Barking, E6
Opposite: Kano, E6

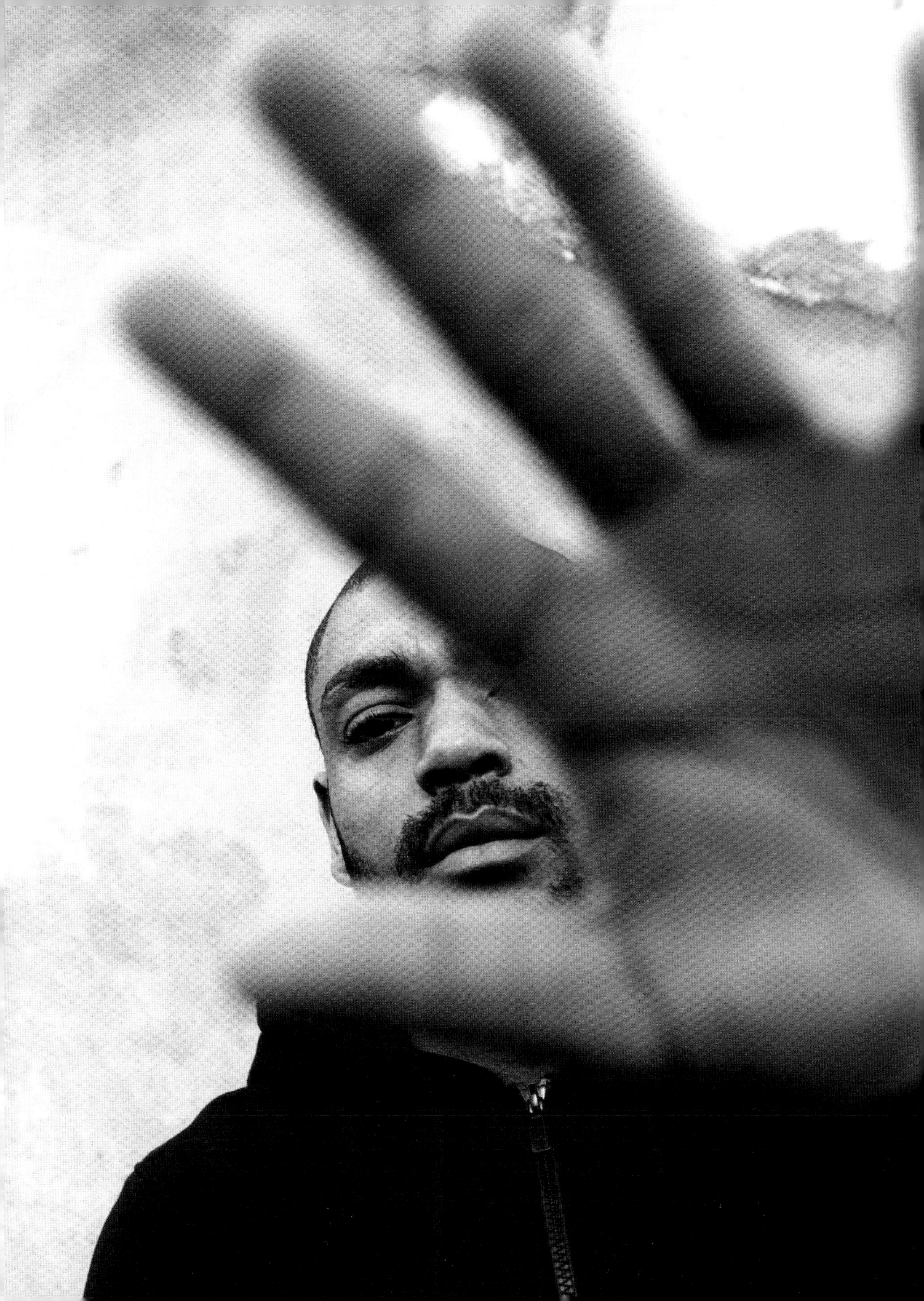

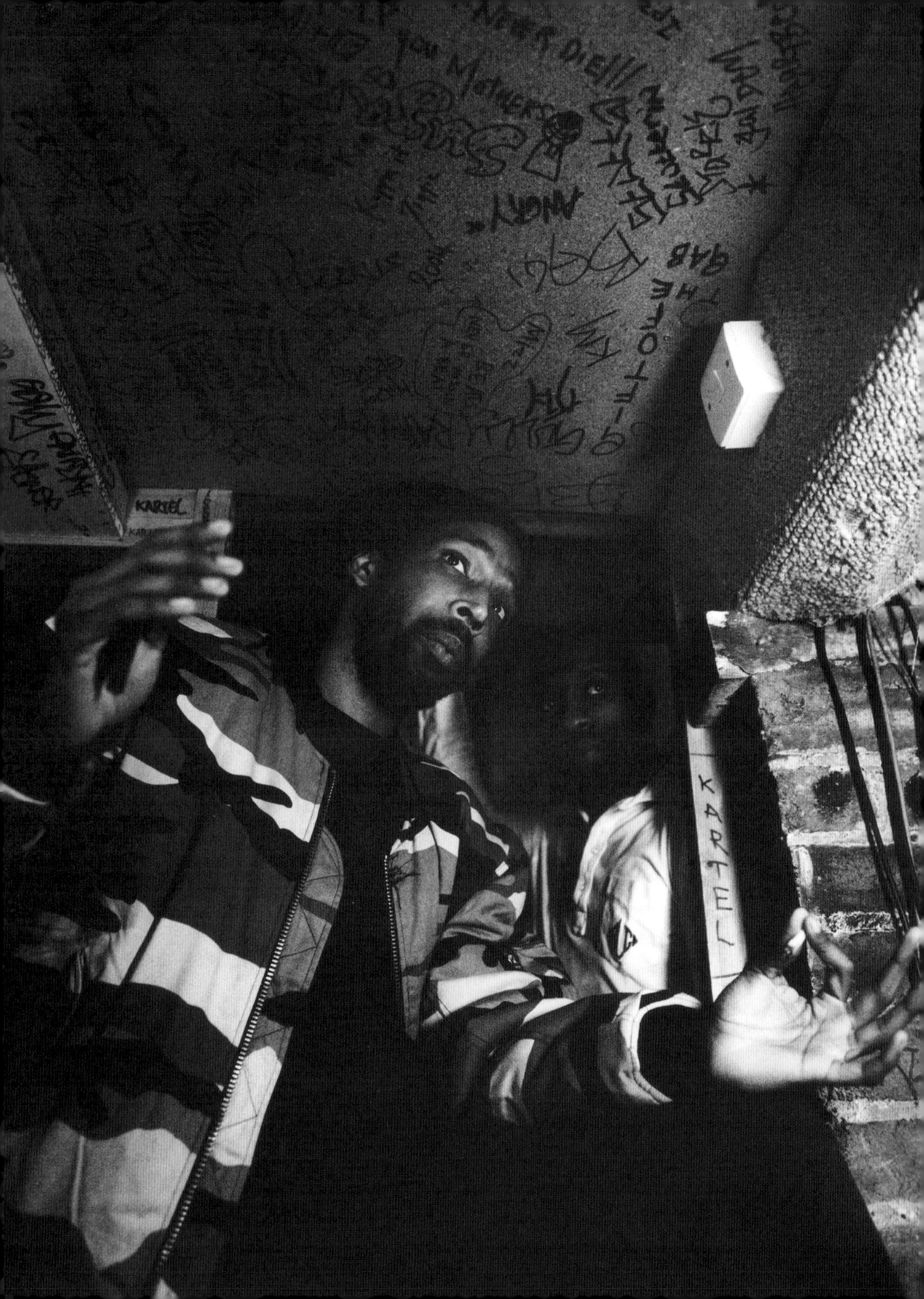
KARTEL
KARTEL

It's The Murkle Man...

Stormin Jammer was very influential, a very important figure, as both a producer and in terms of giving us a place to make music. From N.A.S.T.Y. and the Basement, to *Lord of the Mics* and now to BBK, he's been in this a long time and doesn't seem to be slowing down.

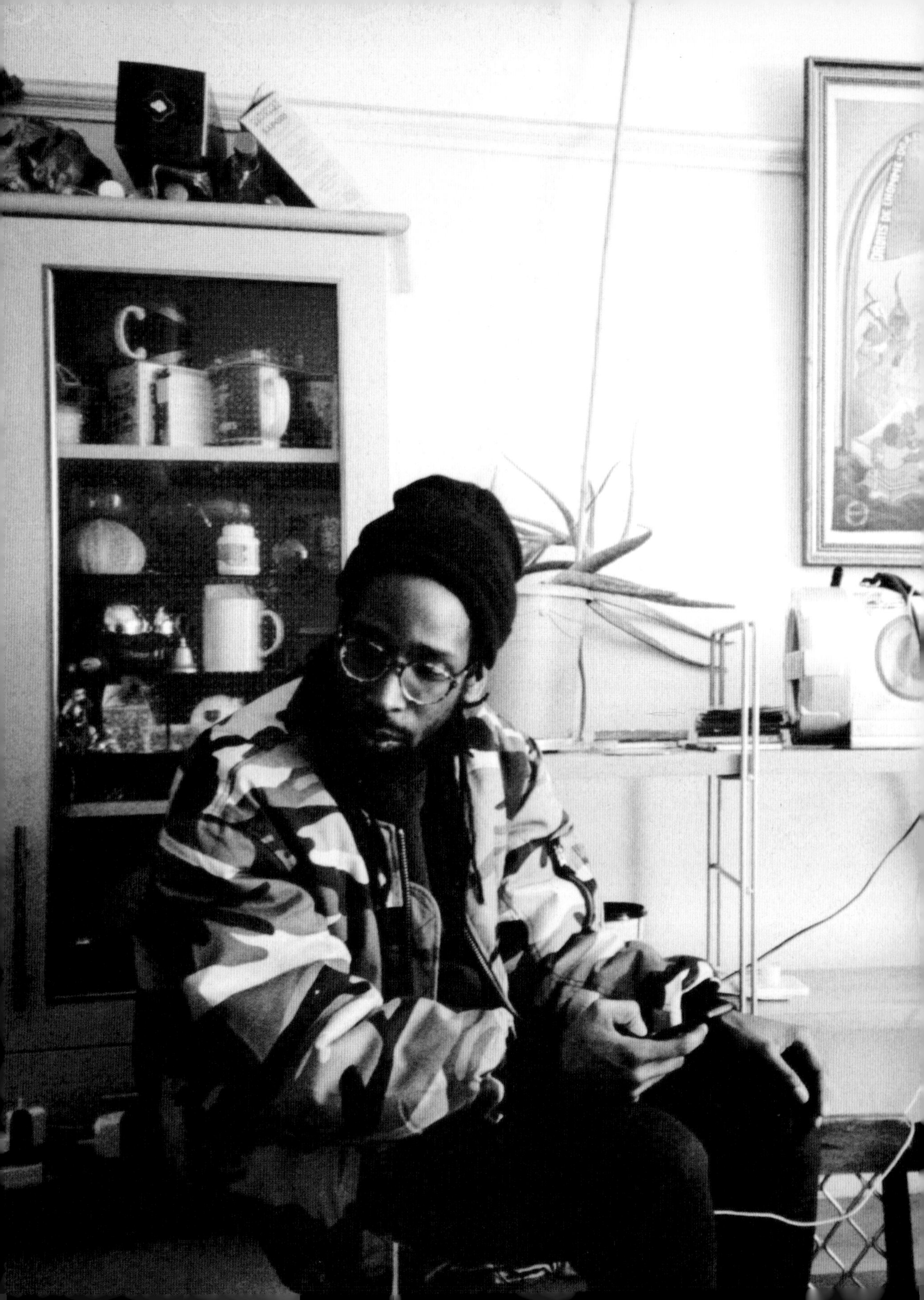

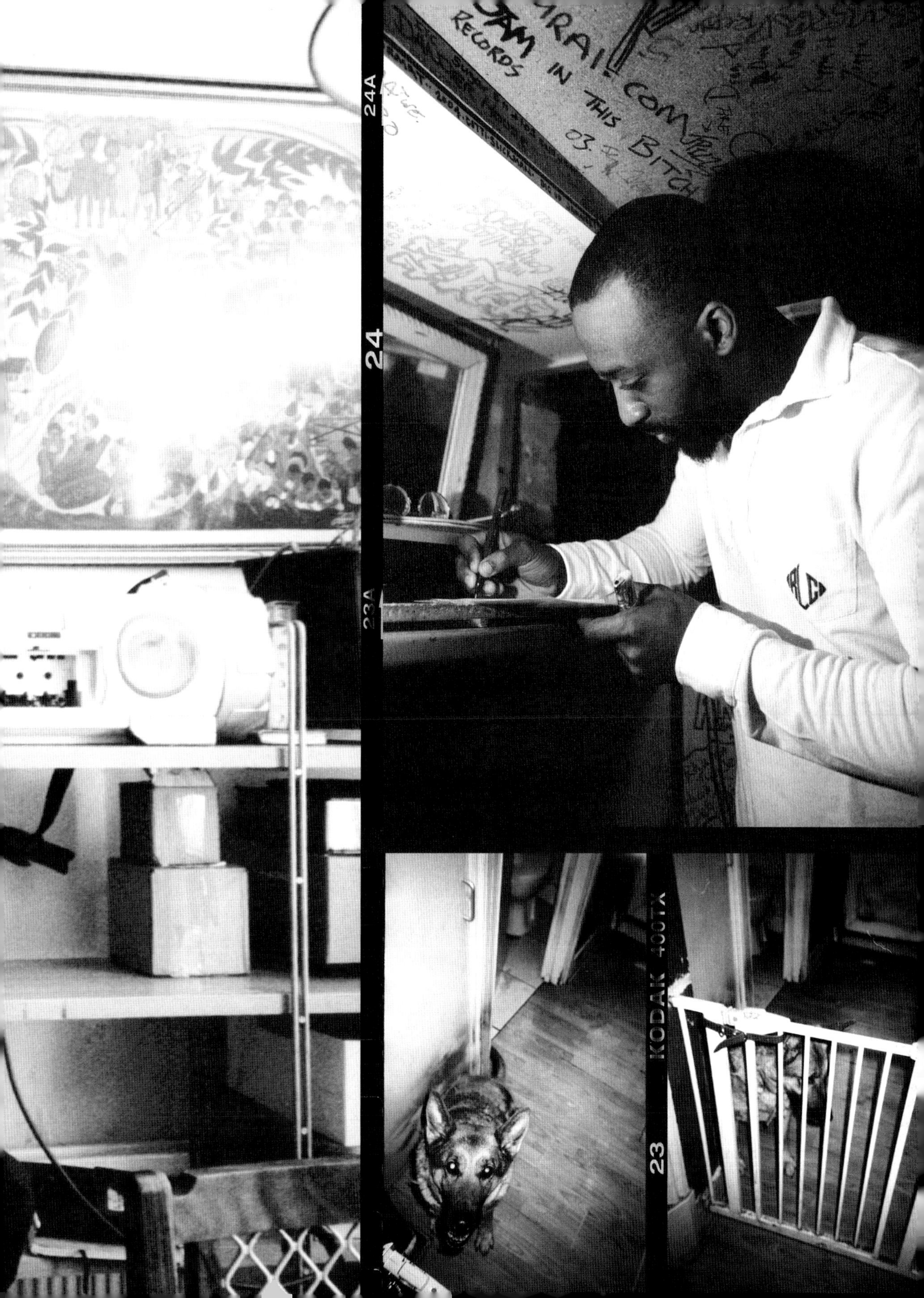
24A
24
23A
KODAK 400TX
23

Queenie We were privy to a lot of the early stuff that he would play to us and we just encouraged that in him. I always said to him, 'Just don't get involved with the law.' Music was probably, I'd say, what kept a lot of them out of trouble. When Jahmek was growing up, we ran a support group in the community and part of the project was to give people from the community a platform to perform on. We'd do three, four shows a year and invite all the people in the community who wanted to showcase lyrics, music, poetry, dancing… whatever it was, we gave them that platform. A lot of the guys now, in grime, that was their first performance, so it's good to see what's come out of that. A lot of people think a lot of negativity comes from grime, but it's no more negative than any other genre of music. A lot of the time, it's that people don't want to hear what's being said. I know sometimes it's aggressive, but sometimes you need to shout to get the point across and you need to say things that people don't like to hear. We need young people to vocalise what's going on. It's empowering; it empowers them as young people too.

Lewi White My friend Cain knew Jammer and he took me to Jammer's Basement. [The Basement] is a legendary place. I can remember countless, countless hours in there with Jammer and Ratty and the rest of the gang just knocking out music and just wanting to get on pirate to play it. These times grime wasn't grime, it wasn't 'cool' or anything. It was Jammer working in Essential Direct, distributing and what not. So I used to go there and buy records off Jammer and that's kind of how our relationship started. I used to come there, buy records – he used to get them from the distribution company and give them to me for £2 each or whatever. That's how our relationship built up and that's how I met most of these grime people that I know. Big up to Jammer always.

Mizz Beats One day, my mum asked me to go the post office. I didn't want to, but I done it and in the post office there was a guy called DM, Jammer and Ratty's friend. I'm in the queue and he has the first *Lord of the Mics*, he's trying to sell them. So we get talking and he asks me what I do, I tell him I make beats and he says, 'Oh my friend Jammer has this studio, come down sometime and play some of your stuff.' I was around seventeen years old, it was 2003. So maybe a month or so later, I finally get the courage to go to the studio, to the Basement. I get there and there's all these guys there smoking. I'm terrified. Jammer was there, Wiley was there, D Double. I knew of Double from Deja. I had this old Nokia phone with the radio on it, on my way to school I used to tune in and listen. I was blown away, I fell in love with it straight away 'cause it was our sound, a London sound. Anyway I guess Jammer pops the CD or the disc or whatever in his computer and everyone's like, 'Sick, this is sick.' At the time, there wasn't any female producers – was I the first? Maybe I was the first. There was a few beats – 'Signal' was one of them. There was something that Ears wanted to jump on. It happened so fast; a few weeks after that, Double vocalled 'Signal'. Double was my favourite MC – still is.

Queenie The Basement was being used for music anyway. My husband's a musician – it's not his day-to-day job but it's his first love – unfortunately he couldn't make enough money to keep a family. What's happening now is watching that progression from my husband to my son. It's two completely different genres of music, however the music is still the same. It's just being said in a different way.

Jammer To be honest, the Basement, OK, so my dad had a five-piece band here. This house, I get it from my mum basically, was just a place where people would come and chill. When my parents found out that we smoked weed or whatever, they said they'd rather us smoke here than smoking weed out in the street. I used to have decks and play music, man would come chill and smoke.

Stormin Jammer's house was the N.A.S.T.Y. Crew meeting point; if you was gonna make the tracks, you'd go there. Sometimes we was sleeping in the Basement and all sorts. We didn't care, the tracks had to be finished. It was a good journey, a good time. You got brought to that Basement, you get put on the spot. We literally used to sit in that Basement and before lyrics was even going, we'd have cussing matches. We'd be there for hours cussing each other, yeah and we'd get so angry with each other and start writing. Imagine what that's doing to your head and the lyrics that was coming out. Jammer was the best at it [laughs].

Sharky Major Them times he didn't even used to write, he just used to cuss people!

Mizz Beats Jammer does a lot of stuff behind the scenes. He knows everybody and he's very, very kind. He's always helping people, from what I've seen. Jammer is a sweetheart and then he's also fucking mental [laughs]. Everyone seems to have a Jammer story. But his heart's in the right place. I love that guy, man. There isn't anything I don't think I'd do for him.

Chantelle Fiddy Jammer once said to me something about grime being a way of life, and I couldn't understand how that applied to me, 'cause I'm not an MC, I don't go studio everyday, I didn't have a hard life. But I understand in the sense that there's a mentality in grime. That is a certain honesty and you can apply that to yourself as a grime fan. The way I manage Fusion and Jammer and *Lord of the Mics* is completely different to how I manage other artists in other genres. It's family, it's love. If I ever need anything from the man dem, I could ring them. You can't say that for a lot of your friends. I've learnt a lot about being around MCs and producers and people in grime, in terms of the way they treated each other. Don't get me wrong, they don't all come correct, there are a lot of pricks. That's part of the reason I don't write anymore. I didn't want to validate pricks. I miss writing but I'd rather share my words with the man dem. I don't feel like I've got anything else to say to anyone.

Lewi White Jammer probably deserves a lot more respect than he gets. He's a legend, in my eyes. Jammer was making so much music for all of these MCs. Before they were even MCing properly, he was releasing grime. I remember his first

Contoller Lewi White in the studio in Stokey – Shelford Place, N16
Opposite: Contact sheet of Jammer's Basement – Leytonstone, E11

31 KODAK 100TMX
30 KODAK 100TMX
25 25A
24 24A
25 KODAK 100TMX
24 KODAK 100TMX
19 19A
18 18A
Cheques Cashed

vinyl, it was called 'Family Thing'. I remember listening to it thinking, 'What the fuck is this? This isn't even a sound like human music, this is just different.' Jammer is massively important to the grime scene. He's brought so many people though, he's made platforms for people, like Lord of the Mics and Lord of the Decks. He is a legend.

Mizz Beats In regards to my career, sure I made my own beats and crafted my own sound, but in terms of behind the scenes, I don't know if I would have been there if it wasn't for Jammer. Jammer definitely brought me through. Chantelle [Fiddy] as well; she hooked up the [Lady Sovereign] 'Hoodie' remix, through Island Records. I'm pretty sure Chantelle was responsible for a lot of my early press. The two of them did a lot for me, a whole lot.

Chantelle Fiddy People forget with Jammer that at the same time Wiley was building his unique sound, Jammer was doing the same thing, providing one of the first consistent sounds with a crew (N.A.S.T.Y.) – his sound just didn't have a specific name. Part of the reason I think Jammer has suffered as an artist, and I've said this to him, is because he's so in it for everyone else, for the scene and love, his heart's too big. It's just how he is. If he sees something in someone he likes, if he recognises talent, he'll embrace it fully. I've heard the man dem tell him he's too quick to let people in but I don't think Jammer can change. It's just the way he is and if you've met his family, you see that open-door policy applies in Jammer's life too. He's done a lot of stuff without credit and without wanting anything in return. Look at Chip; Jammer put his neck out for Chip and if he hadn't, I don't think Chip would be in the position he's in now. Chip had gone off and done his thing, done the major label deal, made the music he'd made... Jammer stood next to him, did a couple of tunes and slowly Chip regained people's respect. I hope people within the scene, and the fans, understand Jammer's importance. Lord of the Mics, that's a challenge, trying to do that at the same time as your artist career is a lot of work. I don't think people realise how busy he is. And he's a producer, a DJ, a creative and a businessman. He's dyslexic, so again, people look at his mistakes online and think he's a tool. No. He gets misunderstood; he's got a lot of heart and he doesn't always know how to hold his feelings in, so that can come across the wrong way sometimes. But it's driven by passion. Prior to me re-connecting with Jammer properly eighteen months ago, I thought he was a madman. But he isn't. He's Peter Pan; he acts like a child sometimes but he's actually so wise, When's Jammer focused he's a problem for a lot of people.

Queenie I'm happy that it's gone from where it started, to where it is now. I'm very proud to see where he has gone and not just him, but the music. Kano, Wiley, Dizzee, the whole lot of them have been through here. When I see them on the TV and doing stuff, I'm proud of them. It's not like there hasn't been problems – you know when they have a clash, things happen – but it's definitely kept them grounded, being in a place they needed to be: here. It's a family home, there's a lot of respect that comes with it. Having the opportunity to come into the family

Dear Grm,

Love is always the answer, love what you do and be yourself. Continue to push the envelope even when others doubt and say it's not the fuck believe in you. Be fearless on you quest to be heard and you'll be bless. Truss!

home, you have to learn to respect that. We've had twenty, thirty of them come through at any one time and I can't really complain, apart from a couple of times when it's kicked off. But they've been very respectful of the household and me and my husband and that's why we've allowed it to continue. If there's nowhere for them to practise their artform, there's nowhere for them to create.

Love is Love   EARS

This Is Grime 131

Mizz Beats on Depression

I started music when I was about twelve or thirteen; it was just me messing round trying to find my sound. It wasn't planned. If I'd had it my way, I wouldn't have done anything until I was in my mid-twenties when I felt I would have been ready. I wasn't that cool kid. I didn't go to my first rave until I was eighteen, I used to just stay in and make music. I didn't go out raving, none of that stuff. I was shy. I was extremely shy. I don't think I knew how to deal with it all, to be honest. One minute I was this kid in my bedroom making music. All of a sudden, MTV are in my house, all of a sudden everybody wants to be my friend. It was a shock to the system.

It was around 2007, 2008 that I fell into a deep, dark depression. I was still creating, but not as fast and as frequently and as much as I would like to. It became a viscious cycle. I was depressed so I couldn't create. I couldn't create 'cause I'm depressed. That lasted for a while. I used to get bullied really badly in secondary school. That wasn't a happy time for me. I came into music around college times, seventeen, eighteen, not long after school. I did that first record, 'Signal' and it was D Double E, so it's not like I was eased in gently. It all exploded. I had some serious confidence issues, dealing with the effects of that. In the music game, you have to have some idea of who you are otherwise it will define it for you. I think that's what started to happen. I didn't know who I was, I didn't know what I was doing. I didn't have a direction. Being bullied makes you question everything. I was told now I was 'cool' but I didn't believe it. I felt like people were taking the piss out of me. I'd go home and cry. I didn't have proper management at that time, so when all that went on it was very much me trying to navigate and support myself. I just didn't have the skills at the time. I remember [Lady] Sovereign when we were recording the 'Hoodie' remix, and she had a moment. She just said she couldn't do this and I related to that. I remember very much feeling that not only was I letting myself down, and my family, but all of these people that believed in me. So my thing was, well if I just disappear then I can't let anyone down. I remember feeling an extreme amount of guilt, 'cause I knew so many people who would have loved to have been given that platform I had, and what am I doing with it? Family, friends would say that to me all the time. 'What you doing, where are you?'

I was on anti-depressents for a while. They're the worst. They're so hard to come off. I had to go to the Caribbean for three months to get off them. There were days when I couldn't get out of bed. It was awful. It got to the point where there wasn't much anyone around me could do. There wasn't much anyone could do for me. I don't think I got out of it, I think it just passed. This time around, I don't have any expectations. I'm older now, I've lived a bit of life, been through some things. I think the fear I have now is a more normal fear. It's not that deep anymore. So I'm not scared. There was a time a few years ago, it was after Meridian Dan came out, from then, everyone started getting hype again and at first, I remember thinking, 'Could I do grime again? Do I deserve to come back? I left grime, I can't just come back, can I?'

Opposite: Mizz Beats outside Balfron House – Poplar, E14

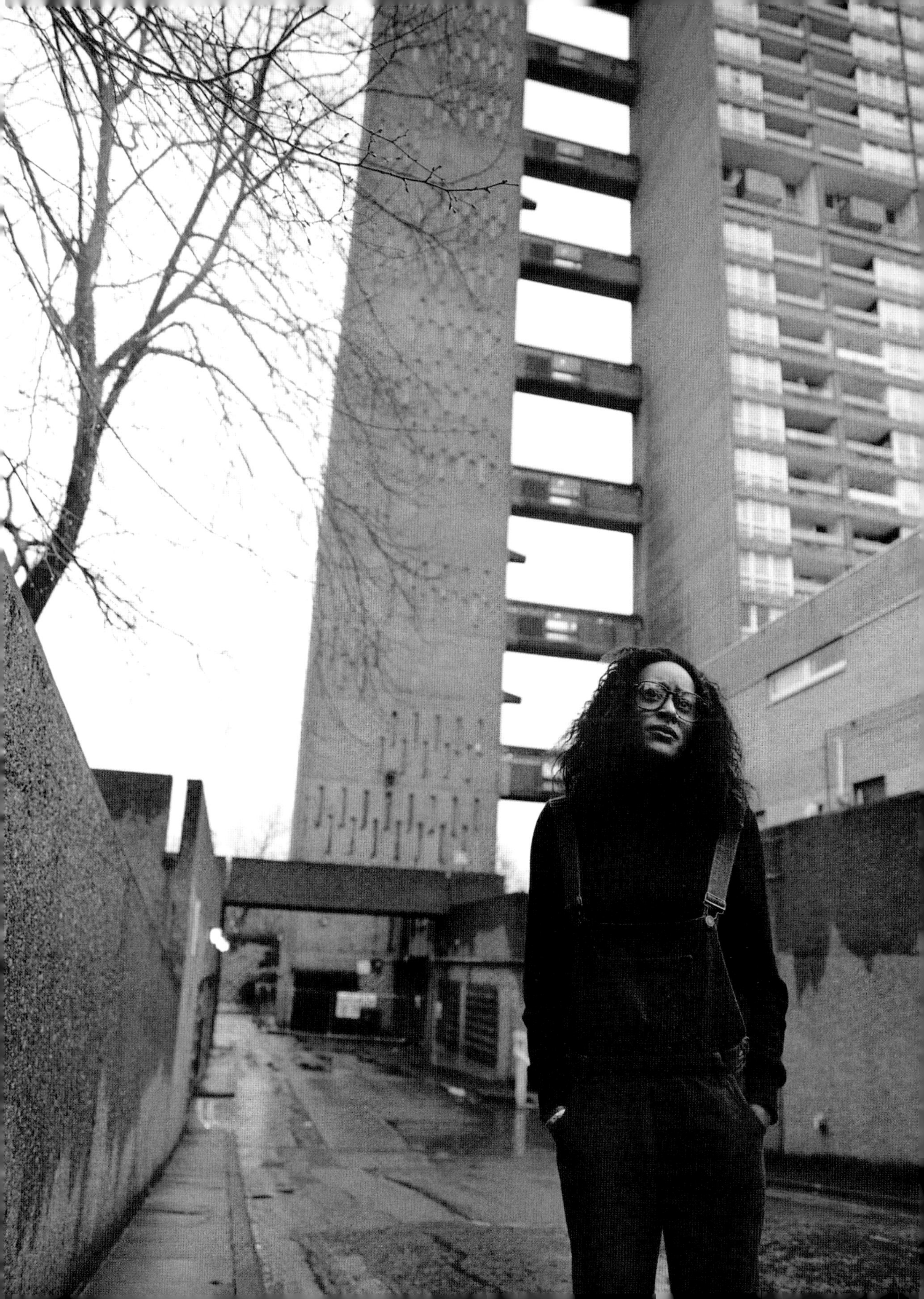

Oh My Diddy, I Load Magazines Like....

Hattie Collins I've chosen to 'break the fourth wall' just once in this book and add my thoughts to the many memories that the subjects of this book have so kindly donated to me. There is just one person I wanted to really talk about, not only because she is one of my very bestest of friends, but also because without Chantelle Fiddy, I very much doubt this book would ever have been written. When I first met Fidz in 2002, we were both fledgling journalists. We had bamboozled our way into *Touch* magazine, a glossy black British monthly that I had read for years growing up in Birmingham. *Touch* took a chance on us, neither of us had had much published – the sum total of my experience was a review of the B-Boy Championships in *Hip-Hop Connection* and Chan had worked on a *Time Out* Carnival special. However, they bestowed upon us both the grand and impressive title of Staff Writer and paid us £35 a week to interview everyone from Ms. Dynamite to Missy Elliott. We had no idea what we were doing – well I didn't – but we dove in head-first. From the first day we met, Chan and I immediately hit if off and became fast friends, the only two women writers in the office and, alongside Rozan Ahmed, Jasmine Dotiwala, Elle Jay Small, Adenike Adenture, Jacqueline Springer, Amina Taylor and Matilda Egere-Coope, among the few within British 'urban media.' In May 2004 we became flatmates when my then landlord (and good pal) kicked me out to move in her future husband. In true Fiddy style she said, 'Oh just move in here.' I didn't so much as share a flat with Chan though, more, I moved into Fiddy's world.

A year before I arrived at the infamous Pelter St, she had played me a new tune by a kid called Dizzee Rascal, 'sixteen, seventeen years old from Bow'. It was called 'I Luv U' and I remember pulling a face and telling her to get if off. I thought it was terrible, utterly awful. Just unfathomable, horrible noise. My tastes back then were strictly American; I wasn't interested in garage with all of their 'Miiiikey's and meaningless (to me) lyricisms. I had previously tried to make pals with UK rap but, well, yeah, UK rap. The song she played stayed with me though – this cacophony of belligerent drums and shrieking synths. The bark of this young MC howling about skets. A couple of days later, I asked Chan to play it again. There was something about its insistent, anti-social sonics that wouldn't leave me. 'What even is this?' I asked her, 'is this garage? – I don't understand.' She couldn't name it then either – it was still the nameless genre after all – but she played me more of it. Jammer, Wiley, a guy called Danny Weed. 'Creeper', 'Igloo', 'Eskimo', 'Birds in the Sky'. What strange, weird music this was.

Living with Chan, I soon put faces to names. Danny and Target would come round for tea – we'd make them eat couscous and avocado. Wiley would drop in on the way to his mum's with a bottle of his beloved Blossom Hill. Terror Danjah, one of the nicest men in grime, would pop by. One day Chan wrote Titch's biog, so he came over and we watched Channel U for hours while he regaled us with his many, many stories. We media-trained (terribly) Lady Sovereign on the same sofa that Titch, Doogz, Wiley and others sat on. This was Chan's way; open house, food, music, chat, relax. She bought me into that world, trusted me with it, guided me while I wrote early pieces for titles like the *Guardian*. She would read my words to make sure I hadn't said anything stupid and immediately pointed out when I had. In 2005, we did a feature together in *i-D* and invited everyone from the scene to come and get their picture taken by Jason Evans (assisted by Tim & Barry). I don't know whose idea it was – probably hers – but we wanted to open it up to the whole scene and include the bloggers, tastemakers and managers that we felt were important – an idea that I continued in this book. We put on *i-D* Live at Cargo and everyone from Wiley to Skepta, Tinchy, Titch, Roll Deep, Kano, Jammer, Ghetts, Essentials, Lady Sov, Katie Pearl – I could continue – came and performed. Later on, Chan went onto do Straight Outta Bethnal; I helped by DJing with her (badly) and I guess just by being about on the night. I found putting on nights way too stressful; would the artists turn up? Would anyone come? People ringing your phone all night because they're not on the guestlist and can you come to the door to let me in. Chan was fearless about these nights; she just went ahead and did it. You could count on one hand who didn't come to one of those three infamous Bethnals. To my memory, Dizzee and maybe Lethal B were probably the only significant MCs of that time not to put in an appearance. BBK was even formed there; the morning of the rave, JME had the first lot of Boy Better Know t-shirts delivered, and they mobbed down, forty, fifty deep, in their BBK t-shirts.

Chan has played so many roles within grime; she's been an advocate, a promoter, a disseminator, a fan. She's mentored so many people – not just artists but journalists, DJs, A&Rs, PRs, multitudes of young people that came through *Live* and *Ctl Alt Shift*, and other avenues that she took time out to advise, guide and, more often than not, lend them bus fare, buy them lunch. Fiddy is one of the most generous people I've ever met.

Without Chan, sure, I would have heard about grime at some point, maybe come to like it even, inevitably written about it somewhere at some point. But she took me behind the scenes, into the heart of the culture. Chan co-signed me and it's through Fiddy that I was able to build relationships with the many brilliant MCs, producers and DJs of this scene. As a hip-hop head, I'd always yearned to be able to go back in time to 1970s Bronx so I could have grown up among that. Now, I realise, I was lucky enough to live in the heart of grime as it was born and became what it is today. How incredible to witness a whole genre of music gestate, grow, fall, fail and rise again.

Chantelle, as testified in this book by various people, has been a connector, an influencer, a fan and a critic. She's helped so many people and steered so many careers, but rarely gets the acknowledgement. But if you know, you know. I hope this in some ways makes her know how important and influential she has been to this culture.

I would have loved to have written this book with Chan, but as she says herself, 'I'm not in that place in my life right now'. One day she will do her own book and it will be a masterpiece. Just make sure you go and buy it.

Thank you Chantelle Fiddy, you little shit.

Opposite: Chantelle Fiddy in her zen – Walthamstow, E17
Next page: Still Life of *RWD* Magazine grime covers (as shot by Artjaz, Jamie James Medina, Kwame Lestrade, James Pearson-Howes, Andres Reynaga, Carnegie and Conway, Response London, Glen Burrows)

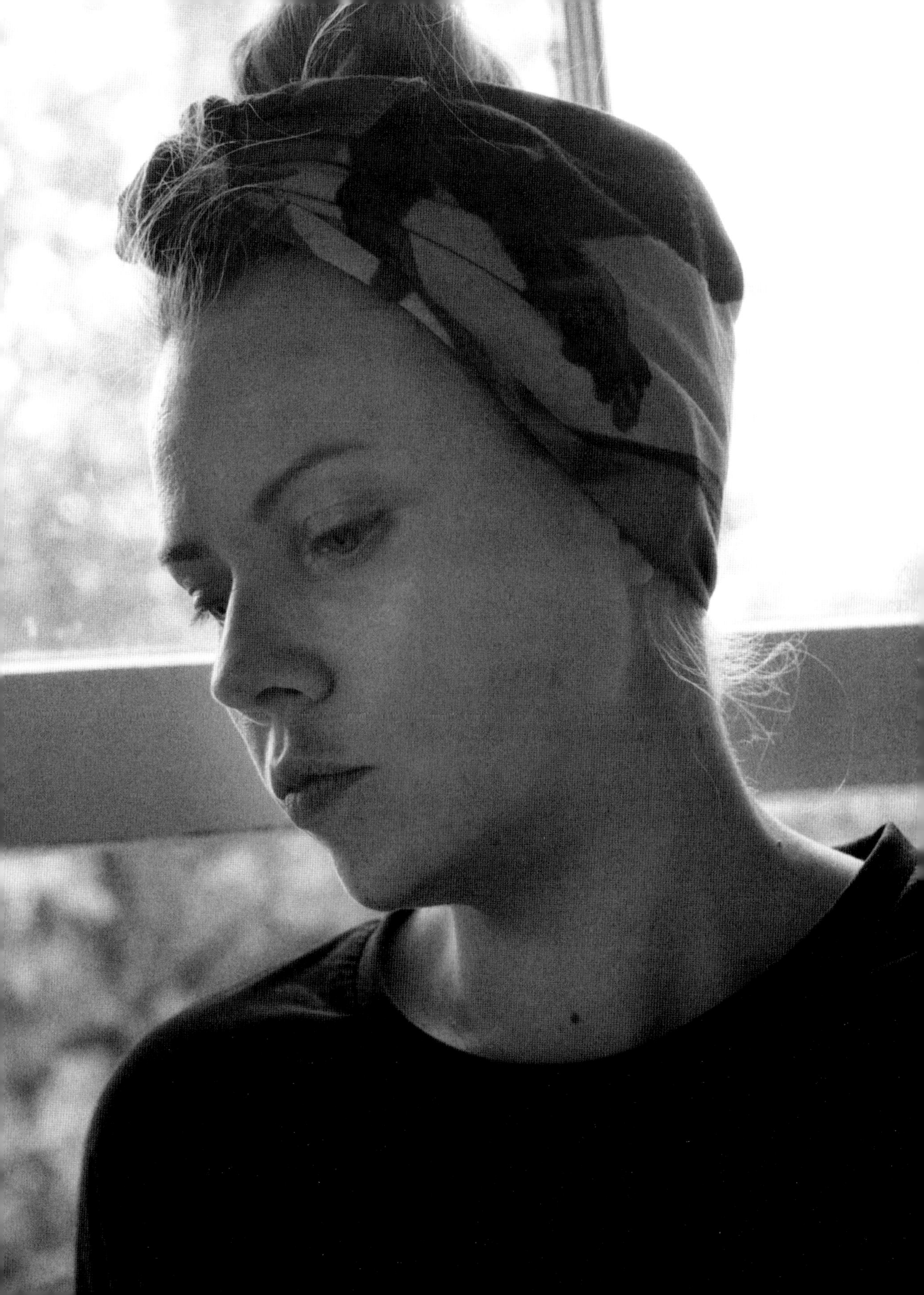

ANNIE MAC
NICK GRIMSHAW
D MONEY
RWD
NEW YORK
RUN THE ROAD
GRIME COMPILATION...
RWD
WE STILL RUN THE ROAD
WITH NO LAY & DOCTOR
KANYE WEST
VIOLENCE RECORDINGS
PARA BEATS & CARMEN REECE
OMARION
18 PAGES OF FASHION AND STYLE
LIL WAYNE
T.I.
SUGABABES
NADINE GIRLS ALOUD
JAY SEAN
DANIEL MERRIWEATHER
JANELLE MONAE
SHAUN WRIGHT-PHILLIPS
ALEX ZANE
MASTER SHORTIE
LUPE FIASCO
WAKA FLOCKA

MATRIX &
FUTUREBOUND
MUMZIE KNOWS BEST
PLUS:
GEORGIA GIRL
ROBIN THICKE
MISS GOD KIDD
TRIM
KATE NASH
SKEPTA
TIMBALAND
NEW YOUNG PONY CLUB
25
PAIRS OF THIS SPRING'S FRESHEST KICKS
Wiley
Serious Times
App Store
10
MUSIC STYLE SPORT GAMING FILM
RWD
WRETCH 32
CHIP
SKEPTA
THE LEGACY
RWD
PINK
CRAZY COUSINZ
DONAEO
ROLL DEEP
UNDERGROUND HEROES
STEED LORD
+ BRITAIN'S GOLD MEDAL WINNERS
GIGGS
AND
TINCHY
STRYDER
BATTLE ON
RAPSTAR
N-DUBZ
JLS
CHECK YOURSELF!!!
JUICED!!!
ON WHY GAMING'S ABOUT TO GET GRIMY NOW...

Grime begins to spread outside of the scene and into the hands, hearts and minds of cultural commentators...

Chip I remember the first *RWD* I got was from a chicken shop, Kansas Chicken, the best £1 chicken and chips in Hornsey. It was on lunch break, Year Seven, around eleven years old. That's where I would pick up my copy every month from then.

Nigel Wells (MD, RWD) *RWD* was the first, the inspiration, no-one else did what we did. You weren't part the scene if you hadn't been covered in *RWD*.

Wiley RWD was there at the beginning, obviously – it stemmed from *Sass* magazine. It definitely helped me; it was a strong magazine in my time.

Nigel Wells I was working selling cars and was in-between jobs. A then-pal had already put out an issue of [*RWD*, then called] *SASS* from money he had borrowed from [a friend called] Palm and asked me to help him out. The first issue had no money from ads, so I got ad money through getting record shops to advertise in the magazine and distribute it. It worked and quickly *RWD* grew. Palm introduced me to DJ Chewy (who had all the music knowledge) and Dacre (the ex flyer designer); I covered sales and managed everything. Things were moving forwards. Jimmy at Public Demand and I got on well, so Warners, via London Records started supporting with adverts from people like Artful Dodger and Craig David. But there was a problem with the boss – he wasted the little money we had on kicks for his girl and parking tickets, to the point where we couldn't even post *SASS* out to the advertising clients. Long story short, a lot of shit went down and we started *RWD* in competition with *SASS* with £5000 from the Prince's Trust. Matt Mason found us and put his experience and skill behind us. I would love to say we never looked back… but, you know the truth.

Matt Mason There have been a few moments in life when I felt that I was looking at the future. That I had to stop what I was doing and throw everything at making that future happen. I was at a meeting with Ice FM in Camden and a pallet of magazines arrived. It was issue one of *RWD*. It had female garage act Ladies First on the pink and yellow front cover. There was a Versace ad (it wasn't real, they booted it) on the back cover. It was glossy and perfect bound – really high production value. It looked like *Teen Vogue*. I instantly got it. People had tried to start 'zines for the garage scene before and they had always looked gritty and grimy – black and white, stapled together. But that wasn't us. This wasn't heavy metal or punk. *RWD* was a success because it looked as stush as its readers. As soon as I saw it I knew I had to get involved. It was the right format and the right time. I called the number in the front, told them I wanted to help and I had experience in magazines and advertising. I met the founders, in their first office in the back of Marvel City Records in Crystal Palace. They didn't have an editor and they asked me to join. They told me they'd give me a cut of the business. They'd pay me in cash, when we had it. I was twenty-three and I joined as the founding Editor-in-Chief on issue three, October 2001. I never had a second thought. I knew it was the future.

Rozan Ahmed (Deputy Editor, RWD, 2000-2004) Everything about *RWD* was small, except our vision. We literally blazed through the industry and became the number one urban music and lifestyle title within three years of solid grind. We broke boundaries with our content and brought a sense of pride to local creativity and musical wizardry. We weren't afraid to call out the bullshit. We incubated artists whenever possible. We broke their stories. We helped them shape their stories; Wiley, Skepta, Kano, Lethal B, Dizzee, Ms. Dynamite, So Solid… they all used to come and just hang out in *RWD*. We became a hub and a safe haven. *RWD* didn't just document. We lived. That's where our power came from, in my opinion.

Alex Donne-Johnson Staff debates got heated. Filing cabinets got thrown around.

Matt Mason Some crazy shit happened at *RWD*. Crazy shit. Drug deals going wrong and guns getting pulled in the office. The constant weed cloud in the office. The banter, the fist fights, sleeping under our desks on deadline day. Having to pull out all the computers and hide by the bins at the back of the office because the debt collectors were at the door. It was one of the most intense and creative periods of my life.

Chantelle Fiddy We looked at *RWD* as a scrappy, irritating little brother; there were always spelling mistakes, barely any grammar, you paid to be on the cover, etc,... It was such a chaotic set-up, but a very loud and bolshie one, which definitely wound us up at the time. Perhaps we had our heads up our arses a bit? They would boast about their numbers, print and online and actually, they were totally trouncing us at *Touch* and *Deuce*, although *RWD* was of course free. But Matt Mason is right; the mistakes really were part of the magic. RWD needed to be as rough and road as the scene itself; those early years were its glory years, in retrospect and most writers from that era would agree they have the utmost admiration for what they did.

Simon Wheatley I chose the title *Don't Call Me Urban* [for my book] because I wanted people to look beyond the hype of 'urban' music, beyond the magazine spreads and the CD cover, beyond the chart successes of Dizzee and Tinchy and to see what grime really represented in its origins – where it was coming from, which socially was quite a dark place. The book is a critique of the times as much as a celebration of grime one might say, especially because I began thinking of my work as forming a book around the time that the knife crime crisis was emerging around 2007 – and yes there was (and is) definitely a strong confrontational element within grime that can spiral out of control in unstable minds. At the same time, there was also an element of hope that I sought to capture too – Dizzee's *Boy in da Corner* had proved that success was possible. Many people write to me and say the book is an inspiration and while this always touches me I feel that the message has yet to penetrate our society which is way too materialistic and on the whole grime continues to reflect that. But grime MCs have a power that UK hip-hop acts before them didn't, they have a big audience and their voices hold considerable clout. I'm surprised no one stood up during the riots in 2011 – and there are a few well-known ones from the Tottenham area – to say, 'Fam, this isn't about nicking some more garms and creps, it's about the tragedy of a young black man being shot by police.' I hope that my book stays there as a reminder of what grime represented in its infancy and remains relevant so long as the social conditions from which grime came from persist.

Crazy Titch If it wasn't for people like Chantelle delving into the past of grime and explaining it to people, I don't know where it would be. Chantelle pushed it out there for people beyond just us lot. Her and people like [booking agent] Rebecca [Prochnik] really helped; Chantelle wrote about us and Rebecca got us bookings. It's all good us lot making music, but who cares if no-one wants to help us to get it heard; they made people care.

Nolay I can't tell you how much Chantelle Fiddy has done for me, man. I love her! I love you, Fiddy!

Chantelle Fiddy There are two iconic pictures of Wiley and Dizzee around 2002, 2003 in Three Flats, taken by David Tong that I set up. I fought and fought to get

Opposite: DJ Lolingo in front of Crazy Titch on the cover of *Don't Call Me Urban* at Simon Wheatley's 'Golden Boy' Screening – Screen On The Green, Islington, N1

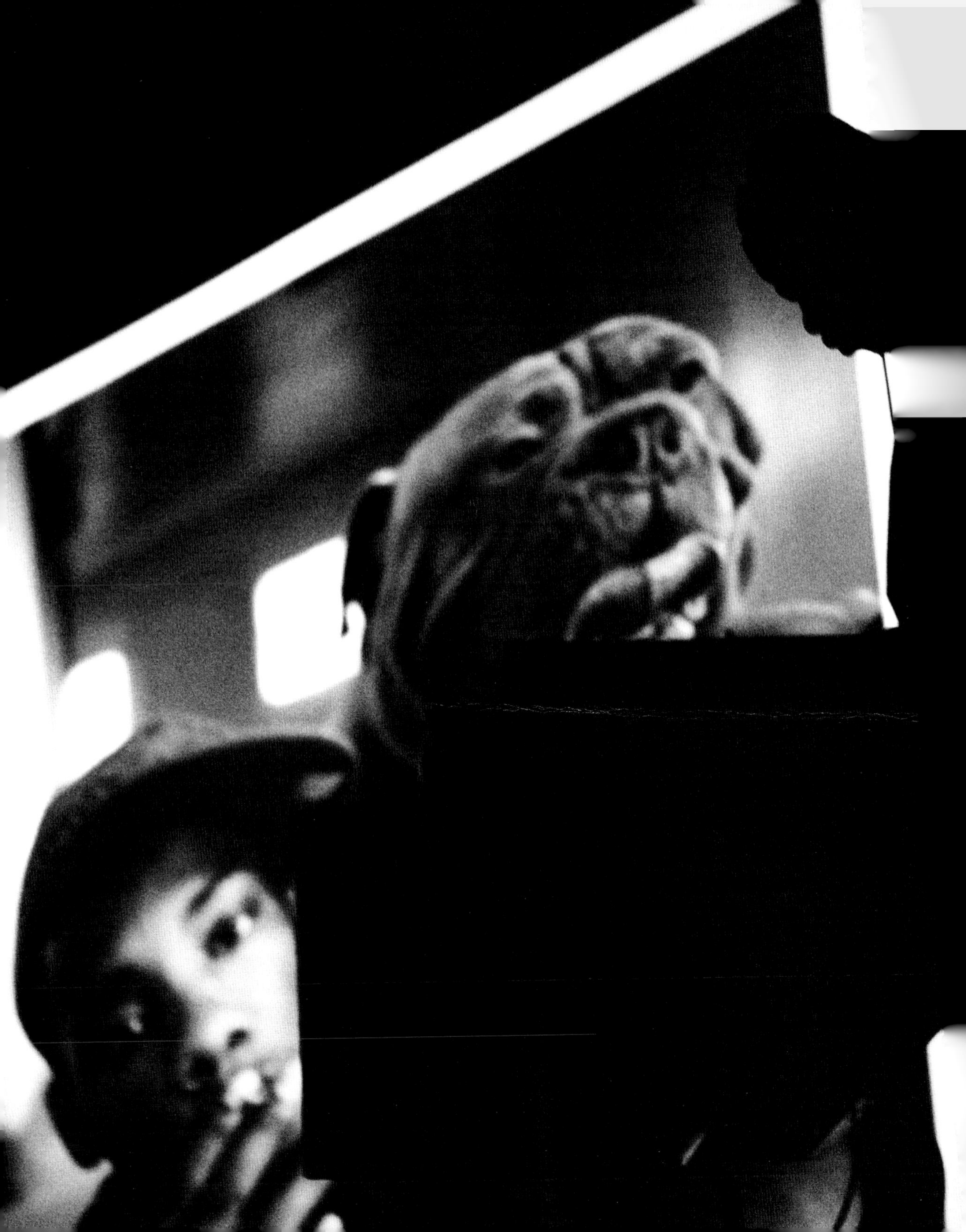

them in *Touch* magazine for months. I was so pissed off. *Touch* really didn't get what was going on, despite the fact that it was supposed to be a black British music magazine. I really wanted to set the shot and interview up, so I just went and set it up with Wiley and went down to the Three Flats. Dizzee was really shy, really quiet. I remember Wiley kept pushing Dizzee, telling him, 'You should talk bro, you've got stuff to say.' Dizzee kept looking to Wiley, very unsure of himself, but when he did speak, he was really articulate. I knew what we were trying to achieve with those pictures – they are some of the most iconic pictures ever taken in grime. I was excited that I was going to put them in a magazine and put them in front of people. Not in an arrogant way, I just wanted people to feel what I felt – I was so excited by the music.

Martin Clark At that time I was writing for magazines like *Jockey Slut, Deuce, The Face* and *Mixmag*. I'd like to think, amongst other people – Chantelle and Prancehall and so on – that I helped to document moments in time. Turns out memories can be re-written. Turns out memories are not permanent. Who knew? It's easy to write things later, but I hope that at the time, when I was there, that I wrote things as accurately as I could, as things were shifting. I hope I gave some attention to people who I thought massively deserved it. I went down and sat on a wall in Mile End in 2002 and just asked Wiley about what the hell was going on and I realised that this dude was an absolute genius. And the same with Dizzee; as *Boy in da Corner* was emerging, I think I put Dizzee in four magazines in the same month, including one under a pseudonym. I tried to give it as much blanket coverage as I could and I hope I gave those people a boost. I'm proud of helping those with talent get to where they were going – and conversely, not writing about people that were terrible – very subjectively!

Chantelle Fiddy It was mad for me meeting Martin Clark around '03 because I used to collect Martin Clark's reviews and columns before I was a journalist. Martin was one of my music writing heroes. I couldn't understand how he wrote the way he did, until I found out he was a producer and that made more sense. I would have first met Martin at FWD>>. Martin has always been so bless, such a lovely, lovely person.

John McDonnell (Prancehall) I started Prancehall in 2005. At the time there were loads of new genre names flying about – crunk, baile funk, Baltimore club etc., – and 'Prancehall' was the silliest name for an imaginary genre I could think of. A lot of other music blogs around then were really dry and analytical – they seemed to be used by aspiring *Wire* journalists to share their 'theories' about music.

Chantelle Fiddy All I wanted to do was tell people about grime. There were other blogs about at the time that were really good, but they were too deep, there was too much theory, it was all very intellectualised. I wanted to make it more accessible, more real. I was seeing these guys every day, let me just give it to people in a real way. 'Here's a chart from Logan,' or, 'I spoke on MSN with Plastician last night.'

John McDonnell (Prancehall) As you know I was just slagging off everyone. Maybe I took it a bit too far. I look back on it now and it was all a bit, kind of a bit too harsh really. I didn't really think about the fact that this is people's careers and you're slating them. I didn't really care at the time, I just wanted to take the piss.

Chantelle Fiddy From '01 or '02 when I moved to Pelter [Street], Wiley's mum lived opposite me at that time, so a lot of people would just pass through. Wiley came round for an interview with Tinchy and I remember Tinchy was so shy he sat on the stairs for two hours and wouldn't come in the living room. I became good friends with Target, Danny Weed. Geeneus and Slim used to roll around; Gee always gave me Slim exclusively, he wouldn't let no-one else talk to him. Because Gee was telling people they could trust me, I was getting what I wanted, when I wanted it. So I ended up writing about grime everywhere from *i-D* and *Arena* to *Smash Hits*. Then *Vibe* magazine, via kris ex, put me in their 'hot blog' list. It took on a life of its own, and I was able to spread the word. It was really exciting. Until I woke up in 2006 with nothing left to say.

Sian Anderson The first time I met Wiley was in a park with Chantelle Fiddy. I don't even remember why we was there, but I just remember him being so distracted, couldn't hold a conversation, like, he was on his phone, texting someone, trying to talk, walking around at the same time, trying to focus on whatever photo shoot, all at the same time and that pretty much summed him up for life for me. There's so much going on in his mind and he's trying to please everyone all the time and it's impossible to do, but he tries to do it anyway. After that day in the park he remembered me. Chantelle really has that effect on people, if she brings you around someone or co-signs you, people remember you, 'cause they feel like this is going to be the next up, in the same way that if Wiley cosigns someone, people believe they're going to be the next up.

Prancehall At its peak, prancehall.blogspot.com got maybe 20,000 hits a day, never anything massive. After a few months of blogging I got an email from *VICE* inviting me to take over their Grimewatch column (previously written by *RWD* magazine editor Matt Mason, who had departed for the US). The majority of early coverage of grime in other publications and online was astonishingly high-brow (stuff like essays about how Dizzee Rascal and Wiley both drinking cartons of Ribena in the epochal *Conflict* DVD was a subconscious display of visceral, unblemished fraternité). So as a dig at the people who partook in this practice, I came up with a ridiculously grand alias, Clarence Stately-Holmes, hoping to paint a picture of a Brian Sewell-type broadsheet arts critic. But Grimewatch was written much more in the style of a tabloid celebrity gossip column. It was throwaway and stupid, which was fitting since at the time, grime was nothing more than a bunch of kids in East London messing about and having fun. Kano was still sharing a bunk bed with his kid brother, Scorcher was living with his mum out in the suburbs and Chipmunk was in secondary school (I waited for him at his school gates in Tottenham before our first interview). I'm pretty sure Jammer still lives with his parents. I tried to make the column as immersive as possible. I spent a day smoking weed and playing pool with Trim in the Isle of Dogs. I flew to Barcelona to DJ at a festival with Jammer and watched him chase dogs through the street and screech at locals like an autistic hyena and I made the pilgrimage to South London to check out the porn collection at the newsagents run by Mr Wong's parents. I'm not sure how much of my life I wasted waiting at Tube stations for MCs to show up.

Joseph 'JP' Patterson I came across grime music about 100 miles away from London in a place called Wellingborough. I moved there when I was around twelve/thirteen with my mum – my parents split up and she was pregnant, obviously needed help and decided to take me with her. When I was settled in school, I made friends with some of the cool kids from the ends and they were all MCs. I came from listening to hip-hop, R&B and gospel – my dad's a minister – and so this shouting down the mic thing was foreign to me. But being around it day after day, I grew to love the music and as I grew older and life kicked in, I could definitely relate to the angry lyrics they were spitting about on a more personal level. The connection really clicked for me and grime when I went to an over-eighteeens rave

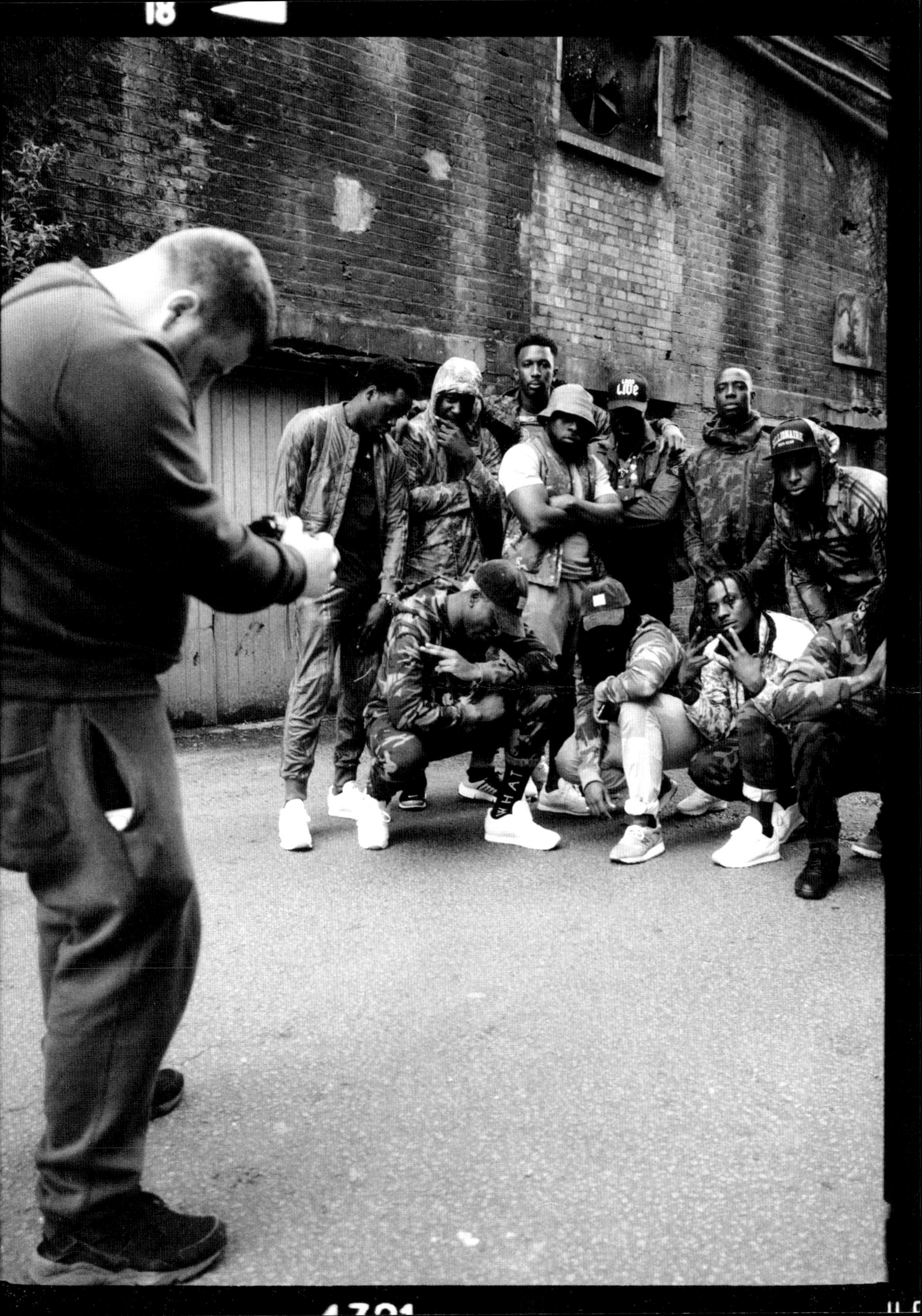
18
WHAT

when I was sixteen. The line-up came like a mini Sidewinder or something and the music grabbed me. I held a rave called ChockABlock after that night. April 27, 2007, I booked out the social club in Northampton and had Skepta, Logan Sama, Tinchy Stryder, Bok Bok and more come and shower it down. That same year, in September, I just randomly decided to put a blog together to put rave flyers up and videos I was rating. Then the love for writing kicked in. I didn't grow up wanting to be a writer, but God has a plan for everyone! I'm still humble with it, but I guess that all comes with hard work and I appreciate all the love. It's a must that I shout out Hattie Collins and Chantelle Fiddy – they were the first to call this music grime! And for that reason alone, they'll always be legends. I liked Prancehall's stuff at VICE as well; those were the main three for me. Bring back the blogspot, Fiddy! But on a real, we've seen many come and go and it's good to see that the originals are still about. Big up us lot.

Laura 'Hyperfrank' Brosnan (Journalist) I'd say myself and JP, when no one gave a shit about grime, when everyone said it had 'died', I'd say we kept the foundations bubbling. It was a tough time and it was hard getting money to put on events and pester publications to put artists on – but we did and now it makes me so happy that it's being welcomed back again.

Joseph 'JP' Patterson I met Hyperfrank at a Dirty Canvas rave in 2006. Dunn know the ICA massive! I had read her blog before then, so I gave her a big up and we hit it off. I think I moved to her slyly but she wasn't having none of it [laughs]. Then we became good friends, worked together on a lot of great projects and we're still going today. She's one of the realest road guys I know [laughs].

Sian Anderson It was my hobby, it was my lifestyle. It was just what I liked to do. I might write the odd piece and get paid for it, but not often. It just made me happy that I got to talk about and play grime. When I did start to get paid for it, it was just a bonus. I never noticed the periods when people say grime died or there's a resurgence of grime. I'm like, 'it's a resurgence to you, to me, it was always there.' When I started it was the Skepta/ Wiley phase and then they kind of moved up in the world and it was Kozzie and Merky Ace and Rival and all that era, and now it's Jammz and AJ Tracey and everyone's all gassed up and acting like they're saving grime and bringing grime back. It's just the third generation, in my eyes, of people who are doing that. I didn't see the beginning phase, but I've learnt about it through you [Hattie Collins] and Chantelle.

Laura 'Hyperfrank' Brosnan (journalist) Around the time I got into grime I was caring for my mum who was extremely ill, so reflecting back now I feel like I used grime as a huge escape. Late 2002 my mum passed away and the next year (2003) I remember getting Dizzee's *Boy in da Corner* album for Christmas. His aggression, articulate, original way of story-telling and fierce industrial productions just comforted my sadness and anger at the world. Every time I take myself back to that moment I realise just how integral that album was for my personal development. I also really want to share that while being a queer gender non-conforming person working in grime – I was really scared when I decided to come out because I had seen and heard so much talk about homophobia. While I may have some privilege by lesbianism being a lot more culturally acceptable, the scene as a whole has been very open-minded and accepting, I have had some really forward-thinking conversations and find grime especially, to be a lot more ahead than so many other movements. Music can bring so many great people together that might never have met – myself and JP are true examples of that.

Joseph 'JP' Patterson Late 2009 to the beginning of January 2011, me and Hyperfrank were pushing a group of producers and MCs we branded as the 'new wave'. Kozzie, Scrufizzer, Marger, Rival, Darq E Freaker, Big Shizz, J Beatz, Dream Mclean and a few more were the guys we booked all the time for raves, did photoshoots with, A&R'd songs for and just kept pushing them. Apart from these guys, nothing was really going on because the scene's legends were off making pop records for the mainstream, except for your odd P Money or D Double E tune here and there. I have to shout out the instrumental grime lot – Butterz, Oil Gang, Mr Mitch etc. – because without them, the scene could have died that death everyone was talking about.

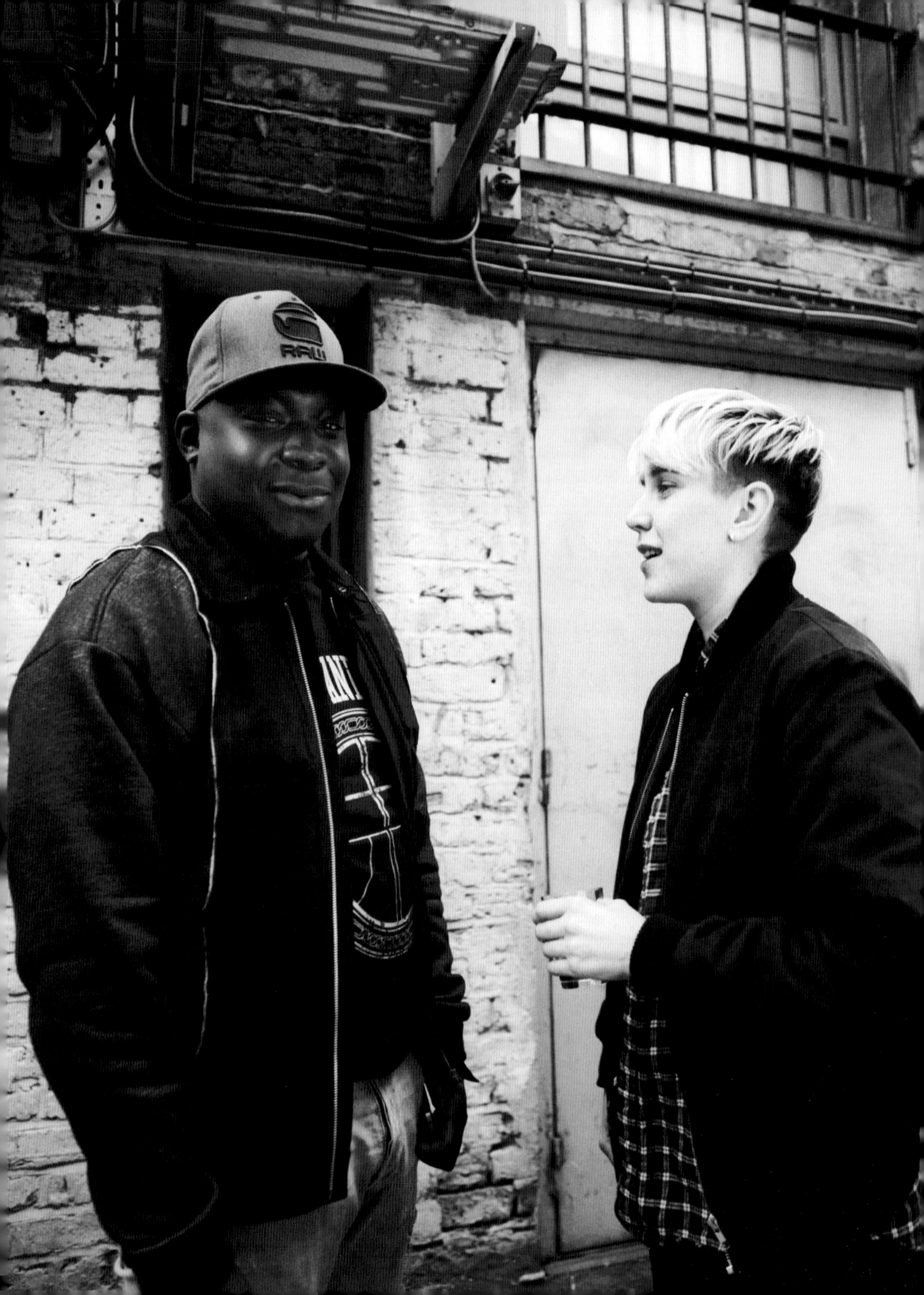
RAW

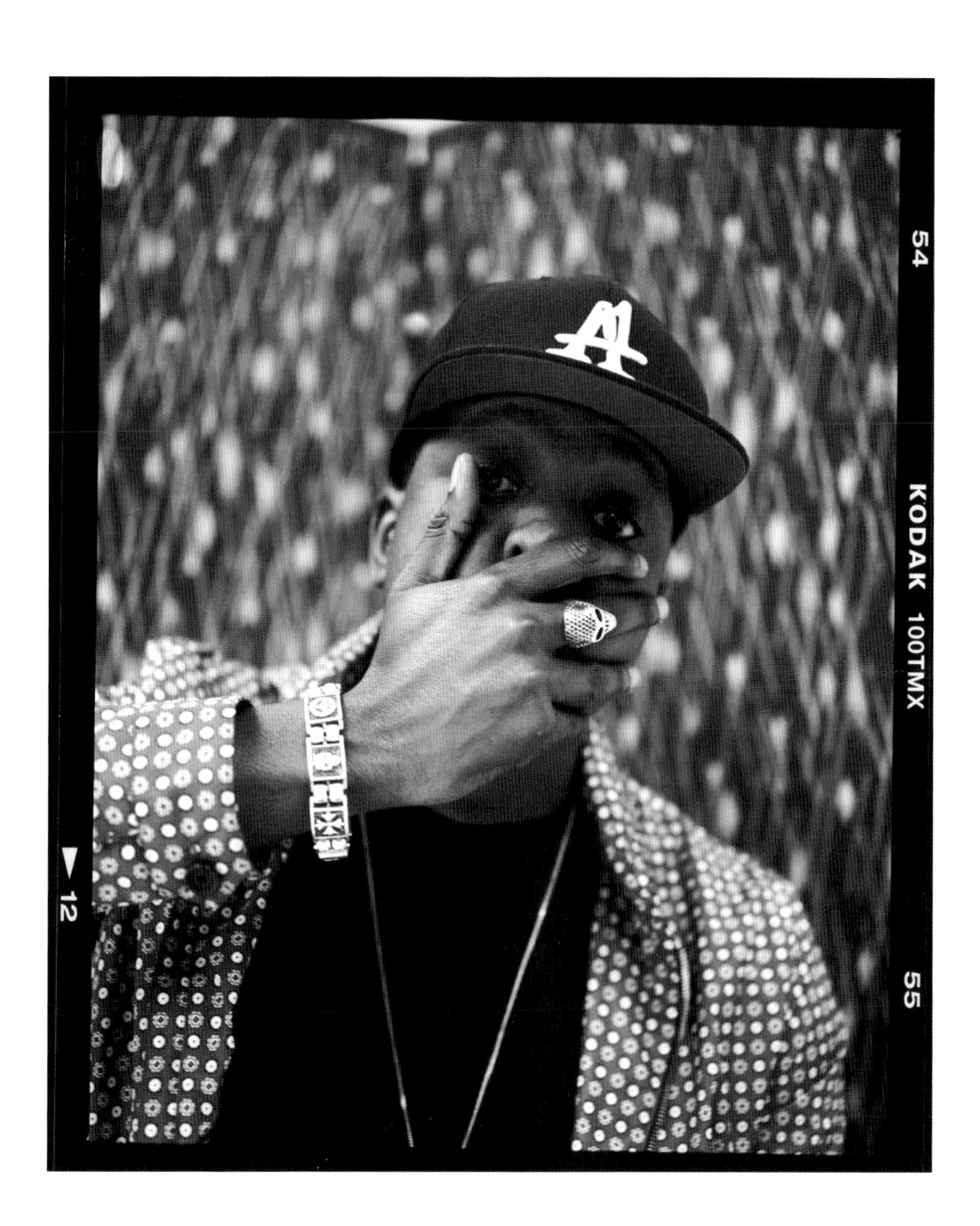

Opposite: Joseph 'JP' Patterson and Laura 'Hyperfrank' Brosnan wax lyrical outside of Dalston Pier Studios – Dalston, N16
Jamal Edwards, MBE *SB.TV* – Dalston, N16

This Is Grime 151

Nothing wa
comes ea

Democratising the broadcast experience, Channel U made stars of the scene and its sound

Mr Wong Channel U helped me because it was basically the whole of England watching Channel U, so the platform helped me get on. It was showing everyone in the UK about me, which was good. The power of television is crazy, everyone just knew about me from then and they still know me and recognise my face now, so yeah it's a nice feeling man. It helped me 'cause that was the only main platform that was helping UK music at the time, other than radio and stuff like that, but that was the main thing at the time.

Riki Bleau (Music and Promotions Manager, Channel U, 2004-2007) Being number one on the Channel U chart was an achievement and a major influence on other platforms such as 1Xtra and Choice FM to support an artist, which amounted to more exposure. The notoriety of being number one would be felt in all inner-city communities around the country and so it was very competitive. You would have the likes of Dizzee Rascal, Lethal B and Kano charting nationally with songs we were championing on the channel months before. The contribution that Channel U made on our scene was that of having an identity and the industry that developed off the back of it – creating work and careers for not only aspiring musicians but also managers, A&Rs, marketers, journalists etc. These were young people just like me who found their voice off the back of this platform. For me, that is Channel U's biggest achievement.

Crazy Titch I was the first unsigned grime MC to have a number one video on Channel U. Before me, the first two grime videos were Dizzee's 'I Luv U' and Wiley's 'Wot Do U Call It'. 'I Can C U', that was the third grime video. Those two did theirs with XL, I did mine on my own. I met this kid at the 'Wot Do U Call It' shoot, he was the one getting the teas and that, running about. He said, 'I love "I Can C U", can I direct the video for you?' I was like [laughs], 'Yeah go on then.' Did I want my own video? Course I did. We put it out and it was number one on the Channel U charts for weeks. That led onto a lot of things for me.

Riki Bleau In my opinion the channel stopped evolving and became a bit stagnant. An ownership struggle led to a name change to AKA and other competitor platforms, inspired by what Channel U had originally done, were born. Inevitably, the Internet and YouTube made U irrelevant. It still exists as Channel AKA, however it no longer sits as the major player in UK urban music that it was once widely considered to be.

Opposite: Mr Wong – Dalston, N16

The incubator of the scene, without pirate there would be no grime

Matt Mason Grime would not have happened without pirate radio. Nothing in the UK since rock 'n' roll would have happened the same way without pirate radio. It is more important than any one sound or scene. I worry that the Internet has sidelined the pirates. Maybe we've lost something. But it's too early to say – maybe we've gained something. I hope so – but no scene is ever going to emerge from Spotify.

Tinchy Stryder When I think of grime, I think of pirate radio. I think of raves. That's what grime was to me. Pirate radio is so key; to do grime, you have to have done pirate radio. You have to.

Tinie Tempah Without pirate radio I wouldn't be where I am today because I met some of my music friends and some of my idols on rooftops and in sweatboxes. It was a place we all socialised; it was also a place that made me realise in this game only the strongest survive.

Manga You've got to think, there was no streaming, no ripping to YouTube. If you wanted to hear Wiley's new beats, or Target or Danny Weed's new beats, then you had to lock into Rinse FM between 9 and 11pm on a Sunday night. That was the

Former location of Rinse FM, Shearsmith House Estate – Tower Hill, E1
Opposite: Ingram House – Daling Way, E3

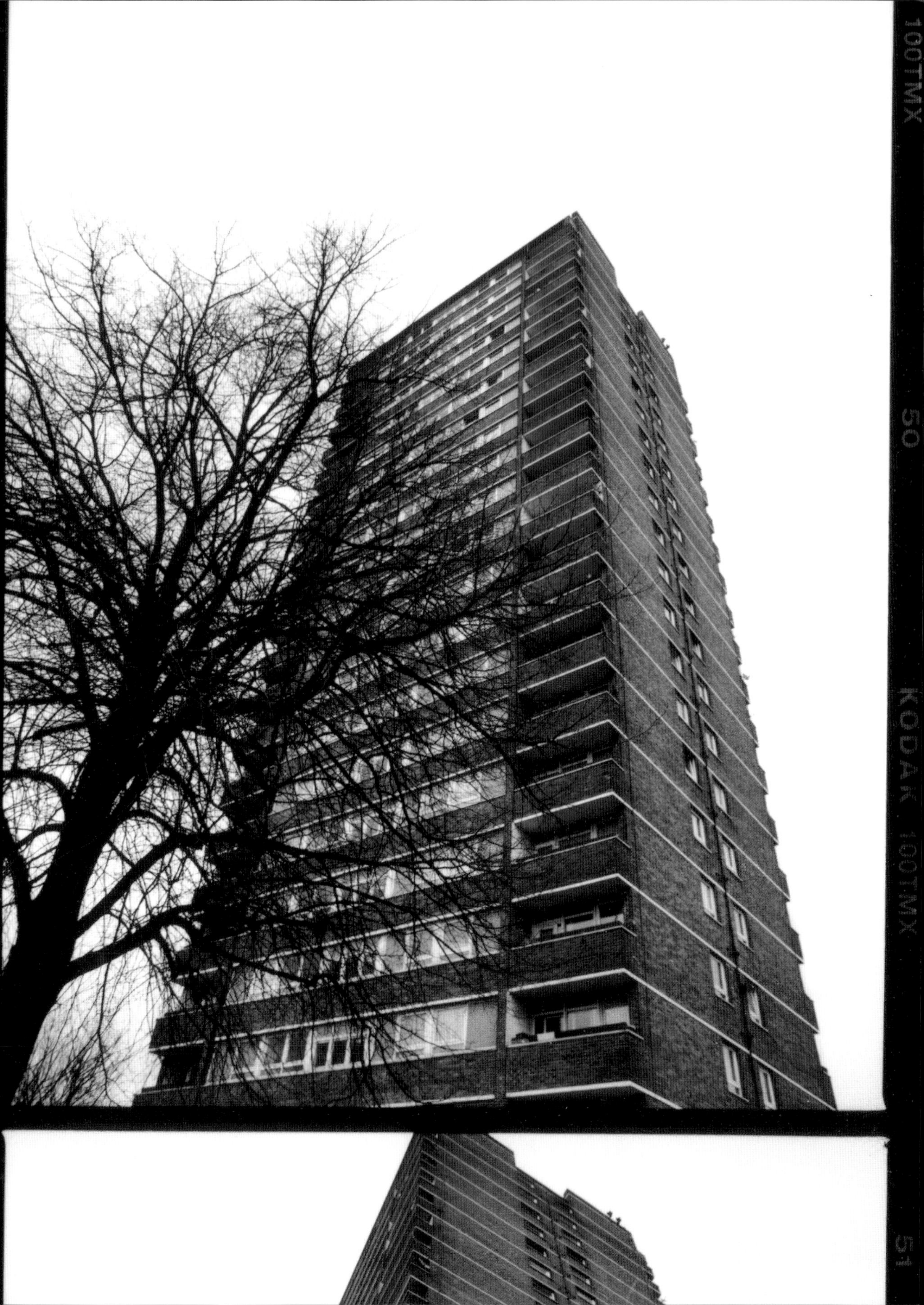
100TMX
50
KODAK 100TMX
51

only place you was gonna hear Riko or God's Gift or Dizzee spit over the newest Roll Deep instrumentals. If you want to hear N.A.S.T.Y. and Double spitting over Jammer's beats, you had to lock into Deja.

Tinchy Stryder Pirate was the only platform we had. You needed pirate radio 'cause that's the only place where you can exercise, get skilled, practise, get better. If you weren't on pirate, then you weren't getting booked for the raves. There was only a few raves as well. There was so many crews, it was all crews back then, whoever came on after you, even if they weren't sending for you, you might feel like they were, so you'd want to go back home and write a new 16. Them days, it was different. You always had to be so prepared, like a boxer, ready to go.

Plastician I can't really put into words the importance of Rinse to grime. I think it is safe to say without it, we wouldn't have grime. Without Rinse there's nowhere for Wiley to do what he did. No weekly slot for Slimzee to play all the dubplates he had exclusive rights to. Nowhere for Logan Sama to grow into the institution for vocal grime as he did. It's such a big part of grime's history.

Manga Rinse was the Mecca. The Hot 97. Once you got on Rinse, you had made it. It's where everything happened.

Flirta D Pirate then was different. You're going from your area to ends you don't know, off a phone call, 'Yeah, where do I go now?' You hear the music, bang on the door, DJ opens the door, get in there and spit. It was different. Radar and 1Xtra are all constructed different. It's nice, but back in the day it wasn't like that. Where radio was would be a hotspot. You risked your life just to spit bars. There was bare sick radio stations – Lush, Flava, Heat, Mystic, Y2K in North – Heartless and them all them used to be there. That's why I rate Rinse, 'cause they went from flat to flat, underground, and now they've got their own place and it's legit.

Richard Cowie I'm walking up the stairs, in Clare House, where we lived. The lift wasn't working so I had to walk up to the ninth floor. All these kids are passing me by, all respectful, saying, 'Hello uncle,' all of that. There was loads of them, I'm thinking, 'Why are there so many guys here?' As I'm going up each flight, I could hear the music getting louder and louder. I didn't think anything of it until I got to the door of the flat. I pushed the door and it was open. I walk in and there's people spitting. Rhyming. They'd set Rinse FM up in my flat! You know, I made some noise about it, but it's a difficult one for me. I knew he [Wiley, Richard's son] was into his music and I didn't mind, but maybe if he'd asked me. He wouldn't have done, but maybe I would have said yes. Well, I wouldn't have said yes, 'cause that could have got me kicked out of there. But to me it's all about encouraging music, all the time. I wanted him to get there but I didn't really understand that it had to be a pirate station operating out of my flat. That was a bit too far, even for Kylea.

Wiley [Laughs] Yeah, that did happen, it did yeah.

Plastician We had to move the studio from place to place to keep it as incognito as possible. Every now and then there'd almost be a new cycle of artists coming on the station or people leaving and I think Geeneus liked as few people knowing about where we were broadcasting from as possible. Back then there was a strong sense of community between the DJs on the station. We were all responsible for the safety and secrecy of the station, so we had a sense of purpose which is different to what you really have on legal radio. For two hours a week it would literally be just me in the studio broadcasting to London in full control of Rinse.

Bashy The first time I went to pirate was Deja Vu on Waterden Road, Stratford E15. Westfield's there innit, but back then there was a club called Club EQ. A lot of grime raves took place there because the station was upstairs, or right next door. I remember getting the cab from Stratford station because it was long to walk, it was far. Those early Deja sets were sick. For me it was like being in Mecca like, 'Rah, I'm fucking here, I've made it' [laughs]. The atmosphere, it was mad because you had to walk into the building, up some mad stairs – like loads of stairs – and climb through a hole. Remember I'm fifteen, I'm still quite small, so I was like, 'Where the fuck are we going?' It was in a little room, just tiny. There was a DJ, and decks on a mad wooden table, paper stuck on the wall with the Nokia phone number and maybe some rules like, 'If you don't play the ads on the hour you're getting kicked off.' You know what's mad, that was illegal wasn't it? But I didn't think it was. It's mad – ignorance is bliss. But for me, this is just how you get on the radio; you climb through holes, go on the radio, spit your bar. It didn't occur to me that you could be arrested for that.

Tinchy Stryder The first pirate I did early, I think, was Mystic FM. Mystic FM and Heat FM. I was about sixteen. I remember I got bit by a dog there. The owner had a dog that looked after the place, the dog was always there, but one day I was on the mic and the dog came around. I think I maybe got a bit of fear because the next thing it jumps on me, locked jaws. Everyone at home can hear the screaming, everyone's jumping on me trying to get it off, but the dog is locked onto me. Eventually the owner comes and punched the dog off me. That's when I knew that I loved MCing, 'cause after all that, they just patched me up and I jumped straight back on the mic. Mad man. Just straight back on the mic.

Crazy Titch Pirate was everything. You can't get that again. I don't think they can build that MC again. And I think this is the revolution behind Stormzy 'cause he actually, to me, sounds like someone that was on Deja. He has a vibe that I could have been on radio and walked onto a set and he's on the set. There's something about him, it's like he's studied the scene. I heard a lyric the other day, I was laughing. He was on a tune with Ghetts and he says, *I'm a real bad boy ask Carlos*. I was bussing up, people that don't know about that clip of Ghetto and Bashy clashing, they probably don't know what he's talking about, you might think it's just a bar, but it ain't. It's a reference to a point in time where you had to be about to even know it. On that clash, Ghetts said, 'Call Carlos, I was a bad boy in jail!'

Novelist Me and my age group, we bought back pirate radio. I was doing pirate from when I was fifteen – putting podcasts online. Creating a buzz. Pirate radio is so important 'cause that's where you practise. 'Cause no one is sounding like a proper grime MC for all of those years, it become like people were just rapping over grime instrumentals. It didn't sound like the authentic, original sound. It didn't sound like four-bar repeats, simple grime. But that's the essence that everyone enjoyed; the jovial mess to it. When everyone was rapping from, like '09 to '13, it wasn't the same thing and 100% that was because there was no pirate radio.

Crazy Titch That's what a lot of these new boy MCs don't have, [the pirate radio environment], they don't. Without radio, it's a bit diluted man. I listened to that Sian Anderson the other day. They had a Midlands set and it was so poor. They wouldn't have passed in 2003! Not one of them earned a reload, not one of them. This is why I love Slimzee. On that set you needed Slimzee. Slimzee's the only DJ I know, he don't pull up shit. If you get a reload from Slimzee, you've really nailed it.

Mistajam For someone that grew up outside of the M25, the first time I heard grime on a proper scale was via 1Xtra, via DJ Cameo and his Pirate Sessions. If it wasn't for 1Xtra, when there was no such thing as Soundcloud or Twitter, the only way that people outside of London could hear grime was if you knew someone who could tape one of those sets – or you listened to 1Xtra.

Polaroid screenshots: BBC Radio 1Xtra, Fire In The Booth, L to R: Bugzy Malone, Ms. Banks, Wretch 32, Kano, Stormzy, Devlin

This Is Grime 159

Plastician on Dubstep

I think for a while there was not a great deal of integration between the two sounds [dubstep and grime]. Growing up in Croydon I was around dubstep from really early. My first job in the industry involved doing telesales on the early Tempa Records releases, as well as all the other labels run by Ammunition Promotions. Hatcha was everyone in Croydon's go-to guy if you wanted your tracks played on a pirate station. My main problem was that for the very early part of my career, I was only really making 8-bar grime and it was a bit too simple for Hatcha and the early dubstep crowd. It wasn't until Slimzee started playing my tracks that it began to click more with the Croydon lot. Given my contact with Sarah Soulja and the Croydon heads, when I got the chance to play FWD>> for the first time in 2003, I was worried about how my music would be received by FWD>>'s more dubstep-oriented clientele. So I decided to try and build my grime tracks the way that dubstep was built – more as instrumental music, with structure. At the time grime instrumentals were really simple and tended to be built with pirate radio sets in mind, simple patterns for the MCs to ride. Dubstep influenced me to build music more intricately and to shape tracks with proper intros, breakdowns and outros etc. I think around 2005 when I was playing a lot of shows with Skepta, other MC's started to pop down to FWD>> to check it out. Jammer, Wiley, God's Gift, Riko and others would come by and eventually some of them were asked to get on the mic. FWD >> up until this point, had a no-MC policy – turning up unannounced never gave the MC a chance to actually spit. Only Crazy D was allowed on the mic with the exception of a couple of others. It was around this time that 'Midnight Request Line' by Skream was getting spun on dubplate, most of Roll Deep were in the venue and all of them were so hyped about that track. Skream got hit up by a lot of the East London-based grime DJs and suddenly you were hearing Skream and Benga dubs on Slimzee sets on Rinse. It was the first crossover track in that sense really. Because even though Slimzee had been playing my bits before that, I still consider the bits he was playing to have been grime tracks. 'Request Line' was a dubstep anthem, so to hear that cross over to grime really was the start of the relationship between the two sounds flourishing. I had the opportunity to throw some parties around that time with promoters in Europe and we'd have Jammer and Skepta, Logan Sama, me, Virus Syndicate, Mala and Coki all playing together on the line-up. The relationship between the two sounds and the artists really flourished once we were all gigging together and it's still a strong one to this day.

Around 2006, once the dubstep and grime scenes had started to cross paths more, FWD>> was a natural meeting place for producers of both grime and dubstep. Besides record shops, FWD>> was the key place to go to get new tracks or CD's off the people whose records you'd been playing. For that reason I'd have to say FWD>> definitely played a key part in grime history, even though it's always been more associated with dubstep. Around 2006, when FWD>> really was at its peak, it was more about the celebration of London's musical mark up than a specific genre. Back then, it was a really, really exciting time to be in London.

Opposite: Plastician holds early dubplates – Dalston, N16

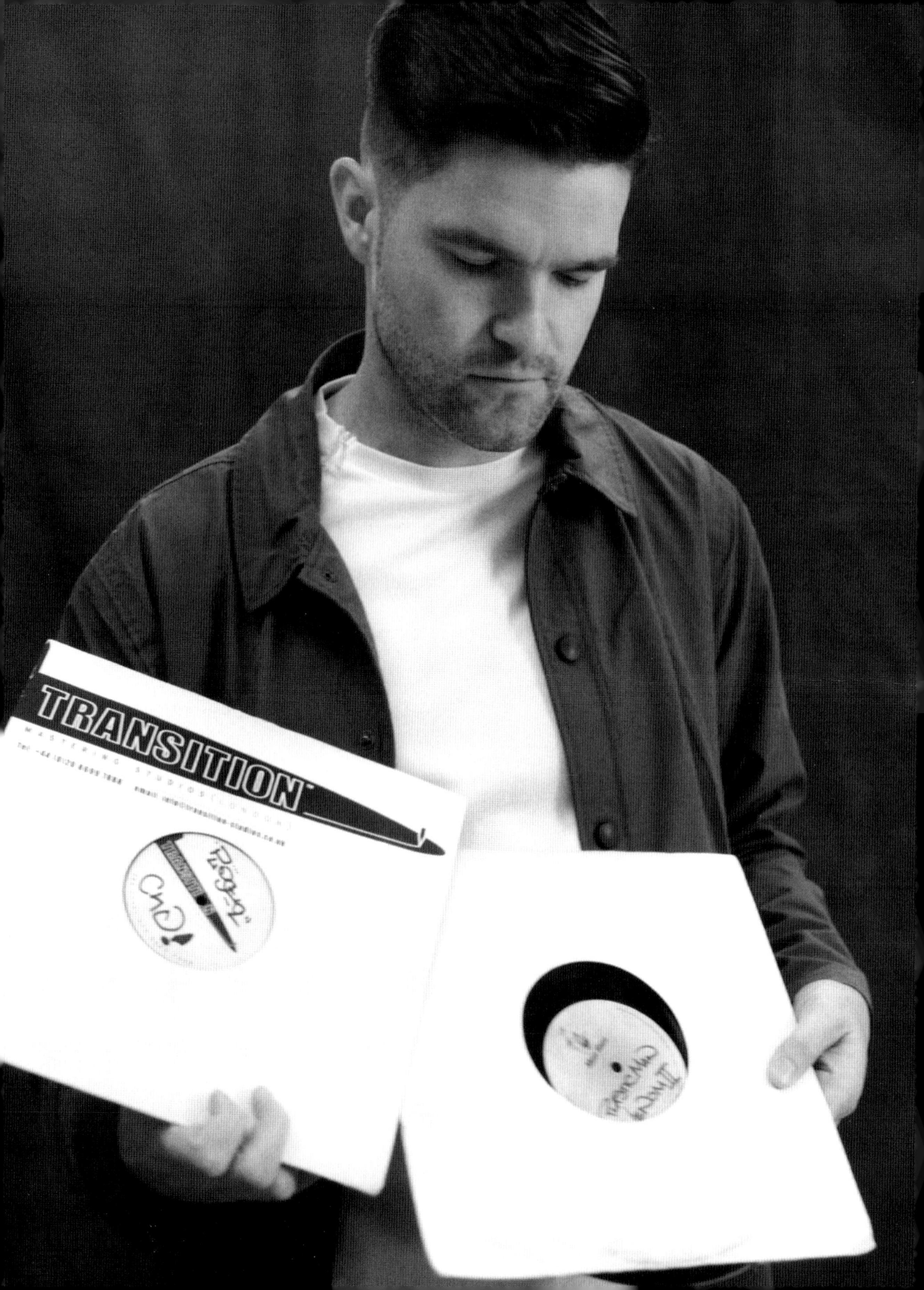
TRANSITION

Let Me See Ya Gun Fingers

Matt Mason They were amazing raves to be at. The energy was crazy. The Sidewinders and the Eskis, where everyone was on stage together... man. Looking back now, it feels like being at Woodstock in the '60s or The Loft in the '70s or Ibiza in '88. History was made.

Riko Dan To other MCs who don't chat patois I don't know how important it is to them, but I know to people like Doctor, me, Gift, Flow Dan [Jamaican dancehall culture] is very important. Without that kind of teaching, I wouldn't be half the MC that I am. That's played a major part in the making of me.

Maxwell D That whole Eskimo thing – that does come from Jamaican dance culture. Me, Wiley, and Flow Dan, we used to watch all those videos at my flat. We tried to turn our Pay As U Go stageshows into that. I would come on and get reloads, Wiley would come on, he'll get reloads. We saw that was how we got impact in the raves.

Doctor It all stems from the Saxon Sound days, it's the same thing. In Jamaica, the DJ will play a riddim, and people will jump on and spit. So I'm coming here from Jamaica in the early '00s and I'm hearing the same things. It's not the same type of beats, but the energy is the same.

Ghetts Reloads is a very important part of the culture. It might not mean to me now what it did back then 'cause I've been doing it so long, but I remember getting my first reload. You feel superhuman. You feel sick.

Richard Cowie Reload culture comes from reggae culture. MCing in youth clubs, everyone grabbing up the mic, wanting to be next to spit, spun into this, into grime. Jamaican music and culture is a big influence on grime 'cause it was a big influence on us growing up. We would listen to reggae music and rap music and that's what our children listened to.

DJ Target I used to look forward to Sidewinder so much. Getting that primetime slot, fucking up Sidewinder and getting loads of reloads, that was as good as the phonecall we had when we went to Number One. It was such a sick feeling. I go to Eskimo Dance or other grime raves and you see their version of what they think that Sidewinder energy was. But that day and age, you can't beat it. If you wanted to see Wiley or Dizzee or Roll Deep or whoever, you had to go from wherever you lived in the country to Milton Keynes. Now people can't be bothered, they'll just go and watch YouTube or a livestream.

Danny Weed People talk about doing promo; promo then was doing Sidewinder.

DJ Target Making the tape-pack. They used to get everywhere. That's how it spread so quick. People were taping Rinse in London and posting it to their cousins in Birmingham. I was getting calls from people in Birmingham, 'Who's this kid Raskit?'

Ghetts It was about the feedback; you see tapes yeah, when someone will say 'Ahh you don't get a million views all the time', I'm like 'I'm from a different day man, that's the new school ting.' Tapes, yeah, tapes was leaving London and ending up in Manchester. They was flying through the school system, like, tapes was doing tours – TDK was on tour! Sidewinder used to move tape-packs like crazy.

Maxwell D We started on tapes. I used to get to places like Wolverhampton and they'd be like, 'Ah blud, I've been listening to you for fucking ages, I've got the TDK'. That was when we realised like, 'Oh, we're famous out here'. We'd be coming home at 7 o'clock in the morning, we didn't have a hotel, nothing. We used to just go up there, buss up the mic all night, for at least an hour and a half – none of these fifteen minute sets and breeze out – and we'd just spray out our bellies, sweating. It was the tapes and tape packs that helped spread that and helped make us famous.

DJ Target The internet just made it accessible for everyone, which was good and bad. That deaded the rave scene. Well, not that alone. There was the police locking things off too…

Danny Weed And girls stopped going too 'cause it was way too aggressive.

Manga I remember going to Eskimo Dance, the one at SE1 club and there was a big riot and it got locked off. I remember Wiley jumping in the crowd, everyone was going crazy. Basically, a fight happened, and everyone jumped onstage. Everyone was going mad, there was girls getting knocked down left, right and centre. It was too much. When it kicked off in that place, it went crazy.

Riko Dan When I come out [of prison], my first memories was being taken to a rave by Wiley and then seeing what was going on. That was my first memory of like, 'Rah, this is serious bruv.' The bouncers were pushing everyone out the way. The first time I spat on Sidewinder I was shaking, my knees were shaking bruv. I said *Dead* first and after that, I saw the crowd and it felt a bit easy. Then I just went in.

DJ Target Before the internet and YouTube, if you wanted to hear or see grime, you had to go to Eskimo Dance, go and buy the records in Rhythm Division, you had to listen to the radio. People used to write about grime being a scary scene; there was only a few outsiders that weren't shook to get involved. There was incidents like there would be anywhere, but it was more stereotyping than anything 'cause it was loads of black kids with their hoods up.

Danny Weed But it was full on. It was normal for us; it wasn't normal for a lot of other people. My favourite moment was Sidewinder Bonfire Night. It was me and Karnage on the decks. Wiley, Dizzee, Flow Dan, Scratchy... Jamakobi might have been there. That was the set before either of them [Wiley or Dizzee] had done their record deals. It was so full on and I remember we left that rave and were driving home, almost silent, like, 'That's the biggest response we've ever seen.' That was a moment. We all knew that we had a bit more power after that.

Tinie Tempah I snuck out to my first Eskimo Dance in Year Nine or Year Ten. I shouldn't have even got in. I took the bus there and I remember seeing Lethal B who was wearing this brown leather jacket. It was like seeing my idols, my heroes. People started rushing the door and I managed to slip in and that was my first experience of a grime rave. It was proper scary but one of the most exciting experiences ever.

Bashy You see those days, the scene was very, very black, very Afro-Caribbean. It was African and Caribbean kids for the first couple years and obviously you're gonna have the bad man Irish yute who's there as well giving zero fucks, not feeling intimidated at all. It was fifteen to twenty-four year olds in one club and the energy was buzzing, it was sick man. It had a dark vibe and those times you could still smoke in the club, it was legal still. There's a fucking cloud of weed in the club... It was different, it was in a different time. Eskimo Dance was mad still.

Cheeky I started Audiowhore, which was going really good. I rang up Wiley around

2012, and said 'Lets bring it back.' Wiley loves a crazy idea, so he was on it. At the time, no one thinks it's gonna work, the police won't let Eskimo Dance happen. In the end, Proud2 said yes. They gave us the worst date, the third week of January, but it ended up being the best; everyone was bored and wanted to get out. The police put the risk at high, but it went ahead. And it was a great night.

Lilz (Eskimo Dance) Before, it was a shoobz, now it's like a concert. Before it was authentic, and ok yes, you can't recreate that, but now it's a lot more professional.

Cheeky No-one was earning money in the old days. It was, 'Let's go radio, let's go rave.' There wasn't agents saying, 'Don't play this rave 'cause you won't sell out your tour.' That killed off the authenticity too. I think agents really killed that. But, look, grime is pop now, we're in the bubble. The crowd back then was hood. It was the back end of what garage was, when garage started to go bad, they moved onto grime. When I say hood, I mean, there was a more than likely chance of it getting locked off. Now, it's students.

Zack (Eskimo Dance) The difference between the original Eskimo Dance and this one, we can recreate the vibe now in pretty much every city, it's the same sort of vibe. In the original Eskimo Dance, you could never, ever recreate what was happening then 'cause it was so organic. A lot of the artists that came there, the styles they had, the flows they had, the energies they had, the hunger they had, some of the MCs we had all on the same night, we can never get all of those artists together on one small stage. It's never gonna happen again. We had, in Area, Dizzee Rascal, Megaman, Asher D, that garage/grime crossover. That was when So Solid realised, 'We're gonna stay with the garage thing and let the grime MC's do the grime thing.'

Cheeky Whenever anyone asks me my story, how I got this, I always say it's luck. You can work as hard as you like, but you need luck on your side. Luck of timing. Right place, right time. The luckiest thing to happen to me was December 2014. The venue at Indigo2 didn't want us to come back because of all the drama we caused and I was about to give up, but in the end I forced them to do the party. And that was the resurrection of grime. That was the first Eskimo Dance in over a year and the numbers, in terms of sales, was crazy. Up 40, 50% on the previous event. The numbers were dying before, but this one, boom. And it's gone up from then. It felt like, straight away, lets book Bristol Academy. We've sold out London, it's time to take this on the road and do it properly. We sold out Bristol instantly. Then I knew. Not just that Eskimo Dance was back, but that the scene, grime was back.

CRAZY T. INTERVIEW
FIRE CAMP & CISSE
GIFT INTRO + SLEW DEM EDITED
Panasonic
DVC
JVC
Mini DV
60

JAMMER + SLIMZEE INT.
Panasonic
JVC
Mini DV
60
Target Danny Weed Wong
SAMSUNG
Panasonic
DVC
60
90
DV
RWD Rhythm Division
chaingang
Panasonic
DVC
DATE

From Lord of the Decks to LinkUp TV, putting the scene on screen played an important part in cultivating the culture

Rooney (Risky Roadz) My mum and my nan, they've had the entire scene come round my house, so they've got to know lyrics over the years. My nan saw D Double a couple of weeks ago and was like, 'It's meeee, meee' [laughs]. It's been part of my life and my family's for fourteen years.

Ratty (Lord of the Mics) It was just good to have something to turn up and do. I came out of jail, I linked Jammer, we knew each other from the area. First time I went to jail, I came out and I'm in studio, in the Basement and I'm seeing all the stuff that was going on. Jammer was running up and down selling all these vinyls and I saw that rhyming was like weed. We can make it ourselves, we can take it to the shops, distribute the vinyls. That's how Hothead Promotions started. We started distributing all of Jammer's vinyls, Wiley's, JME's, everybody. Coming from where we came from, I believed that you could hustle to make your money and do that all your life and you'll be alright. And the lightning bolt for me was realising that there are other things in this world than just selling drugs. That was the learning point for me. From the vinyls, Jammer did *Lord of the Mics* CD and then we came with the idea of *Lord of the Decks* and to be honest, that changed everything. Me and [my cousin] Capo saw all of those American *Smack* DVDs and saw the potential. I started filming everyone and I remember when we passed them out to Wiley, Target... everybody was so gassed to see themselves on TV. Remember, this is pre-internet, pre-Channel U; this was the first time that people, outside of anyone going to the raves, could actually see what Wiley looked like.

Rooney I used to DJ before I started filming and I used to go in Rhythm [Division, record shop in East London] to buy my tunes. That's how I got to know Mark and Sparky [from Rhythm] and I ended up with a Saturday job in there. From that Saturday job, seeing the MC's come in, it built up. I already knew a few, I knew Dizzee and Wiley from around the area, then when more and more used to come in, say like Hyper, 'cause I grew up listening to Pay As U Go and N.A.S.T.Y. I'd be like, 'Oh *that's* what he looks like.' Then I thought, 'If I wanna know what they look like, everyone wants to know what they look like.' So I started uni, and someone mentioned something about a program called Adobe Premiere, so I got hold of it, and I asked my nan to lend me the money, about £300 I think, for a camera. I bought a camera and *Risky Roadz* was born. Nowadays, you've got the GRM Dailys, SB.TVs, Link Ups and they always say, 'It's because of you that we picked up a camera'. To me, that's pretty monumental. It's good to still do what I do – as well as driving my cab, I just passed The Knowledge – and to be involved in it and know I've had that impact.

Jamal Edwards, MBE (SB.TV) My mum got me a camera in 2006 for Christmas, that's when I started. I just started off filming stuff on my estate, foxes and stuff like that [laughs], 'cause they were making so much noise. Steve Irwin, RIP, that was my inspiration. If I didn't get into music, I could have created a wildlife channel! But I put this video of the foxes on YouTube and it got like 1000 hits. I thought, 'Hmm, OK.' My first video was just raw, there wasn't any colour grading, no fading. It was rubbish quality – no sound control and shaking hands. But I taught myself, I learnt the little tricks you need to learn, stay out the wind, don't shoot with the sun to the back.

Rooney YouTube essentially killed the DVD game in the sense of people were given the chance to see footage instantaneously rather than waiting for say eight to twelve months for a DVD to be produced. It was film, upload, watch, and as people wanted things so rapidly attention spans also diminished and essentially killed the DVD.

Ratty A regret for me was not seeing the transition from DVD to YouTube. That's the number one regret, because we were the first people to do anything on DVDs and put these people and their faces there. And obviously SB.TV and people have come along and done what we were doing, but for free. I wasn't about to give it away for free, because I'd spend every day and night with these guys, filming. And plus we were getting paid. We were young and getting money. So I was like, 'I'm not putting it on YouTube!' I didn't understand it then. Fuck it, live and learn. It's given us brand strength at the same time.

Jamal Edwards I was inspired by all the DVDs, Channel U, pirate radio. I got the DVDs from an older friend on my estate, and then I started going radio myself as an MC. My mum banned me from going to the market, where I had started getting the DVDs for myself, so I thought, 'OK, let me just try and film my own ones.'

Postie (GRMDaily, Not For The Radio) Before we came, there was *Risky Roadz* and stuff like that. While Risky was on holiday spending his DVD money [laughs], we was deprived, we needed something to happen. YouTube was becoming quite popular, but YouTube then was kinda like how Snapchat has been for the last year. Like, there's still some people who ain't on Snapchat. It took a while for people to catch on. So we jumped on there, started filming everyone and because there was such a big gap, it took off straight away. We brought regular content, daily content – that's why we called it 'Grime Daily'. J2K, he was our first interview, we filmed him for twenty minutes, cut it into five pieces, dropped a piece a day. Filmed four more people like J2K, I've got twenty-five pieces; freestyles, interviews, funny parts, controversial parts. Because it was such a rarity to see these people that often, anything they did was entertaining. Until then, you'd see them on a DVD for ten minutes and then you wouldn't see them again for months or years. So we made it like a business because we approached it like a business. We wanted to make something out of the culture, as well as supporting the culture. We wanted this to be our life. Now you have cameraman, website entrepreneurs... A whole new facet opened up. I feel like that's what we brought to the game, as well as good videos and entertainment. As an entity, I can only go as far as the artists go, so it's based on what the artists can do. The limits have really opened up. It can only get a lot bigger for a lot more people.

Jamal Edwards I want to keep on finding these artists and allowing them to tell their stories, but still go overseas and localise it as well. I don't have to be at the front of it, or the back or the middle, I just want to be a part of it and just continue to help it grow. I hope I will always get messages from people who've been watching it since they were eleven or whatever, telling me I was their source to discover new grime. It's funny, I feel like I also have a job to educate people about the history of grime as well, like you should know about *Risky Roadz*. I feel like I have a job to, as well as entertain people, to educate them so they don't get it twisted between what's grime and what's not and where it's actually come from. Hopefully I'll make some cool little documentaries and keep on unearthing these talented people. I had no idea that filming foxes all those years ago could lead to everything that's happened. It's surreal, that I'm an MBE, it's nuts.

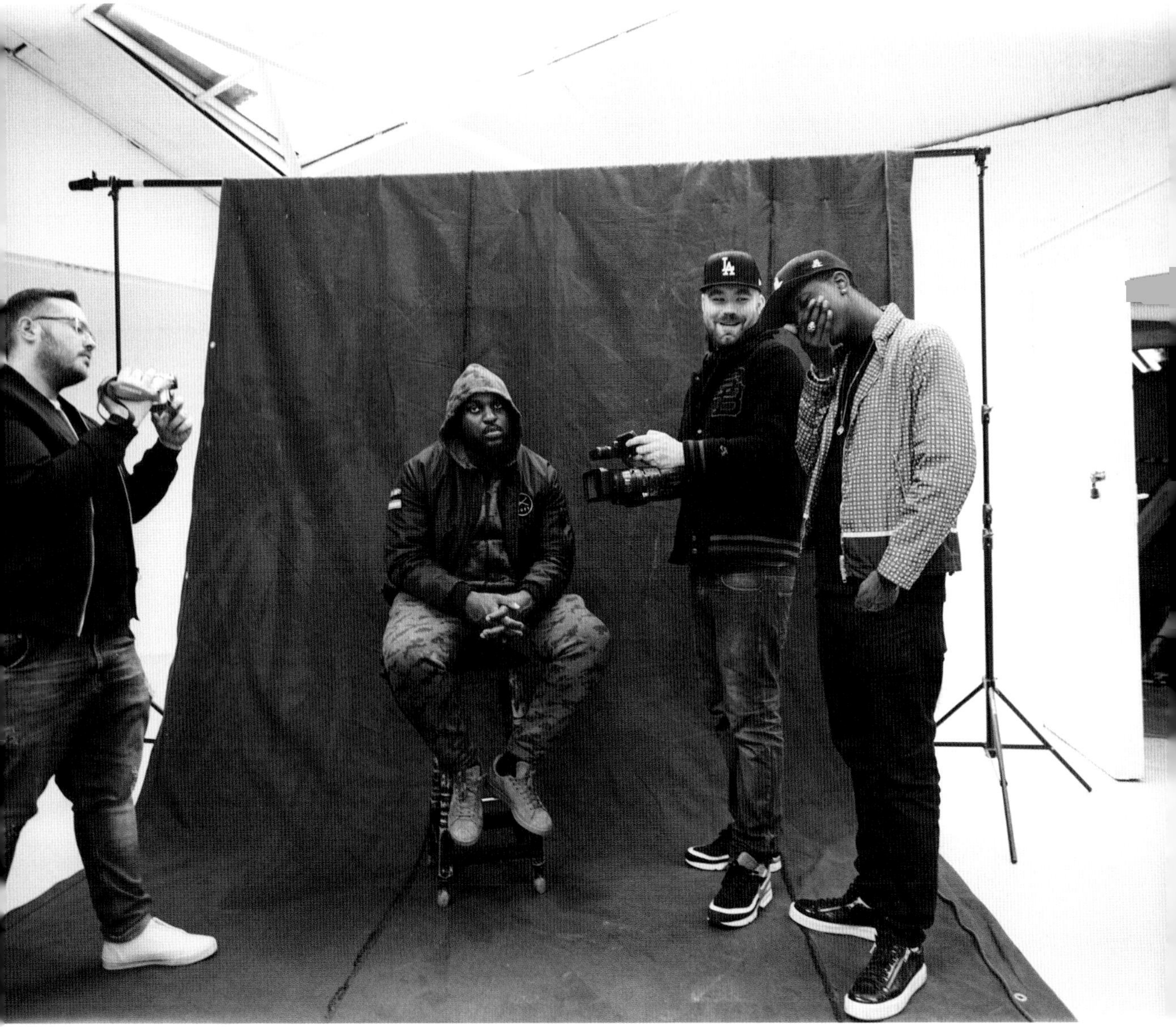

The Internet's early forums were a space where fans and MCs got up close and very, very personal

Alex Donne-Johnson In its heyday, the *RWD* forum reached 50,000 members and the website was getting more than one million unique users per month. The main competition was a site called 2sg.co.uk (2StepGarage), which had 40,000 members but less of a site to back it up. The strength of *RWD* was definitely the grime focus, something which other people shied away from at the time. This was a deliberate decision pre-mediated by [Matt] Mason and myself.

Rozan Ahmed (Deputy Editor, RWD, 2000-2004) Alex would show us the controversy on there. It was great. To see that level of exchange in one place was a big deal for the movement. It was almost like grime's first Twitter moment.

Alex Donne-Johnson The forum caused so much trouble. There were people on there threatening to kill each other. There was a big sex scandal involving a footballer and DJ... The stories that came from the forum were amazing: it attracted such an eclectic group of people. We had sex scandals, marriages, disputes, in-jokes and memes. Lady Sov's sister met her future husband on there. It became an addiction for many members as it was like taking part in a real-life soap opera. This enabled it to grow organically into a beautiful melting pot of personalities and musical opinions. It was a self-sufficient community with people making true friends, deep connections, promoting their music and making their own rules. To me this epitomises underground music culture.

Matt Mason The forums were huge. They reflected the back and forth of grime so well. Grime has always been a conversation. And they were huge. Alex, who joined us when he was sixteen, really understood this and grew *RWD's* forum, which made *RWD* one of the most popular music websites in the UK. Grime was the last thing to happen before the Internet and social media really became the dominant platform for all emerging music and culture. Grime happened on radio and in clubs and print more than it started online. I worry that now the Internet exposes new sounds and cultures too quickly, before they've had time to gestate in one place and build a foundation. Ultimately the Internet has really helped grime, but it definitely got overexposed and portrayed in the wrong way for a minute.

Nigel Wells (MD, RWD) Investors couldn't believe our traffic. We had over two million uniques a month, plus. We were like the KSI of today. *RWD* was the first UK social media platform – stars were made on that forum.

Alex Donne-Johnson Some of the biggest stars from the budding scene started to post on it and interact with their fans.

Wiley The *RWD* forum was a good place because it allowed everyone to talk about what they wanted to talk about. People went up there to explain different stuff that was going on in the scene. It was like a newspaper. Sometimes it got heated but it was jokes. When I was on there, it reminded me of college and school. When I first went to college and the email and stuff happened and we would be in the common room and see that girl on the computer and send her messages and stuff, or man dem arguing and one tryna draw a next man's girl, it's all that type of stuff. So that's what it reminded me of even though there was a lot of man talking about grime.

Alex Donne-Johnson My personal highlight, which I feel gave the forum more prominence in the scene, was when the artists started to engage in discussions with their fans. Wiley, JME and Skepta, to name a few, became regular posters. Wiley's posts are still remembered to this day as he always had the best comebacks for his disputes. My personal favourites being, 'Your mum is a lorry driver, bruv,' and, 'You are a two face watermelon head…' Not much you can say after Wiley says that to you!

John McDonnell (Prancehall) I never got too heavily into using forums but the highlight for me was when Wiley signed up as a user for the *RWD* forum and spent about six months trading insults with twelve year olds. His best put down was probably: 'Both your parents are experiencing the credit crunch. I ain't.'

Found down the Roman Road, the hub of grime was Rhythm Division

Rooney I miss Rhythm. It was a bit more personable then, you had to go places to get stuff done, you had to go to the shops to get your stuff into the shops, unless you had a distributor. You had to go to the people to get their music. Artists used to have to bring their music into Rhythm, some of them would bring them to Rhythm, write 'Slimzee' on it, and wait for him to come in and he'd get their tune. Now it's all Soundcloud and email and whatever, it's a completely different world. Back then, you had to meet the person to have their music.

Plastician Hanging out in record shops, that's how everyone met each other; you'd spend an hour in a record shop and you'd meet other producers bringing their boxes of vinyl in. As a DJ, I'd wait for them to come in and I'd always want the one of the ten copies they might have of a test press they wanted to put out. It's no surprise to me that most of the people I met back then are still here doing things now. You had to work so hard just to make the slightest name for yourself back then. It did take a little bit of business acumen, even though we didn't really know what we were doing. But it was fun and that was the driving force for me keeping at it.

Opposite: Rooney *Risky Roadz* holds out his taxi vehicle license – Dalston, N16
Next page Left: It's Reaaaal, Doogz under the A40 – Portobello Road, W10
Next page Right: Durrty Goodz in his emperor hat – Portobello Road, W10

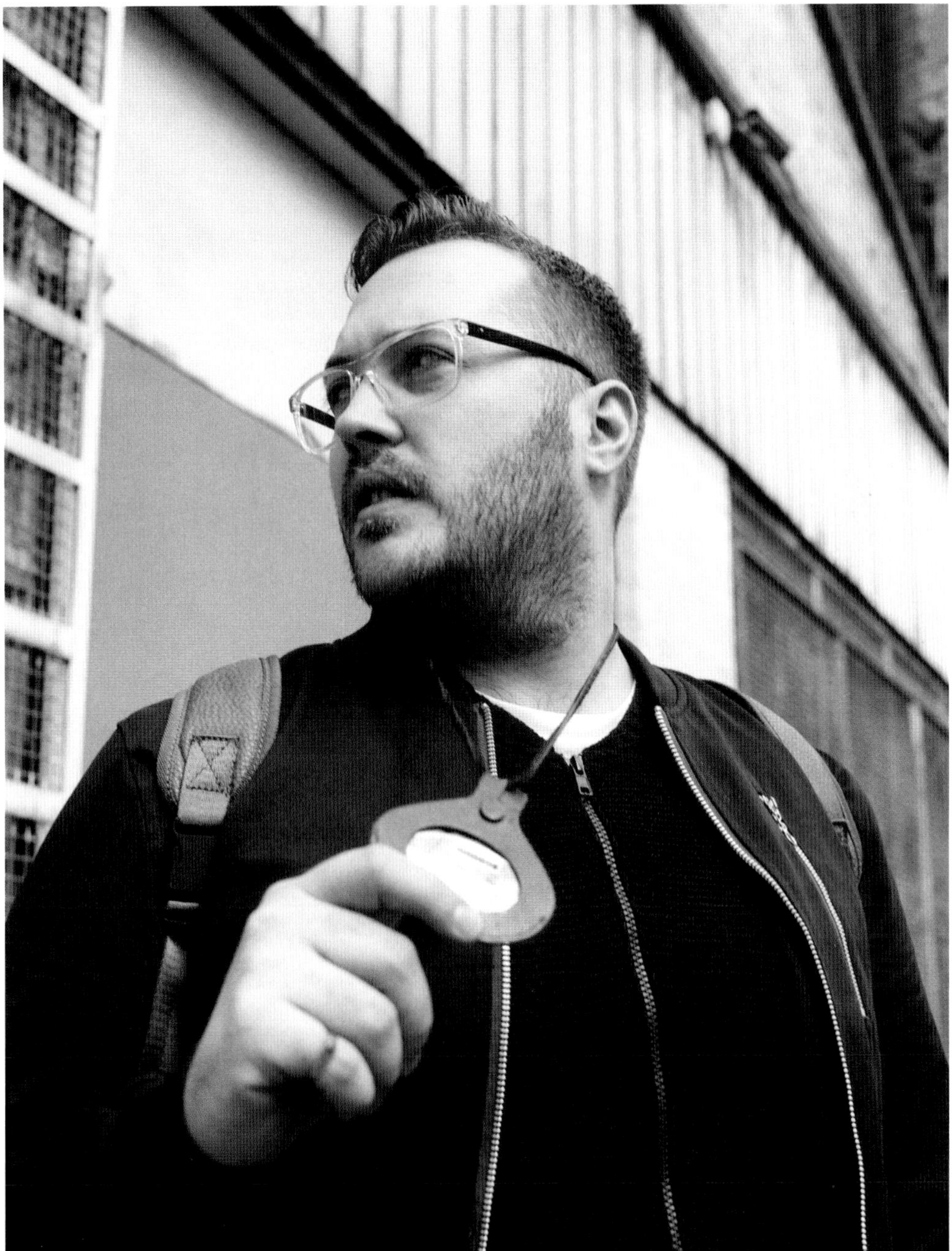

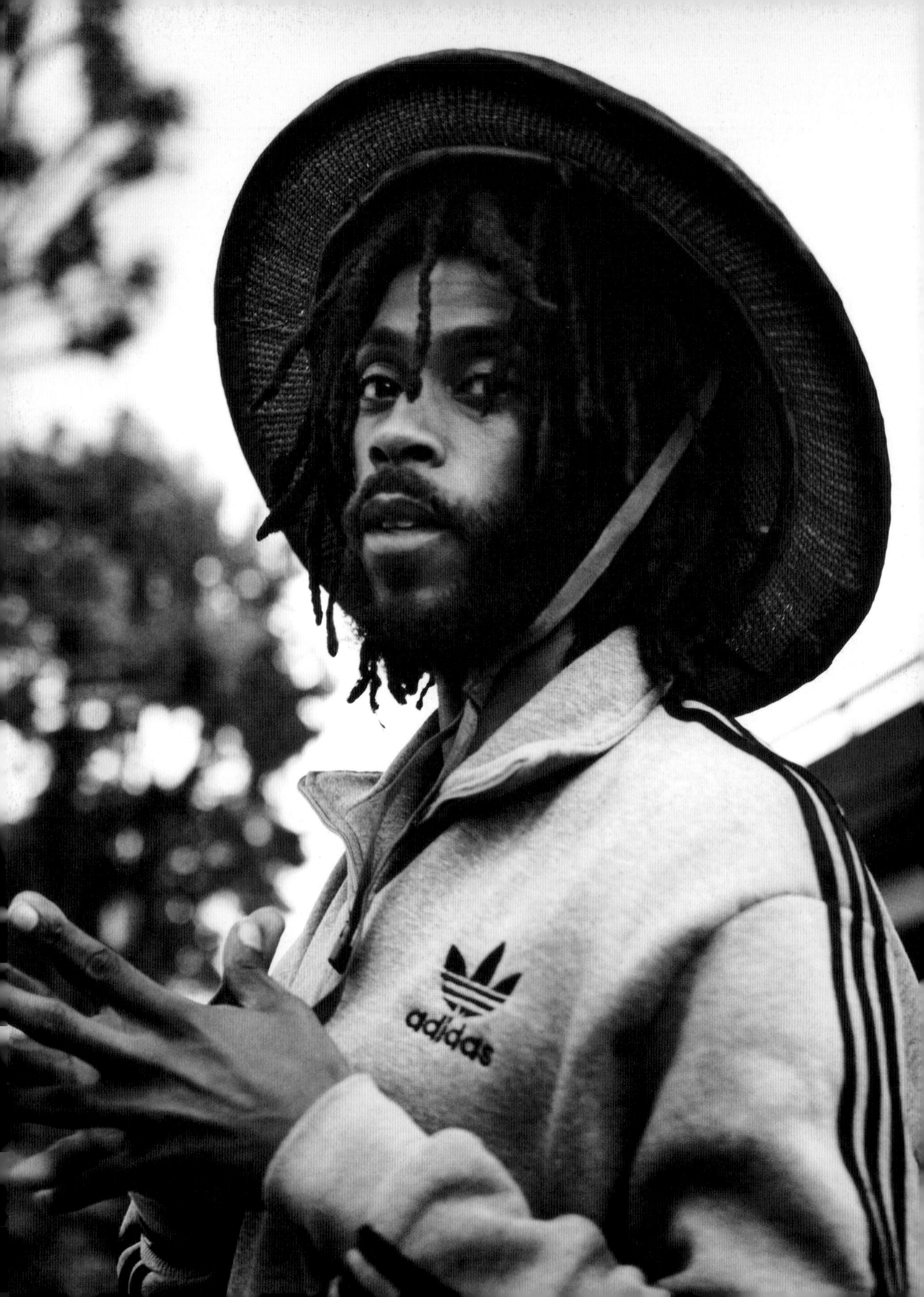
adidas

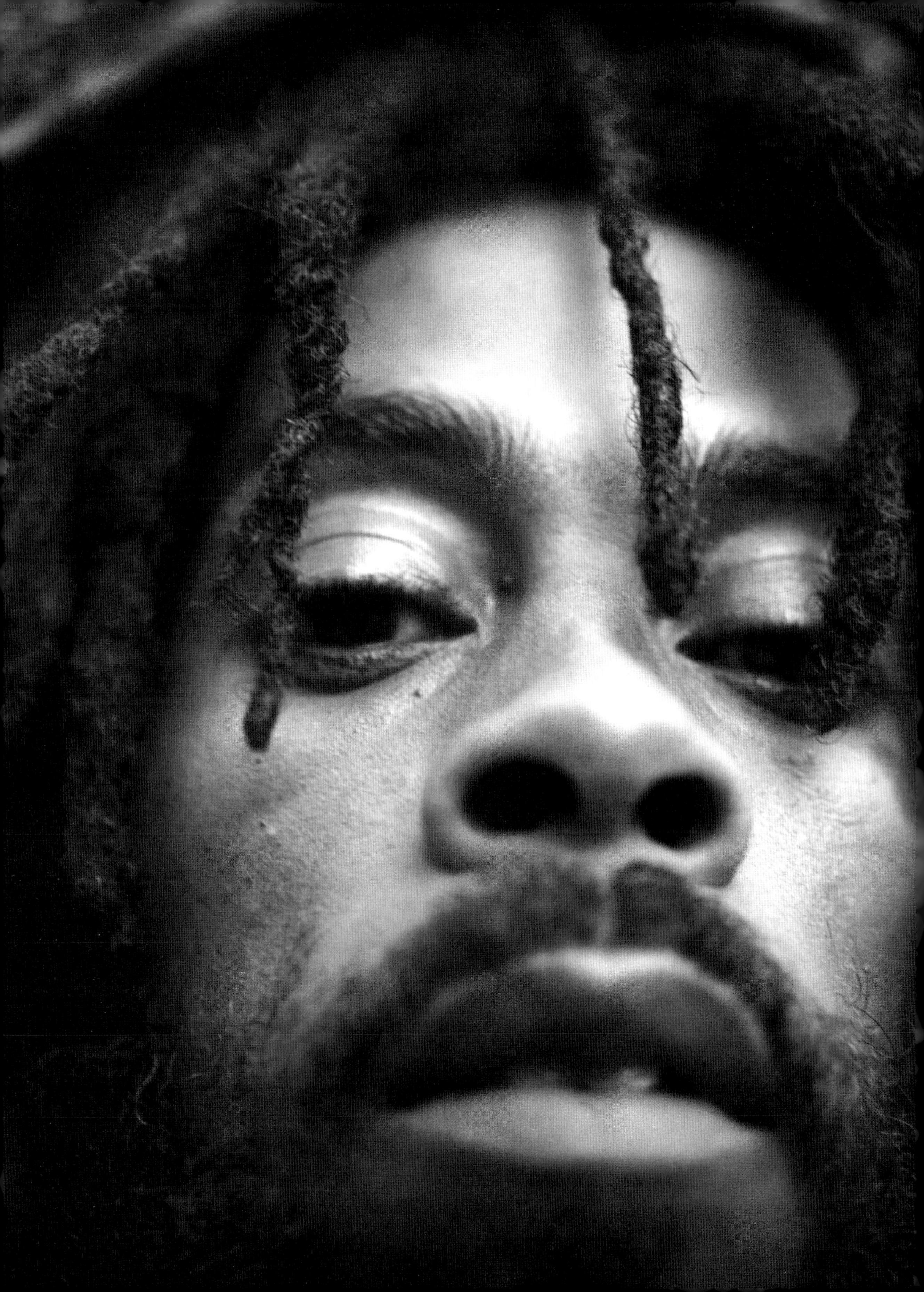

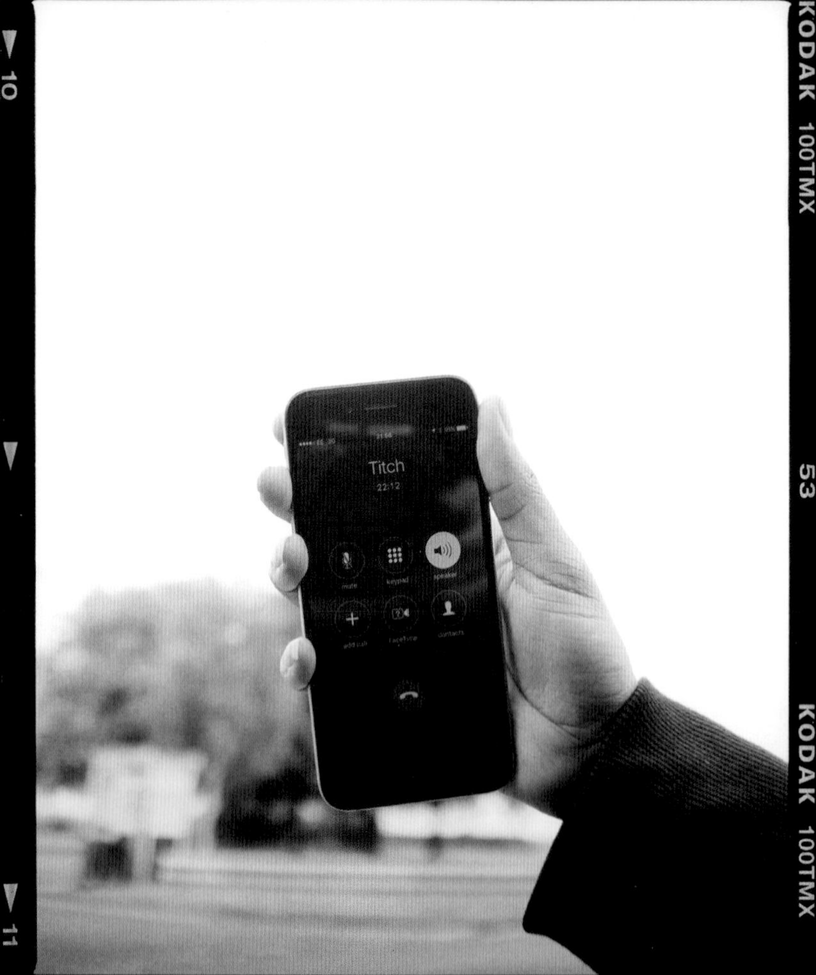
Titch
22:12
KODAK 100TMX
53
KODAK 100TMX

I Can C U, U Can C Me, Say My Name It's...

Crazy Titch Maybe they did make an example of me, coming from the grime scene. Especially 'cause they think kids are trying to be American. That's the whole thing they got wrong; we did not want to be American. There's nothing American about me. I'm from East London, I talk Cockney 'cause that's how we all talk round 'ere. This is me. This is us. This is England. I'm so British, I'm fish and chips, I'm pie and mash. I can't leave England and not miss it. Any country I've been to, give me forty-eight hours, I want to come home. I'm weird that way. I don't like taking a left turn and not knowing where I am. I don't like being a tourist, I really don't. Crazy things happen to tourists. I don't want to be one of them.

Bashy Titch came out and changed the game. When he landed on the scene there was a shift in lyrical aggression – instantly. So many people added a more aggressive approach in response to what he had added to the scene. That's my opinion. When he come out with *Shut up! You don't want beef so shut up! You don't want war so shut up!* Understand, no-one had heard it like that. *You don't want war, PRICK!* Man hadn't heard something like that before. That was crazy. Instant change. Everyone was like, instant reload.

Crazy Titch Blame it on ADHD. ADHD and a lot of sugar [laughs].

Double O Titch, look, we had clashes. We didn't see eye to eye all the time. But what he did do was bring energy. He used to go in and hog the mic. Everyone was scared of him, he was a bully and although I don't like bullies, I did love that. He was a character and all these characters make grime. Titch came in and turned the game upside down with his one-line flows. Yes, it was basic but it worked. It bought a different element to the game. A lot of the better spitters might have looked down on him, but Titch was shutting down shows, getting all the reloads. Credit where credit is due.

Crazy Titch First time I went jail was when my daughter was due to be born. I saw the price of a buggy and I robbed a post office the next day. A buggy is, like, £600. Are you drunk? I went prison in 2000 for three years.

Ghetts Titch came out nine months before me, January 2003. In all honesty, he showed a man that was in jail the possibility – remember he shot up to the top quite fast – of what you could do. Titch is a very persistent person and his belief system is not hindered still until this day. Someone could be somewhere and be more talented but not believe in themself – he believes. If you look at what Titch was doing from an early stage and you look at how he marketed himself, he was a borderline genius. *Crazy Times* was a DVD, a documentary he based on himself before anyone had done that. Before SB.TV, before we knew what YouTube was.

Opposite: Crazy Titch incoming call – One of Her Majesty's Establishments

Let the Records Show
I Was the first un-signed Grime MC
To be Voted one of the 50 Coolest
People on the Planet 2005 by N.M.E Mag
Fact!

Let the Records Show
I Started filming My own DVD Crazytimes
Vol.1 when load of the decks was just
A mix tape CD being Sold in Hackney/
Market (and I got the footage of it) Fact!

Let the Records Show
I did More than Just Slew Mcee's
Or bullied Grime I loved Making Music
I love Grime let the records show

CRAZY TITCH

Please Get My trumpet & dust it off as
I'm about to have ago on it.

Let the Records Show
That I Crazy Titch from Stratford &
Plaistow in East London am a Original
Top boy Grime MC, Fact!

Let the Records Show
That I was the First Grime MC to Send
Directly for a MC (in actual fact it was tha)
live on Pirate Radio (D-Doubles birthday Set
on Mystic FM 19.01.03) Fact!

Let the Records Show
I ran up on everybodies Radio Set by
Myself un-invited & Slung everybody around
If You was on a big Station ie Roo.5 or
9.23 & was a top boy Crew you got it.
Fact!

Let the Records Show
I was the First Grime MC Un-Signed
To Put an Chart topping Singer on
A Grime track, big up Jamie Middleton. Fact!

Let the Records Show
I was the first un-signed Grime MC to
Have a Music Video on Channel U 1.
Dizzy Rascal I Love You 2. Wiley Wat do you
Call it 3. Crazy titch I can C u Fact!

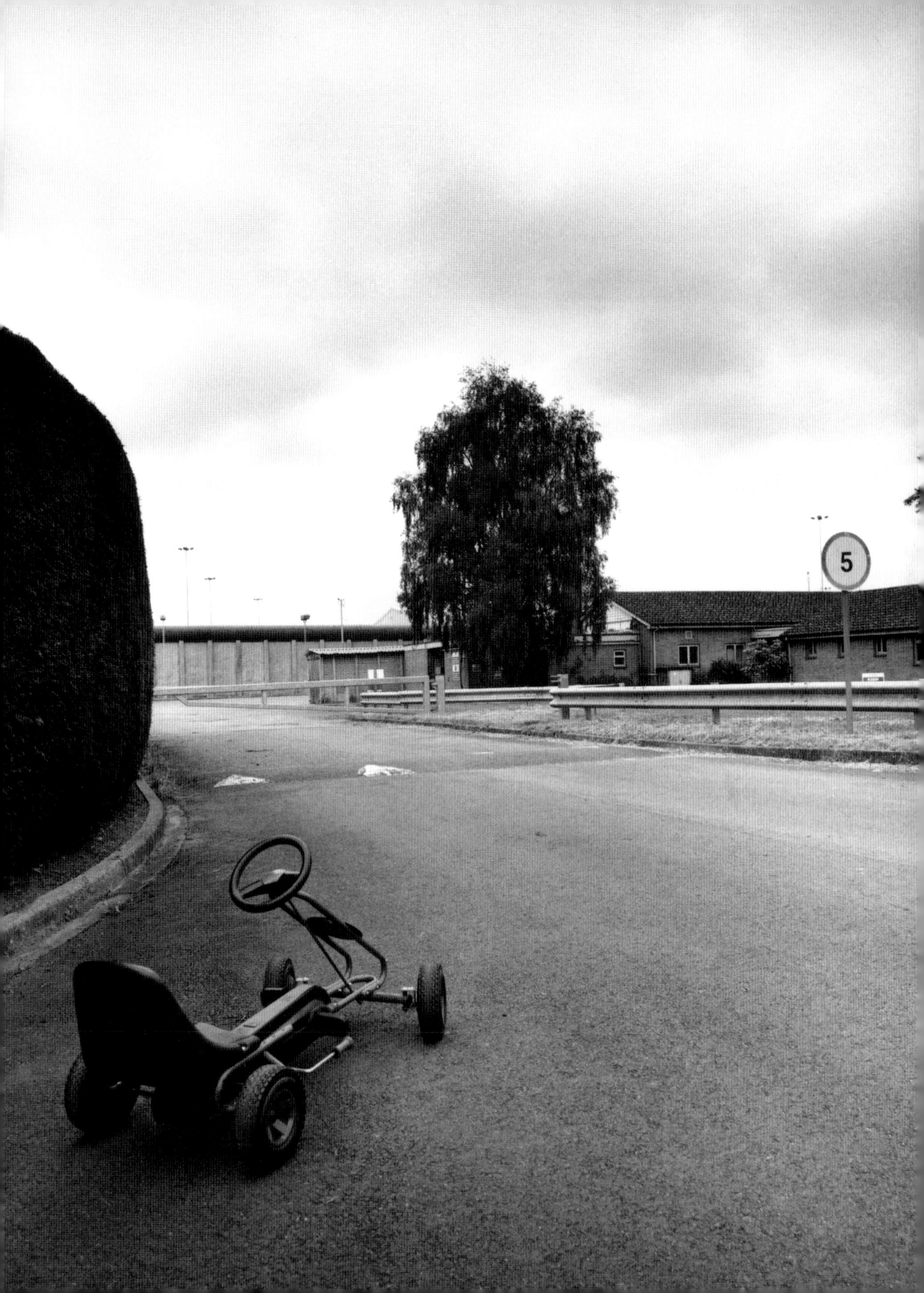
5

He knew that his character was one of the most powerful things he could possess, He was very, very, very clever. We've remained good friends. I speak to him all the time and I seen him about a month ago.

Crazy Titch I came out in January 2003 and I did D Double's birthday set on Mystic, and I sent for everyone. I went Napa that August – everyone knew me. In the space of eight months, people from, like, Manchester, recognised me. I didn't understand it. It was nuts. From there, in 2004 I was on tour with D12, I went to America, I did Glastonbury – all that in a twelve month period. I was on *NME*'s Cool list. Today, it seems more like, 'I want to do grime to make money,' but then it was passion. Passion. Obviously I wanted money, no one wants to be poor, but we spent more money going to the rave then you earned spitting in the rave.

J2K Me and Titch started buckin' from like '03, '04. He's a cousin of one of my good friends around my area. I knew of him as an MC, but then we clicked and really started getting along when we all went to Ayia Napa – you know what it's like, fun and frolics and madness. We just clicked in that way and ever since then we started rolling. Titch was Titch, innit, you had to know who he was at that time. He was making a lot of noise for himself; he was a very vocal character, very animated. We were different in the sense where he was very animated, I'm known to be kinda cool, doing my ting. It met in the middle somewhere. We were both troublesome, we liked the same banter. We were both MCing, he was doing his ting, I was doing mine. Then we started making a few tunes together, we started rolling together to bookings and then we made the Alliance. Obviously he had Boyz In Da Hood, then there was Kidz In Da Hood, it was really organic, it was just built through rolling together around them times.

Crazy Titch J2K, him and Ghetto come to see me, they came a couple of months ago. Other people come, but those two I particularly care about. Before I started trial, he [J2K] turned up to the prison, unannounced – before my life went to shit. He just turned up, by himself and I was like, 'Ah you're actually my friend you know'. Whatever happens, he's my friend. He tells me, 'When you come home, everyone will go mad, the whole world will be at your feet.'

Jammer The first time I met Titch [laughs]. That's very mad that story [long pause]… I don't think I can say it. I saw him in a house rave and yeah, basically, that was the end of the rave. Yeah. That was when we was young fifteen, sixteen years old. He had so much energy, but you've got to love him, he brung that energy to the scene. If Titch was on road still, he'd be one of the main players now, guaranteed.

Chantelle Fiddy I've got a love for Crazy Titch. For his wild side, he also had a really good way with people. One thing that emphasized that is that Y-3, at the time, chose to only gift Titch their clothing. No one else in the grime scene was given Y-3, only Titch. Y-3 only patterned Titch. There was a lot of love in the industry for Titch. He knew how to handle himself, despite his wild ways.

Rebecca Prochnik (Live Booking Agent) Titch. I find it hard to answer how I think of Titch now because it's so tangled in how aggrieved I feel for him about what's happened in his life. I would describe him as an intelligent, funny, quick, brilliant character. And obviously he was a badboy MC, all of that, big following in his area, big following in grime, but as a person, he was changing week by week as everything was moving. I mean, that's travel isn't it? It expands perspectives and I feel like that was really coming across in his lyrics. Really it's such a dumb shame how things played out. Kids looked up to him as a role model and when he got on the mic on stage, he had a power, he was one of the powerhouses. Similar to Skepta, there was this explosive energy, a kind of compelling violence to his vocal and his body language – like a bark. He had so much confidence, physically and mentally, so when he went, it was like an explosion. His swagger and humour were out of control, but in the best way, and we always just got each other. We used to talk a lot.

John McDonnell (Prancehall) I guess Titch is like grime's ODB – he's kind of remembered more fondly because of his abrupt absence from the scene. Never liked him too much as an MC. Too manic.

Simon Wheatley If Crazy Titch had stayed around he would have run the streets. I wonder if the phenomenon of Giggs would ever have happened, or at least whether he would have achieved such reach? Titch would have doubtless been huge – even back then before he went to jail, many youngsters on the roads said he was the main man, regardless of Dizzee or whoever. Titch was hype. To be around him was to be in touch with the essence of 'grime.' Everything seemed to be a hustle and one thing would lead chaotically to another. The last time I saw him he was on a motorbike while I was hanging around with some of the N.A.S.T.Y. Crew around Pudding Mill Lane in the Stratford area. He said hi to everyone and then rode off. That was autumn 2005 and after that I heard what everyone else did.

Nick Huggett Obviously him and Dizzee had that beef. I met him and I really liked him, liked 'Sing Along'. I considered signing him [to XL] and then a month later I phoned his manager [Zak Biddu] and told him I wasn't going to sign him because it was too much grief – with the Dizzee and Titch thing – and he was like, 'Cool, OK, understood.' A few weeks later, he'd been charged with murder.

Wliey I think had he not gone to jail he would have blown up and been massive. He's the bad boy MC, the rude boy MC, he was the king of shouting and jumping around and badding everyone up. He shouldn't be in jail for thirty years but he made a decision that any brother would make. We're not gonna hate on the situation 'cause I would expect nothing less from a brother, but both brothers should be in jail. I hate to say that, it's horrible to say that, but…

Rebecca Prochnik People were intimidated by him and his lyrics were pretty rugged. It was obvious that people who didn't get him were easily going to be intimidated. If you saw how it played out in court, it was almost funny, if it wasn't so sad. I remember him saying to the prosecutor, 'Don't put words in my mouth, I'm the MC here, I'm the one with words in my mouth.' Because he was smart, and because the guy was trying to twist him up, his natural response was to call it with a play on words, like in a clash. So in truth, Titch clashed the barrister, 'cause he couldn't help himself. With hindsight, not so smart maybe, but it seemed so impossible, the case they had against him. I don't know really what went on but I just listened and listened and there was no way it was beyond reasonable doubt. He was confident too at the time, so when he said that, it really made me laugh but in truth, it made the jury breathe in. That was it in a nutshell. He fulfilled, without meaning to, the *Daily Mail* stereotype of the dangerous underbelly that had to be stopped. The way they built the case against him, it played heavily into that too. If you didn't understand or accept all the posturing of the grime scene and you take it literally, then you're going to reach a guilty verdict. For Titch, it really was a very dangerous position to be judged in. I know that everyone in the scene has their opinions about what did and didn't happen that night. I wasn't there and I will always say I don't know. But I did go to court day after day and all I can say is the legal system let him down. He was not convicted on evidence at all, but on a stereotype. It's not the first time it's happened and it won't be the last, but it's a tragic thing to see someone's liberty and rights be thrown down the drain like that. If the police wanted someone to make an example of, they sure went around it a dumb way and let themselves down too. Anyone can see now how influential Skepta has become, changing his follower's approaches through his lyrics. Titch had that capacity too. But he was fed to the lions.

Crazy Titch See, this is what pisses me off about jail – these are my best years getting pissed down the drain. But I'm hopeful that they're maybe about to change this law called Joint Enterprise, 'cause that's what's got me in prison, you know that? On the contrary of what people think, I'm a unique case. It was the law at the time. They're talking about changing it, so we'll find out what they're saying. Hopefully they'll change it. People are in here for all sorts of reasons: love, family, money. Family. I'm in here for family. Jail is tiring. It's meant to be tiring; prison is far from easy, despite what you read in the papers. 'Oh, there's PlayStation 3s'. One: there is no PlayStation 3, and two, I don't care if there's PlayStation 10, nothing can beat being home with your family. So that's poxy anyway. They make out like it's all easy. It ain't. Prison is far from easy. I've had to show my teeth more than a few times. I survive it because it's what I know. I know this life. I know it's not real life. I know this isn't living because I've lived. I travelled a lot through my music. A lot of these people ain't left their estate. People would never believe what has happened in my life in these thirty-three years. I was such a road yute, to then trying to balance road and music and then being in that crosspath of my own life. And then having a chance, throwing it away and having to live a whole other life in prison. I don't know, it's fucked. It's fucked. Some stories are like that, I suppose. This story isn't finished yet. Not just yet.

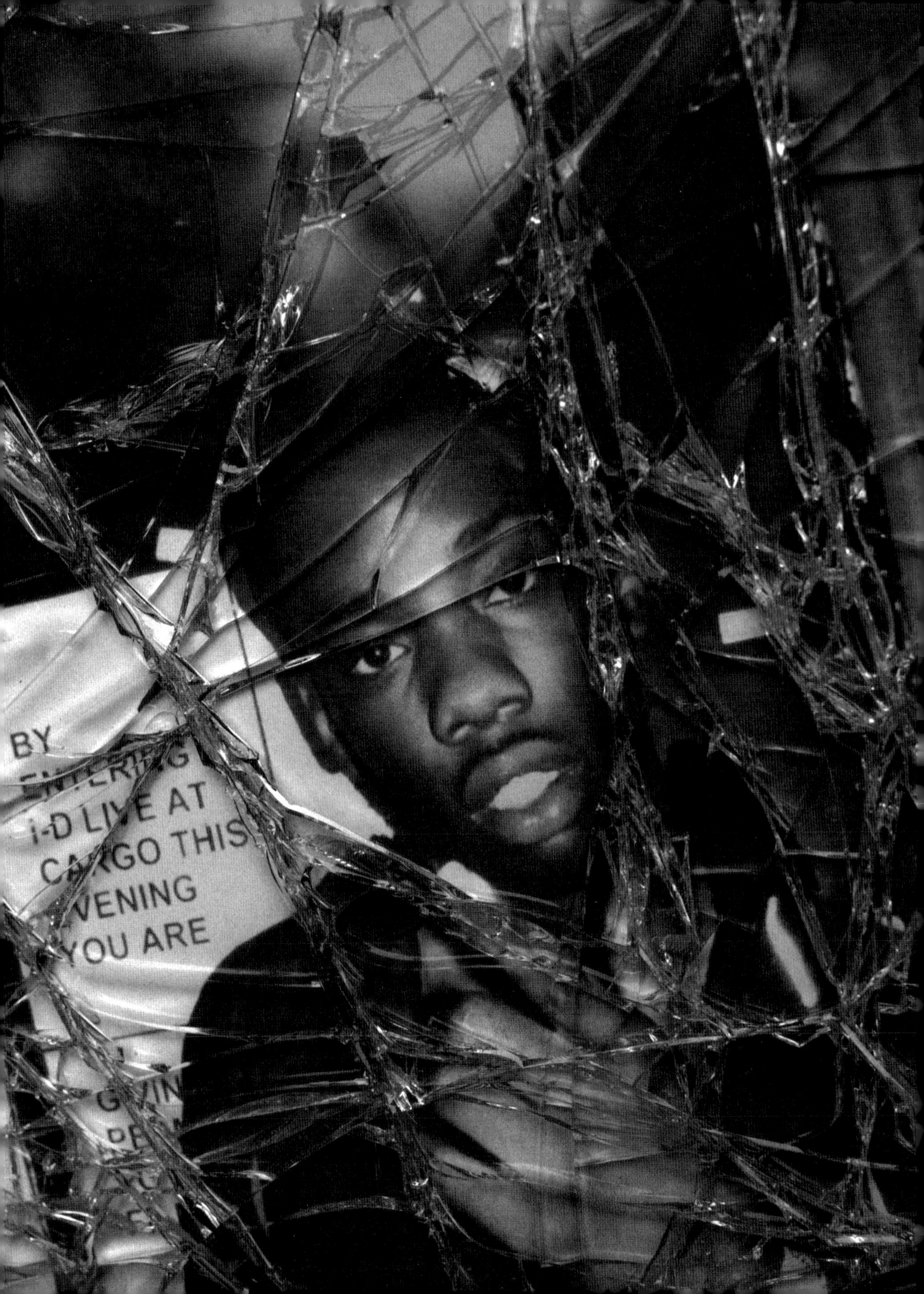
BY
i-D LIVE AT
CARGO THIS
EVENING
YOU ARE

Crazy Titch on Religion

I first got interested in Islam when I was twelve, thirteen years old. I wasn't into other religions. See, my nan used to take me to church and that, she would be like, 'Jesus died for your sins,' and I can't wrap my head around that 'cause that means I can do what the fuck I want, really, 'cause someone's already paid for it. Do you see what I'm trying to say? Everything I did was being cleared by someone else? No. That I couldn't really fathom. I also couldn't wrap my head around Jesus being the Son of God. Some one or some entity so powerful doesn't need a son, he doesn't need a living, breathing being. If he can make the world, he don't need that. So that's what baffled me.

When I got into Islam, everyone was like, 'What you doing?' My mum was onto me as well. Them times, it was unknown really. If a woman was wearing head-to-toe burka, no one cared. It wasn't until 9/11 that people started to paint it in a bad light. Before that, no one really cared. Islam is taken many different ways. There are extremities and I don't think extreme anything is good. In the middle is where I want to be. Because I wasn't born in Saudi Arabia or one of these countries, I can be that way. 'Cause over there, you know, it can be extreme.

I take Islam for what it is, a peaceful religion. Any country you're in, you should be living by them laws as long as the laws don't contradict your religions beliefs. It's not for me to say, 'I want Sharia Law,' 'cause really I don't. All I know, when I started this stuff, when I was twelve, all I really wanted to do was go to Mecca, make Hajj and get rid of all my sins. That was my my mindstate as a twelve year old kid. There was something I could do that started me afresh. That's really what drew me to Islam. The media has made it all look crazy, but they're just focusing on the nutters, but there's nutters everywhere. There's nutter Christians. There's nutter Zionists, but they've got money, power and privilege. They built a wall around a place that they just got to fifty years ago. They are on one! And they've got nukes. No one says a thing. That Kim Jong Un is trying to get nukes and they're all over him. He must be thinking, 'Hold on, my country's been mine from time, they just made that a country the other day and no-one says nothing!'

But the media has made Islam into something it's not. I got into it to clean off my sins, but then I fell off and I racked up more and I'm still racking up more. I still want that one chance to get them all gone. Just once. I'm not perfect, I'll rack them up again, I probably will, but I just need to get some done and I'll be alright.

Religion is two things. It's either, it could be wrong and there's no God, or, it's right and there is a God. If it's wrong, and me trying to be a nice person and cause no-one no harm and take no-one's wife and not steal from my neighbour and these types of things, that has held me in a good stead. So even though I was wrong about God, I've still not lived like a bastard – even though I have lived like a bastard! But, say I'm right. I'm alright then. I may still burn in hell, but I will get to heaven at some point (God willing). I've tried to live as righteous a life as is possible for me.

Religion is the most divisive thing 'cause it falls into the category of something with sides and as long as something has sides, then people will never really be one. You've got to be one or other. You've got to be black or white. You've got to have a religion, you've got to be from a place, you've got to have a football team. I understand why it's divisive, but for me, religion works. If I'm wrong, no harm done, is there?

I never wanted to be nothing but the same kid who wanted to be on Deja Vu, getting people to learn his lyrics. That was it. I wanted for people to know that whatever I was spitting wasn't an exaggeration, it was actually the truth.
Crazy Titch

Competition is healthy, as long as it stays in the studio and not the streets

Wiley Sadly, clashing is a big part, it is. Today, battling is dangerous in the sense that if someone says something to you that you don't like, it's iffy. Back in the day, if someone says to me 'Suck your mum,' I can't even hear them, I just say 'Suck your mum' back, but today if someone says it, I might punch you in your face. It's weird. It's different. They need to take it back to the sport. You can bar man back, you can. Yungen and Chip, that surprised me. Yungen surprised me, he didn't just have it off him at all. Also, nowadays, someone can send for you and your career can get dunn. Before, I will clash Doog, or Kano and if I lost or won, I could carry on working and trick people into thinking that was them. 'Yeah I battled them, I won.' Today it's different, there's nowhere to hide. Online. There's no getting away from it.

[ASHER D V. DIZZEE]

Donaeo I wanna mention Commander B, because there was a period with Choice FM that also rebranded grime. The clashing was very important to grime. It made everyone choose artists and seek personalities; it created more of a fan base, which then created Eskimo Dance and that was because of Commander B and the platform that he made. Because Commander is not around anymore, everyone has kind of forgotten about that and that was a very important part to the culture as well. I think that period is actually what turned everyone into artists.

Rozan Ahmed I set up the clash on Choice with Commander B. I knew this would be a game-changer and it went beautifully – apart from Ashley's [Asher D's] lies over how the story came about. The guy was fresh out of jail. He was a friend and he called me asking if I could interview him for *RWD*, the first (and only) voice that was truly representative of the British underground. It made total sense for Ashley to call me. We were trusted as a title and I regularly featured So Solid as an outfit that I felt were leading this definitive new sound we now know as grime. Ashley knew what he was doing.

Maxwell D I didn't think that was a proper clash really; Asher was a rapper, Dizzee was an MC.

Rozan Ahmed Ashley wanted to battle, that was clear. Using the new hype of Dizzee's name to resurrect his own from the prisms of prison was also clear. I asked him, specifically and repeatedly, if this was his intention: to battle Dizzee Rascal. Does he want this banter included in the story? Does he want me to tell Dizzee/Commander B to set up a live clash? Do So Solid, as pioneers of this game, really want to do this? Is *he* sure he wants to do this? Because it will set off fireworks – much needed fireworks – but I would obviously make sure these fireworks popped positively for our movement. He said yes to all of it. Yes, yes and more yes. He knew what he was doing. So did I, and so did everyone involved. Ashley's decision to then back-track live on radio was a surprise to the rest of us. Mincing words and spewing untruths was just sad and unexpected. Both as an artist - who knew I had the entire conversation taped – and a friend. Anyway, despite the many times he still brings up his self-gratifying delusions around this, we all know who lost.

Harvey It's an iconic clash. GRM Daily always throw in that clash, 'cause it was the blueprint for what started; now we've got *Lord of the Mics*, Culture Clash… There's always a root to something.

Asher D I think it was good for music really at the end of the day and I think it was one of the platforms for Dizzee's career. I'd just come out of prison and people were tipping Dizzee as the next big thing. They come from a place where clashing was the thing. For Wiley and them lot, it was all about clashing and that's why they were really good at it. When they came through, that's where the divide really was, between us and them. We didn't come through clashing, so when Dizzee was clashing me, I think I may have taken it a bit more personal than he did. That was natural to him, it was his culture. But I felt it went down right and it did good things for their side and our camp.

Rozan Ahmed Everyone saw what happened after the battle. It was a landmark moment. It brought new relevance to our culture. It elevated skills and garnered so much attention to our local music, pumping a lot excitement into everyone. Folks still talk about it today, which means it meant something. There were no real fall-outs. Most of us made the best of things and moved on to bigger and better. A year or so later (2004) I worked with the Prince's Trust in orchestrating the UK's first Urban Music Festival. It was the first time both British and American 'urban' artists were celebrated equally, on the same stage. That was a battle to make happen in and of itself, but we did and I remember taking Dizzee to meet Jay Z backstage after we wrapped. Onwards and upwards. Only.

[TITCH V. DIZZEE]

Crazy Titch If you look at the whole of that *Conflict* set yeah, they're all mates. It's all a friendly atmosphere and then I turn up. I turn up with Sharky Major, people see me in the doorway and everything changes. Dizzee retreats into the corner – boy in da corner. Everyone started scattering and it was no longer, 'Smiley face, spit into the camera,' it was, 'Oh shit, he's here.' What happened basically was, I wanted to give him [Dizzee] the mic, but I also wanted to par him and carry on. He touched my hand and I overreacted. Sometimes I think I shouldn't have overreacted like that. But I was in a place in my life where I didn't want to be touched by nobody. That wasn't even really a drastic overreaction for me, 'cause I didn't like man touching me. Being locked up so much, I'm not used to people touching me. Even with girls and that, I'm not touchy feely, I really do not like to be touched. It's a fucked up thing 'cause obviously you get that from being incarcerated. If I was him, I'd probably be like, 'Rah, what you going apeshit for, I just want the mic fella, I didn't hit ya! I didn't even pinch ya! All I did was touch your hand, like, pass me the mic!' [laughs]. So that's his point of view, but from my point of view, I don't like to be touched. So that's all I really remember. And someone had my car keys and wouldn't let me have them, pissed me off. But that's another story.

Maxwell D I was there that day when they clashed. I was on the roof, trying to stop them. That's when grime became very competitive, everyone wanted to get to the top, everyone wanted to get them reloads, everyone wanted to scream on the mic and get heard. It wasn't about no girl lyrics, no reality, conscious lyrics, it was all about, 'I'm the best, shut up, I'll shank your neck, back, ankle, side,' [laughs]. That was the M.O.

Crazy Titch Honestly, I've only ever had one clash and that's me and Dizzee. I've not been challenged – or felt challenged – by anyone else. That felt like a challenge. Only a few people know this, but I was going to quit grime. I actually did quit for a minute. I stopped. It was about two weeks before Dizzee went on Radio 1. I told my close friends, 'I'm not getting any money from this, I need money, I'm going back to road.' I wasn't getting nothing from it. I needed to live. So I stopped. And then one day one of my friends rung me and said, 'Bruv, turn on the radio. Dizzee's dissing you on Radio 1.' So I listened and then I went and did 'Just An

Arsehole'. I didn't want to do 'Arsehole', I didn't want to do the 'Lean Back' diss, all I wanted to do was fuck him up. I'll be honest, I didn't want to do music, at all. Not one fibre of me wanted to do music. I wanted to go to his mum's house, kick off her door, tell her to call him and wait for him to turn up. That was my plan. But then I told Doogz what I was gonna do – the only good information that Doogz gave me. He said, 'Look, you're better than him, and beating him up doesn't show no-one you're better than him lyrically. So you're gonna have to go and diss him back.' The thing with Dizzee, he was talking about my life. That's what I felt like. Everything he said was a reflection of me. Everything; from robbing banks or jacking people, being a bad boy. He's not a bad boy. I am actually one of those people who would be referred to as a bad boy. He ain't one of those people. And plus, he was friends with Wiley and Doogz was against Wiley so I thought this is what the scene would need. 'Cause they wasn't gonna clash. Until I came out, they was just fannying about. Doogz would say 'Why He', he wouldn't say Wiley's full name, but it was more friendly beef, more subliminals. You can be subliminal if you want, but I'm from Newham and most MCs grew up on clashing, we clash each other. And it's just for fun, it's not even aggressive or anything, it's just fun. In a nutshell it's just 'Your mum,' but not everyone can say 'Your mum.' There's rules. Dizzee can't tell me to suck my mum, I can't tell him to suck his mum. If he tells me to suck my mum, I'm gonna go nuts.

[BASHY V. GHETTS]

J2K Bashy versus Ghetts' clash, that was hilarious. Me and Titch were there. It's mad because obviously Ghetts didn't expect Bashy to be that ready. Bashy is a trained actor, improv is their thing. So whether you're better than him lyrically, or you're able to do better things, he's trained to do that kind of stuff. Freestyling and improv is a whole different skill. It's mad, it's mad. No one really saw that one coming, it was so jokes to watch that.

Ghetts [Clashing is] something I want to stay away from just because of how I am as a person. I haven't got the composure for it. I'm all for like the friendly sparring, like me and Kano and me and Dev[lin] spar all the time, me and Wiley. It's all good for keeping the levels up, but for me, I find [clashing] counterproductive.

Bashy Back then I know that if someone wanted to clash, man was saying names back then! There was none of this subliminal shit. It was names, out and out saying names, innit. Clashing right now, it's healthy but sometimes it's mad… sometimes it's good, sometimes it's not. If it stays in the music, it's good. If it spills over into something else, it's not. If it distracts you from your main goal, which is to make good music, which everyone should be trying to do, then it's long. My clash with Ghetts… those things are old because we're friends now. I don't really wanna talk about it because it's just a part of growing up.

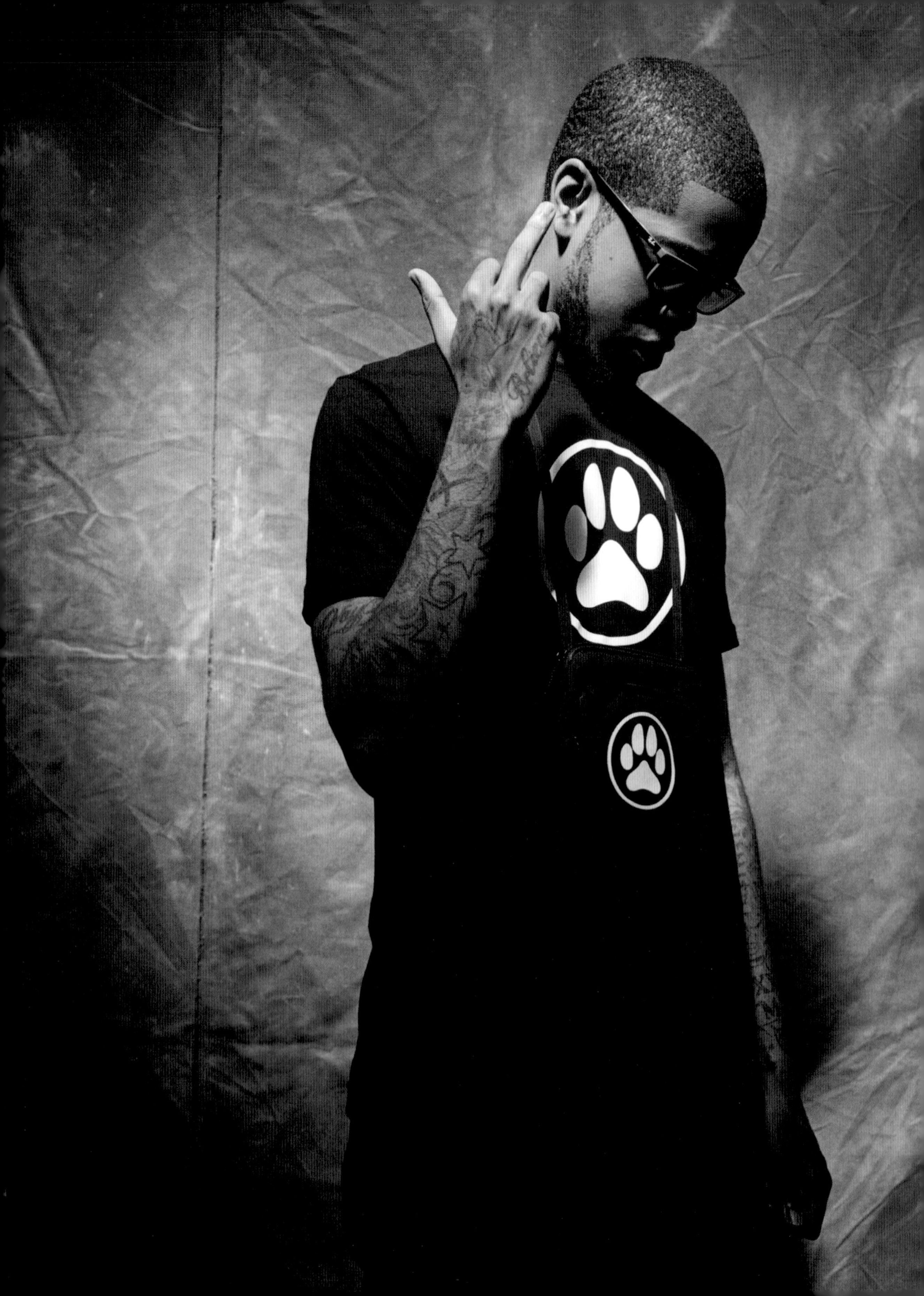

[CHIP V. EVERYONE]

Stormzy [Chip and Yungen] went global there for a minute. I don't get involved. They're both my friends. It doesn't affect who I collab with; I can make tunes with both of them tomorrow. It's fun, It's entertainment, it's good, lyrical war.

Chip I know what I'm doing, trust me. 'Cause these man are taking major L's in front of their idols. Me and Drake are texting each other, bussing up. Checkmate. It's given me such an energy. At this point here, the only way back for me was through. I had to go through. I said it to my mum the other day. She said, 'Son, I'm getting tired of you making people famous and them disrespecting my family. Enough is enough now, Jamaal.' I said 'Mum, I had to do this at fourteen, but you just weren't watching.' Now it's the internet time. There are histories of sets where I'm on my jacks and I have to swing. I'm wearing Nike and I have to go on the microphone and slew Nike. That's how it was. You have to go in, you have to step up and murk and that's the energy that I'm doing what I'm doing now. The only difference is I'm doing it to guys who probably wouldn't have made it to Fuck Radio. The reality of us being in the same building for a set is very unlikely. When I go to sets now, Skep will be there, the new yutes will be there and it's that environment again. These yutes actually might have their knives on them, but you have to normalise yourself and they have to see that you are reachable. If Yungen had to spit his 'One Take' in a room full of MCs not from his ends, he wouldn't get his whole bar out. I swear down. He wouldn't 'cause it's a completely different school these yutes are coming from. If you just have to let negative energy out of your body for me, that's fine, 'cause I'll lead and this time I'm not letting anyone run.

Opposite: Chipmunk in Cash Motto – Dalston, N16
Yungen in the playground – Tulse Hill, SE21

Polaroid screenshot: Skepta's freestyle on Tim Westwood's BBC Radio 1 show, 2008
Opposite: Devilman and his nephew in 0121 – Birmingham

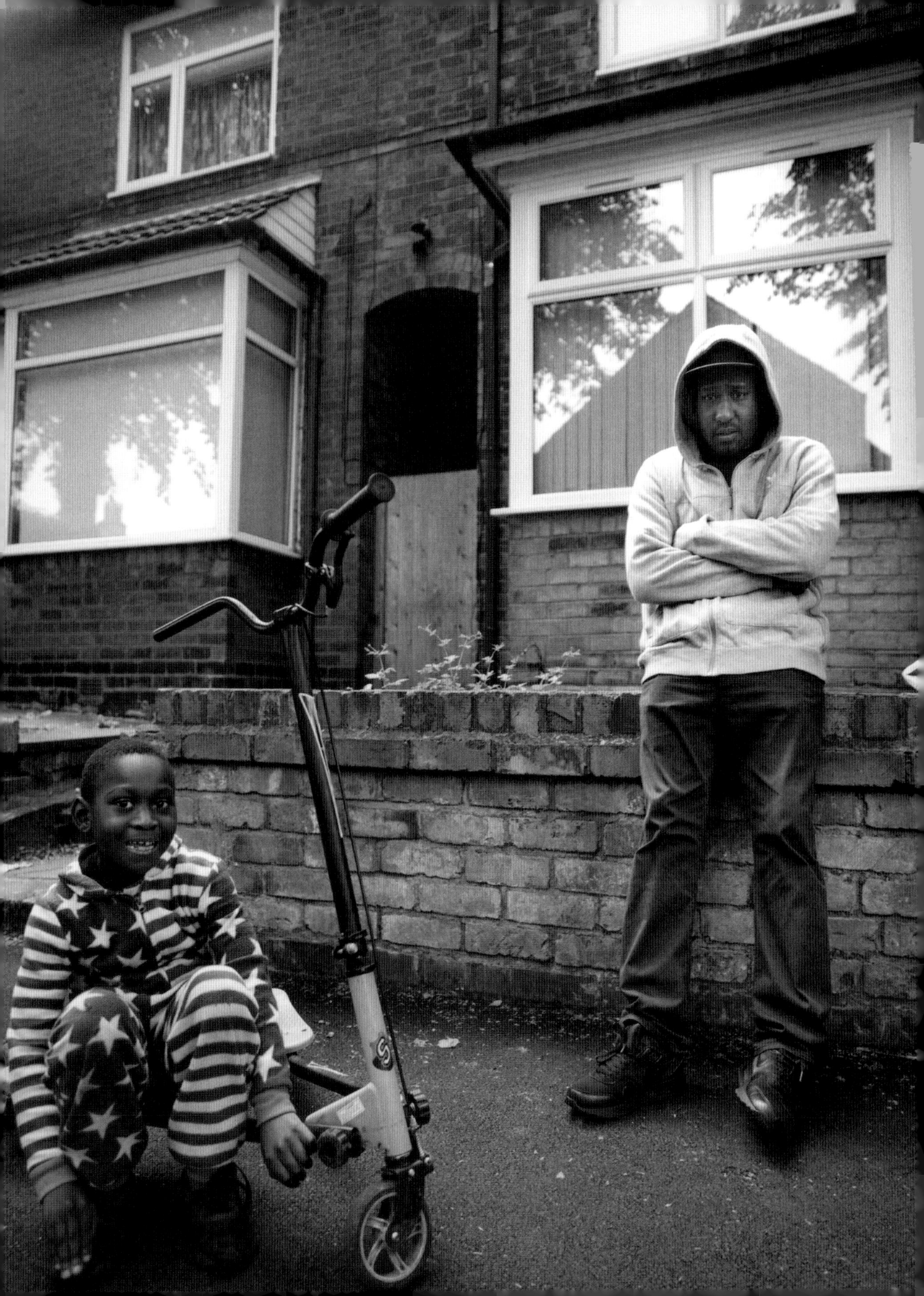

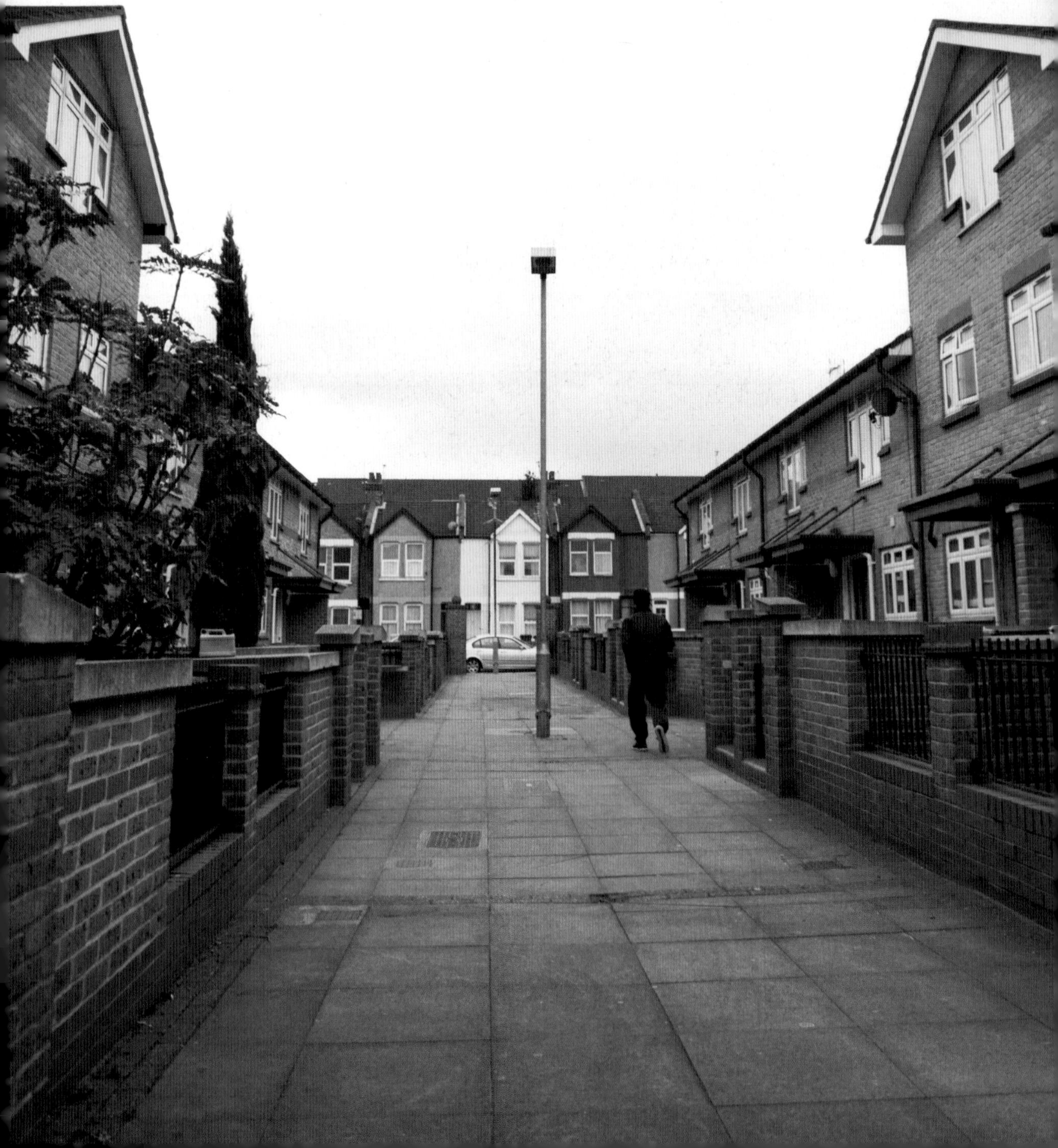

Adenug-shhhhh huh yuh muh

JME I think the only difference is time. We're a really close family, we've only ever been in three-bedroom houses, so we were always sharing bedrooms, two of us, or three of us at times. It's just time apart, other than that, nothing could ever change between us and it's not that we all went our separate ways at like fifteen. We lived together until Skepta was thirty-something. We've been together so long, it's impossible for us to have any differences, no matter how long we're apart. As a family we're done, that's it. Everything else now is just extra, as a family we're solid.

Skepta Meridian Walk; I used to live at number 54. We lived there from when I was seven until about 2001, when we had to move. Jason, Julie, Jamie, me, my mum and dad. Everyone used to come through and spit lyrics, show me beats. It would be all the Bloodline; Dan, Bossman, Big H, JME obviously, just loads of different MCs from around.

Meridian Dan Meridian is such a… [pauses] I don't know how we did it, for that estate and that crew to have all gone on and do what we did, individually?

JME People always ask me about family and I don't know what to say, 'cause you only live your own life. You only have one family, that's all I know. We was brought up normal, just bare respect, a bit – no, a lot – of Nigerian culture instilled into us and we're trying to break free a bit. We're living in the UK trying to do all the things we've got to be doing, with all the respect we've got to be showing to all these people. You know, we're calling everyone 'Aunty,' everything is so cultural, but then at the same time, we're trying to flippin' get Adidas popping jogging bottoms, Reebok Classics, Evisü jeans, we're trying to live that life outside. But then at home, we've still got to be respectful and flippin' no swearing. If I saw my friend swear when his mum's anywhere near? I didn't even hear my mum and dad swear, let alone me swear. I wouldn't even swear if they were in the house and I was upstairs somewhere. So that's the life I know, isn't it?

Skepta Waking up and knocking for your friends every day is good. We used to do regular things, talk shit about our trainers, that whole vibe of knocking for each other every day and having nothing to do but cuss each other and smoke weed and whatever, it gives you time to be creative. We didn't have Twitter and shit, there was nothing to do except play football or whatever, but I feel like now it's too easy to be on your phone. You can be on Twitter with your mates and be in the house.

JME We didn't have a lot, we used to play games, make up things, invent things. I remember we used to play Tunnels. Tunnels was when my mum and dad were out, if they went to a christening or something, we would get all the chairs and tables and all the throws and sheets. We used to take the quilt covers out of the sheets and we used to try and make the best, longest tunnel. You'd turn off all the lights in the house and then you make a tunnel at the door to the front room and you crawl through under the table leg, under the chair and we might put, like, biscuits in there, so then you get to that bit there – see, this sounds funny, but to me this was totally 100% normal – so then you get to eat a biscuit and then you go through the next tunnel under the chair and there might be sweets there. You make your way through it, you might get out and then that'll be the end of it.

Julie Adenuga It was just a creative time. I don't know where that came from, I just know that we didn't have a lot of money. We weren't poor, but we didn't have a lot of money. When the ice cream came round we wouldn't ask for money for an ice cream. There's four of us, that's two pounds. So I think it came from realising, 'OK, we can't have this, but that's not it, it's not over, there's not going to be no fun in the house.' We'd dress up as Mortal Kombat characters and take pictures of ourselves dressed up as Sub Zero. We couldn't afford to have four bikes so we'd make bikes from old bike frames that we found, two different tyres, we'd just make them for fun. We'd make go-karts from string, hammers and nails. That was definitely a thing in our house. Maybe it was our Nigerian background of being loud and having overactive imaginations that we just did loads of things. When we went back to Nigeria at the end of last year it all made sense. In the village that my dad grew up in, we saw how the people hustled to just be there and live. It made sense that we've got that same thing. Junior [Skepta] built his first table to put his decks on. And it's not even money, he could probably have afforded a table, it's just we're used to it.

Skepta You don't know it, but back then not having anything to do, it gives you time to be creative. Sometimes I just wish I could live back there, to see what I'd write. Just chilling every day, having nothing to do. I was about eighteen when I started making music, making beats, my mindset was totally different. It was me, what I knew, Meridian, Tottenham.

Julie Adenuga Junior [Skepta] texted me recently and said, 'Yeah, I want to put the merch store up today,' so I'm like, 'OK, cool,' left the event I was at, come home, created a website, found a theme for the site and got it going. You don't need to wait for anyone to do something, whatever it is you want to do, let's make it happen. Every time someone tries to tell me there needs to be something in place before I do something, I just think, 'That's not how I live and that's not who I am.' That comes from my family, that's always been an Adenuga thing. Jamie [JME] wants to learn piano, so he buys a piano and he goes on YouTube and now he Periscopes himself learning to play classical music.

JME Being an eight year-old kid, I saw my dad bring home four pieces of wood and then they became a desk that was in my house for like ten years, it wasn't a big deal, it was just like making cereal. But that's part of my life, that was in my brain and forms who I am. It's just the life that we lived, everything we've done up until now has just been DIY, enjoying it, trying to picture things that can be better. Picture something that can be better and just see if we can make it. Why not? There's nothing else to do in your life, you're here for a while and you go, so while you're here, if you don't like that and you think you can change it, why not try and change it? I don't think any of us have ever tried to aim for something so big and to change the world, we're just trying to do things that we enjoy and they snowball into bigger things. Julie didn't set out to be on Beats 1. It never even existed, she just wanted to be creative. She was always overshadowed by the big brothers and she wanted to go and do her own thing. So she ended up being her. Me and Skep, we never wanted to be two brothers making music. We just enjoyed making music. That was the only thought – the only feeling – behind anything we did.

Skepta I used to DJ wherever I could, in the Selby Centre across the street, wherever. I used to get a sheet of paper, fold it in half and draw a flyer. I wrote a couple of DJ names – they were just my friends – all by hand, it was so messy. I folded it in four so I knew it was the right flier size and I printed up loads of them in the sweet shop. I cut them up and gave them out and we had a rave in the Selby Centre. I charged a fiver. We must have been in there half an hour and they locked off the electric. We still tried to power through, like, 'It's alright, we all know each other, we can have a rave in the pitch black, no one's going to stab each other or hurt each other.' Then the flipping guy came and told us to get out. That was it,

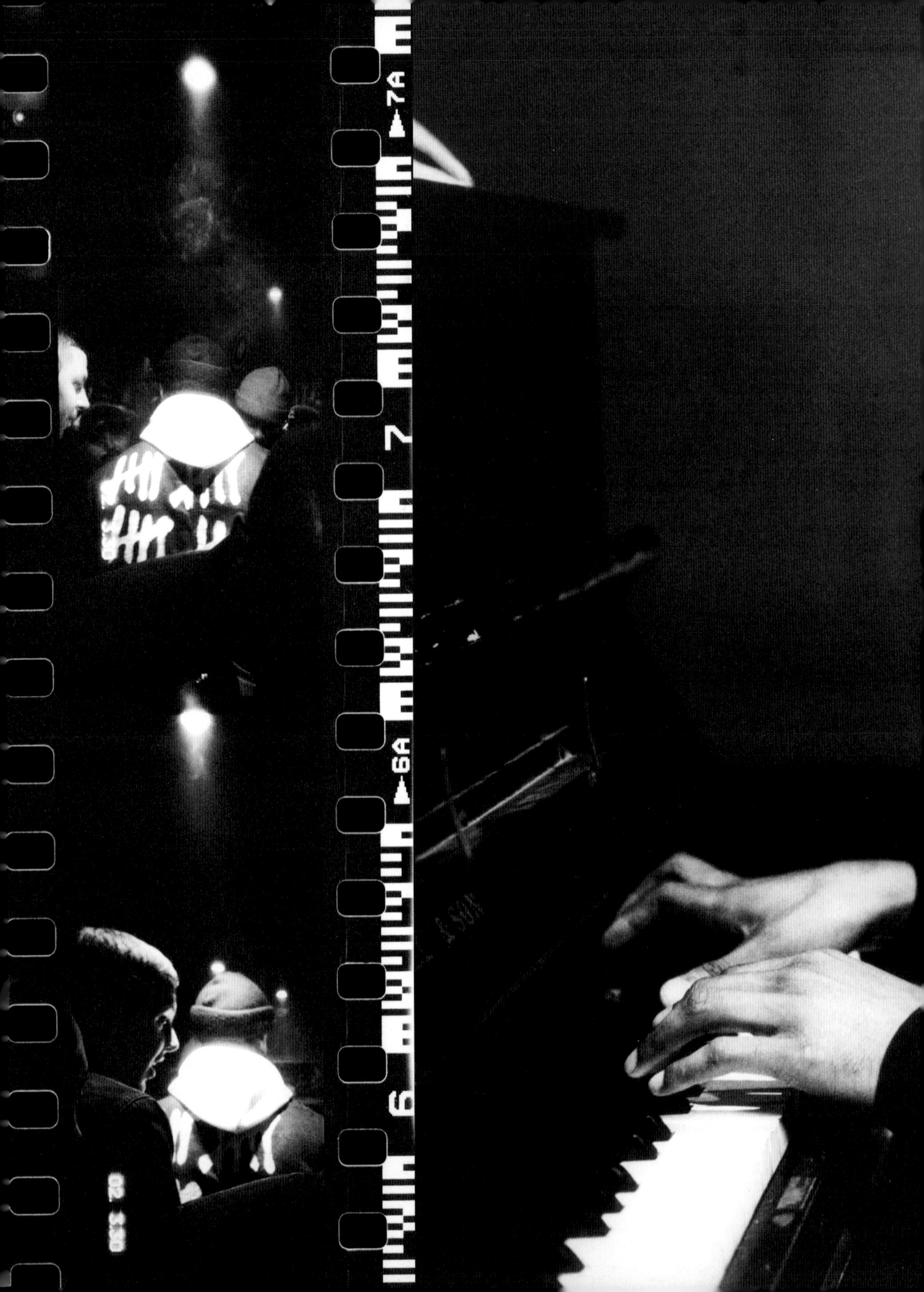

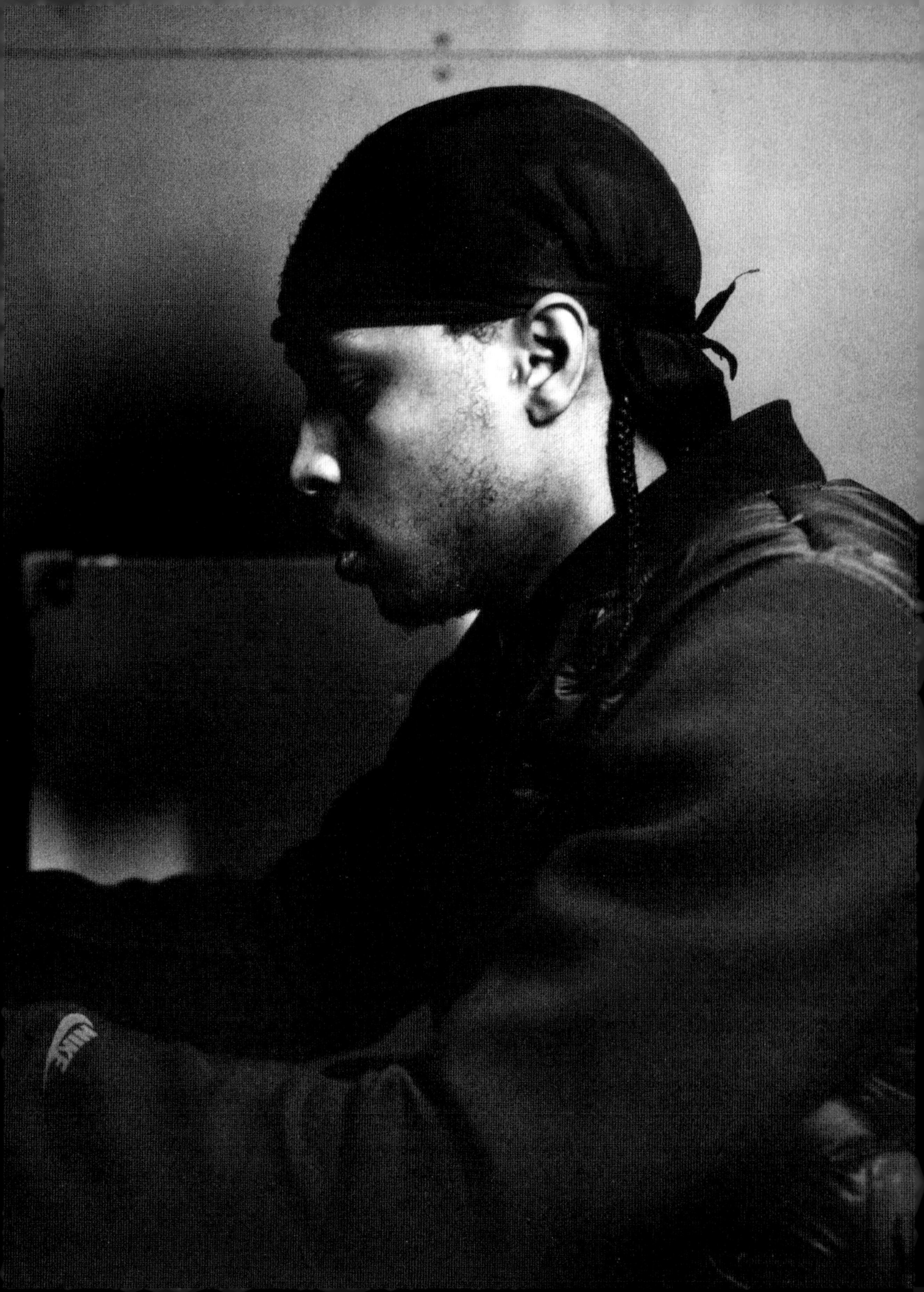
NIKE

game over. I was about sixteen/seventeen years old. Playing garage, putting on my raves. I used to love Heartless, with a passion, so I played all the tunes they would play.

JME He always wanted to DJ, Skepta. He used to mix advert music with a little karaoke machine thing that had a speed tempo to it, play the tape of Heartless Crew or whatever, slow it down and speed it up to when there's like a McDonald's advert on, mixing music. My dad used to DJ too, so we used to hear music all the time. My dad had records, but only one deck, so Skep used to try and play a song on one deck – the Music Centre we used to call it, a cabinet with a glass door – he would play one tune on the record and then mix the tape to it, that's what he used to like doing. He became a DJ. I was taking the mick out of people's lyrics, I wasn't really MCing, I was just mucking around and then I started to write my own, joking around, me, Dan and everyone in Meridian and yeah, it was MCing and then it just snowballed until the point where now I'm some UK artist, Skepta's decided to start spitting, you know what I mean? It ends up being something but it's just about being creative in the first place. Being creative, having fun and enjoying working out how to do something that you don't know how to do.

Julie Adenuga I remember being in the local burger shop and people would come up to me and say, 'Oh, you're JME's little sister.' It happened all the time. We always went to the same school and had the same surname and looked exactly the same. So I went the opposite way. I didn't want people to think I would MC and sing or do anything in music. I would do things that were completely different because I didn't want people to predict what I was doing. For a long time I steered away from that path and it was something I really had trouble with, growing up. It was difficult. I did go through a long period in life where I was doing stuff 'cause I was trying *not* to do the thing that I wanted to do, so people didn't think I was doing stuff because of my brothers. I remember when me and Sian [Anderson] got on Rinse, I read the comments and people said we only got that show because of Skepta and Jamie. That was exactly what I was trying to steer clear of. But things happened that made me start to see that I didn't need to be so conscious of that. Geeneus asked me to do the Drivetime show when I wasn't even on radio. I'd left by that point, and they asked me back to do it when they went legal. I thought, 'OK, this has nothing to do with JME or Skepta. You don't give someone a Drivetime show because of their brothers!' That's when I thought, 'Ok, maybe I might be good at this radio thing, I might have a talent for this'. And then the Apple Beats 1 happened and I thought, 'OK it's time I chilled out with this whole thing.' It took a while though. I met loads of people, did loads of things, got involved in loads of projects, and having the community of music, not just grime, but a music scene in general, having that to be around, that kept me in a good space.

Skepta Meridian Walk made me in two ways. Living on an estate gives you the teachings of life. Being on the estate every day, seeing people's struggles, people borrowing off each other. I used to go to the shop with an IOU note for milk and bread on it. Seeing that, when I MC, I MC from that mindset. When I got kicked out of Meridian Walk that made me as well. I was DJing before, so I don't know if I would ever have started MCing. I lost my records because something happened on my estate and someone went to prison for it. One of the guys was rapping about what he was supposed to have done, so the police said, 'Oh, you must have rapped about some of this stuff on wax.' So they took my records and tried to see if there was any more lyrics they could use. We got kicked out of Meridian, evicted, and I lost my records so that was my DJing done with. I thought to myself, 'I need to do something.'

JME I met Wiley when I moved [after the eviction] from Meridian. My first mixtape [*Shh Hut Yuh Muh*] came out in 2006, so this was around 2005. He rang me randomly. I remember when we had moved and [my friend] Joel showed me *Lord of the Decks*, or *Mics*, maybe, but it had a Wiley tune on there. It was over 'Morgue' and he said, *I'm serious like JME on the roads*. I was like 'Rah.' Joel says, 'Jamie, I swear he says your name'. I was like, 'No, he doesn't!' We listened to it and I was like, 'Oh my God, Wiley knows who I am, how does he know who I am?' This was before 'Serious'; 'serious' was just what I used to say on my radio sets. But yeah, I was confused, I was gassed. After that, I remember he rang me, I don't know how he got my number, but he rang me.

Skepta Wiley had heard of JME and invited him to come to the studio, so we went studio – all of Ruff Sqwad was there – and Wiley was like, 'Why don't you write some lyrics?' I was like, 'I can't do grime, that's for kids' – I was twenty at the time and I thought I was a gangsta, a proper rude boy. I wrote one lyric, *Go on then...* [*draw for the tool*] and it's been a myth since then. I remember writing it in my friend's house, doing illegal things, writing lyrics.

JME Wiley calls me, 'Come studio, make some music, I've seen what's happening, come down.' So then I went down with Skepta, to the studio. It was on Old Kent Road, Tooley Street maybe and we was just there like, 'Rah.' I'm looking at Scratchy recording and stuff, like, this is fucking crazy. It's quiet. But I've got the beat for 'Serious', 'cause I'm making beats now and I've got the all the lyrics, everything, but then I didn't want to record it in front of everyone. I was thinking, 'This is nuts, these are people, like everyone I've heard on radio.'

Skepta After that, Wiley started taking us to Rinse, we're going there with Roll Deep who have been spitting for years and I'm rolling there with one lyric, one 16. But it kinda made me hungry 'cause I thought, 'No, I'm not going there next weekend feeling inadequate like I did last weekend,' and I guess that's why I started to clash everybody. I saw it as a quicker way for me to get into the game.

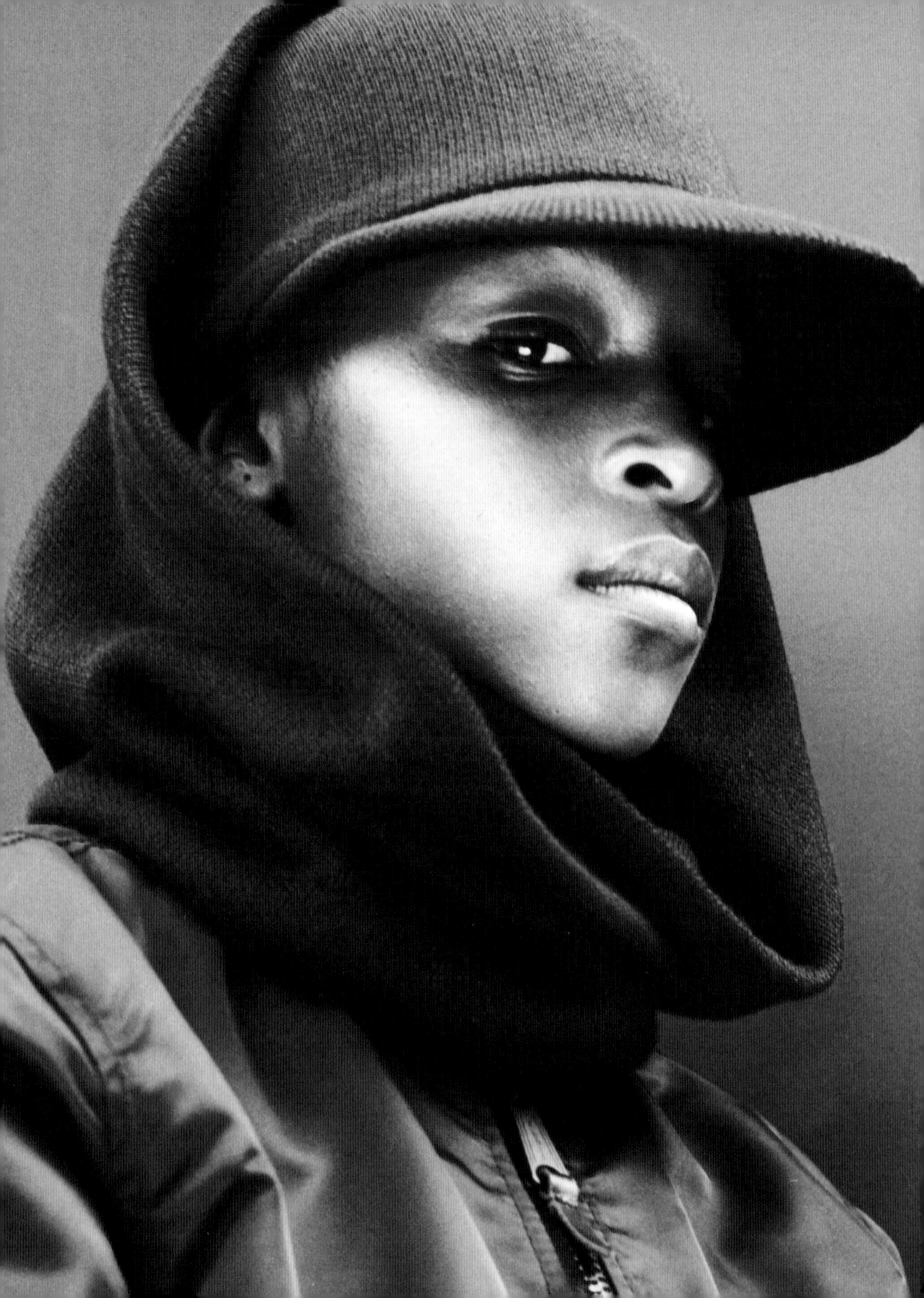

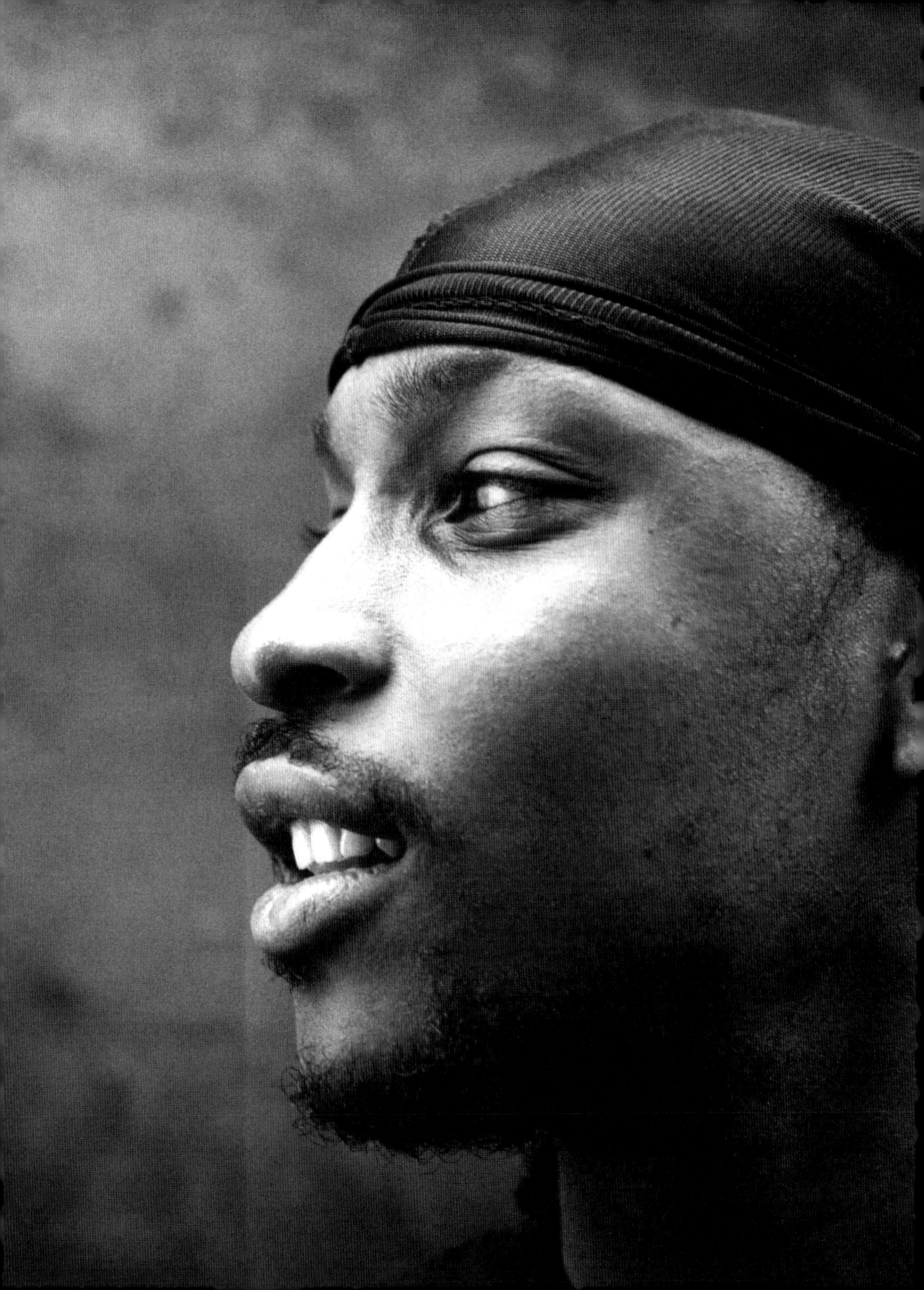

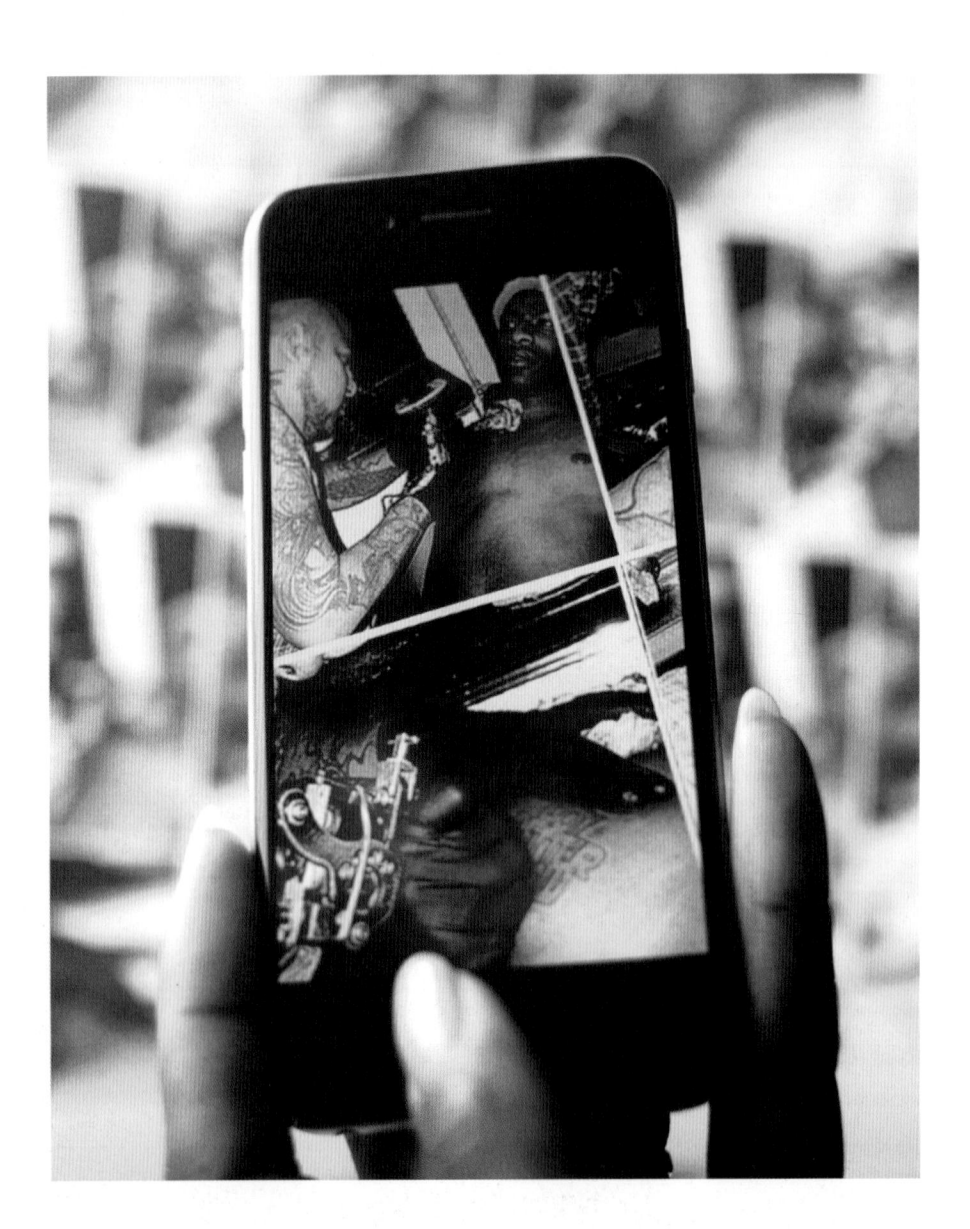

Skepta getting his BBK tattoo, as shot by Hattie Collins April 2006 — Rephotographed 2016

He put it all in the bin and shut the scene down

Chip Skepta's energy right now is just ... he's a beast. He walks into a room and you can just feel it. It wasn't always this way, there's been times back in the day when I was living in the US when he was done, he was fed up. But he's come back swinging. His energy right now is unbeatable.

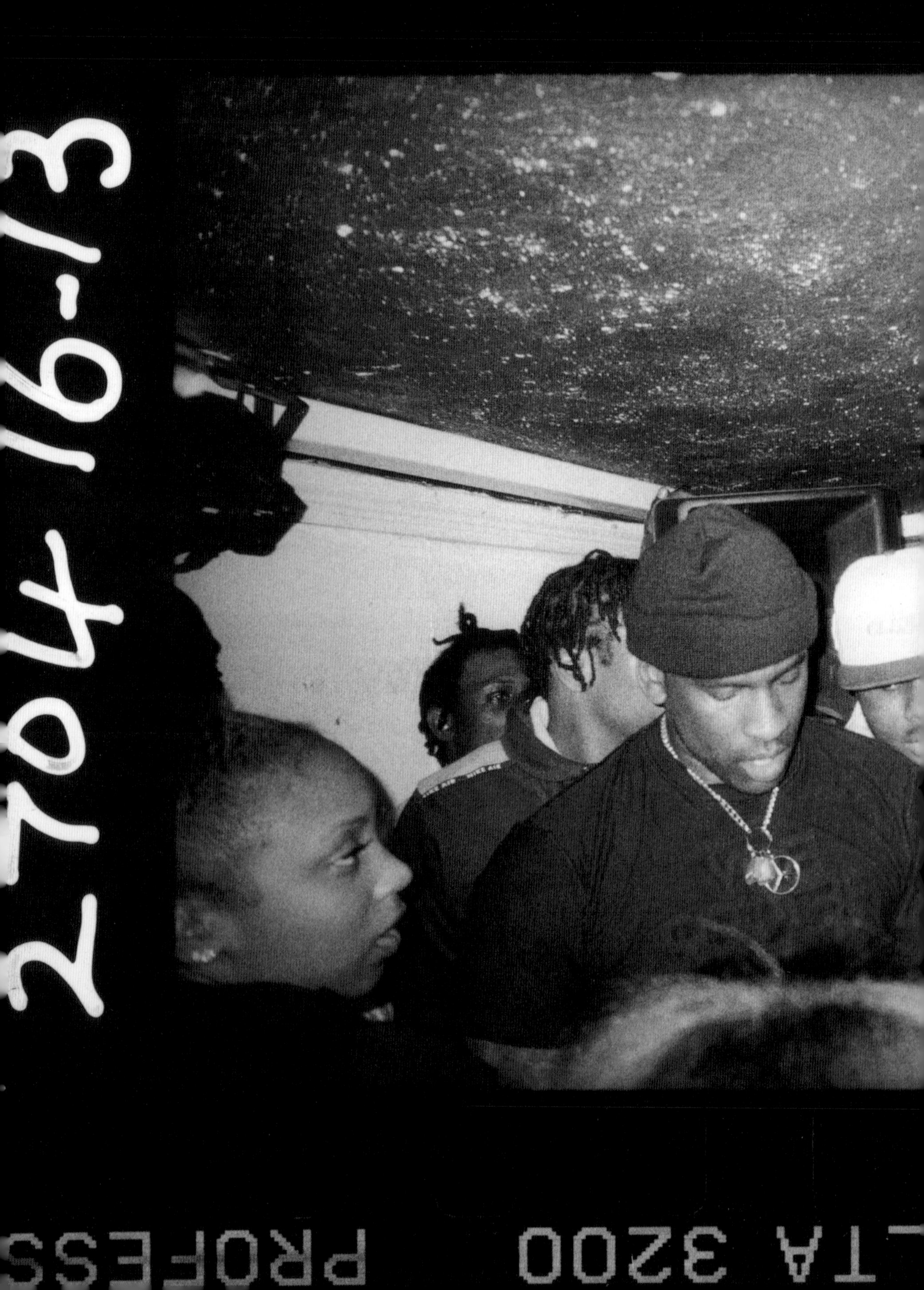
2704-116-13
PROFESS
LTA 3200

SKEPTA

Plastician The first time I met Skepta was at Music House, a cutting studio in North London. I specifically went to cut there in the hope of meeting some more producers whose music I could cut. I was cutting a VIP version of 'Venom', which was my first ever release. Skepta was in the waiting room and heard what I was cutting – he asked me to do him a special and took my number. He was the original moody Skepta many of us know and love to this day. He phoned me in the week asking if I had done it yet and I told him I hadn't – he literally just said, 'Alright call me when you have done it,' and then hung up the phone. I couldn't believe his cheek! We laugh about it now; we were both about twenty years old at the time. JME and Skepta are two of my closest friends in the game. I've known them both for so long now, it's amazing to watch them grow as artists. They are still two of the most exciting artists the scene has, and that's just crazy so many years on. Imagine if Public Enemy were still the most forward-thinking artists in the hip-hop game. That's pretty much what they've managed to achieve in our scene. They're true artists.

Blakie Skepta's a G man. Yeah. He's a G, full stop, exclamation mark. He's already doing loads in the US. I went SXSW and every other person I asked, they're like [American accent] 'Yeah, I know that Skepta. Boy Better Know!'. Even if they don't know the song, they know the name and if they don't know the name, they know this song. It's mad. It's happening, man.

AJ Tracey To me, Skepta is the most important person in grime. The reason I say that, when I started spitting I was listening to Skepta and these man. What they was doing, they've been doing and they're still doing, you get me? They kept it strong. OK, he done his two-two pop thing, but he's always kept it grime. You can't say Skepta isn't a grime artist. You see these rappers with their big chains and diamonds in their mouths, Skepta's made it so you be a grime artist and achieve that lifestyle from grime. You can get rap money off grime. People think grime is a subgenre of rap, but it's not. It's its own genre. Skepta has actually helped to make people see that.

Julie Adenuga Skepta, he's the mad scientist. He is the most discombobulated, unorganised, plain nonsensical person, but because of all of that he manages to pull together this incredibly talented, all-round amazing musician. He's a prime example of being close to someone and seeing that being an artist isn't about making sense and being perfect. To have a conversation with him is the most difficult thing but then he will go away and make probably the best tune I've ever heard in my life.

Chantelle Fiddy Some people might question why JME hasn't done this or that or why he appears to hold back at times… But if you look retrospectively, there doesn't always appear to be rhyme or reason to what [JME and Skepta] do at the time, but it tends to have a way of making sense in the long term. And it's always consistent with them as people and goes hand-in-hand with their respective personalities. I've definitely being massively inspired by Skepta; how I think about a lot of things now and in ways I've developed as a person over the last decade have been motivated by conversations we've had or at times, his lyrics. What I've learnt from them both, in completely different ways, is the idea of freedom from the shackles of society, expectation and conformity. You can choose to be free in life. You don't have to get a job and work a 9-5, you can make you own situation and live it. I know that doesn't work for everybody, but it's the concept of applying yourself and realising that it's not going to happen overnight. It's about having a vision and sticking with it. Don't ever count your worth on what money you've made or what title you currently hold. All that is bollocks. That's why I don't care about much anymore. So much we're consumed with means nothing, it's all just vacuous bollocks. I care about being happy and living an honest life.

#Greatness, 616, BBK, Laigon: Smashed up, graffitied car several days after the Skepta *Man (Gang)* video shoot – Bentley Road, E8

Boy Better Know He's A P.R.O

Chantelle Fiddy JME is a one away. I wouldn't even try and box him into anything and describe him. He's unique and beautiful in all of his uniqueness.

Double O JME ain't the best, he's far from it, but he's determined and he made what he does work. He's a very rich boy off the back of it. He was determined, he came in to do what he done. Now, when you think grime you think 'Boy Better Know'. You have to give credit to the guy. He's not the best, but he's made the best work.

Martin Clark JME is clearly a genius. It really bothers me that I've never really met him, I've never really spoken to him. I'd love to know his IQ levels. He's outstanding.

MSM Engineer He has an extra chromosome, JME. My dad always says, 'That boy is the special one.'

Terror Danjah I think JME has changed the way of thinking. No deal, nothing, he's just put his music out and he's charted enough. He might not sell bucket loads like everyone else, but compare it to the ratios on the business side of things and he's doing very well. Getting that deal isn't what it's cracked up to be. Maybe ten to fifteen years ago when records did actually sell, but the sales now doesn't correlate. Now it's integral to release independently, get bookings for shows and festivals and create a scene. That's what JME's done, he's shown us the format and by doing that, you can be in control of what you're doing. That's powerful, so powerful.

Julie Adenuga JME is the prototype human. Jamie is the perfect human being. He's the prototype that all human beings should be made from and then we can change bits from there. There should be a Jamie base in everyone.

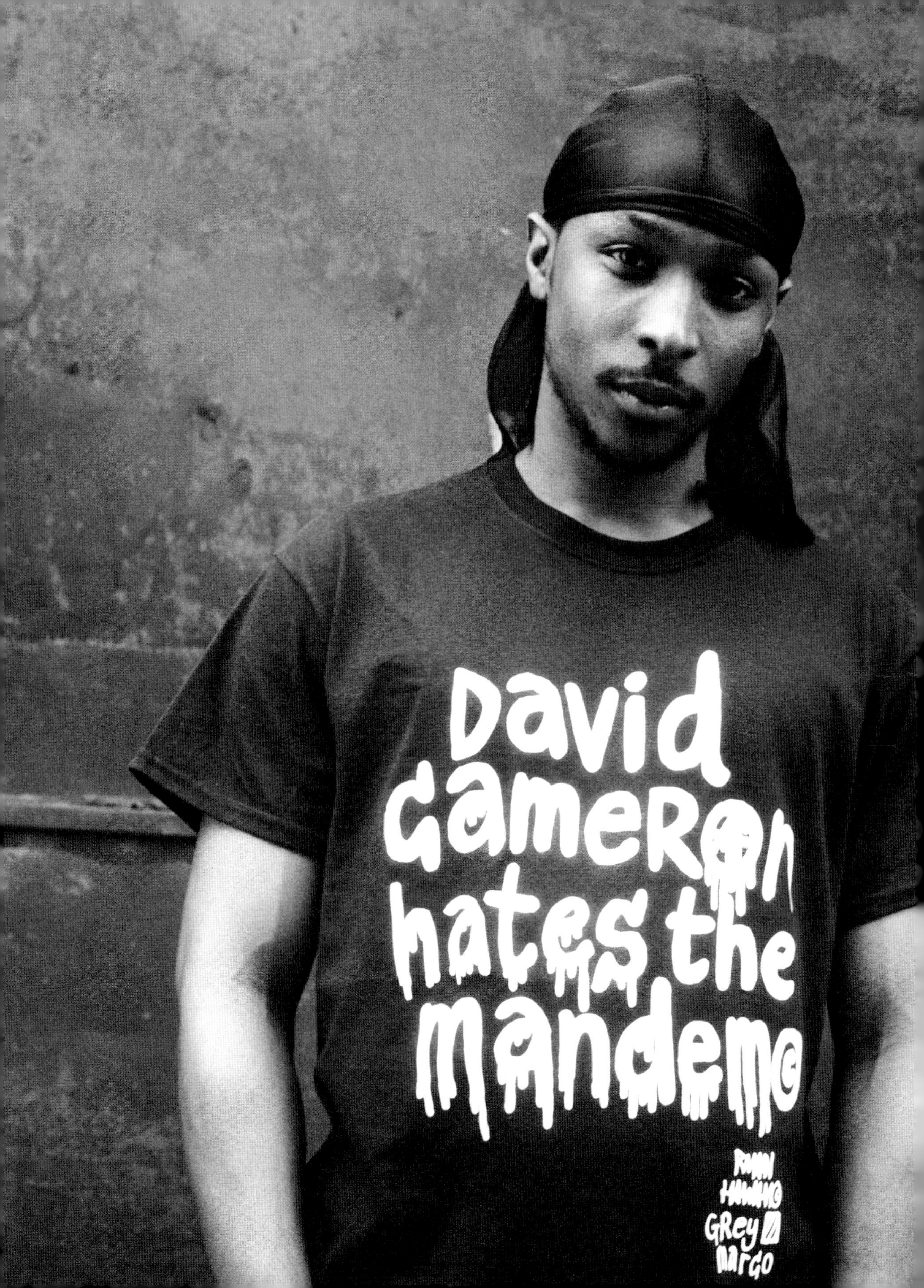
David
Cameron
hates the
mandem
Grey
Margo

Sian & Julie on Sian & Julie

Sian Anderson I met Julie at *Live* magazine. I don't know why she clicked to me but I clicked to her because she was unapologetically black and in my eyes, confident with who she was. Julie was always very – and still is – very assertive, very unapologetic about who she is, at a time in my life where I didn't know who I was, in hindsight. I was told certain things in a certain way and I'd kind of stick to that. Then I met Julie and she just used to not give a shit about any of those things. She'd wear the same tracksuit if she was going to the office, versus if she was going to a grime rave, versus if she was going to work. She didn't care. She once said to me the reason why she didn't wear jewellery is because she feels like people that wear a lot of jewellery are trying to detract from who they are as a person. I looked down and I had fourteen piercings in my ear, four piercings in my face. I took off all my jewellery, just to see and I felt bare. I felt really empty that people were looking at me and seeing into my soul. It made me feel really uncomfortable and I thought, 'Good, feel this level of discomfort because what you was doing before wasn't real, that was not really you.' I realised it's just easier to wear tracksuits and trainers or what I'm comfortable in. Julie became important to me for that reason. I wanted to be as comfortable in my own skin, so that was what drew me to her. I don't really know what drew her to me, 'cause actually I was a bit of a dickhead. Even today, we're still very different, but we have similar things in common. We want to help young people, so we set up our charity One True Calling, where we mentor young people. We like the same kind of music, we're both very logical, we like to try new things and we like to empower our generation, where possible. We can never really fall out because of how much history there is there, it's more like family now. Julie doesn't have any sisters and I don't, but Julie moves like my brother [laughs] 'cause she's older than me and wiser than me.

Julie Adenuga Sian's magical power is her blind fearlessness, I think that's one of the things that's kept us together. When I was in those embryonic years, where I was just doing stuff and having no idea what was going on, she was a really good person to have around 'cause she just didn't give a shit. From where I was sitting, she came across way more powerful than even I think she knew she was. Sian would just do things. I was more calculated; I didn't like to do things unless I knew the outcome, or how it might affect me. I like to plan things really, really well. Whereas Sian is just like, 'We're gonna buy a car and drive here.' 'But we can't drive.' She didn't care about logistics. That was one of the things that really drew me to her. Sian made me push myself. She just dove in headfirst and did it and got a result. She kind of has that Jamie thing. He has that, but his thing is more logical, 'cause he knew he loved music from a young age, he almost had it in front of him. He knew he could teach himself. Jamie and Jason, my youngest brother, taught me if I didn't know how to do something, then just YouTube it. Sian is like, 'I'm not YouTubing nothing, I'm just gonna do it.' She didn't know if it was gonna work, she just did it. That scared me. I didn't like to do things like that, I didn't like to fail. So our friendship has been based on the fact that she's given me that energy to just try it and see what happens. With One True Calling, I was finally at a stage where she had built it into me so much that I knew we could do it, even without a venue or food or anything. We just did it. That's what's held us together. Even her becoming a parent, that was another thing for me. I was like, 'How are you doing this? Where's the plan? We need to sit down and think!' She's like, 'I'm having a baby, great, amazing, we'll go and get this and we'll do that.' Seeing her with Elijah I'm like, 'How do you know how to burp him? How do you know what you're doing?' She's just got that thing where she doesn't care; 'This is what needs to happen to get to here, this is what I need to do to make this happen and I'm doing it.' Growing up, and having someone like that, especially someone younger than me, I couldn't buy that, I couldn't get that information anywhere. Having someone younger than me and someone so fearless to say, 'I'm going to do this, no matter what.' It's so powerful. That is, still today, my favourite thing about Sian Anderson.

JME & MSM on Fruity Loops

MSM Do you remember when we were all in here once [MSM's old studio at his mum's house] when it was me, you, those four girls were here, Sarah, Emily, all that lot, Joel was here and you were on the old computer screen, the big fucking one we had Fruity Loops on and you made that tune? I used to beg you to do something with it. It was red, where you had colour-coded it…

JME I remember, yeah. I'd done it about three or four times and I remember there was a tune I definitely didn't want to forget about.

MSM And I was like, well, why didn't you do anything with that? I remember the day I bought Fruity Loops, Fruity Loops 3.52 or some shit off a CD, off a guy called Deji in school. He used to sell slices of pizza and Tip Tops. This guy would sell you anything.

JME Back in the day, you had to get things on floppy disk or CD. You'd get it and just gas.

MSM Music 2000 was the first one. Music 2000 on Playstation.

JME Yeah, I had both. My dad got a PC and I had on Fruity Loops on there, but it was like a game, Fruity Loops was like a game.

MSM It's the best, I still think it's the one. I miss it, man, even though it's still there.

JME I use every single program like Fruity Loops still, even though you're meant to get Logic and use these programs, like proper equipment. I just muck around. I use it exactly like Fruity Loops 'cause Fruity Loops to me is like a game. You get all the sounds you like and just muck about.

MSM Do you remember when you colour-coded all of ours, edited all the graphics so that when it loaded up…

JME Yeah, yeah, yeah, yeah.

MSM He edited everyone's program, so when it loaded, it had your custom logo. That's what I mean by Jamie though, he would do these kind of things.

JME That's boredom. Listen, brother…

MSM It don't matter, you learnt how to do it.

JME That's boredom, doing it…

MSM But bruv, if you build a house and you're bored, you're still talented, it doesn't mean that you were bored, it means you're talented.

JME But everyone can do it, that's the thing. Everyone could do it. People was, I don't know…

MSM I tried to do it.

JME People were just not as bored as me. I just got a bit more bored in the house.

Opposite: Jamie Adenuga and MSM outside the old studio at MSM Engineer's mum's house – Enfield, EN1
Next page: Original BBK t-shirt, 2005

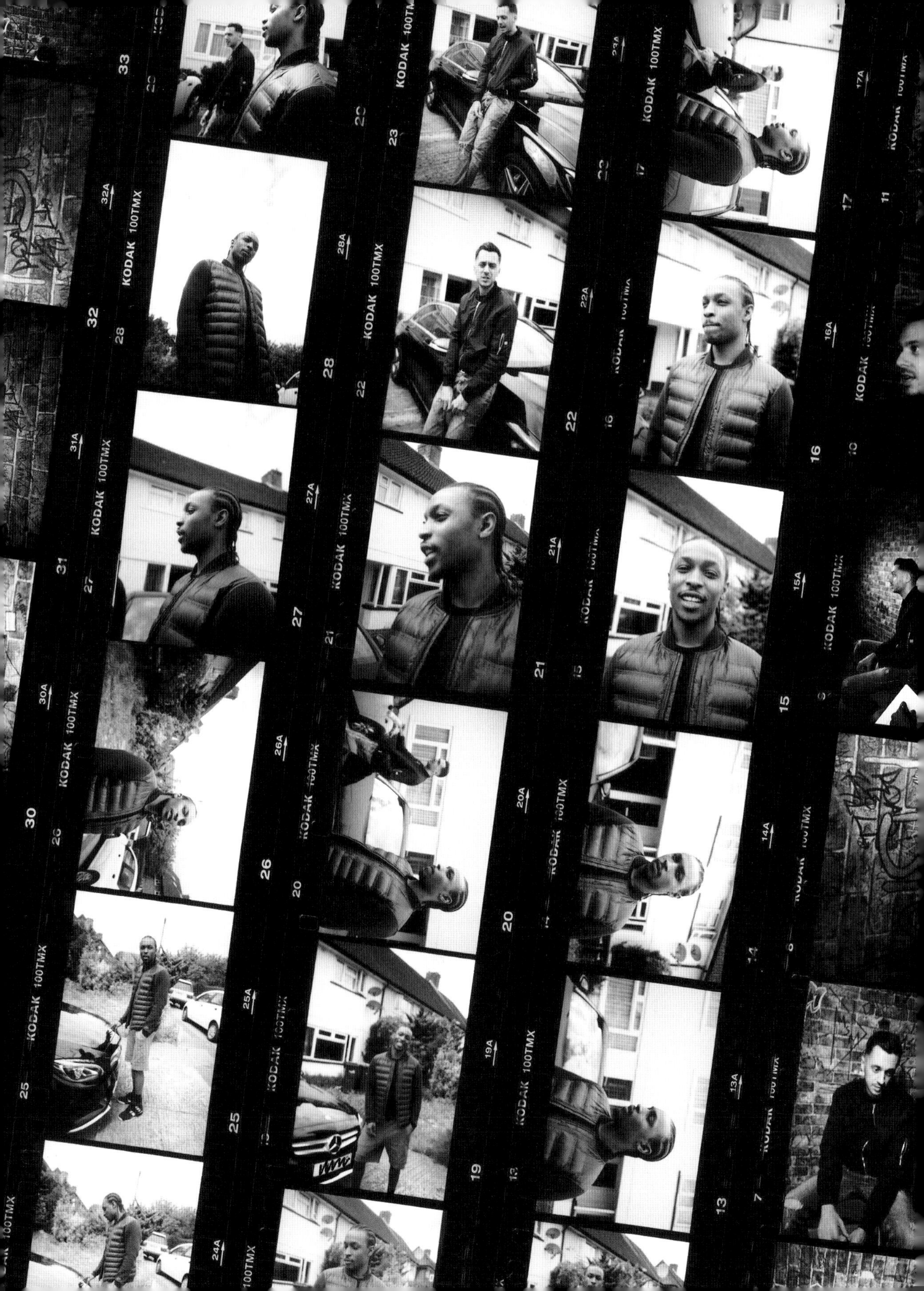

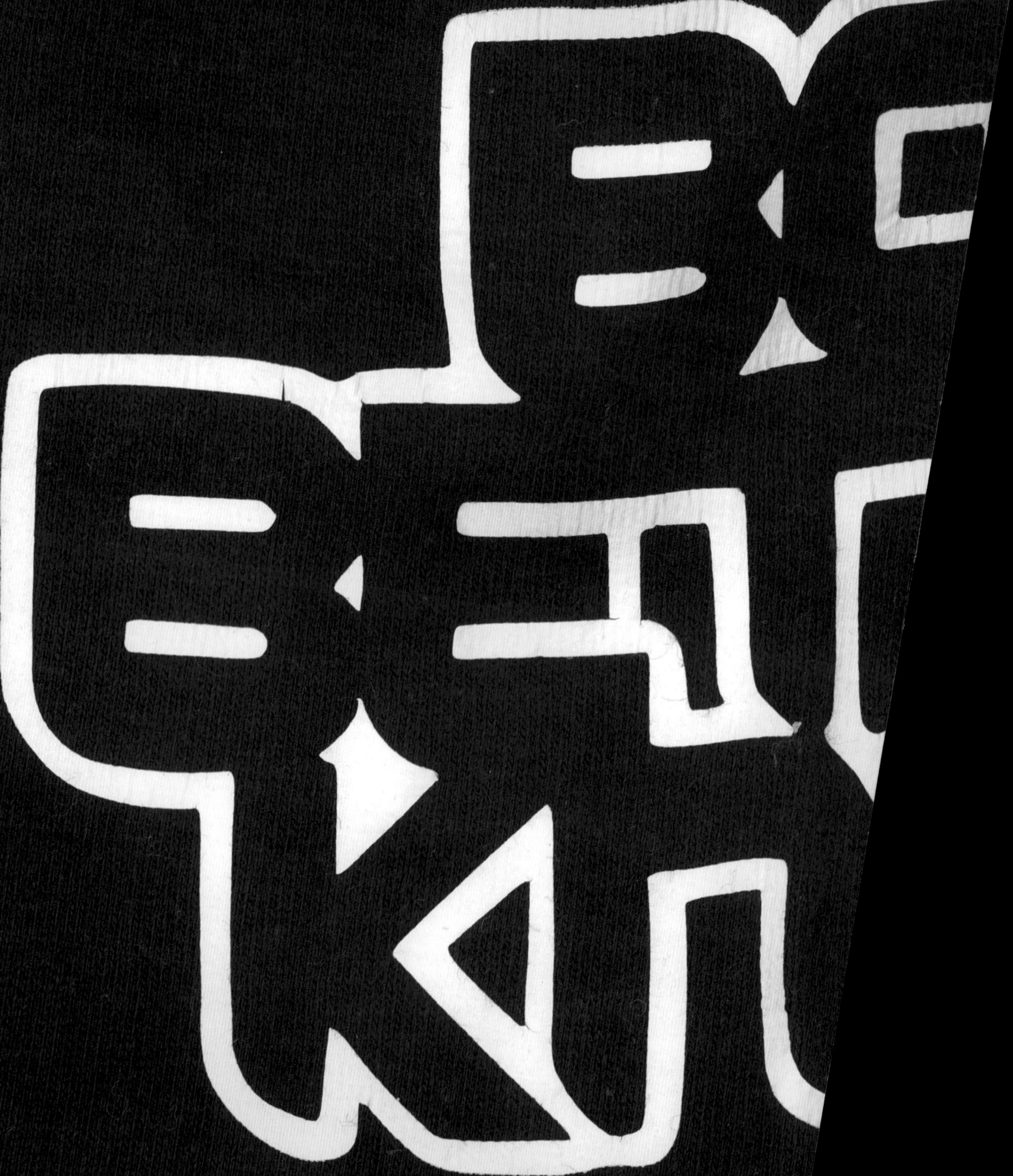

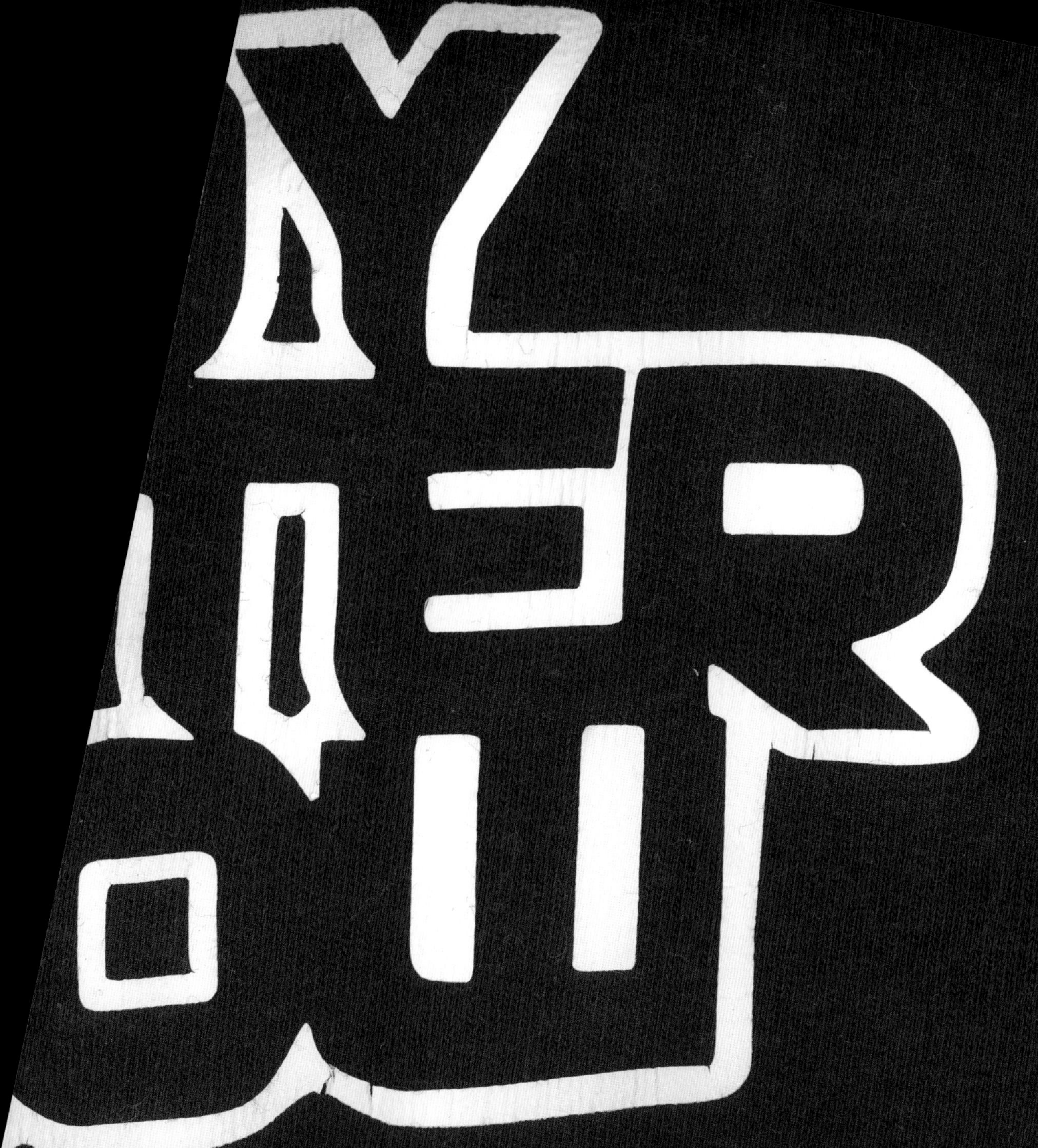

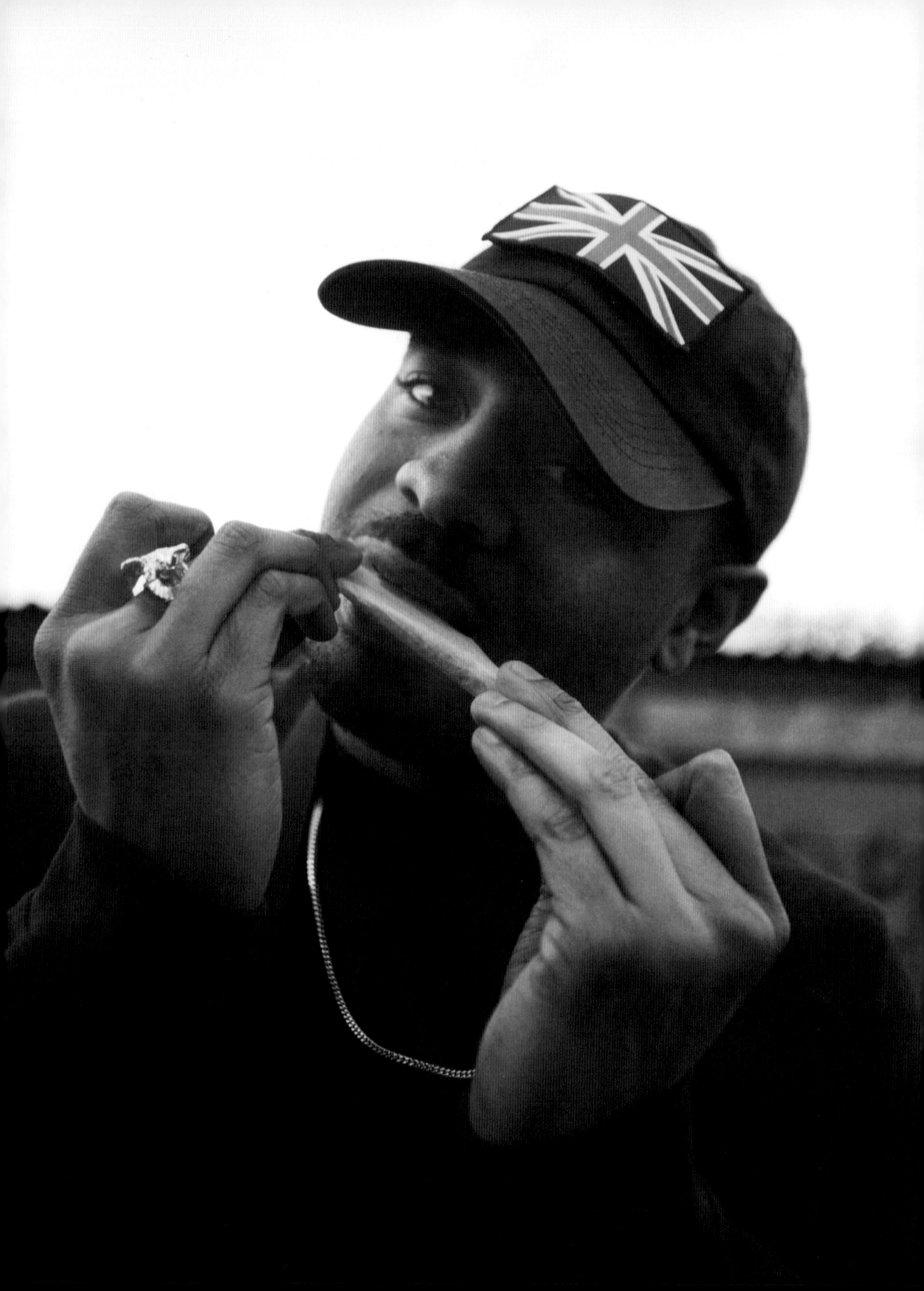

This Ain't A Culture, It's Their Religion

JME It was just what we all used to say at the time, 'Boy Better Know'; Bossman, Big H, me, Dan, everyone, we used to say, "Man Better Know", 'When I come around', 'Boy Better Know'. When I did the mixtape, I didn't have a picture. Mixtapes were American anyway; at that time no one in the UK had anything called a mixtape. I didn't even know what a mixtape was. I thought a mixtape was meant to be on a tape. I thought I'd have to get a picture of me with cars and money, 'cause I really thought that's what a mixtape was. I thought, 'I ain't got that,' but at uni, I was using Photoshop, so I thought, 'Yeah, cool, I'm going to design a logo and put it on the front, that's it; a JME logo.' Then I thought about a Boy Better Know, logo 'cause I had a tune on there called 'AWOH,' which goes *Boy better know, CEO*. So I designed a logo and made it like a flippin', glossy thing. I didn't know what I was doing at the time. From there, it spiraled, it got big. I did CD number two and Wiley said, 'Let's put things out with that logo, that's big.' But Skepta's the reason why it ended up being a *thing*, 'cause it was just a mixtape cover really. Wiley said, 'Yeah, Boy Better Know, me, you and Skepta, lets keep putting things out.' So Wiley put out *Tunnel Vision*, then Skepta said,' Yeah, let's make it into a crew, let's bring in Shorty, 'cause he's younger, he's the youngest guy, bring him through. Frisco, he's from Tottenham as well, he's repping, he's doing his own thing.' Then Skepta brought through Solo [45]. Skepta always brings through people. Jammer

Opposite: Shorty BBK perfects his spliff round the back of the newsagents – Palmers Green, N13
Eskimo Dance L to R: Frisco, Maximum BBK, Wiley, Solo 45

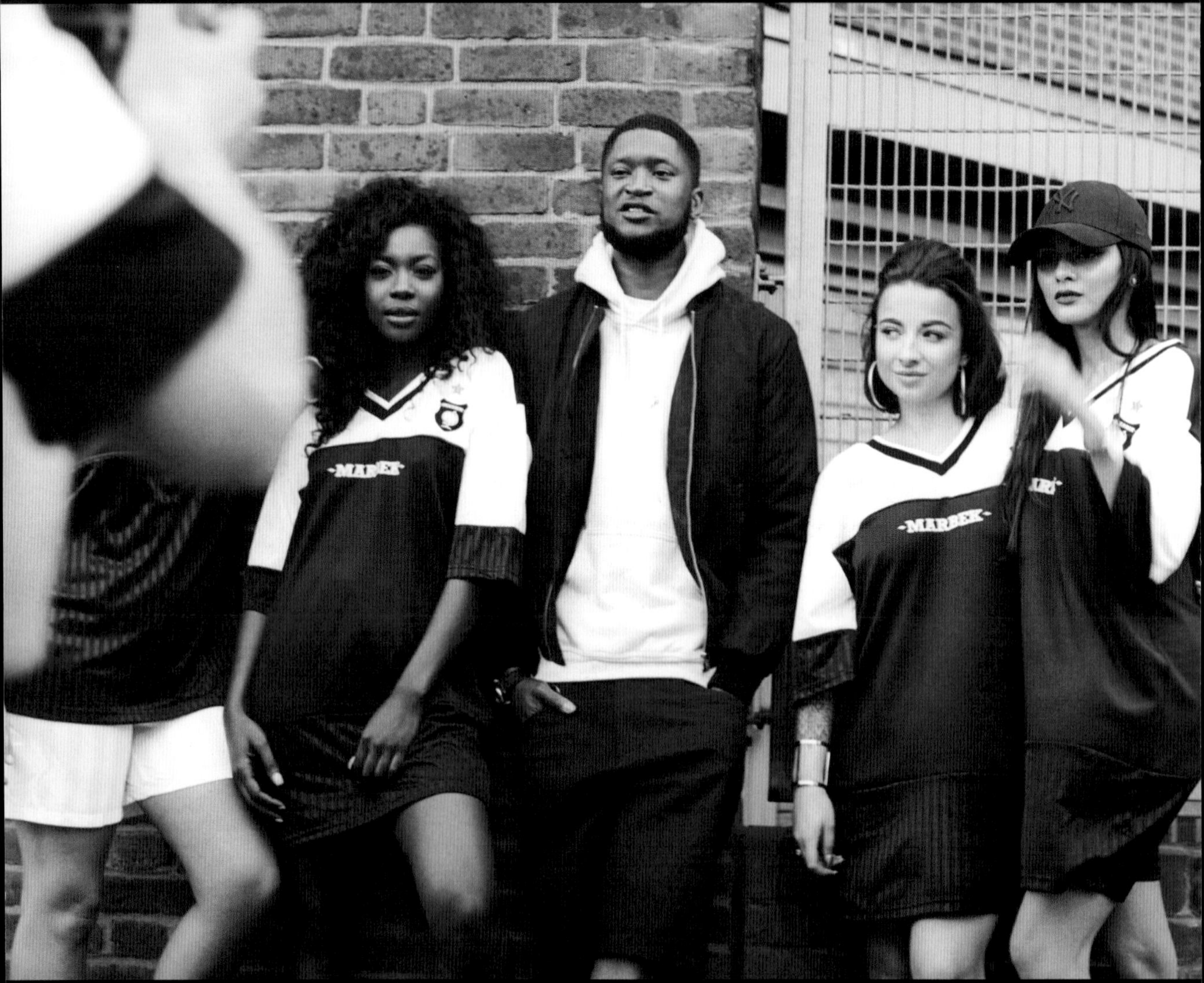
MARBEK
MARBEK

ended up joining organically, but he was always around a lot. But it wasn't a crew, it wasn't a record label, it wasn't nothing, it was just a mixtape.

The t-shirts came from [Chantelle Fiddy's night] Straight Outta Bethnal, like, random. The t-shirt shop was round the corner from the 333 [where Straight out of Bethnal was held]. So on that day of Bethnal, I made my own t-shirt. It was white with 'Boy Better Know' with a metal mesh kind of effect that was from this transfer paper the printer used. I was wearing it, and everyone was saying it was so sick and how they wanted one. I thought, 'OK, I'm not going to go and spend money doing bare t-shirts with this transfer paper 'cause it's expensive.' I decided to get a cheaper one done. The minimum they could do was fifty – I only wanted like ten. But I took the fifty, paid, got them, I had the boxes at my house and told everyone to come and get them. Everyone comes to my house, trying on all the sizes, gassed, like, 'Lets go Straight Outta Bethnal tonight.' Everyone's gassed. Sometimes, the thing I've got in my head, it clicks, like, 'This DIY thing that you're doing for fun, it's actually a thing in other people's lives'. Everyone was trying to get a t-shirt, they wanted their size. That was it, we went to the club, all of us together, we all had a t-shirt on and we had a sick set. That was the birth of Boy Better Know and the t-shirt game being healthy [laughs].

Opposite: Frisco and his video shoot girls wearing Marbek – Greenwich, SE10
Jammer and Skepta – Visions, Dalston, E8

Black The Ripper smoking the dankest of England, backstage at Chip's gig – XOYO, EC2
Opposite: Chip shows off his tattoos and wears Cash Motto at home – Essex

4305
3
ILFORD DELTA 3200 PRO
4
4305
5
ILFORD DELTA 3200 PRO
Believe

Grime Goes Pop and Eats Itself

Dizzee Rascal Some people forget I had three albums before all that happened. This day and age, guys are going straight to that. But whatever anyone thinks about the direction I've gone in, I've put it in the grind. I had to build the thing up properly.

Wretch 32 It all starts from the underground, like Chip wouldn't exist if he wasn't doing 'Fire Alie' and if he wasn't going back to back with Griminal and Devlin on radio. If he wasn't shining in that room, then it wouldn't have happened as big as it has did for him. You can tell which artists have really come from the root. You work your way up, up, up, until you get to a certain level and I think the sky is the limit. Running around with The Movement with our backpacks, with our lyric pads, going from studio to studio, that's definitely sharpened my skills. I would have been swallowed in that crew if I wasn't good, that's the truth. I'm thankful for everything.

Chip I could see the artform changing. I saw the change coming and I adapted. It's all about *adapt*, bruv. That's what this ting has always been. It started out as S.O.R. – sale or return. If it sells, you get your P, if it don't, you don't. Songs we learned to do later, the original essence of the ting was swinging. It was £20 for an hour in the studio. If you had a score, you had a key to a bill. The key to a bill was the key to a grand and from there it was lit. From where you had £20, that was the key to a bill. You get them three dubs done in that £20, then you're gonna get a booking, that's a couple of bills, you do a couple of those, and it's a bag [£1000]. It's lit. That was the mentality.

Dizzee Rascal For me, it's just, I left it behind when it was *that* and haven't really been a part of it since. I dip in every now and then because I know Jammer, I know D Double E, so I'm around it every now and then and it's not that it's not my field, but I'm not trying to get the biggest reload with my bars. I've moved onto other stuff. I'm exploring music as a whole. I know what I can do as a spitter but to me I thought [grime] was more limited. [*Sixty Minutes* with Mistajam] to me, that's nothing. Not that it doesn't mean nothing, but that's the easiest shit ever. Me going in and saying my bars from fourteen, fifteen years ago, I do that in my sleep. That's nothing. But writing a fucking smash hit, that's actually hard. As easy and as simple and as cheesy as some of them people think it might sound, that's harder.

Chip Do you know what's hard? Writing a hit song. That's hard. For me, I can perform straight bars onstage for eighty minutes, no hooks, no choruses, some of those songs I won't have performed since I wrote them, but I won't forget a word. I can't. It's ingrained in me, it's embedded. You know how people speak in tongues? It's like that, it's blind, it don't leave you. All of that training, all of that swinging for ten, twelve years, it's part of me. But to sit and write an 'Oopsy Daisy', or a 'Champion'? That's actually a test of artistry, musicianship, bars, and imagination. I've only ever made songs that are authentic to me.

Ghetts Grime was looked upon as a dirty word, people distanced themselves from it. See me, I'm all about the culture. I want to help the culture so when youts come through, they don't have to do what we had to do. I didn't get mad when Wiley makes a 'Heatwave' or something like that, I didn't get upset. When Wiley made 'Wearing My Rolex', what you have to understand is, I witnessed that first-hand. One day Will [Wiley] was struggling and three weeks later he had a Bentley; that does a lot to the mind. I saw it. Then you just start panicking. But now I feel like man would rather be Stormzy than Tinie today. NANG! No disrespect to Tinie, but a kid that wants to be Stormzy rather than Tinie is nang for the culture. Man would rather mean more to the culture than the mainstream, blud. That's no disrespect to Tinie. People say to me, 'What are your thoughts on Tinie?' and I'm like, 'A cool bruddah.' 'Nah, not as a human being, the mainstream thing?' I say, 'Bruv, listen, you see when Tinie was here, he wasn't embraced, don't think he was.' He wasn't embraced, so let's have that right.

Wiley The 'John Woolf years'. He's a powerful figure; John Woolf [Wiley's manager] can walk into an office and have a conversation that more often than not will lead to money. In '07/'08 he went in and had those talks, he got into meetings with people that probably wouldn't want to talk to me. I don't like them years though because my country has bigged me up for them tunes and then shat on me for them. 'You sell out, that's shit, why did you make that tune?' But bruv, no one's listening to grime, you're all in house raves and garage raves. I've got two kids, however I'm gonna make money I'm gonna do it and I don't really like the fact that's what's popular no-one likes. People like it when it's not popular, they don't like it when everyone likes something. That's why someone like JME is a don, for ignoring everyone's bullshit. I hate them years because my country's made me hate them, but otherwise I made enough money there to do what I wanna do. I spent every penny of 'Take That' on grime anyway.

Tinchy Stryder I would never say grime sold out because personally every time I made music I saw it as growth. Writing a so-called pop song, it's hard. It's hard to make a good song. When 'Number One' went to number one, it was number one for a whole month in the UK. If it was that easy, we would all do it. It's cool 'cause everything goes around and I guess the hype is back on grime. I'm happy that it's cool to be grime again, but the realness of it though is, how much is about pushing things forward? How many songs are actually selling? Is the scene able to sustain itself? So it depends. You have to stick to your heart. Wiley done 'Rolex' and 'Heatwave' but that doesn't make it any less grimier; without him there wouldn't be grime. If you take it there, the main man's done it, what's the problem?

Ironik It was fun; I don't regret anything I done in my career, especially that time. A lot of people saying it was us lot trying to be pop. But for me it was just going from producing when I was about fifteen, recording in my bedroom for MCs like Wiley, Black the Ripper – Chip came up after school – and wanting to be at the forefront. I was sick of being in the back. Tinie, by that point, had done 'Tears', I saw him making stuff for the girls and thought, 'Yeah, I want to do that.' I liked girls too! So I started trying out things, writing about girls and got signed off the back of it.

Chip and Stormzy backstage at Lethal B gig– Koko, Camden, NW1

I didn't sit there trying to make pop music, it just ended up being popular. My first song was called 'So Nice', Rude Kid produced that one, which went to number one on Channel U for eighteen weeks. Me, Tinch and Chip, we'd all come from grime, DJing, mixtapes. I DJd from early, I supported So Solid's '21 Seconds' on tour at thirteen, fourteen years old. We'd been in this for years.

Tinie Tempah I first saw Ironik get a record deal, which was cool, cos Ironik was my DJ so it was really interesting to see that happen. He went on to chart really high. We'd seen other people chart too, like Dizzee and So Solid, but that was a long time ago. Ironik came and got a number five. Then after that Tinchy came and got a number one. Being a grime artist, coming from that grime world, it's not only equating to them being more popular and having more exposure, it's equating to more money. We're all kids from the street, we're all kids from council estates, we didn't have any silver spoons in our mouths – not only are we seeing success, we're seeing money. At that time Tinchy was the biggest-selling male of the year, black or white. I remember thinking, 'This is great, he's shining, look at him.' While that was happening, that raised the level of aspiration. Before, people just wanted to get on pirate or get a reload or get in a popular crew. The aspiration changed to being able to get yourself a record deal, to tour, to do all these things in a manner that a pop star would. From there, I was still independent, getting on with it and then eventually I had my time via a combination of releasing underground music via 1Xtra, Channel U and having my own blog. The way a YouTuber would do now, I was doing that with MilkN2Sugars and eventually I signed to Parlophone Records, (home to the likes of Coldplay and Lily Allen), and the rest is history. I released 'Pass Out', it went on to be the biggest selling song of that year. When you sell that much, regardless of your origins, it becomes a popular tune in the same way as '21 Seconds' is a popular tune.

Riko Dan As a musician that's why we started to MC, to become worldwide superstars, not just to spit on grime. I don't know about anyone else, but I didn't start MCing to just be a star in one genre. I wanted to be a megastar. The people that went away, I say good luck to them.

Dizzee Rascal I just know that I made a conscious choice to make pop music. Where else could I go? On my second album I was touring with Justin Timberlake, but it wasn't until 2009 that *Tongue n' Cheek* dropped, a full six years later. And that was on my label, independent, no one, nothing, just us. And that's when it really went bang, on that fourth album. It's never been seen before; someone that came from the bottom and lasted.

Julie Adenuga Because of the people I've grown up around and my family, I have to look at both sides of the spectrum. From the artist side of the spectrum, I appreciate they did what they had to do, at the time. I appreciate that they allowed themselves to be guinea pigs, in a way, because if they hadn't done that, Junior wouldn't have had his *Underdog Psychosis* realisation. They wouldn't have known how far they had to push before they realised they didn't have to go that far. And I think that's a brave thing to do. A lot of them could have said no and the music might not have got to where it is. So I appreciate they took that step and although they might have had to do things that they weren't 100% happy with, I appreciate their bravery to do that 'cause I don't know if I could have made that decision. I think because of them, I'm allowed to make the decisions that I make today. I say no to a lot of things because I know that people now recognise how powerful our culture and our music is. They may not have realised that if them lot hadn't done what they did. But from the other side of things, I don't think music took a loss because we had JME and Big Narstie who said, 'I'm not doing it, I'm not getting involved, so fuck it.' From a fan side, I don't think it's a loss, but I can understand hard feelings on it. I can see why people were upset about it. I understand where they were coming from, when you have no idea how things work, you just want to hear a grime tune, but Chipmunk's releasing this, or Stryder's releasing that. But there could have been more empathy for the situation. We could have had more empathy for the artists.

Tinie Tempah Bar now, that was the biggest time for the culture because it meant it was being seen by people outside of the culture for the first time. We were only limited to certain platforms before, i.e. pirate radio, independent TV stations like Channel U, which is now AKA and DAB like 1Xtra. We've definitely had a resurgence of an underground culture again via Soundcloud and Spotify etc. but at the end of the day, people are still looking at what chart position it got to and how much it sold, which in my opinion means that it's relative to what is pop and what is popular. As an artist who has come from the grime world and to have been able to have that success, it's one of the best things to have happened to my life. It's exposed me to the rest of the world, it's enabled me to work with everyone from Dizzee to JME, Stormzy and Bugzy as well as Calvin Harris and Jess Glynne, Katy B, Zara Larsson, 2 Chainz, Big Sean... That's definitely down to the sort of music I made. I couldn't have asked for it any other way and you know I'm always a big advocate of that. Why shouldn't we compete with our contemporaries from other genres by way of chart positions and record sales and sold out tours?

Plastician I don't think any great damage done, perhaps a little more confusion if anything. People forget that grime was born out of living in not-so-great conditions or areas. When a major record label offers you a five or six figure advance to record on their terms, they knew it would be hard for anyone in our circumstances to turn it down. That led to a few acts being moulded more into pop stars, but as sad as it was, I don't think any of the artists who enjoyed that success are really suffering now for it, luckily. They've been able to detach themselves and refresh what they are doing. Grime fans seem to have given them all a chance to come back and remind us all why they caught the eye of the majors in the first place.

Ironik They called 'Stay With Me' the 'Anthem for Broken Britain'. It was a crazy time. People still now tell me that songs are played in funerals.

Tinchy Stryder We put in the shifts. I'm so happy for grime now and we're all doing what we love. I was always making grime tracks, it just wasn't what was being pushed, people didn't always hear it. Even now, I have people ask me when I'm dropping new music and I just had a song out with JME. But, yeah, I've been pirate, I've had a Staffie bite my leg and I've carried on MCing. People don't always see the graft. Paying subs. Now, you just do YouTube and you get booked for Eskimo Dance, which is nothing like the Eskimo Dance back then. It's not the same. *Boy in da Corner* was sick, the album was so homegrown, but then Diz did 'Dance With Me', 'Bonkaz' and yeah they sound different to 'Ho' or 'Jezebel'. But you've seen the world and you realise you're influenced by music. It's a double edged sword.

Jammer We believe that if you do what you do and do it best then one day it will be big. We don't see our careers on a spreadsheet, that's not why true musicians do music. It comes from a spiritual place, a creative place, so it being translated into business is another problem. No one can take away Tinchy Stryder's history. He clashed in this very Basement, he recorded some of his early tracks here, he's been through the thick and thin of it. He's come from there to being a millionaire, but at the same time under the pressures of those labels that might not enable him to live relaxed and live how a free artist wants to live. There's a lot of ties that come with it. To understand that making music, firstly, and being yourself is the most important thing, that's what grime is. That's what grime is.

Tinchy Stryder on Snapchat outside the Link Centre youth club in his Mercedes – Devons Road, E3

Chronic on 420, near Big Narstie's pitch at Speaker's Corner – Hyde Park, W2
Opposite: Tempa T at home – Somewhere up the M1 near Milton Keynes

232 This Is Grime

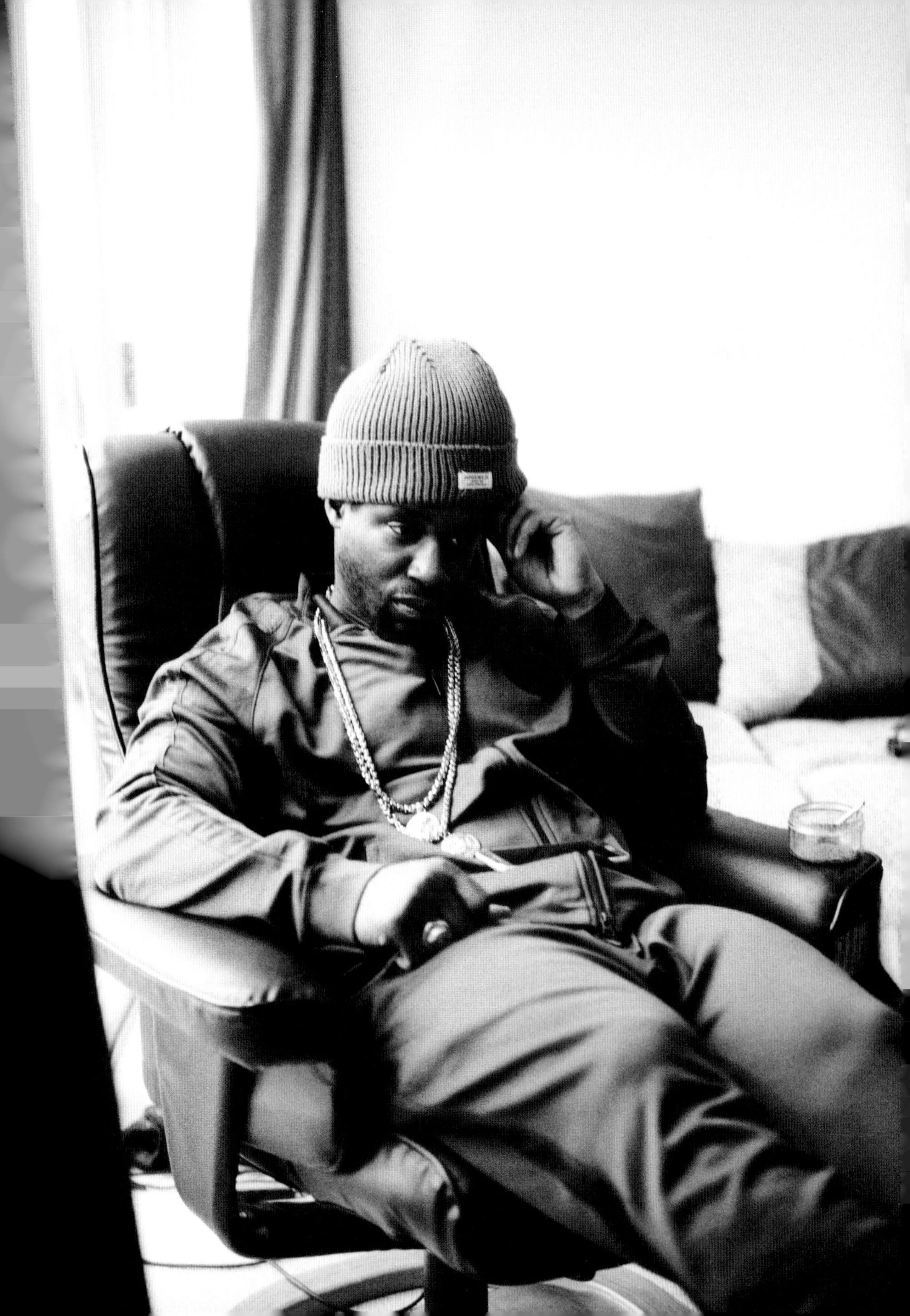

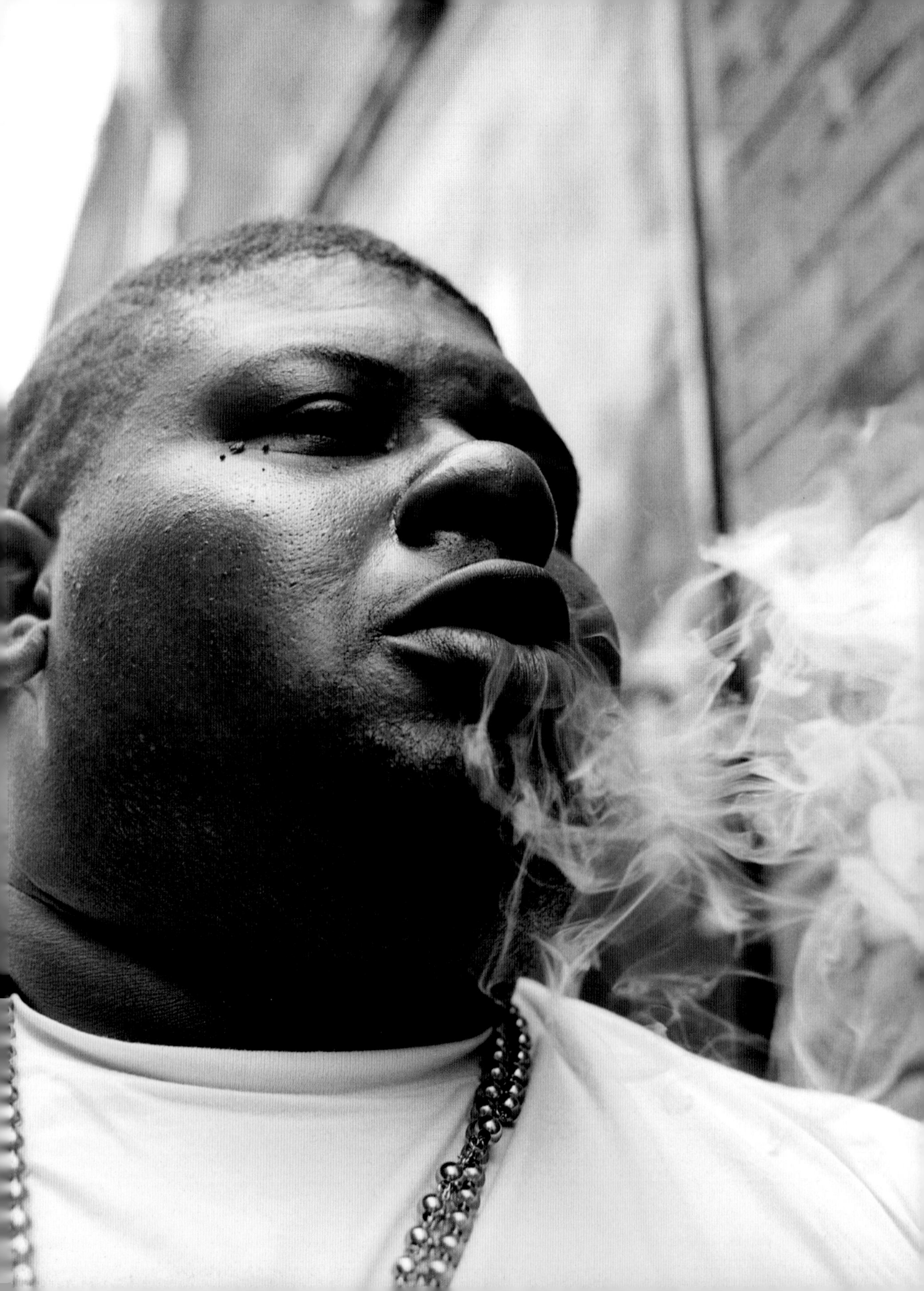

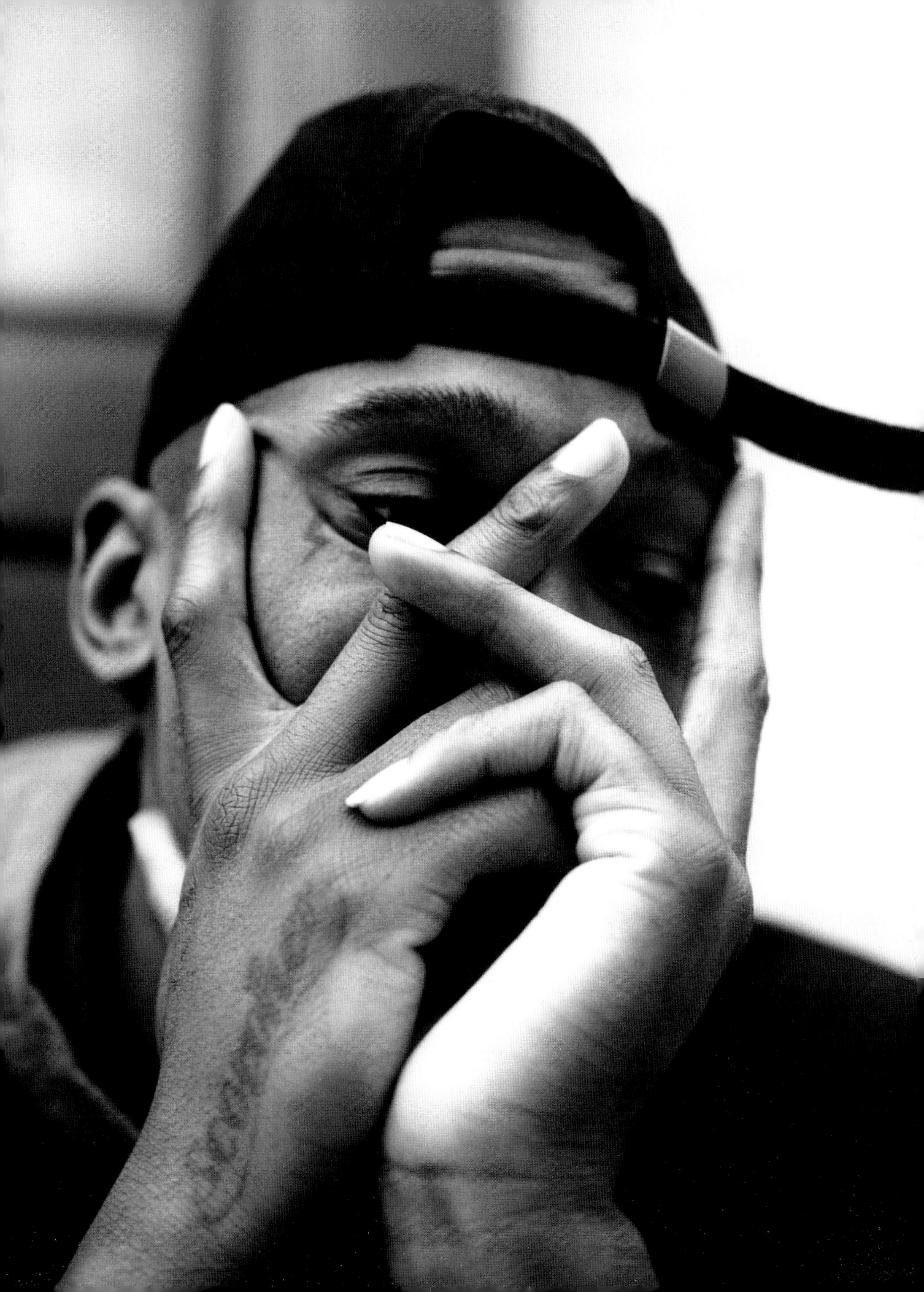

Ironik on Violence

I got stabbed in 2010. I was twenty-two years old, and I'd had a few hit singles, some success. It was, essentially, an incident that didn't have to happen, but it was set up and orchestrated by a few guys. It was kinda my fault. I was wearing a lot of jewellery at the time thinking I was 'the guy' and I probably shouldn't have really. I came back from a show and they was waiting outside my mum's, balaclava's and all that. They kept saying, 'Give me your jewellery, give me your jewellery.' I thought it was a joke because it was around Halloween, so I thought it was one of my friend's messing around with a mask. One of them hit me and I realised it wasn't a joke. I started running up the hill and I saw a car coming towards me, I thought that would be my chance to get help. But they were trying to drive into me, so obviously they were in it together. I had to run round them, I ran up the hill, got up to the top of the hill and I couldn't run anymore. He said, 'Give me your ring,' so I took it off and threw it as far as I could so they'd go after it. Just before that happened, it felt like he had punched me, but I didn't clock. I ran back home, I got back down the hill, ran into my neighbour's flat and she sad, 'Are you OK?' I was like 'Yeah, yeah, I'm fine'. I could see her looking at me. 'There's blood everywhere'. That's when I realised I'd been stabbed.

It's hard, because you want to be in the places where you grew up and hang out with your mates, but then this is what can happen, people try and take advantage of that. And you can ask anyone, I'm one of the most clean artists you can meet; I literally just do music, that's all I know. So this was crazy for me, this wasn't why I wanted to get into music. It made me think perhaps I should have stayed in the background after all and just left the 'superstar' stuff to other people.

I still come around here, but that took me a while, to be able to come back around the place I grew up. At the time, I moved into a hotel for months, just hiding out, trying not to be seen. Then I moved out to Essex. I didn't realise it at the time, but I started going through anxiety and depression. I was young then, the police would call and ask me if I wanted to speak to someone, but I said no. I just wanted to get on with what I was doing. But now, looking back, I was probably in a dark place. It messes you up a bit. I'm just a guy that wants to make music for the people, that's all I want to do. For someone to try and take my life over that, it's mad. It was quite a hard thing for me to get my head around and to stop feeling that it could happen again at any time.

I'm 100% alright now, I'm in a good space. I've got a great girlfriend. I speak to her about a lot of stuff, which helps. And my mum, my friends and family have been a great support system. I feel like I'm in a good place, my energy is right, I'm as happy as ever. I don't regret stepping into the spotlight anymore; what happened, happened, and I can't be defined by that.

Previous page Left: #BDL Big Narstie smoking outside the studio – Dalson, N16 Right: Scorcher – South Tottenham High Rd, N15
Opposite: DJ Ironik outside his mum's house – Muswell Hill, N10

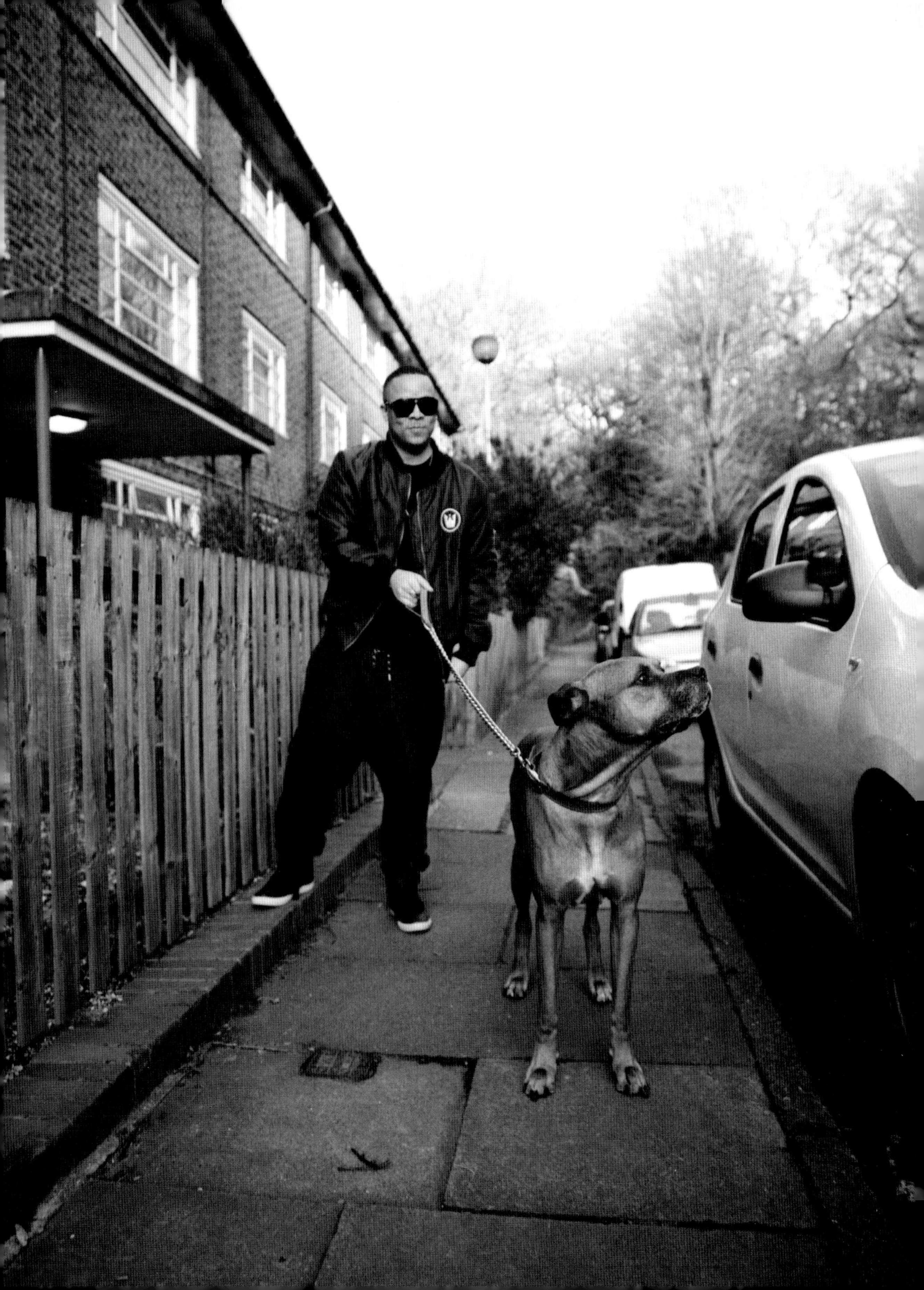

02. 3.30
02. 3.30
ILFORD
8
9
02. 3.30
02. 3.30
ILFORD
DELTA 3200
PRO
12
13
02. 3.30
02. 3.30

Opposite: Wretch 32 backstage at Lethal B – Koko, Camden, NW1
Views from Tiverton Estate, childhood home of Wretch 32 – Tottenham, N15

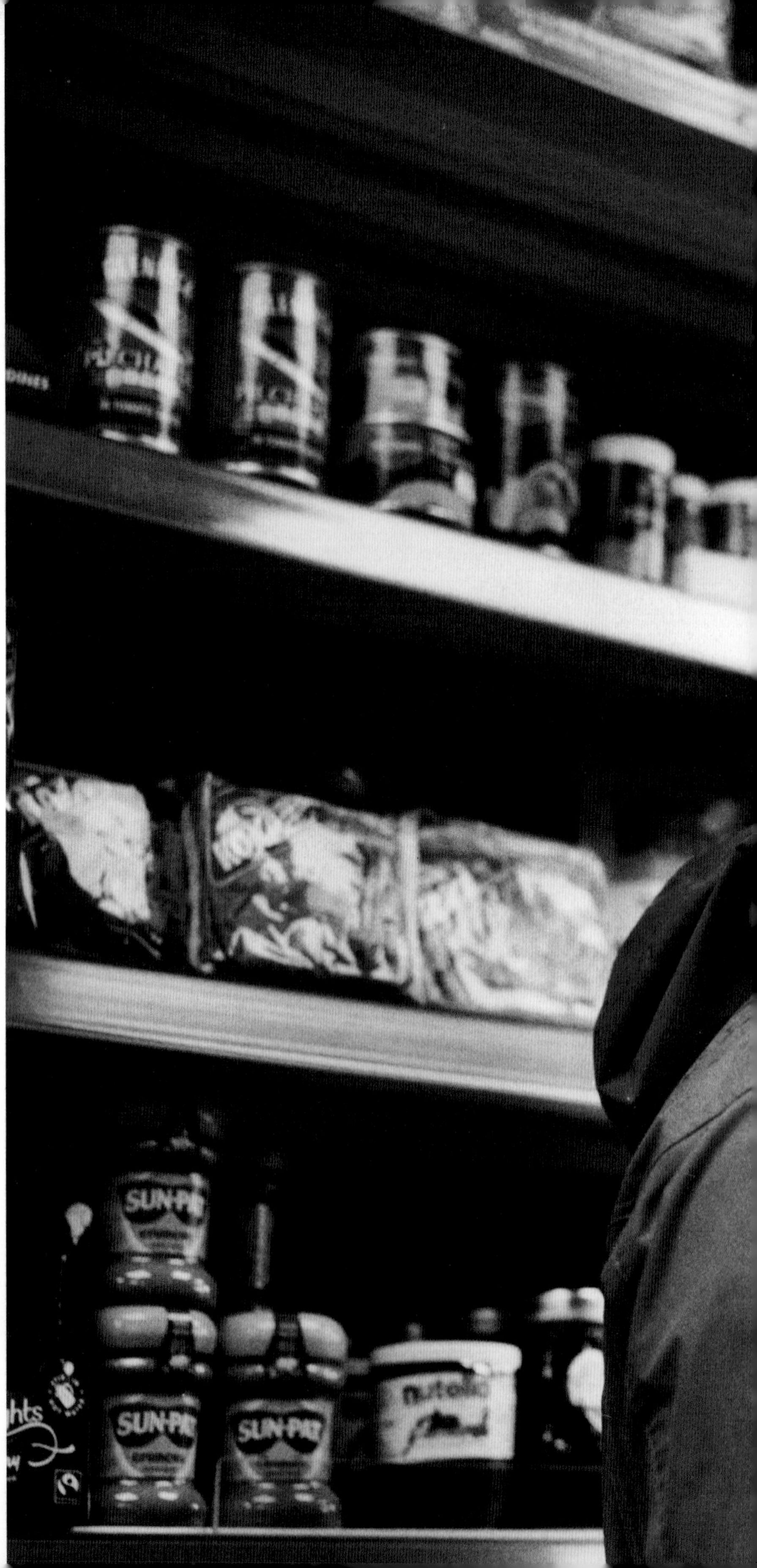

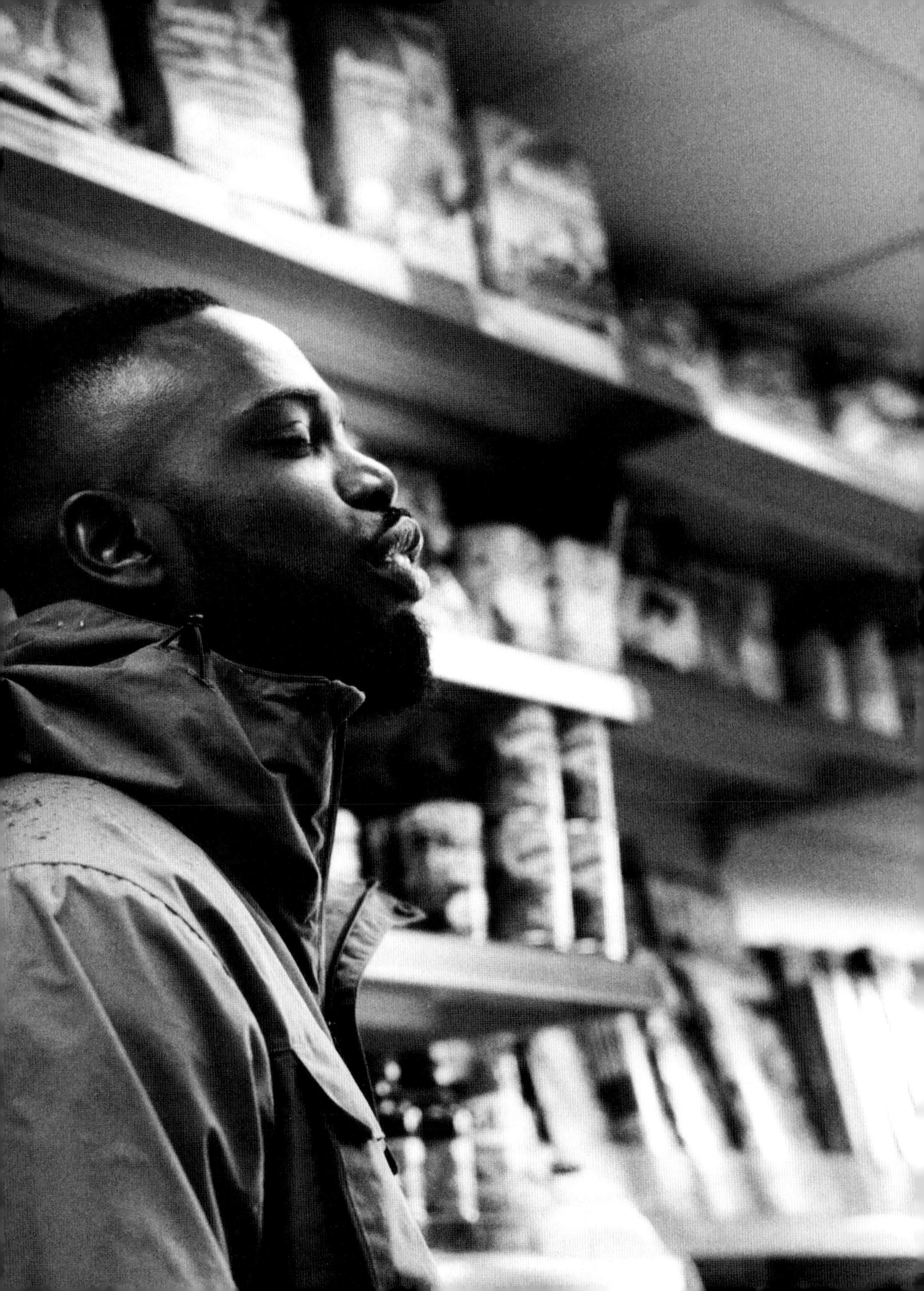

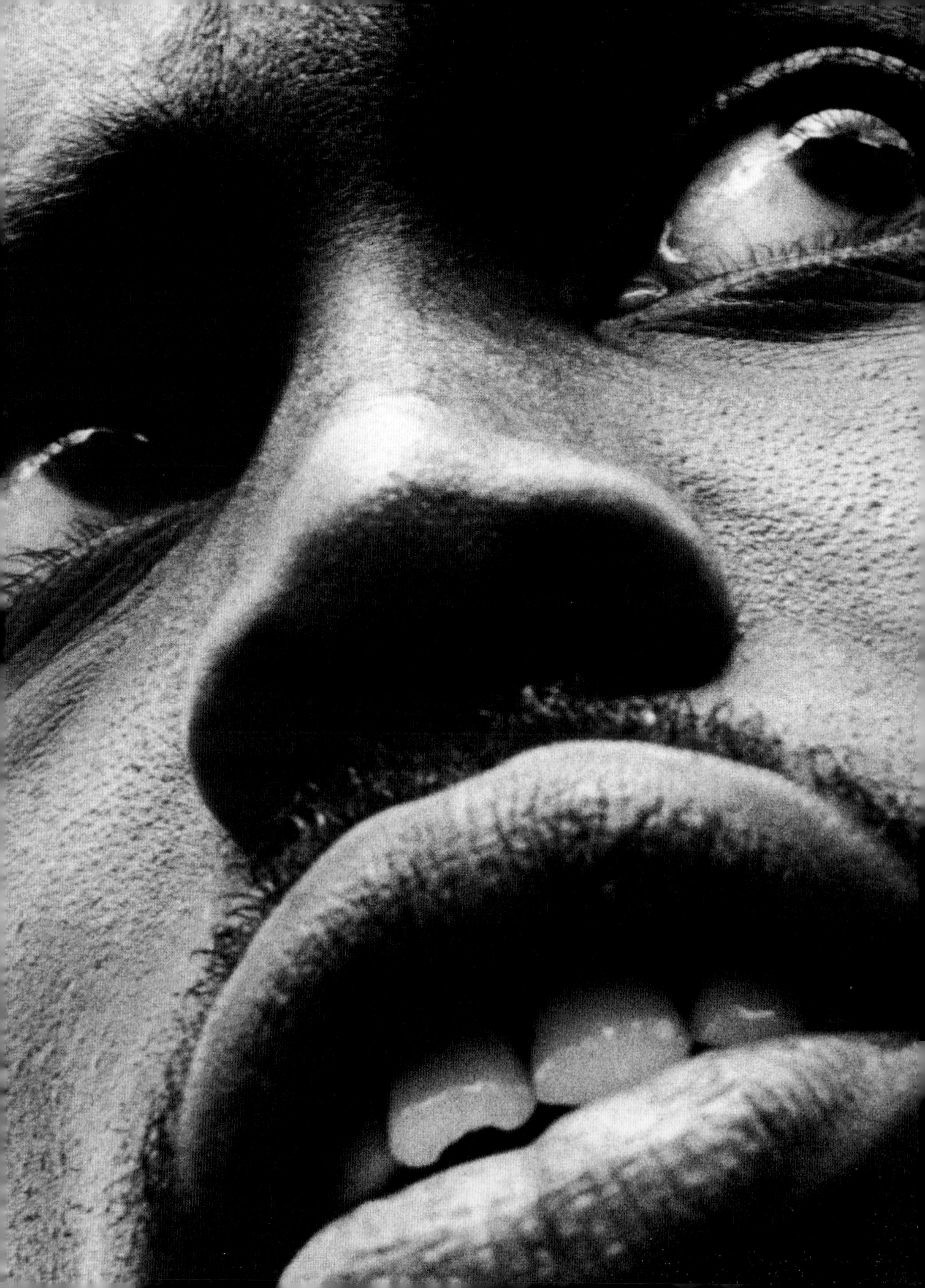

Ghetts on Religion

I'm from a very religious background; my mum, dad and my whole family on both sides are Seventh-Day Adventists. We go church on the Sabbath on a Saturday and I feel like the only people that have kind of strayed from – well, not strayed from because it was still strong – are me and my brother. I've been church every Saturday this year [2016] so far, except for two weeks.

As human beings we have to believe. Well, you don't have to believe, but I just feel like I've had situations in my life where I can see there's a God. I'd be a fuck boy to talk about all this stuff that people think is cool and not say, 'Bruv, you know what, one day this happened to me and I don't believe it was an accident'. I've been like this from time, if you go back to *2000 & Life* you can hear I'm saying certain things on my first CD. When I was in jail as a kid, about seventeen, I got stitched up and they said I caused a riot at Hollesley Bay, which was in Ipswich and they were gonna ship me out. I thought they might send me to Feltham, which would been cool. Instead, they sent me to a very racist jail in Scotland. I got there and stuff was happening – I was fighting and that – but it weren't nothing I couldn't handle. But they had an older side and I was turning eighteen that October. It was August, and I was thinking, 'You see over there it's different, I'm going to have a real problem.' I was holding my own in the younger bit with people my age, but when I used to walk past the older bit, and they used to start, I'd think, 'I can't go over there'. I was praying all the time, like, 'I've got to get out of here', because I was fighting every day, like every single day I'm proper fighting.

I got moved two days before my birthday.

I still had two years left on my sentence and it felt like they told me I was going home [laughs]. They kept saying to me I wouldn't get moved unless I behaved, but I couldn't behave because I didn't have the chance to behave. It was fucked. I just didn't know how to handle it. But then I got moved.

Then another situation; I had something in my house, I'm not gonna say what, but imagine my missus was pregnant [with my daughter] and I had something in my house that I shouldn't have had in my house. So imagine, it's six o'clock in the morning, GRMDaily is outside because I'm getting ready to shoot a video and then I heard boom! My door got kicked off. I was thinking, 'Why the fuck would these man knock my door like that?' I've come to the door to go mad and I just heard, 'Get down, get down!' I thought, 'What have I done?' They said 'Looting,' and I'm cool because I'm thinking, 'They've got the wrong person.' But now you're not cool because they're checking the house. My aunt come and they showed her a picture of the person who obviously was not me and she's like, 'Yeah man, you're cool, you're alright, don't worry.' She's smiling, she's cool but I'm thinking, 'Yeah I'm not cool 'cause I'd rather get shifted for looting right now.' I was praying like, 'God please, I swear if you just… I'll get rid of that and never touch one again.'

They never found it. I didn't know how, because I would have missed this whole… everything.

You know what that taught me? Sometimes when you have certain things around you, or carry certain things, it attracts it. When I was a kid, I'd go places and just attract all this stuff, but now it's calm. I see some younger kids that want to do something to me, maybe, but because I'm older I know how to change a situation. 'Have a good day mate.' People that are my age, their thinking is different. It's much easier at this age. So, yeah, I see directly the results of having faith. I feel like I'm closer to God at this point. I'm just easy and I feel like that young thing of 'Fuck them' and 'Fuck that' and 'Fuck this' has kind of gone. I'm just at ease innit.

Previous page: Ghetts in the local newsagent – Newham, E13
Opposite: Ghetto Gospel – Glen Rd, E13

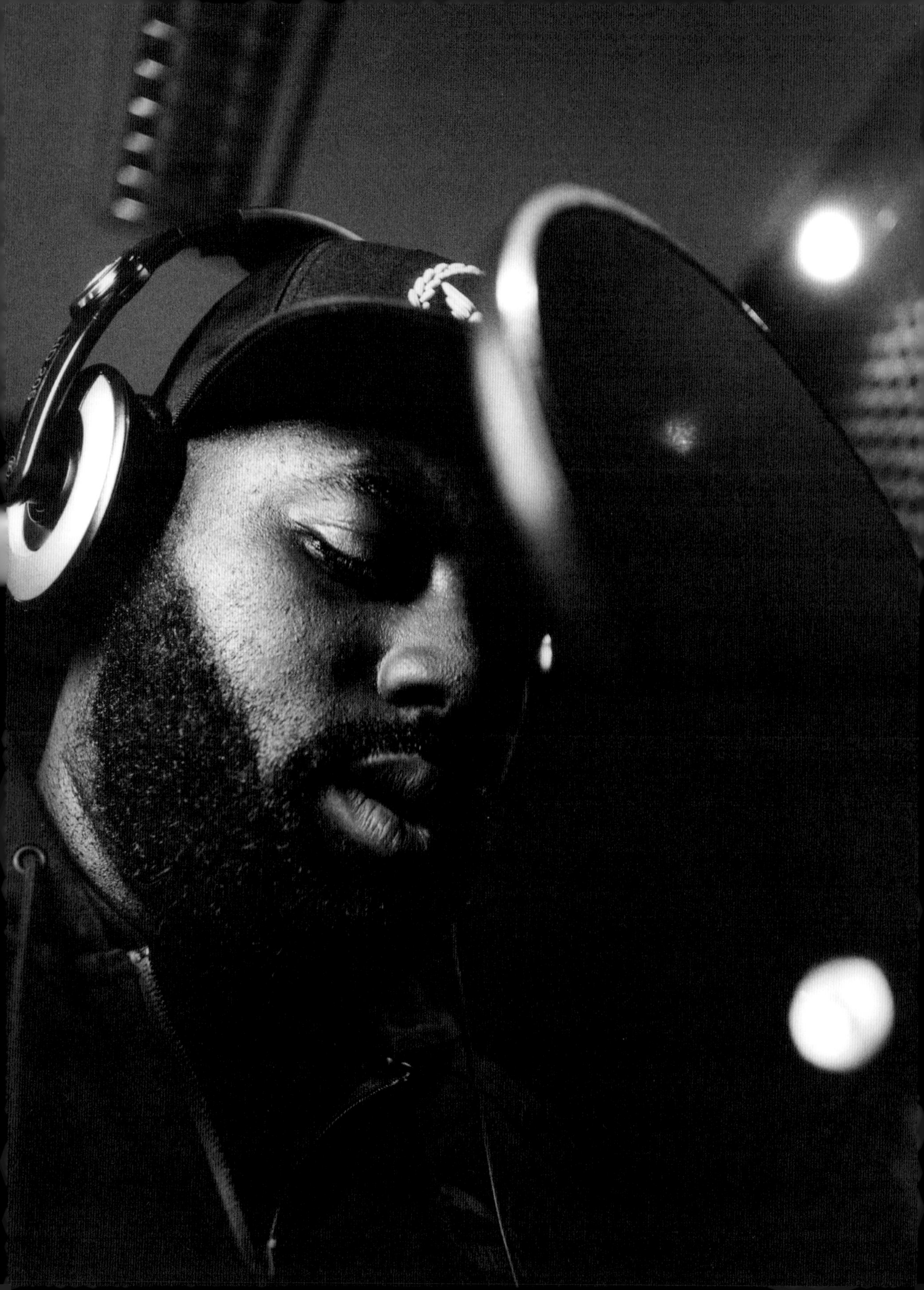

Opposite: P Money in the booth at DaVinChe's Studio – Putney, SW18
Grid L to R: Ghetts lyrics on his iPhone, DaVinChe in the studio, Ice Kid – Northolt, UB5, Griminal in his studio, EN8

Top and Left: Scrufizzer and Maxsta in the studio at Kidbookie's – Lewisham, SE13 Right: Maniac at Cloud 9 Studios – Kings Cross, N1
Opposite: Devlin and Lewi White smoking outside the studio in Stokey – Shelford Place, N16

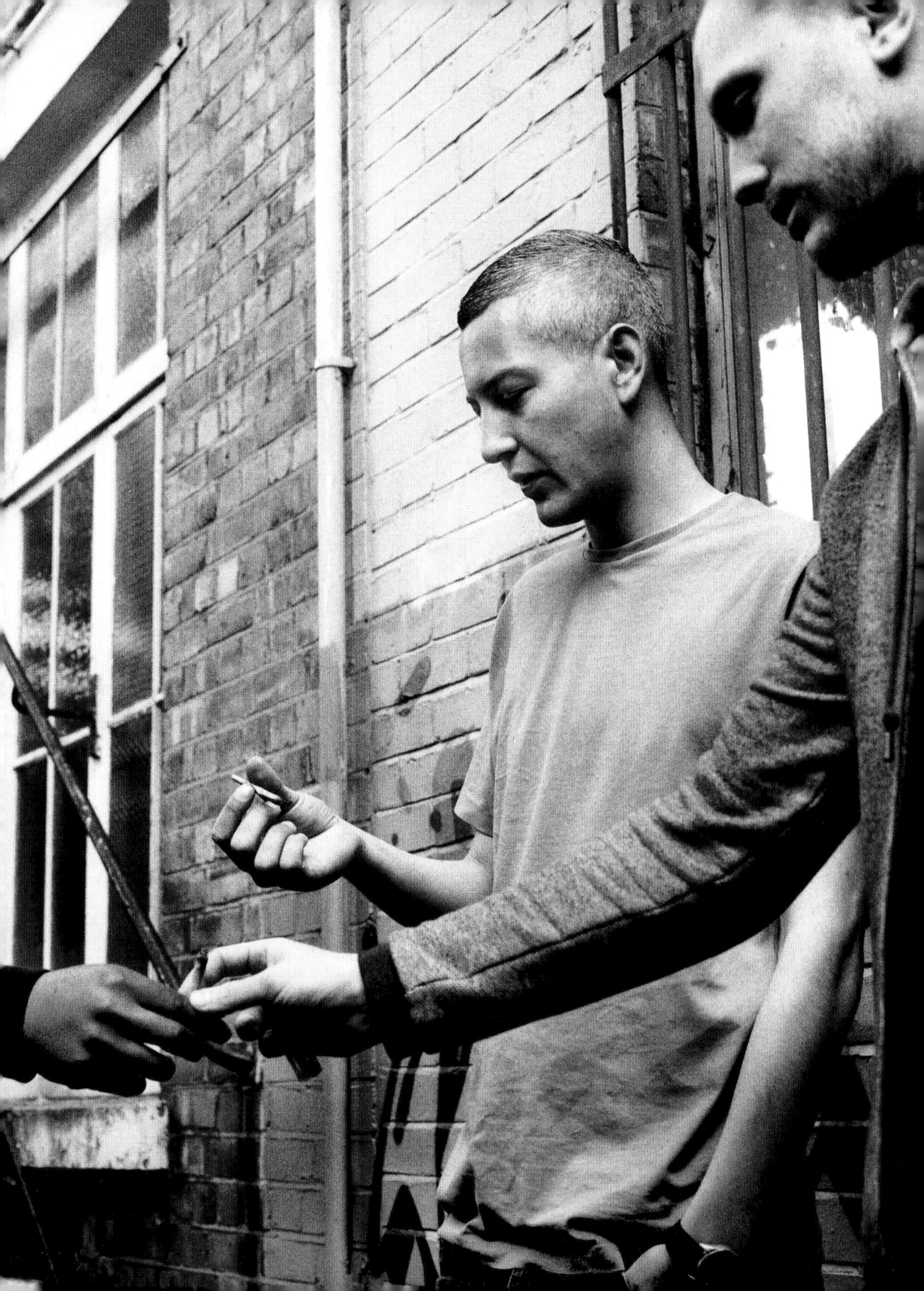

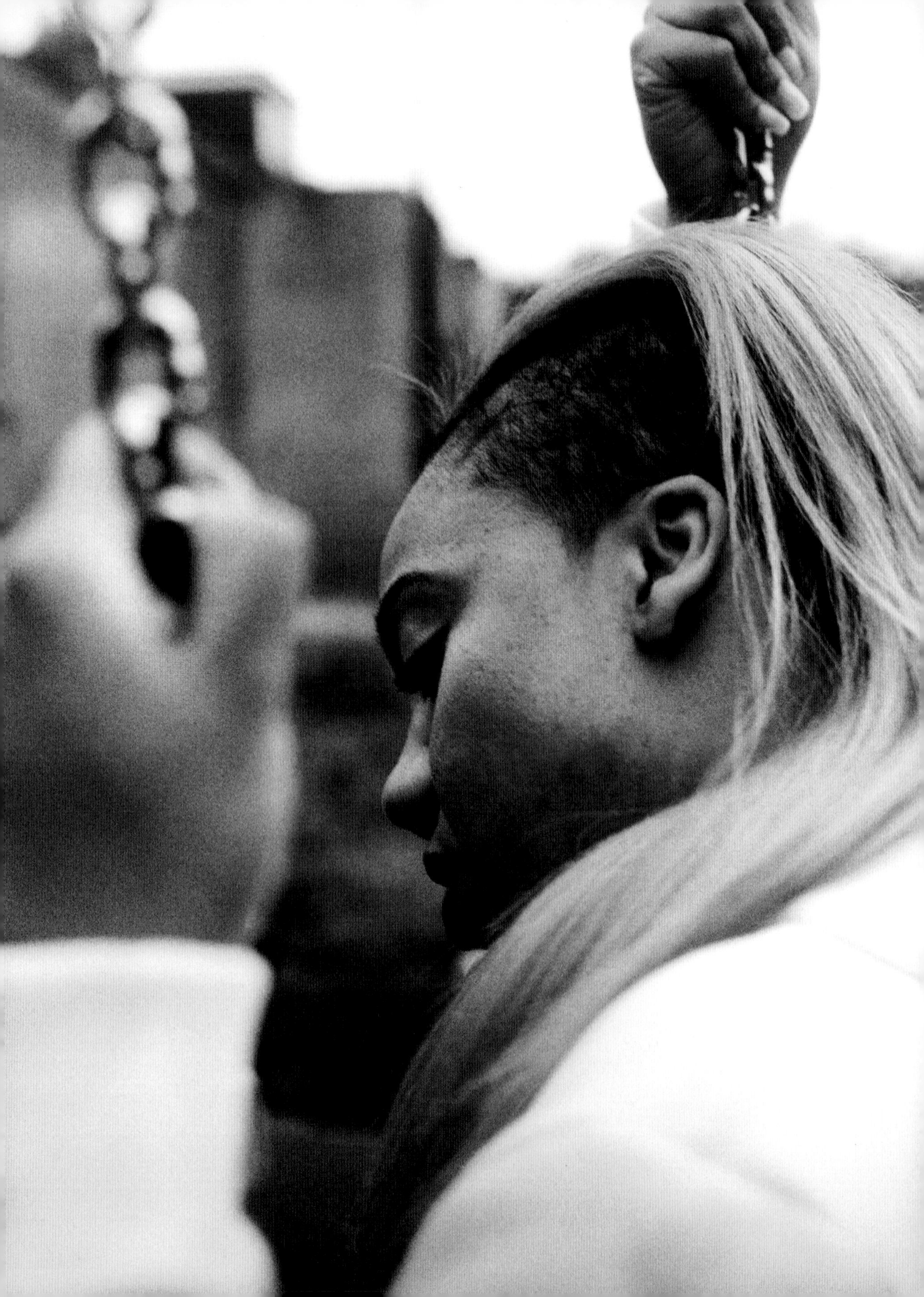

Big up the Unorthodox Daughter

NoLay I'm trying to stand alone, a bit like what Skepta is doing. He's in the scene but he's in his own lane. I'll still make grime, but there's a lot of other stuff I want to make too. It can be quite shallow at times, our scene, I don't feel like there's a lot of reality driven music out there at the moment. I think the grime scene needed 'Netflix and Pills'. I wrote it sat in my front room. I talked about a lot of things, my dad's drug addition, suicide, abuse. My dad's passed now, he died in a mental hospital, but I think it was important for me to talk about his drug habit. Both because I know other people go through it with their parents, but also as a release for myself. Music's an outlet for me, it's pretty much therapy. And crack really devastated our community. When crack came over here, it was just everywhere. I can remember being in raves, at the back, by the speaker box and smelling it. All these young guys, they'd call it 'ting' back then, they'd roll it up in rizla and smoke it.

I also talked about losing my virginity at fourteen to a twenty year old because I feel like a lot of women these days are scared to report molestation or rape or domestic violence. For those people that listen to my music, they can find strength in me coming forward. Women are abused all the time, whether that's rape or mental of physical abuse. The only way to combat that and to make women feel like it's alright to have a voice is through people like me who do have a voice. If you lay yourself bare, it can give people the courage to do the same. If I can tell thousands of people and not give a shit, then they can tell someone, just one person. I don't care what people think of me, to be honest. I don't want to live a lie. My favourite line in the whole song was *You gotta capture the beauty in what is ugly. I swear the art in mistakes remains lovely.* The fact that I put this song out and the content is very ugly, but the beauty that's come from me putting it out, in terms of the reception it's got, the new places that it's taken me, who I'm working with and what I'm doing right now, is very positive. I might fall in a dark hole now and then, but I still do what I need to do. You've got to numb the pain sometimes. Music is an outlet. I find art in honesty.

welcome to the future where even when I'm old I'll still be young forever young and these guys will be forever spun.

NoLAY XXX

HALF BAKED
PAP
ESCAPE
deviation
Dime
DEEJAY LEDISKO
DO NOT SLEEP
SO GREEDY
-VS-
EVERYBODY
SOUND OF DET
SKT

Form 696 basically killed off grime for about half a decade. It stopped grime in its original form taking off by killing the live music.
John McDonnell (Prancehall)

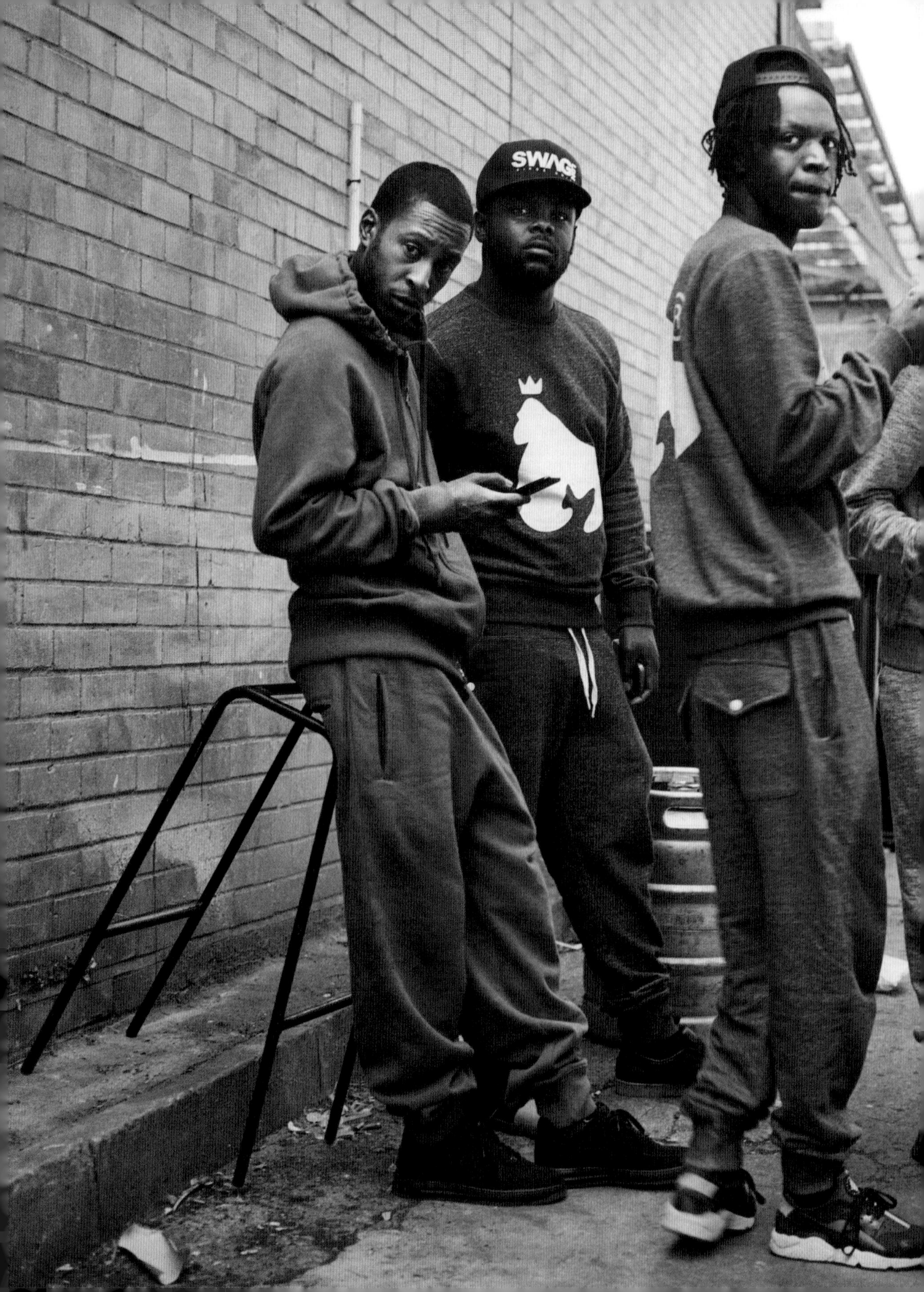
SWAG

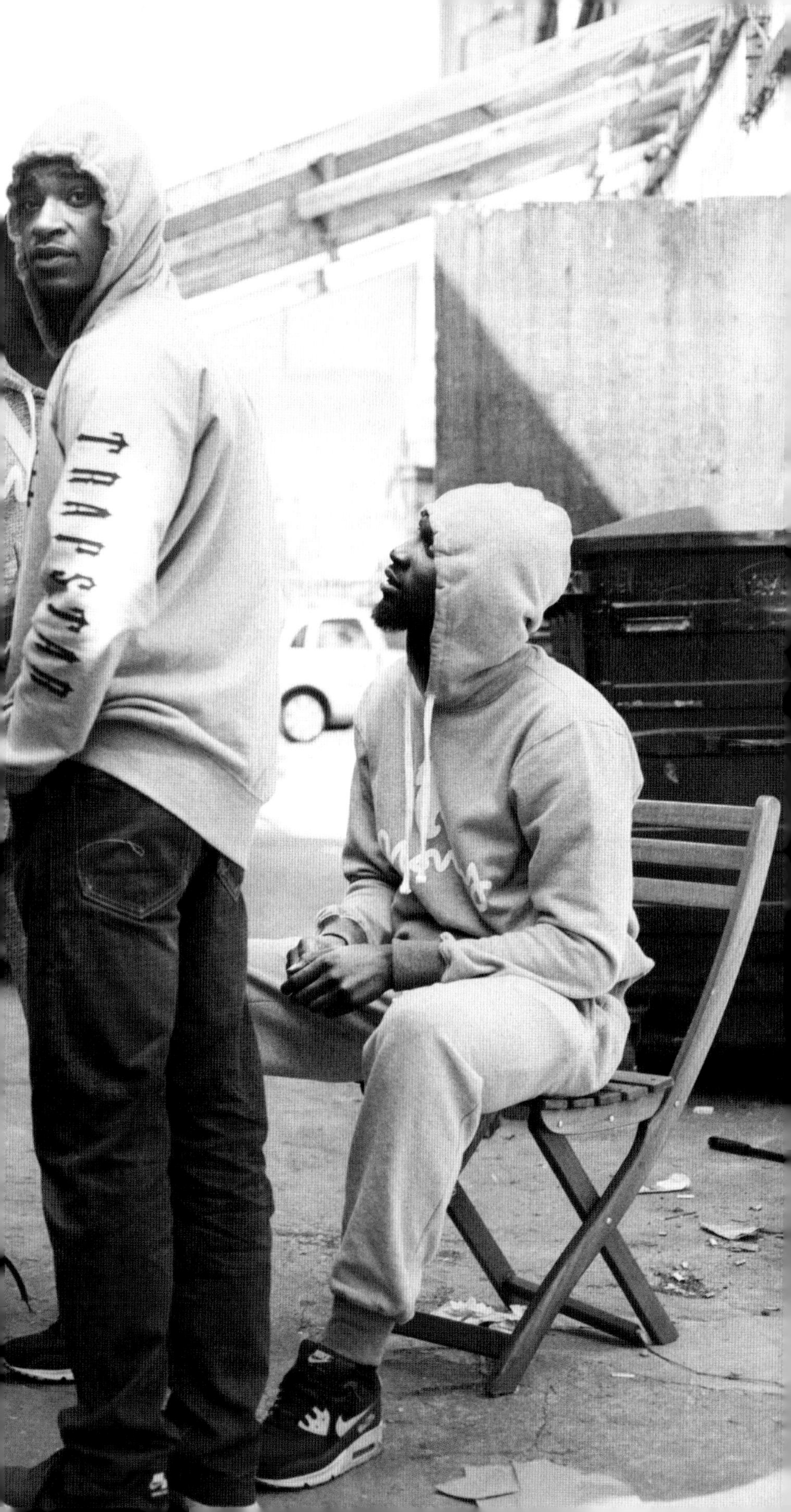
TRAPSTAR

If You're Talking The Hardest, Giggs Better Pop Up In Your Thoughts As An Artist

Krept Giggs, what he done for us, for rap, that has to go down in history, Giggs is my favourite rapper 'cause he's my favourite rapper, but also 'cause of what he did for us rappers. Before him, it was UK hip-hop. Say no more.

Wretch 32 He was the first in-car CD phenomenon the country has ever seen. I know people were listening to tapepacks and radio, but in terms of putting in a mixtape and listening to a rapper – there was a time when you was driving up and down the street and all you could hear coming from every car was Giggs. He had the whole rap game in a chokehold at that point. At that time you might have thought grime was the only option; when you heard and saw Giggs, you saw it was possible to do it that way.

Martin Clark A lot of people said that when certain crews from grime did the commercial thing the first time, that they really lost a lot of the streets. DJs specialists kept listening to grime and thinking it was the thing, but as a grassroots council estate thing, a lot of that audience had gone. I wrote about this a few times. Giggs, he's a genius, he's done his thing and a few other guys who have, arguably, not compromised their sound. But as a mass movement, I've always waited for a real breakout star. If you google 'street gangs wood green' the stuff they listen to is road rap. It's been road rap for five, six, seven years maybe more. Grime isn't blasting out of cars like that. I'm glad that the scene is getting recognition, but it's a non-core audience that are getting into it. The people turning up to Skepta shoots aren't particularly people from Meridian Walk. Maybe I missed it, but I've waited for someone in hip-hop with the identity and the character of someone like Trim, like Ghetts, like Wiley or Dizzee. If all the roads are doing road rap, why haven't more come through? They're implicitly looking to the States for their style and I understand why young black men do that; the success, the energy, the confidence comes from there. The history of great music in London, historically, has been; look to the States, copy it, do it badly, find you own way, build you own genre. That's how garage happened. Road rap always felt very tethered to the States, which never allowed them to be totally distinct. I've waited for someone to break out of that, I was waiting for something to iterate out of that. Giggs has that, but he's an outlier.

Sian Anderson Giggs made it possible for people to not just have to do grime and that was very powerful and I guess still is. Giggs to me is culturally important because whether we like it or not, he's still not allowed to do shows in London. There's still a fight for him; Giggs isn't allowed to do a lot of things despite the fact everyone was behind him. It shows we're still ten steps behind; you can

at the top says no, then it's no. Giggs is the glass ceiling and the prophet. It's proof that we still need to work harder. You can't take away from the fact that he showed man dem everywhere that you can do it. He's important in other ways too; he's constantly on Instagram with his kids, showing people that they're the most important thing to him, his kids and his friends. That's an important lesson to put out there. Giggs is culture personified. Culture personified.

Elf Kid People from my area, I'm from an estate where If you go on to a fourteen year old's phone or ask them if they listen to grime, they'll be like 'What, Section Boyz? 6-7?' Grime has been reinvented, there's a new face for grime. That's their grime, you can't fake that. For them, it's not about the next kid coming from E3 or who is the next sixteen year old kid coming through. When I was fourteen, I listened to Chipmunk, Ice Kid, Griminal, Maverick. But a younger, a fourteen year old kid from my estate, he isn't listening to Elf Kid, Novelist and AJ, he's not. It's youts from outside of London. And that's the truth. And it's crazy. It's mental. I think it's sick, it's meant to be like that. It's changed and change is good. My south London estates, they're not listening to house, they don't know what a festival is, they're not listening to that. 6-7. Section. Krept and Konan, when they first came out, they were popping.

Stormzy I think what it is, is that we all started off doing grime. Even the rappers. We started off doing grime. Something happened, and they all started rapping. Even I started rapping cah I was doing grime. I saw everyone rapping so I thought 'Ok I guess this is what is going on.'

Bonkaz We all knew Krept and Konan since they started, I remember being in school and walking around with an MP3 player listening to Konan doing grime. He was the best in the whole borough, everyone knew that. They used to spit individually – Krept's from Gypsy Hill and Konan's from Thornton Heath – the two areas joined up and since then they've dropped tunes every single year from when they started. They've been consistent for nearly ten years now and that's been something that's influenced all of us lot coming through. Although they rap, we MC, we're all the same crew, we're all friends from the ends. They've inspired all of us from Croydon, definitely.

Little Simz I don't look at it in terms of categories, in terms of labels. I'm just an artist, that's it. I don't like labels, with anything. I'm just not a label person. Even when I'm seeing a guy and he's like, 'So what is this?' It is what it is. Labels are just for other people. In a year's time, I could wanna do an album that is heavily influenced by rock and roll. Then what? I'm a person that likes to learn and likes to grow. I like to be a sponge. With music I'm not scared to take risks or to try new things. Just because I feel like I can. I'm willing to try something and fail at it. I don't mind doing that.

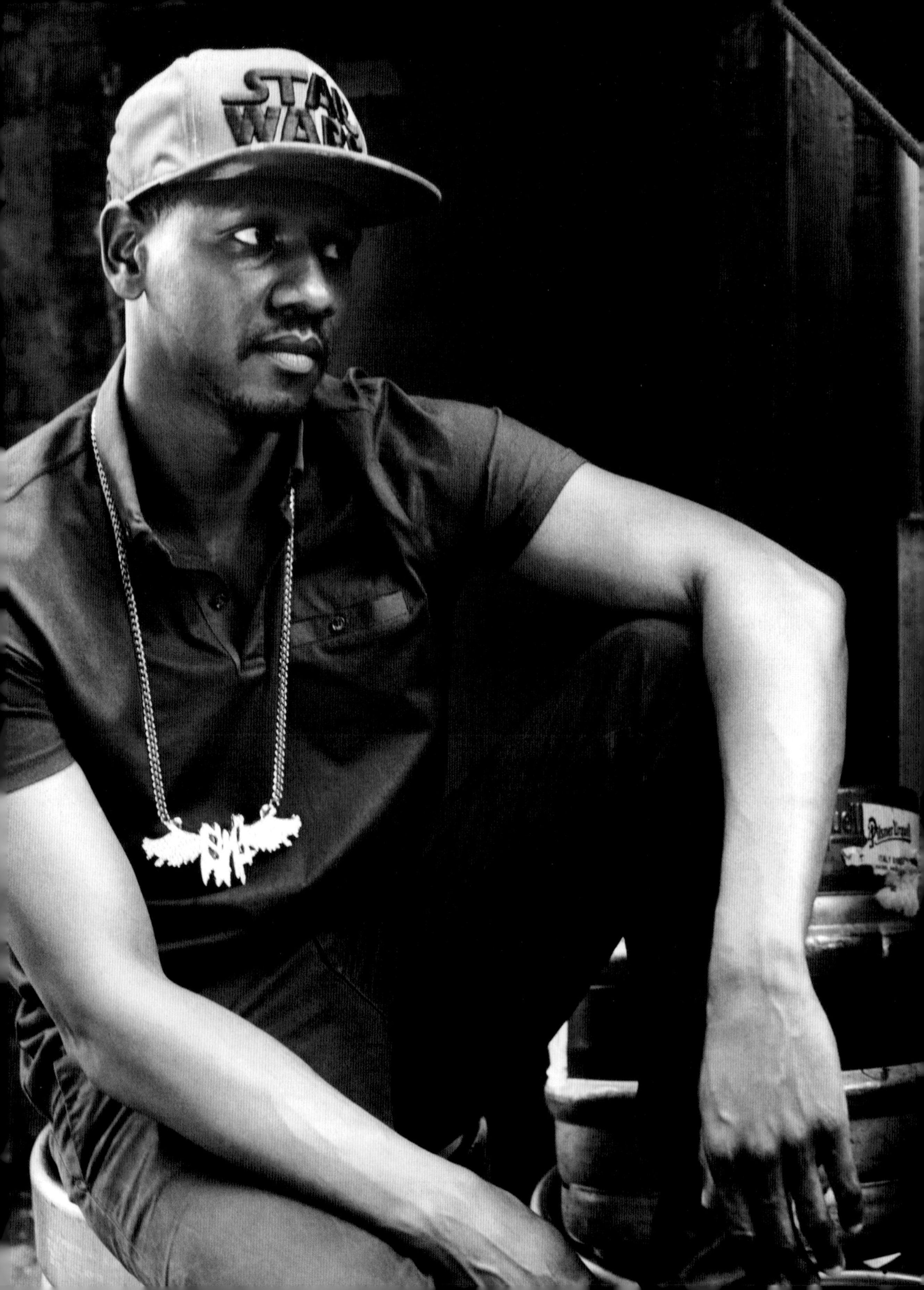

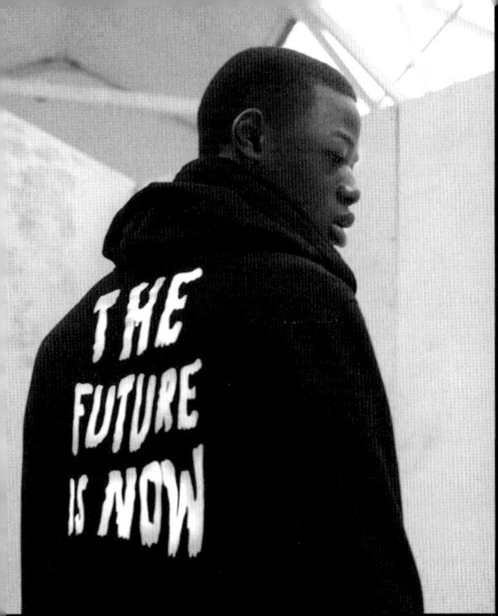
THE FUTURE IS NOW

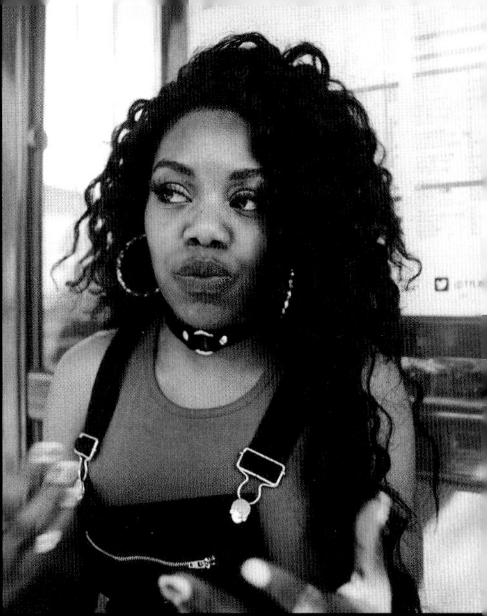

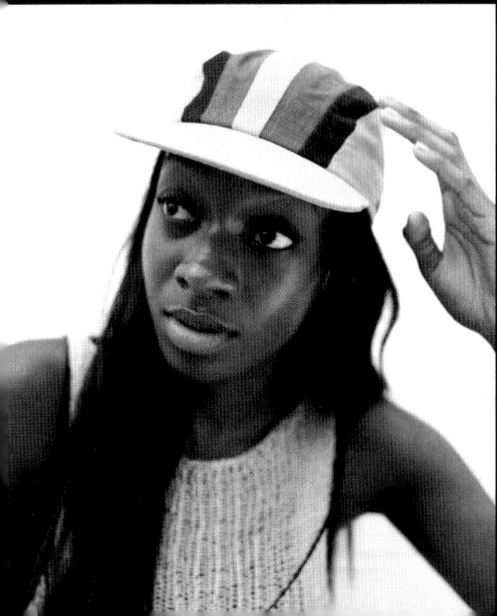

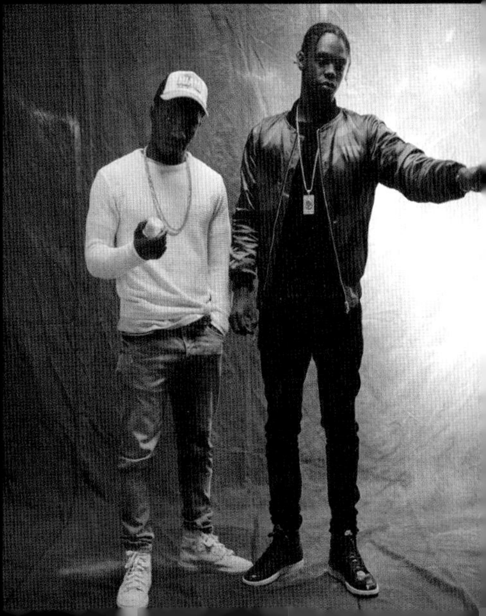

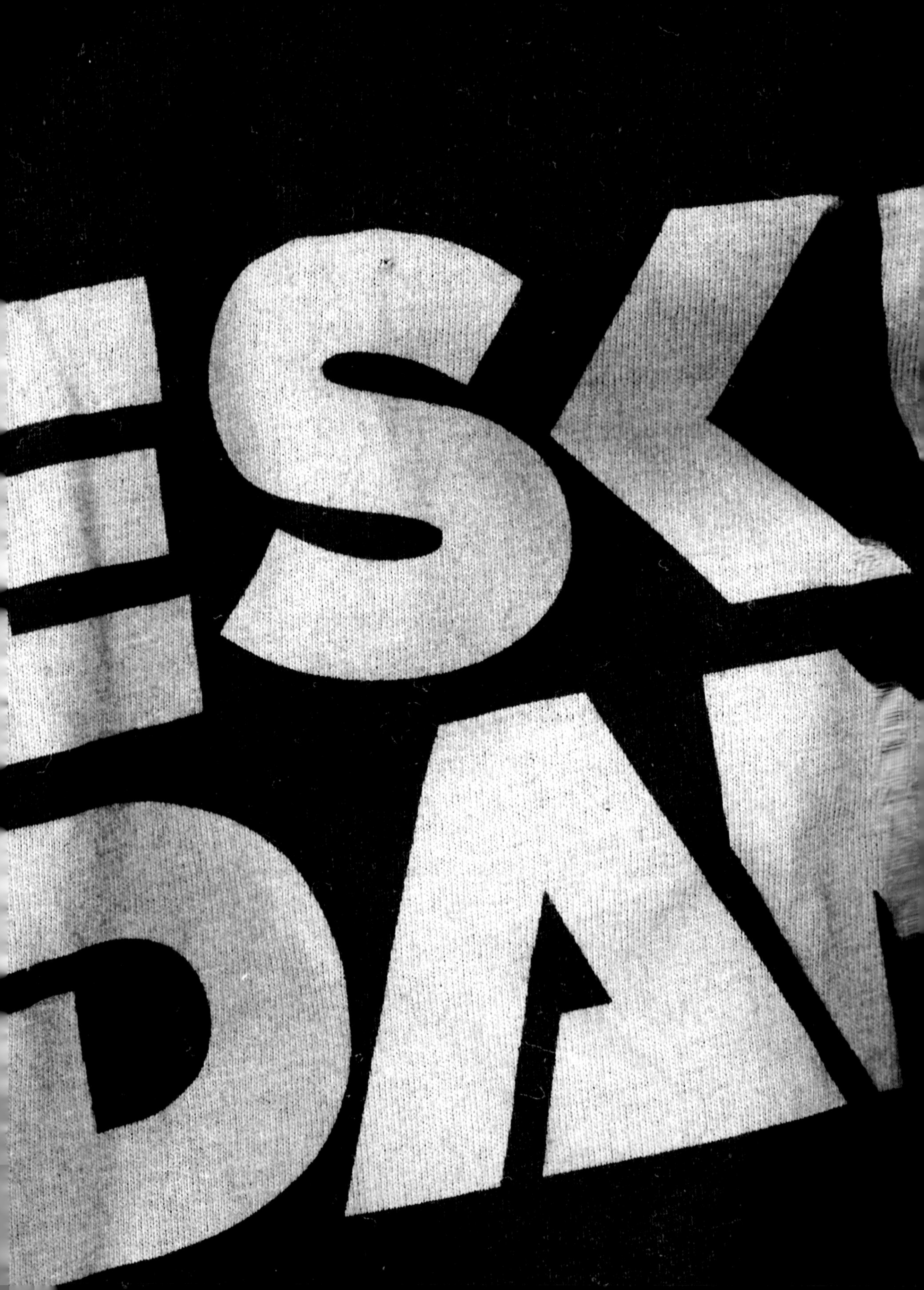

MO
NCE

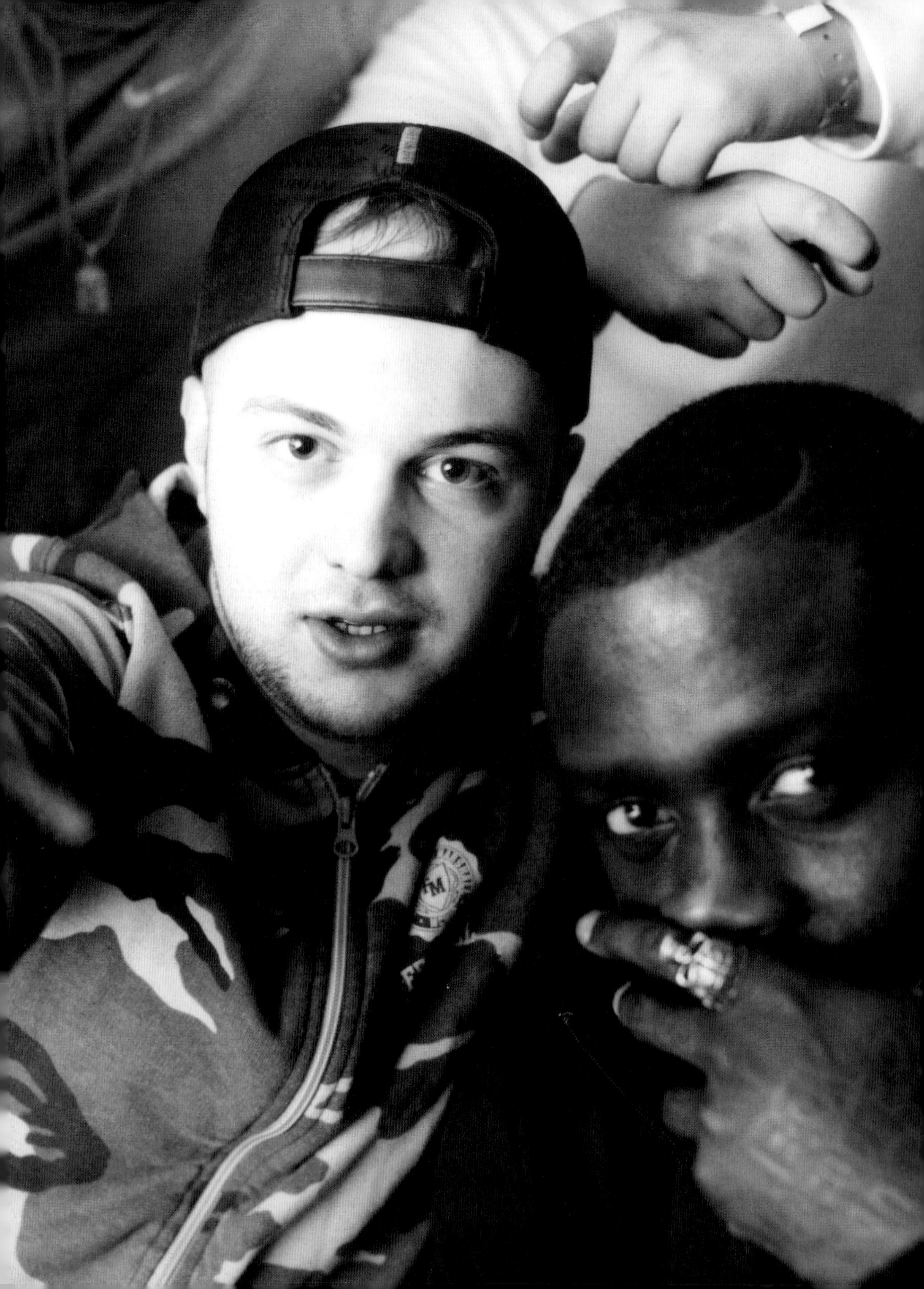

47

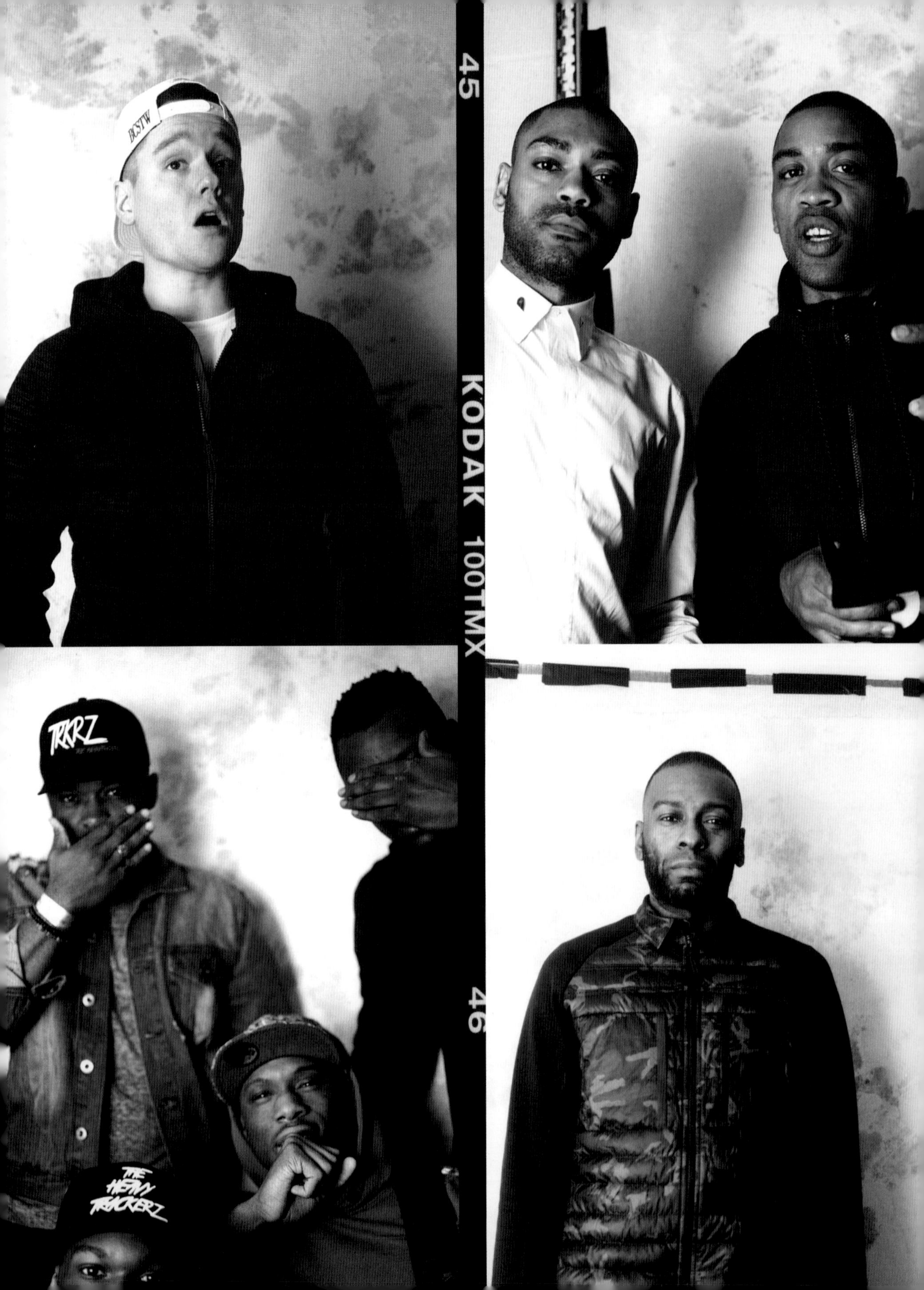

45
KODAK 100TMX
46
TRKRZ
THE HEAVY TRACKERZ

GRIME WILL RULE THE WORLD 2017

CHEEKY (MARCH 2016)

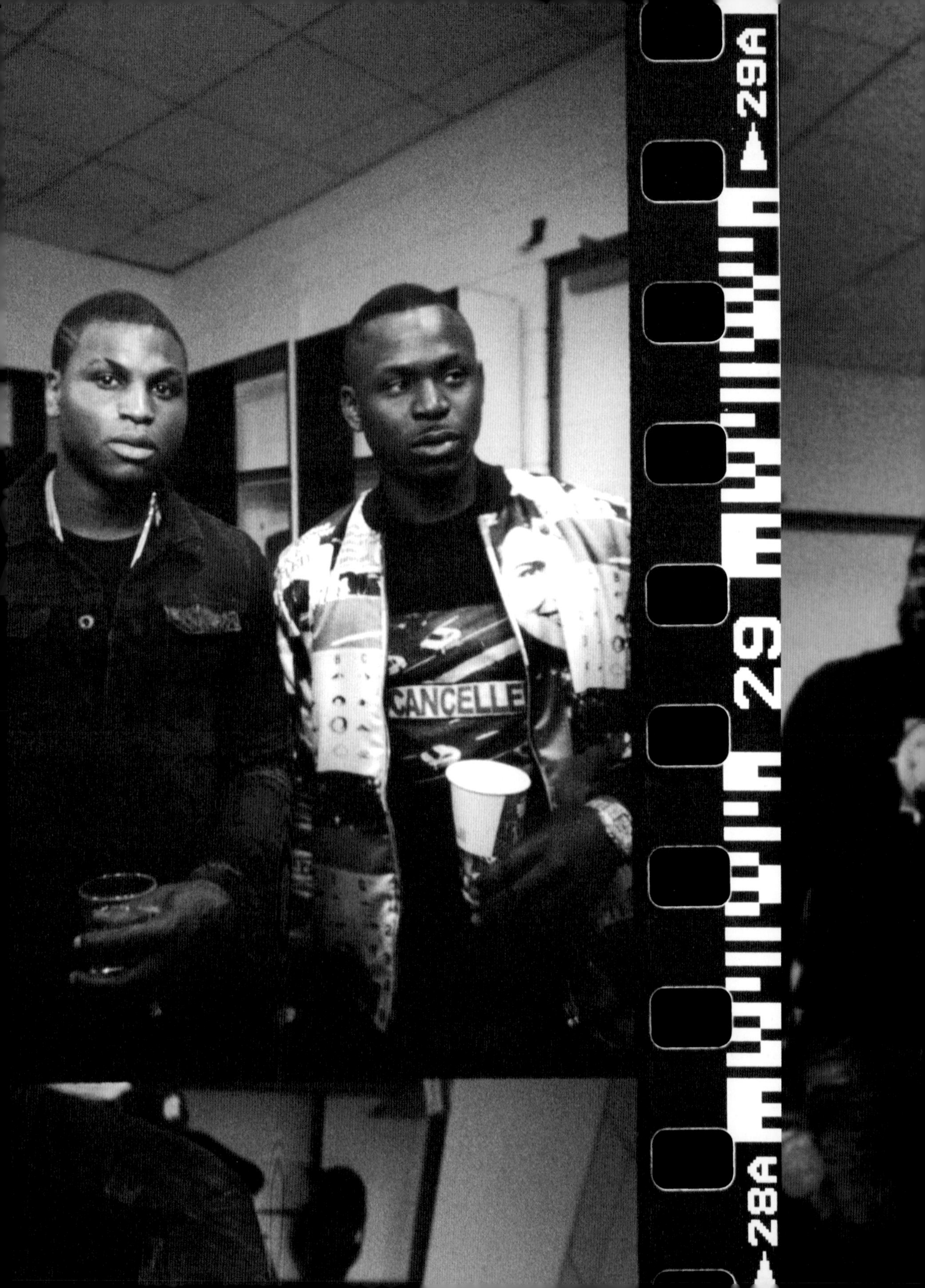
CANCELLE
29A
29
28A

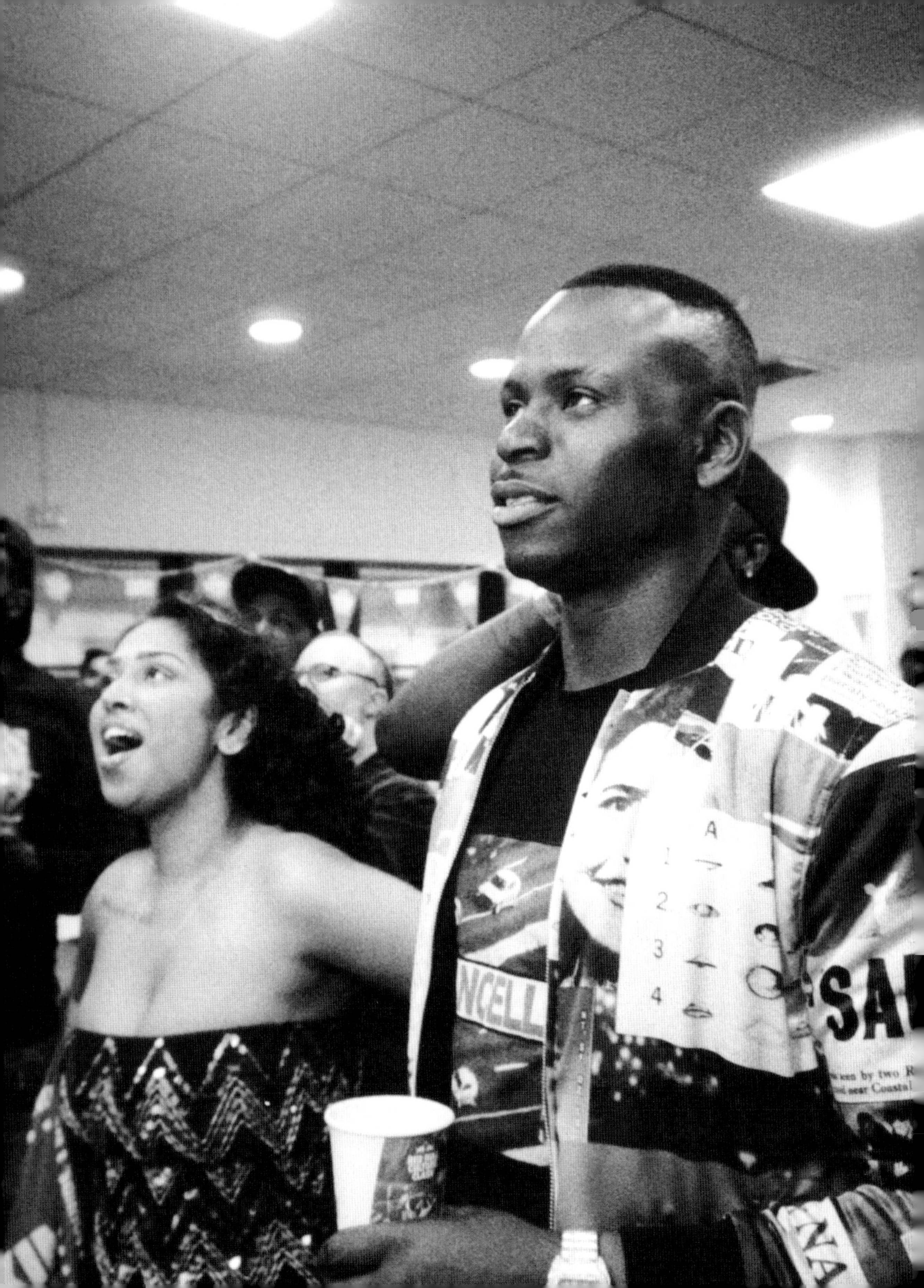

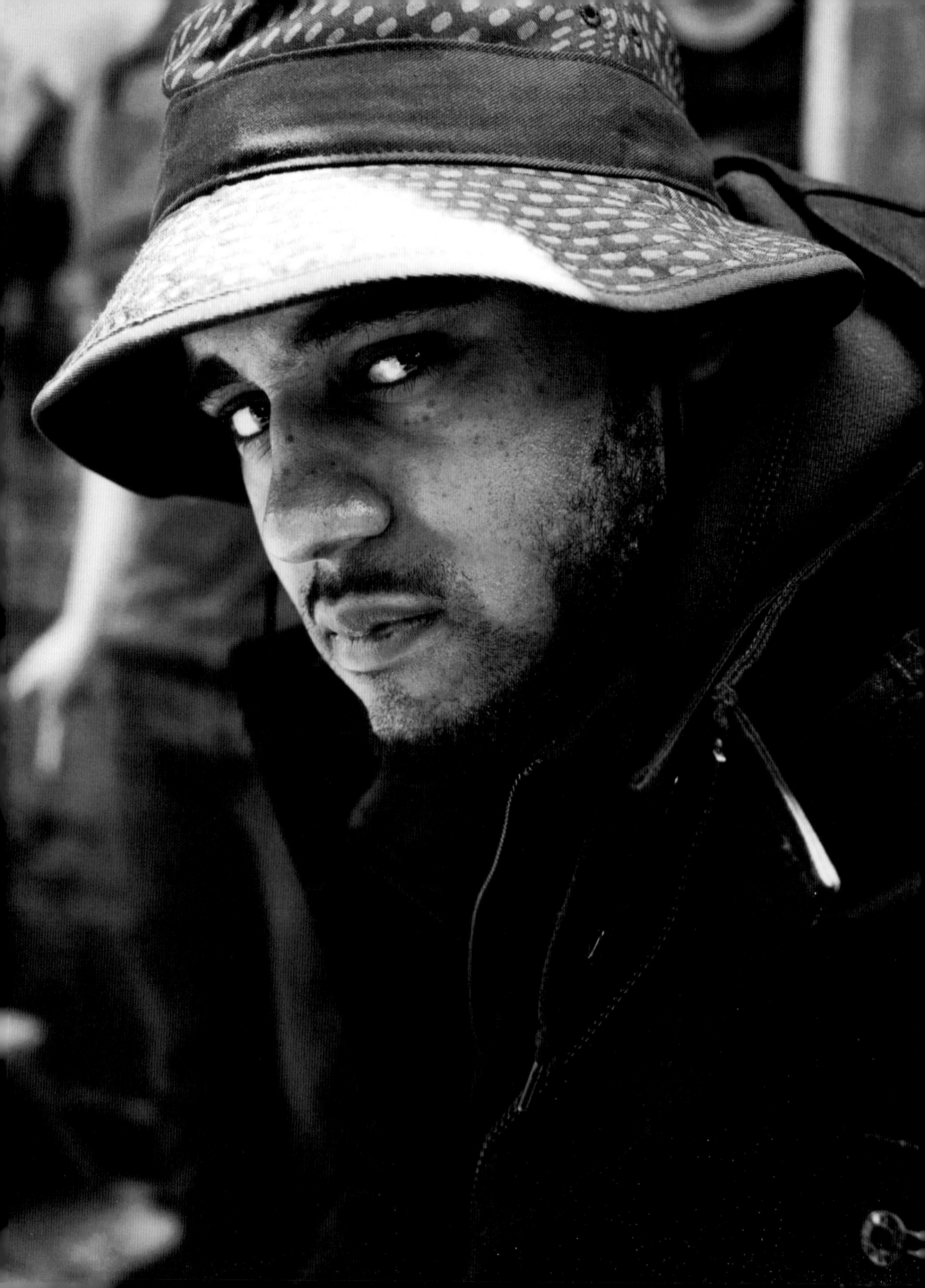

It was broken, it was battered, it was down… but grime was far from out

Skepta It's all well and good to say you're from an estate and to say you're broke. But do you really remember? Do you really feel that passion? Do you really remember when you were spitting not for money? Growing up in an estate and being in a crew have kept me. I can't lose myself. JME's around me, Frisco, Shorty, guys that are hungry, they want to be better than me. Every day. And I want to be better than them. Having that kind of competition in my crew and coming from where I've come from, even if I had ten number ones tomorrow and had a thousand commercial tunes, I'd always be able to make 'That's Not Me'. It's in my soul. 'That's Not Me'? It's like riding a bike, you can't ever forget that. It's lifestyle though, you have to take time sometimes when you're hanging out with bare famous people, you look around you and you can't see one friend that's been there since the beginning. We all go through the same thing, we're all trying to make music and get paid for it as good as it feels working for it.

Wiley Meridian Dan re-energised the scene. 'German Whip'. Yeah, yeah, yeah, it was. It made people look at us again. Imagine that! Dan! He never knew he was gonna do that.

Joseph 'JP' Patterson Grime definitely didn't die. It dozed off a bit, but it never

090616 - 3

died. Meridian Dan doesn't get near enough credit for throwing water on grime's face to wake it up and move forward with his track 'German Whip'. That track was instrumental in this 2.0 phase, if you want to call it that.

Ras Eye (Heavytrackerz) The first beat we made as Heavytrackerz was on Chip, Black the Ripper and Cookie's *Motivation Music Volume 3* mixtape, around 2007. From there, we've just built and I guess we hit hard with 'German Whip'. I think grime came back so much 'cause of the break. Grime wasn't the in thing for a bit, hip-hop took over, but it needed a break. The resurgence was due to new talent and new blood. It's fresh. Nov, Stormzy… although Dan is from the older generation, he's still new to a lot of people. I think the producers like us and Z-Dot helped too.

Wiley Meridian Dan didn't know that he could come up with a hit that would bring it all back. Imagine. Skepta and JME saw and they knew. JME already knew, but Skepta saw and thought, 'Rah, that's not me, bruv!' Trust me, Meridian Dan brought it back. It went back to the roots, that's part of it, but also grime needed new people. It can't just be the same people, it can't 'cause it gets boring. No-one ain't trying to test no-one, and no-one ain't trying to lick no-one out the sky. It can't be like that. There has to be the elite and then whoever's coming up, that's what they're aiming for. You don't want to lick them down, but yeah, your aim is to lick them down, really and get to where they are and surpass them. That's what grime is about, bruv. You've got to battle. It's sad, but you've got to battle and make sure you're doing all you can to get there.

Jammz I think the resurgence or whatever you want to call it is about lots of other things coming together in a sort of perfect storm. There was Culture Clash, Stormzy winning the MOBO, 'German Whip'… all these things bubbling up over time just created what we're seeing today. Before that, for a long time, a lot of MCs were having to do what labels were telling them, as opposed to making the music they wanted to make. Now people are making the music they really believe in.

Mez I don't think anything has changed, I just think the Internet changed everything. People from all over the world are able to see what's going on. As long as everyone individually works and does what they're supposed to do, the scene will be alright.

Jammz I think it's a fashion thing. It goes out and comes back round. One day black trainers are cool and the next day they're not. But people will keep wearing black trainers. A lot of MCs carried on doing grime and now it's benefitting them.

Izzie Gibbs I think for once in quite a long time British people are looking to Britain and not to the US for inspiration and culture.

Blizzard I think we're at a point where the music scene isn't London-centric anymore. Manchester has been smashing it recently but you had my cousin Shifty back in 2009 doing tracks with Wiley, JME, Devlin. The fact that you don't need to be from a certain part of town to get your music heard is what helps. Because of things like *Fire in the Booth* and Target's *Homegrown* show, it's made it more geographically democratic. But I've wanted to MC for a long time, I didn't let the fact I was from Manchester put me off. From thirteen, in school, I knew what I wanted to do. I didn't care about bunsen burners. I just cared about music.

Mumdance There's a new generation of kids brought up on UK music. When I was young, people were listening to Snoop but kids now been bought up on a very UK-centric scene that they can identify with. It helps that people are making good grime. And different sorts too. There's the more 'mainstream' grime and then there's your instrumental Boxed scene, which really helped the music receive the attention it deserved. MC's have realised they don't have to be a washed-out version of an American sound. Everyone was making trap, but what's the point, when we innovated our own sound?

Ghetts In the grime scene, do you know why people bounce back, after they come out of their deals? Because we never had nothing to start with. We never got signed to a label and had everything done for us. I had to phone the video person, I had to phone the plugger... When you get pop people dropped from labels, they don't comeback because they don't know how to. We know how to. You can never keep a grime artist down.

Laura 'Hyperfrank' Brosnan I find it offensive when people say that grime died for a bit. It didn't die at all. These were the moments of Wiley's *Zip Folder* release. Tim and Barry's *Just Jam* ran through 2010 at the Alibi – which were possibly the most intimate moments pre-golden era I've been to – D Double E, Footsie, P Money, Chronik, Darq E Freaker, Faze Miyake, Tempa T, Spooky were all regulars. Logan's Kiss 100 show was popping off weekly with and Mistajam hosted the epic Soundclash on Radio 1 between all UK sounds – basically Culture Clash 2010 – and grime won. It all comes down to the theory of 'If a tree falls in a forest and no one is around to hear it, does it make a sound?' Yes! The way I see it is everyone who wasn't invested from pure love ran off, some glided away out of label manipulation and need to survive financially. The state of grime at one point was that all the artists that developed their craft in the grime scene began making more electronic, house, euro trash and house style music. So we needed a new cycle of MCs and producers to come through and the only way possible for the likes of Novelist, AJ Tracey and Faze Miyake to deliver such authentic styles of grime was to dig back down to the roots of the movement and start again with stronger foundations. Grime 2016 that we know today would not be without those dark deep rooted community moments. It was a struggle, to be yourself and be heard, there was so much pressure and barriers to put on nights, to be played on mainstream and even pirate radio and document what was happening – which is why GRM Daily and SB.TV are so integral to our set up now.

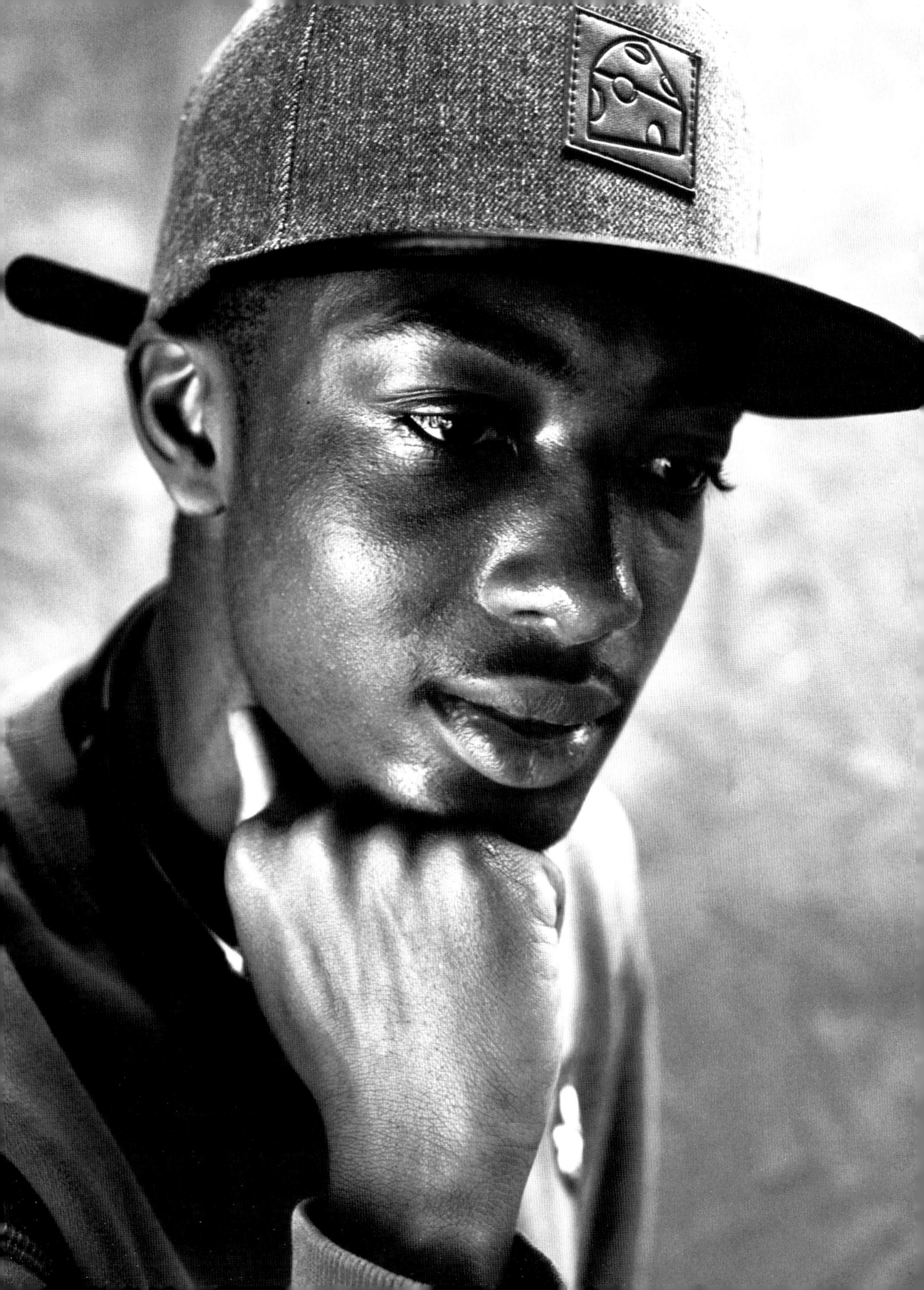

Go On, Go On Then, Draw For The Tool

Wiley A main song for me was 'Shutdown', 'cause 'Shutdown' reminded me of youngers. When I was younger, the youngers then, their flow was duh-duh, dud-da-duh-da-duh-duh. So when I heard, *Shutdown, dud-da-duh-da-duh-duh Shutdown*, I thought, that's a youngers flow. He knows it, obviously, Skepta. It's their time bruv, the youngers. Smart.

Jammer We decided to bring back *Lord of the Mics III* in December 2011. Wiley called me and said, 'Yes, you've done it'. A whole breath of fresh air came through, new talent. Then Wiley bought back Eskimo Dance at Proud in January 2012. That was the rebirth of the scene. The final topping on the cake was when Skepta, who was still doing stuff with 3-Beat, because he had power and pull on the young male, and people in general, I felt if he done a grime track, at that time, it would set everything back up. So I called him and he said he had this lyric, he spat it in the car, 'That's Not Me'. He said, 'I need to get your old keyboard.'

Skepta I was at Paris Fashion Week and I was in this club, listening to what was being played and thinking about taking it back to the old sound. I was sitting in the corner of the club, on my own, just recording the rave onto my phone. I recorded seven minutes of the different tunes the DJ was playing and when I came home I listened to it over and over. I thought, 'What grime song would work in there, but also sound fresh and different next to these other tunes?' I had the beat in my head, I knew what I wanted it to sound like. I wanted a proper old-skool sound, I wanted to take it back to all the old grime songs, but I wanted to do it properly. So I phoned Jammer and I asked him, 'Where's that keyboard you used to use back in the day?'

Jammer This is the Korg Trinity that everyone recorded on; I did everything on there, 'Destruction VIP', 'Take U Out', Wiley, Skepta, we all used that keyboard. But I didn't have it at the time; one of the kids from the estate had taken it a few years back to use it.

Skepta I'm like, 'What! Phone the guy.'

Jammer So I called him, 'Have you got that keyboard still?' He said, 'I knew this day was coming,' [laughs].

Skepta So now the guy has given it to someone else or whatever, so we had to drive around the houses, but finally I got it. This keyboard is so heavy 'cause it's got a million songs on it. I turned it on and it's got all the grime sounds on it. All the early Jammer, Wiley sounds, they're all there. All the old grime was made on that keyboard. All of it.

Jammer He put the rest of the melodies of 'That's Not Me', on the keyboard. Then he done that video, in the old hat, in the style of *Risky Roadz* and it just bought it all back. *Lord of the Mics*, Eskimo Dance and then 'That's Not Me' in 2014. It was a kaboom to everybody's head. It all made sense now; this is what everyone should be doing. The MCs started coming Eskimo Dance, and getting the passion back. They see a whole new audience was coming. Imagine seeing a 90% black crowd, goon rave, to Proud2, 70% middle-class white students. So you can see it's happening and it's not old fans, it's new life. That was the rotation, that was the rebirth.

Skepta It's funny that by trying to be as grimy as possible, you end up seeing commercial success. I tried to be as taboo as possible on 'That's Not Me' 'cause it was just for the grime fans – but mainstream radio played it. Nick Grimshaw, Fearne Cotton played 'sket' on the radio, it's mad [laughs]. I saw then that murking and keeping it grimy is what I should do. I'm not trying to live in the past though; I'm doing yesterday in HD.

Chip If we're honest, the songs that got us into that music, you can name them – 'Eskimo', 'I Can C U'. The energy is real again. Now I do what the rass I want.

The keyboard in Jammer's Basement – Leytonstone, E11

Novelist Growing up in Lewisham was mad. Good and bad, man. The good is that it teaches you how to understand more than what school teaches you. I was allowed out of my house a lot so I know my whole hood and I get along with everyone. The summer I left school was a mad summer. My bredrin was linking one girl called Whitney and we used to go to her house sometimes in Forest Hill, at the top of the hill. It looks like it's LA; they've got palm trees in the gardens. It was nice. And the man dem would link up there and just watch the sunset and that and it was just good. I remember we was just talking about life one time and talking about all the things we wanted to do in life. Like, that's never gonna happen again because the warfare that's going on has hit the younger generation, so you can't just walk around anywhere. You can't move the way we used to move. Everyone's got straps now and there's beef and different dynamics.

Bonkaz Thornton Heath's where I grew up with like everyone basically; Stormzy, Krept and Konan, Section Boyz... Everyone just grew up in this area and we were all friends, just playing out. We was all like one gang or crew, but it was separated into friendship groups. Krept and Konan had a group of friends, Stormzy got his group, Section got their group, I got my group of friends. But outside of that, we were all just one big group of friends.

Blakie (The Square) I started making music years ago. There used to be something that came around in the ends, Rolling Sounds, like a bus that used to come around [Lewisham]. This is like 2010 times, I used to go on the bus and make music there. The thing is, I love music. Before I was doing music, I was doing music [laughs] if that even makes sense. Before I even did music, I used to freestyle and after that I started spraying bars. I used to be into bashment; my background is Caribbean, a lot of dancehall, a lot of bashment and the rhythms between grime and bashment are quite similar. Grime comes from that culture, 100%.

Novelist I was in school, spitting bars when I was about eight. Around that time, that's when I first put my hands on music software and started making beats with my uncle. That was good 'cause it eased me into caring about things. That's when all the DVDs was coming out, 2006, 2005, 2004, *Lord of the Decks* and all the pirate radios my olders were listening to, that's why I'm grime influenced.

Bonkaz I grew up listening to American rap 'cause that was what my older sister listened to. But I remember everyone was talking about this grime thing in school. This was around Year Seven, I was about eleven, twelve years old. I kind of felt left out, I didn't know what they talking about and then they told me about Deja Vu. I tuned in to this set, I think it was Roll Deep, back-to-back with N.A.S.T.Y. It lasted about an hour and I taped it and listened to it over and over until I memorised it. It was the first thing I'd heard that sounded like me; the same slang words that I used, the same accent. Wiley, Tinchy Stryder, when his voice was like super high, God's Gift, Jamakabi, Jammer... I think what I loved was that, with sets, you never knew what was coming next. You can listen to normal radio and hear ten songs you've already heard; with Deja, you didn't know who was going to come in next. When someone sick comes in, it's just a mad feeling. You just get so gassed.

Bonkaz I guess grime saved me in a way. It's the first time people have been proud of me for something. No-one's ever really had good expectations of me, teachers or anyone. I was really disruptive, argumentative at school – I was always trying to be funny. When the teacher told me off it was an opportunity to be even funnier. The education was secondary to me. I was all about having fun and making people laugh. So people looking at me with expectation, good ones, that kind of took some getting used to. I found it a bit weird at first, when people were wanting to speak to me, and not moan at me. I remember times sat in my room with no money in the summer and everyone's out doing stuff and I couldn't go nowhere. I remember sitting there and it would get to like 9pm and I'd be like, 'Shit, no-one's phoned me all day, to see what I'm doing 'cause they know that I ain't got no money.' Then I just started really going hard with music and I had to cancel my iPhone and get a little Nokia, 'cause my phone wouldn't stop ringing. It's a weird transition, but it's a cool problem to have, in a way.

PK (YGG) It's more spraying bars really. We've got bars for hours, days, years… I grew up on grime so I just wanted to do what they, the first MCs, were doing. We're a new generation and it's more structured now and everything, so boom, it's like, alright cool, lets just spray bars. And that's what we do; vibes. Everything we say is just jokes, vibes. There's aggressive lyrics too, but that's the combination.

Mumdance I think the secret to our creativity is that the UK is a melting pot of culture. As cheesy as that sounds, there's so many pockets and it all cross-pollinates. People aren't repelled by it, they're excited by it. The lexicon of music is about pushing it forward; it's ingrained in us as a culture, as a country.

AJ Tracey I think we're just different, innit. I've not heard anyone like PK, ever. He's actually his own guy. With me, the way my content is and the type of instrumentals I pick, no one else is like me.

PK It's the clarity as well. People know word for word what we're saying

Lyrical Strally (YGG) We've got a lot of ambition. We want to rob everything from grime that we can. We are the truth.

PK The justice.

Saint (YGG) The Grime Justice League! There's a lot of things that aren't going right in grime, and we're going to correct it.

PK Some people's pedestals are a bit shaky. If you haven't got the right balance, we'll kick you off. Watch out, we're about.

Producers grid, L to R: Mikey J, Stanza, Z Dot, Mumdance
Opposite: Rude Kid – Relentless studios, WC2H

Novelist I want to be influential. I'm mad on this anti-governmental shit. Fuck feds. I'm on all of that. But at the same time, I want to teach people how to govern your money. Know what's going on in the world. It's not about Ps, it's about happiness.

John McDonnell (Prancehall) I honestly don't think grime is any better. It's maybe worse even. I think what's changed is some of the kids who were listening to grime in 2002/3 are now old enough to start record labels and have managed to pick up jobs in the media or on the radio and are pushing the music they grew up listening to. I think it's important that grime stays lo-fi. Look at all the success Stormzy has had with those one-take YouTube video freestyles. Fans don't want million-pound videos, they want something they can relate to. That's always been a major part of the success of grime.

AJ Tracey I think Skepta and them man have opened the door of money but not having to change yourself. You can make money from the sound. So I think what we're hoping to do is establish it fully. Like, bang, on iTunes 'grime' is the category, the genre. Not 'dance slash electronic' but *grime*.

Next page: Preditah being photographed for Selfridge's Shakespeare reCITED zine by P+F – Camden, NW1

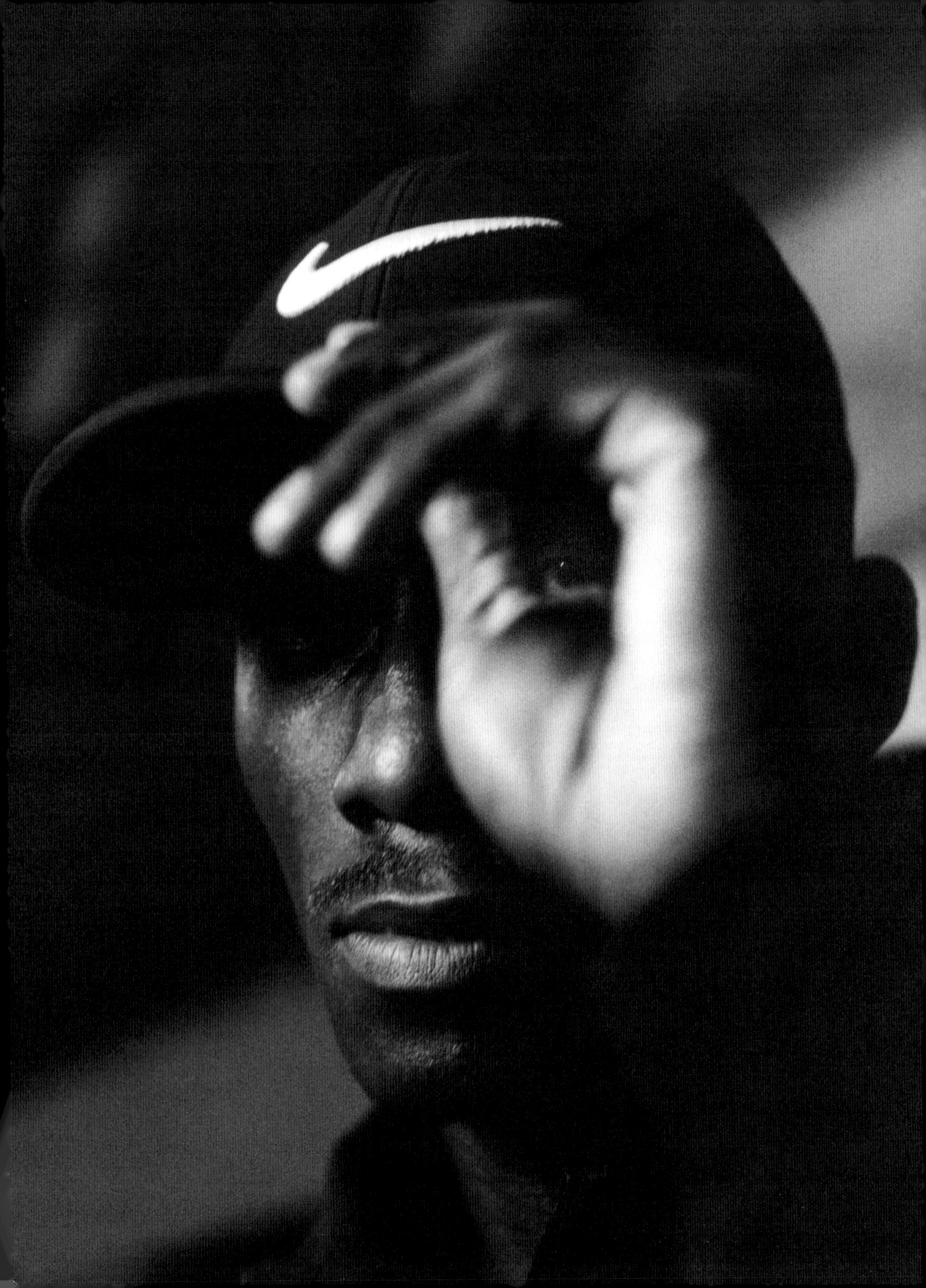

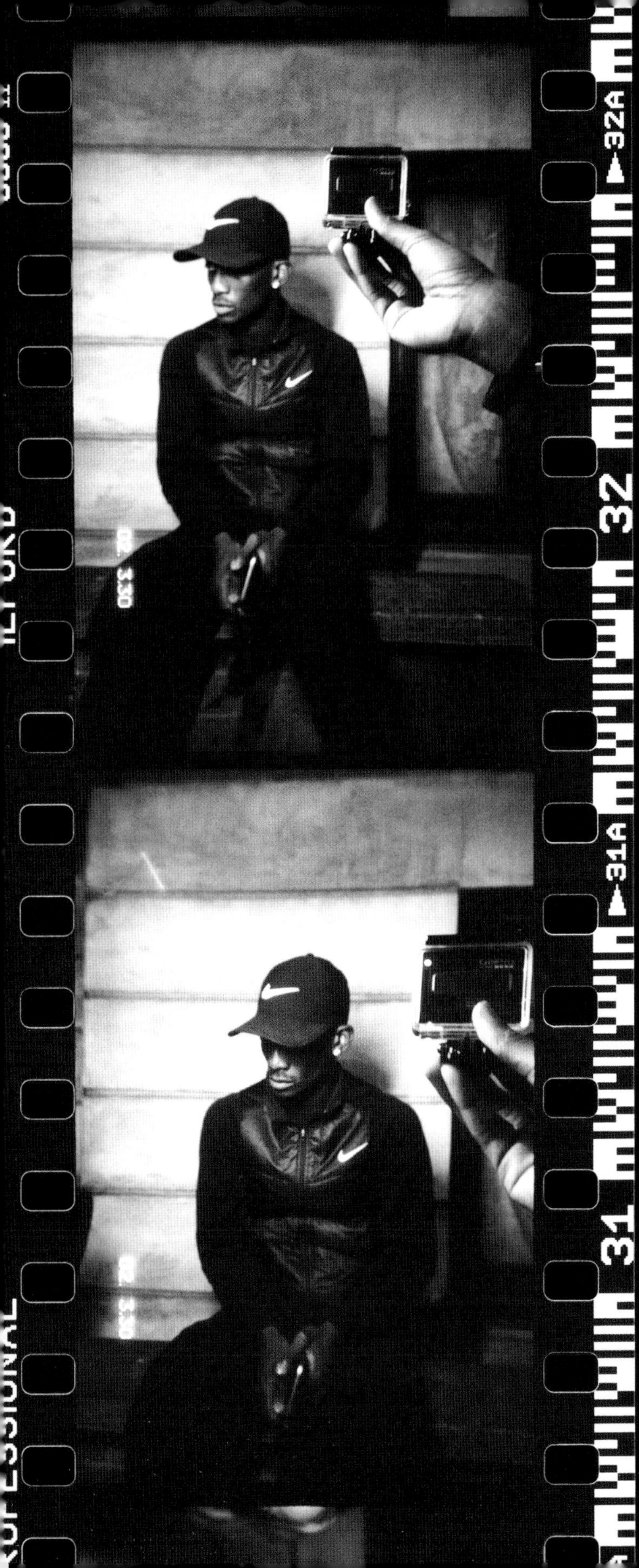
32A
32
31A
31

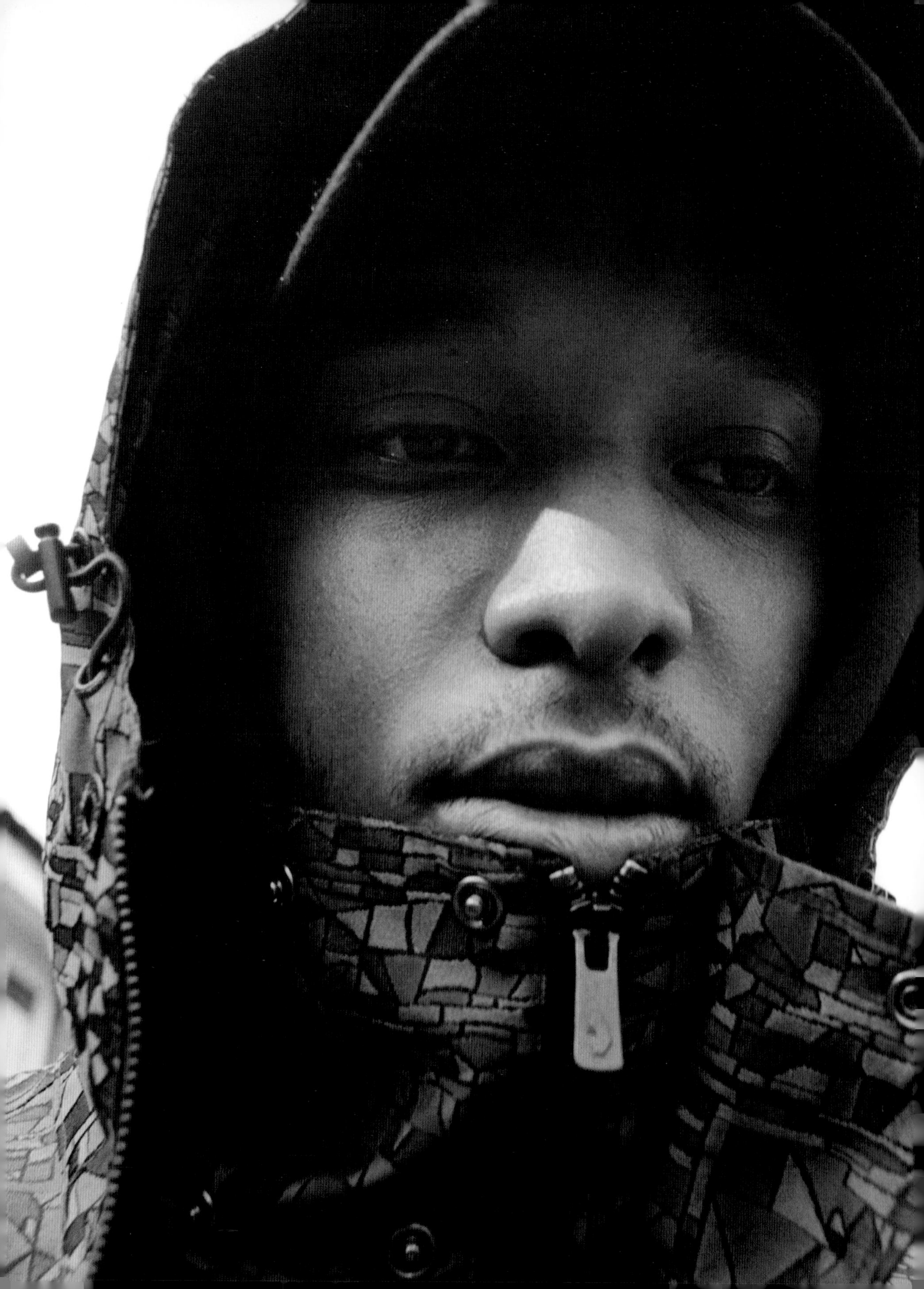

Bonkaz & Stormzy on MCing

Stormzy Year Seven, when I first started secondary school, that's when I got into grime. That was the era of Sony Ericsson Walkman phones and little Nokia teardrops, Bluetooth. It's so mad 'cause back then Krept & Konan was doing grime. They had a little group called Gipset and they're from my area, Thornton Heath. So we used to listen to Krept and Konan a lot. We used to send our songs around by Bluetooth. It's mad 'cause back then I don't remember listening to rap. I couldn't even remember the rappers at the time. They were there but you'd tune into Logan Sama and hear *The War Report* or *Lord of the Mics* and *Practice Hours*. Going back to it [from rap] was so easy because that's all I've ever really known; D Double, Wiley, all of them, the whole scene. A lot of people say they grew up on Mobb Deep and Tupac and Biggie. I don't know about anyone else, but I grew up on Lethal, Bruza, D Double E, Flirta D. That's who I grew up on. I think sometimes they didn't realise that, the grime scene. Our generation didn't listen to US hip-hop, we listened to you lot. You lot are our Tupac and our Biggie. That's why when I'm around them, it's so mad.

Bonkaz I always wanted to be the best at something in school; I was never the fastest or the strongest or the best but I clocked that I could spit. Between me and my friends, I was the one that could spit. I started out blagging it, I never had no bars, I just would freestyle and that's why I can freestyle now, 'cause that's how I started. I pretended that I had bars. I just blagged it. I used to spit other people's bars as well [laughs]. There was olders in the ends who had bars from years ago and I'd go to somewhere far, somewhere out of the ends to like my friend's cousin's house, and I'd spit like a Krept bar! They'd be like, 'You're sick, you're sick!' [laughs].

Stormzy We all started off doing grime, even the rappers [like Krept & Konan]. Something happened and they all started rapping. Even I started rapping cah I was doing grime, but I saw everyone rapping so I thought, 'Ok I guess this is what is going on.'

Bonkaz I definitely started off MCing and doing grime and I drifted towards rap because I started to write bars where I could take my time and make a point, tell a story. I liked that kind of format, so from about seventeen to eighteen, I was just rapping. I wasn't even spitting on grime beats, my soul was with rap songs and slower tempos 'cause I felt like I had stories. I think only some people can master the art of telling stories on grime. Dizzee and Kano were great at that. With me, grime just gets me too gassed, so I can't slow down and tell you a story. I'm just going in.

Stormzy It took me time to adjust 'cause going from fast flows [in grime] to breaking it down [for rap], I was rubbish. I had to learn how to rap 'cause I'm such a proper grime kid; I know everyone's bars, I know all their lyrics, that's why it's so mad to be around them. I've always had a love for grime. I started off doing grime with #WickedSkengman but when you watch the first one I think it's evident that I was doing it just to freestyle; let me freestyle over a grime beat quickly. That was just 'cause of my love for it, 'cause I was rapping, but I wanted to do grime, I couldn't neglect it. So I did 'Part 1', then 'Part 2' and '3' and I realised then that I loved it and I couldn't stay away from it. When you're a grime kid you're a grime kid.

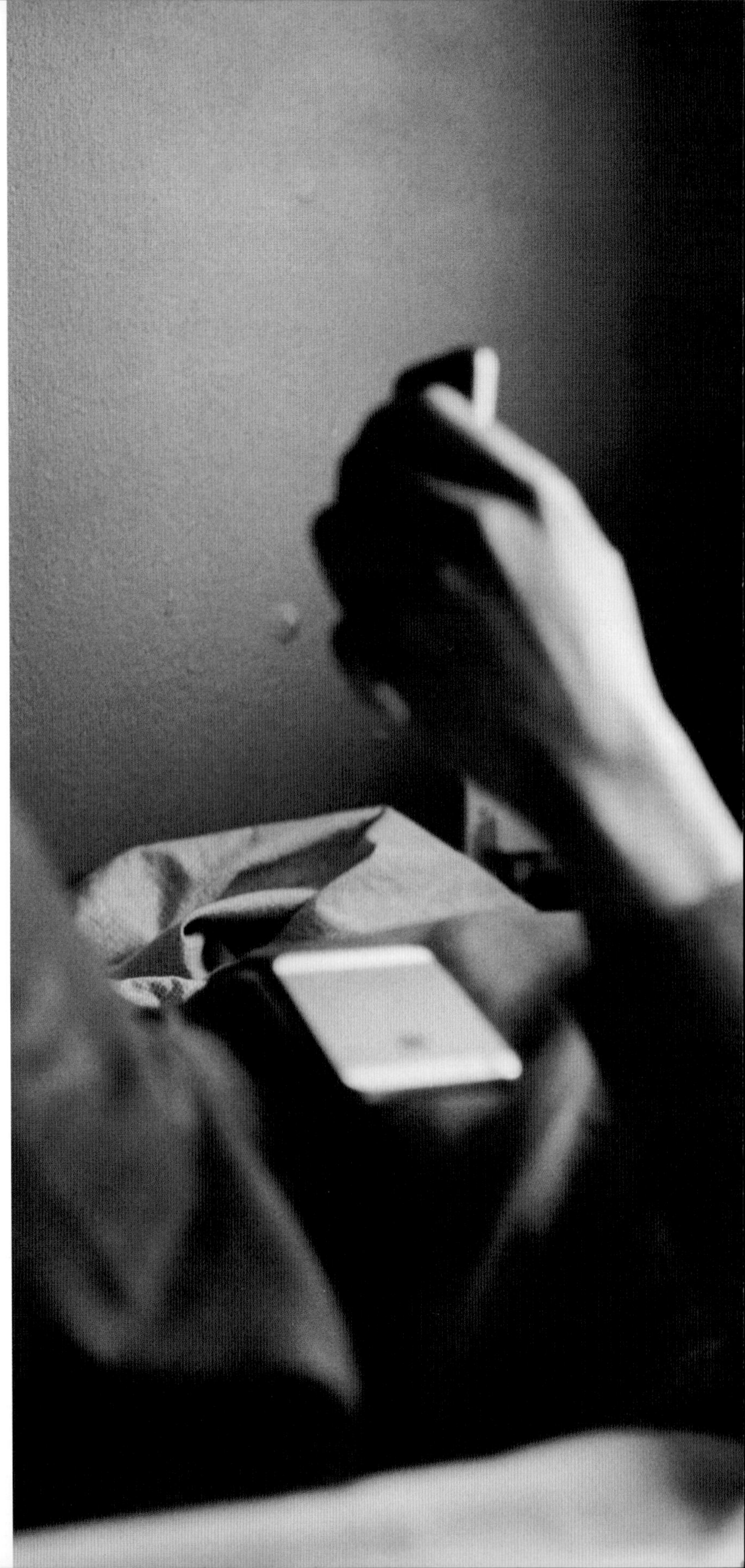

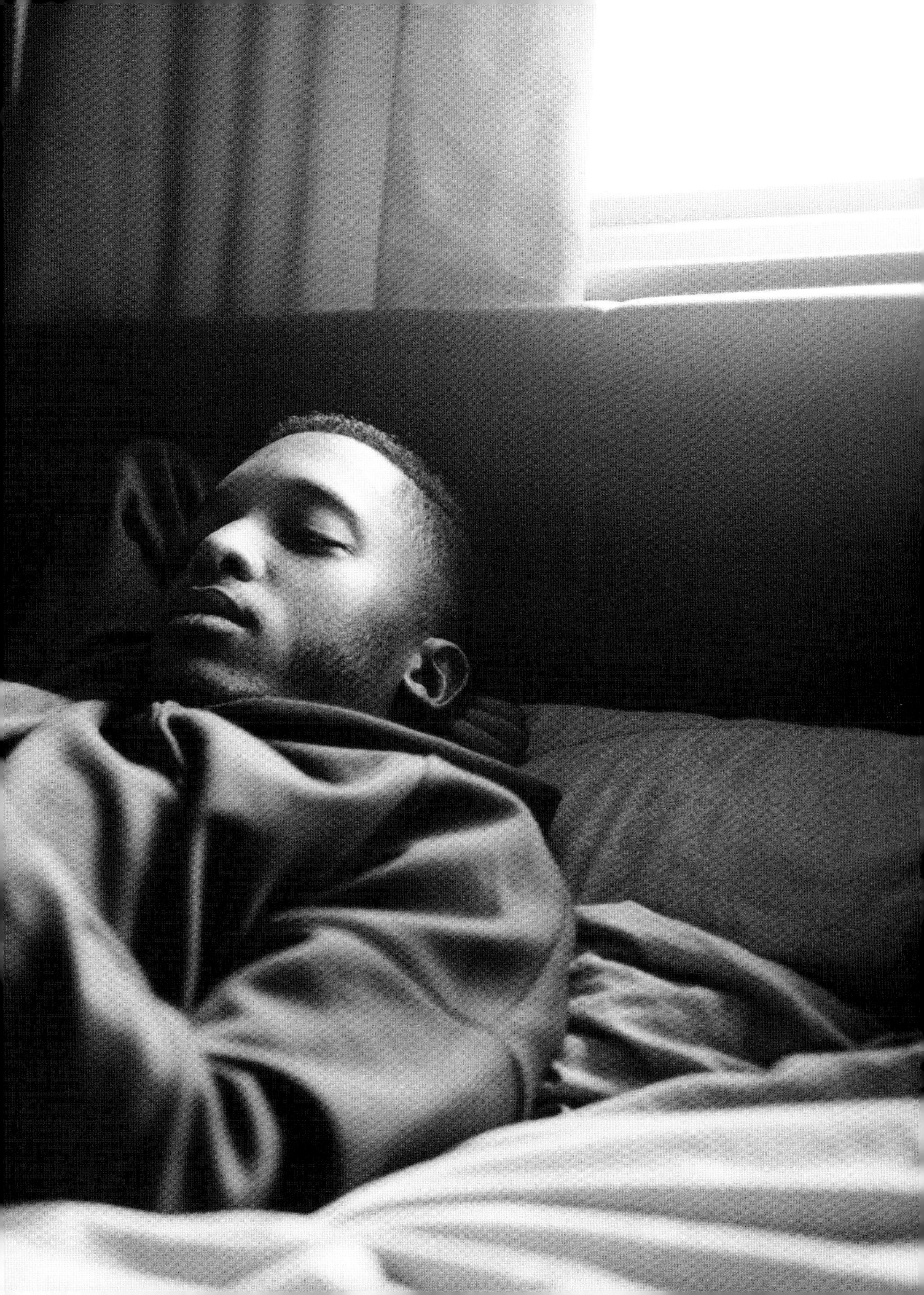

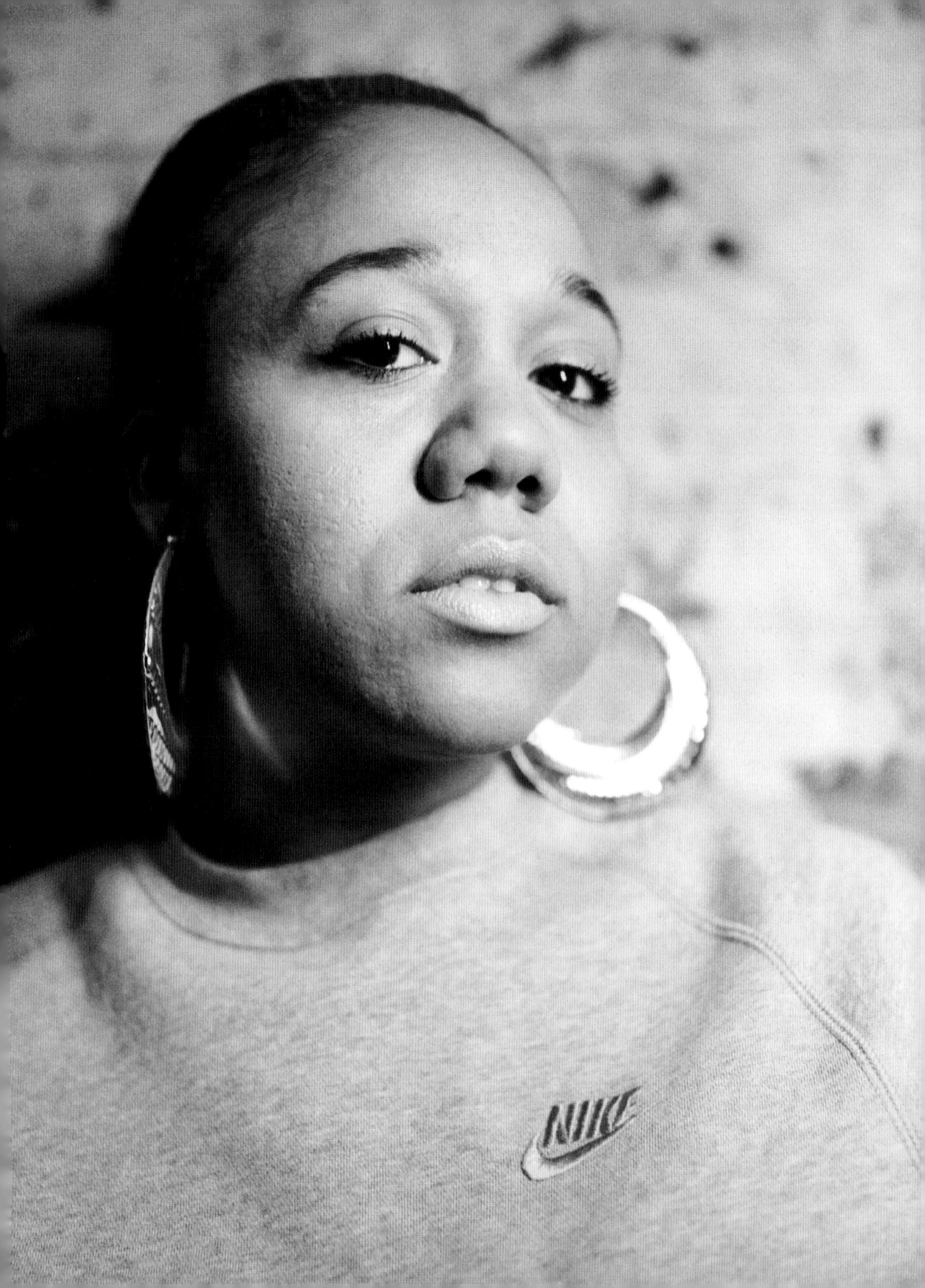
NIKE

Lioness, NoLay, Ny & Shystie on Inequality

Shystie Sometimes it can be disheartening; you want to get to this place in grime and sometimes it might take a bit longer just because you're a woman, that's why there's so few of us. Some women might think, 'It's not for me right now, I'll come back to it.' I've been there before. There's been times where it's been mad for me and I've wanted to give up. But I keep going. With guys, they just seem to crack on.

Lioness You need to have a thick skin in grime. As a girl, you're put in boxes like, 'Yeah, you're good for a girl,' or, 'Girls do this over here and the boys will be over there.' Over time now, we've started to come on the same level.

Ny Other genres of music, there isn't as much as a divide. Reggae, soul, both have prominent female and male performers, but in grime, why is that OK? Why is that allowed? I remember hearing Wiley beats on his laptop and thinking, 'I want to write to that.' I would write for hours, go studio and people would say I couldn't sing on grime. For me, that was the impetus to do it! I'm gonna be the first one to do it and I don't care if it's all guys. Watch me! That gave me that energy even more, people telling me I couldn't sing on grime. Being the first girl to sing on grime was a huge thing for me but also being able to talk about things that I wouldn't normally have been able to talk about in my life. On *Split Endz Volume 1* I talked about writing a suicide note, and the pen talking me down from that place. I had my mum on there doing skits, my aunty; it bought my whole family into my world at a time when I felt quite isolated.

NoLay You always have to fight your way to get what you deserve. There's bare guys who ain't as good as us, but they get more recognition for the fact they're male in a male-dominated scene. One thing I'd like to clear up is that people try to paint me as an unsociable person. I'm not unsociable. I have no problem with any females in the scene. What I don't like is this; say 'Pow!' just as an example, no thing to Lethal B. But they'll contact me and say, 'Will you do the female version?' Well, no, I won't. Not because I don't want to go on the tune with girls – if you do a 'Pow!' and put all the girls on it with the males, then I'll do the tune innit. But don't keep doing this male/female thing. Why does there has to be a female version? Subconsciously, you're trying to say we're not as good as you, that's how I see it. That's why I won't do it. It's not 'cause I don't want to work with females, I am a female, I'm all about empowering women, I like to see strong women, but I have a problem with the males trying to be smart and using it as an excuse. You don't want me to get on the tune 'cause you know I'm gonna burn you. Let's be truthful.

Ny We're the foundation in a sense. Although people say it's a man's world and the genre is male-dominated, the women are always there. They might not get the same love and recognition, but they're there. You check the Sidewinders, the Rinses, the Deja Vus… we might not have got the biggest cheer, but we're there.

Shystie In America, you don't hear them say, 'Nicki Minaj is great for a female rapper'. She's up there on the same level with Drake, Kanye, Wayne, everyone. It's never a problem, it's never a separation.

NoLay I think it's an insecurity thing. In America they care about money and they know what sells. Here, I don't think they have a business mind as far as I'm concerned. You should know that women are going to sell your products and we don't even have to be in skimpy clothes. Women sell. Beauty sells. Who do they use to sell products? Women. That's why men like having women in their videos, because it sells their product. It all boils down to an insecurity inside men. That's why you don't want to get on the track with females, otherwise you'd be all for it. I've never heard a tune with three females on it and three man. It's always separate. So it's not that I'm unsociable, people try to twist it that NoLay don't want to work with no girls. I don't like the pigeon hole. Why can't we have quality control? If the girl wants quality control, she's being unsociable, she's got a problem. Because you expect women to naturally be submissive.

Shystie These guys are leading the scene, they have all this exposure, they do all these big tours and they've never – as far as I know – asked a female to go on tour with them. They always bring through the younger guys. You'll never see the Lethals or Kanos take a girl on tour, yet they have a platform they could help us to elevate, but you never ever hear them bringing Nolay on tour or putting female MCs on tunes.

NoLay They're not all like that though. I got called to do an all-female thing on 1Xtra and I said no. Not because it's females, it's the stigma behind why you're asking to do it. You can't keep saying 'Girl power' and keep doing all-girl tunes. Girl power is jumping on a tune with the guys and being just as good, if not better, than them. You can't keep screaming that you want equality and then when they come allow yourselves to be thrown into that pigeon hole. You gotta think smarter than that. I've had to choose my own lane musically 'cause if I didn't choose my own lane they'd just dash me aside. The whole stigma behind the all-female tune is detrimental.

Ny I do feel hurt when I see concerts and tours and think, 'Oh OK, it's cool for me to be on your mixtapes and albums when you first started out, but I'm not cool for you to call me when you have your deal.'

NoLay I can't say all the guys are like that though 'cause that would be liberties. P Money, for example. I love P Money. There's no insecurities within P Money. Being female don't come into it, you're just a spitter, same as him. Same with CASisDEAd, Devlin, a few others. Sometimes these guys don't even have to say it, I can tell when I walk into the room – whether it's a Radar or whatever – I can tell they're scared. I just want them to be about the lyrics. Some of them need to grow some balls.

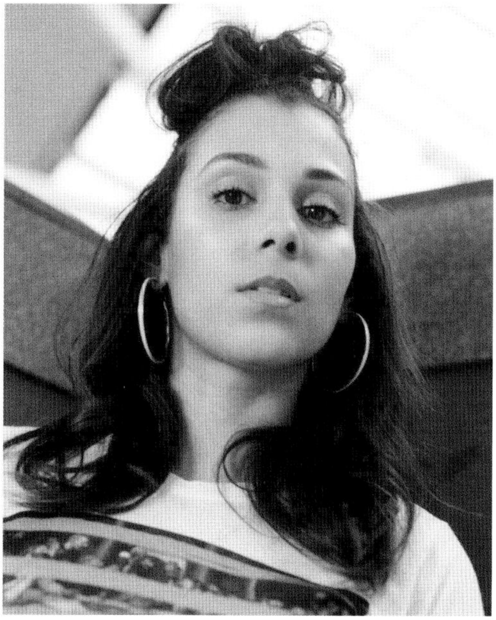

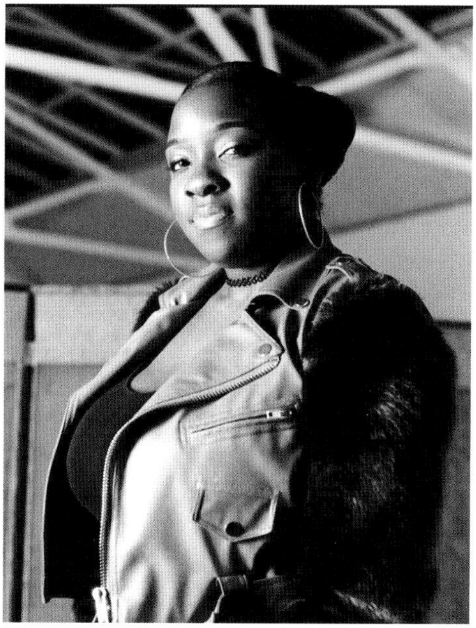

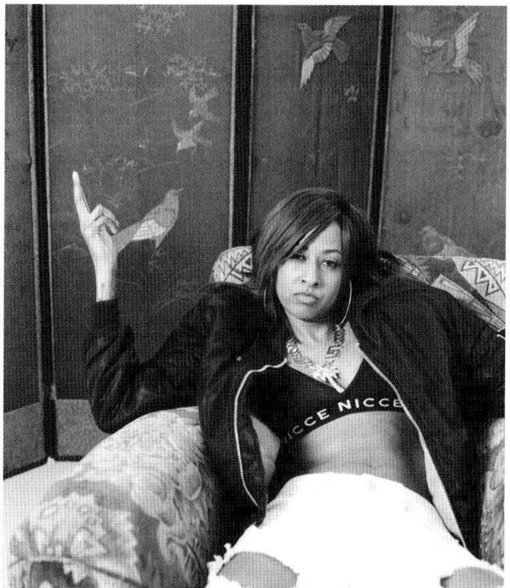

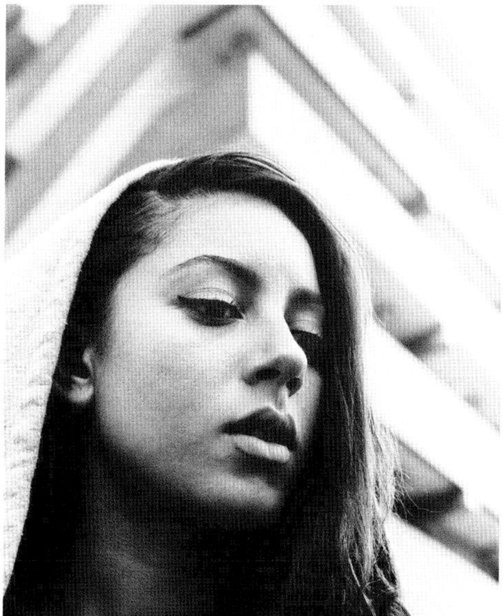

International attention and acclaim thrusts grime onto the global stage

Crazy Titch Why hasn't Drake made a grime track yet? He's BBK, he's bringing Skepta onstage, he's even got a BBK tattoo. So why hasn't Drake made a grime tune yet?

Tinchy Stryder What's cool about it is that it doesn't feel like Skepta is trying to reach out to Drake, it feels like it's the other way round. And now you hear he's signed to BBK, he's part of the team. But he's always repped UK music; Shola Ama, Craig David. Drake gets it and the best thing about it is that it's not forced.

JME Drake understands what it is. People get the Drake thing misconstrued. What it boils down to is, Drake is Canadian, he's the biggest artist popping right now, worldwide. I'm sure when Drake was coming out, he probably thought, 'Rah, man, I want to be big in America,' but he's from Canada. Canadian artists are popping all day in Canada, but they're not popping in America. He wanted to do it and he's done it, he has smashed America. So he looked around, like he does. Remember back in the day, he's referenced Dizzee Rascal, Shola Ama, all these people, so he's looked around, he's found a crew in the UK. He can see Skepta wants to get to where he wants to get to. He can see the similarity between us, Canada and the UK, so yeah, he's 100% repping Boy Better Know, full stop, tattoo, everything,

100%. We've yet to link up on a business level 'cause it's all fresh now, it's organic, so there has never been any meeting held. It's just vibes. I'm sure at some point in the future there will be some kind of organisation behind it and we can actually try and do something, but yeah, until then, it's just vibes.

A$AP Rocky BBK was with the Mob years ago. You know, Skepta was with Yung Lord and little Ian and all of them was always together back in the day. This was when Yams was still alive, you feel me… I feel like everybody seen parallel personality traits; there was a respect and an admiration for both crews, for both cultures. I think Skep's cool man, those guys are family. I can't remember when we first met. From my recollection, we met plenty of times, on plenty of occasions. When I first met them, for me, it wasn't like I was meeting anybody and for them, I don't think it was like they were meeting anybody. It was like meeting a normal person and when you meet a normal person you probably don't recollect. The first time I remember meeting him was probably New York, A-Life. Yams was there and I just remember it feeling normal, you would have thought he was a New York cat 'cause the Mob was already mobbing with him already by then, strong. He was fucking with the Mob before he was fucking with me, personally, so that's why I fuck with him. He legit. The homies say he legit, he legit.

Novelist Why are people thinking about that? Just do grime, innit, what the fuck. Why you caring about where it goes? If it goes to America then cool, do your bookings in America, innit. This is what I'm saying, people are looking at the cheques, they're looking at the shekels and they're looking at the fame. I don't

Drake casually backstage at the Section Boyz gig – Village Underground, Shoreditch, EC2A

8 minutes at Red Bull Studios with A$AP Rocky – London Bridge, SE1

give a fuck if New Yorkers are listening to my music or not. If they do, then respect, love, safe! I don't want people to think I'm anti-USA. I want people to know that it's not about the USA or not – it's about the people doing it and are they getting their just dues. People just need to stop gassing man, that's part of the problem, everyone's gassing man.

J2K People aren't scared to co-sign grime now. Like before – we're not stupid – you'll get these big international artists coming and taking influence from what we do, but shy to kinda back it and be seen to be backing it. They're not shy to do that no more and that's helping us. And it's been deserved because we've been working our arses off for ages, so as long as that keeps happening, and we keep doing our work to keep people wanting to love what we're doing and taking the influence, then I think it's in a good spot.

Joseph 'JP' Patterson We don't need it, but having those big co-signs don't hurt either. We still have work to do over here, because I'm sure there's some people in the Welsh valleys who still don't know who Skepta or Stormzy is. But in the next five-ten years, it'll be a respected genre in the States. Even if the mainstream don't fully understand it, it'll definitely have a place in the market.

Bonkaz If you look at Drake and Kanye, I think it shows that there are two very different co-signs, there are two very different motives. I can't say whether Kanye's motive was good or bad, but it's just two very different co-signs. When Drake was here and we were at the Section show, you can see he's enjoying himself around the man dem. He actually knows all the words to the Section Boyz, he knows who Bonkaz is, who Novelist is, not just who Skepta is. That as a co-sign is much more powerful than what Kanye done.

Kano I never have really cared. I don't want to say I don't care, but it's not a thing for me. Making a song that is important to someone else is more important than any co-sign. I said it in that song: *Jigga said I was the best/ But ni---a act like they ain't hear it…* When you're young, you get gassed over them things, but you can't base your art on pleasing other people or on the basis that it needs a co-sign. Because you have to believe in it yourself, first and foremost.

Matt Mason Grime has completely changed the narrative in the UK. It gave a generation a voice and the country is better off as a result. Grime has got broader and more confident now. When it came out, it was angry and unproven – it wanted to tear everyone's head off. Now the scene is like a heavyweight champ that's been unbeaten for a decade. It's more relaxed. It's become self-referential, developed more of a sense of humour. It feels more open to different styles, more experimental and worldly. But it will still knock you out when it counts. I blast grime constantly driving around LA, where I live now. People give me funny looks. It still sounds really unusual. It's still the future.

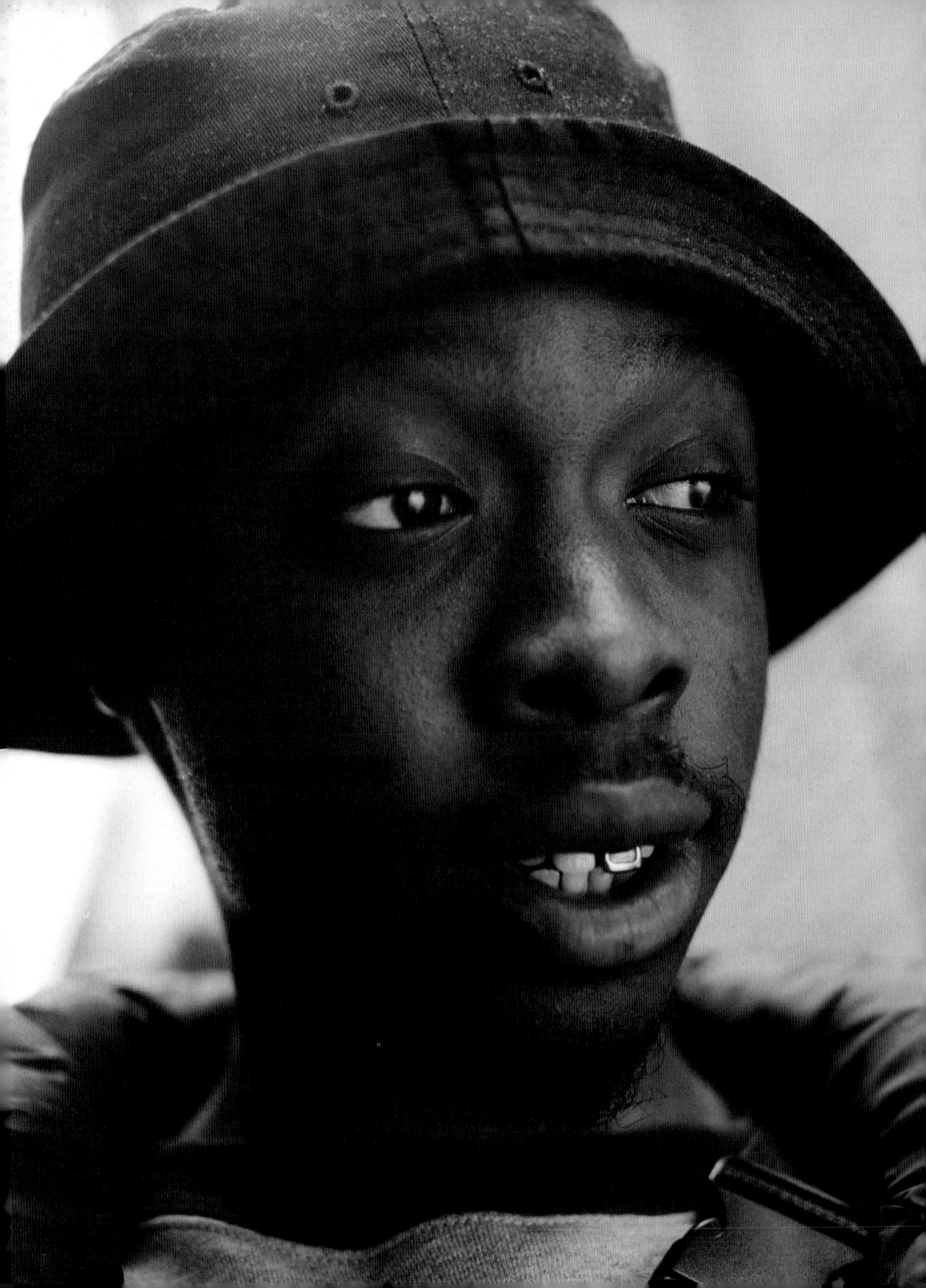

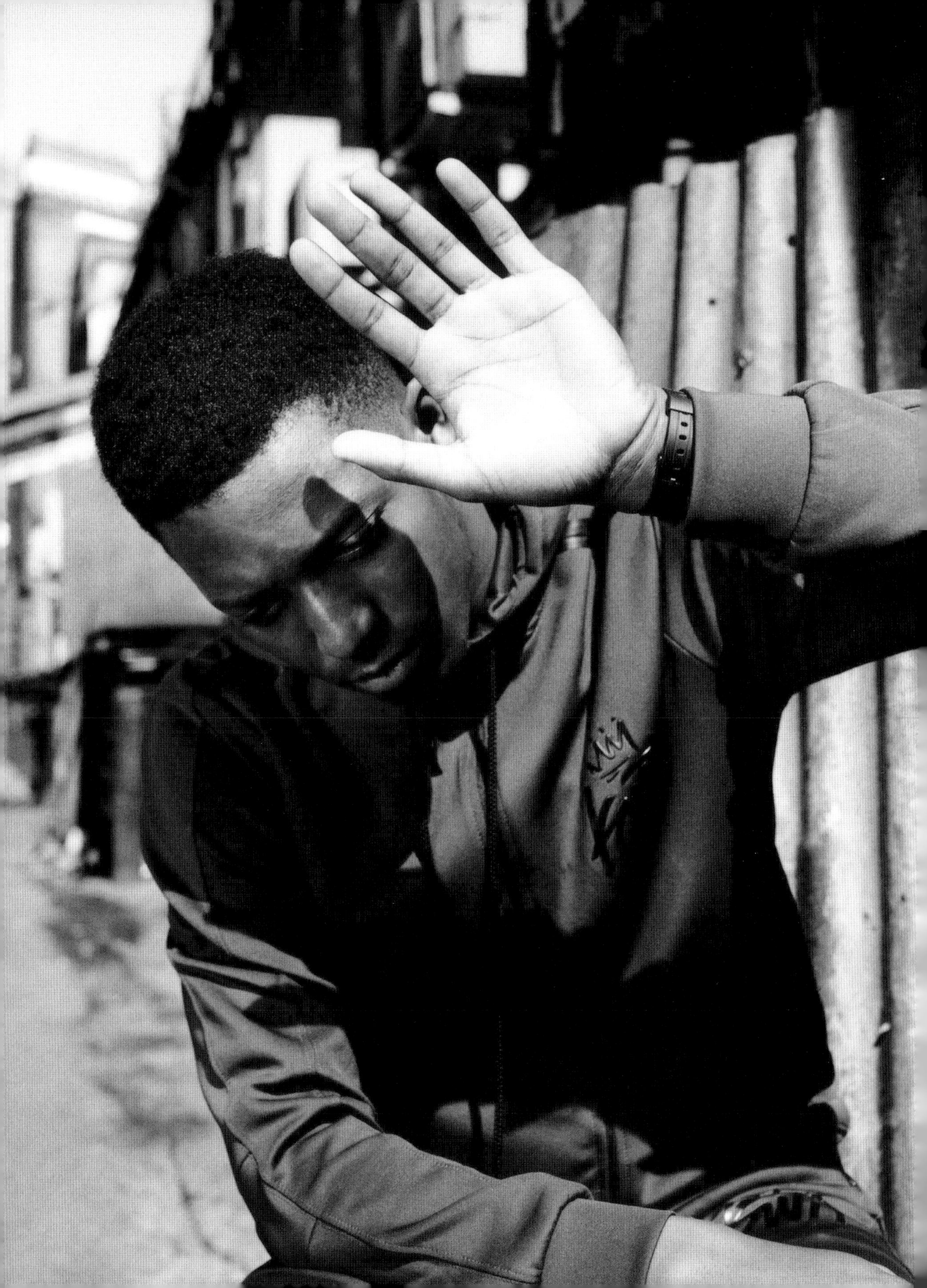

Dear Grime,

Make what you want to make, and don't get lost in the Sauce

x

Opposite: AJ Tracey backstage at Eskimo Dance – o2 Academy, Manchester, M13
Grid L to R: Bugzy Malone, Fusion at Fiddy's, Sir Spyro – Ace Hotel, E1, YGGs

Blakie on Ambition

Blakie My ambition in life, yeah, is to have a qualification, yeah, for flying a airplane. I want to be a pilot. I've wanted to be a pilot since I was four years old. I enjoy planes a lot.

Konkz That's your dream but you haven't done nothing to do it.

Blakie That's the dream. Yeah man, I've had a couple of flying hours, flying lessons.

Konkz So you've started your journey then.

Blakie Yeah, all the time, I'm building up my hours. When I have Ps, that's going to my hours. I just like airplanes. But when I'm doing all these bookings, it's mad how life works. For instance, say what, I can't be a pilot, but I'm doing these shows, I'm doing these bookings, I'm going on planes. It's mad. When I went America the other day, ask Elf Kid, ask the man dem, the best part of the journey for me was the plane. I'm up and they're like, 'Chill, sleep', but I'm telling them bare information. I'd like to fly a plane to Dubai. I've heard it's nice when you jump off the plane in Dubai. 'Fasten your seatbelts'. All of that. Yeah, every second, every day, what I'm doing is building towards that dream.

FAM don't forget who you are !!!
Blakie
01/04/16

Opposite: Blakie wearing Billionaire Boys Club – Dalston, N16
Next page: Blakie and friends with their mopeds at the 'blocks' – Brockley, SE4

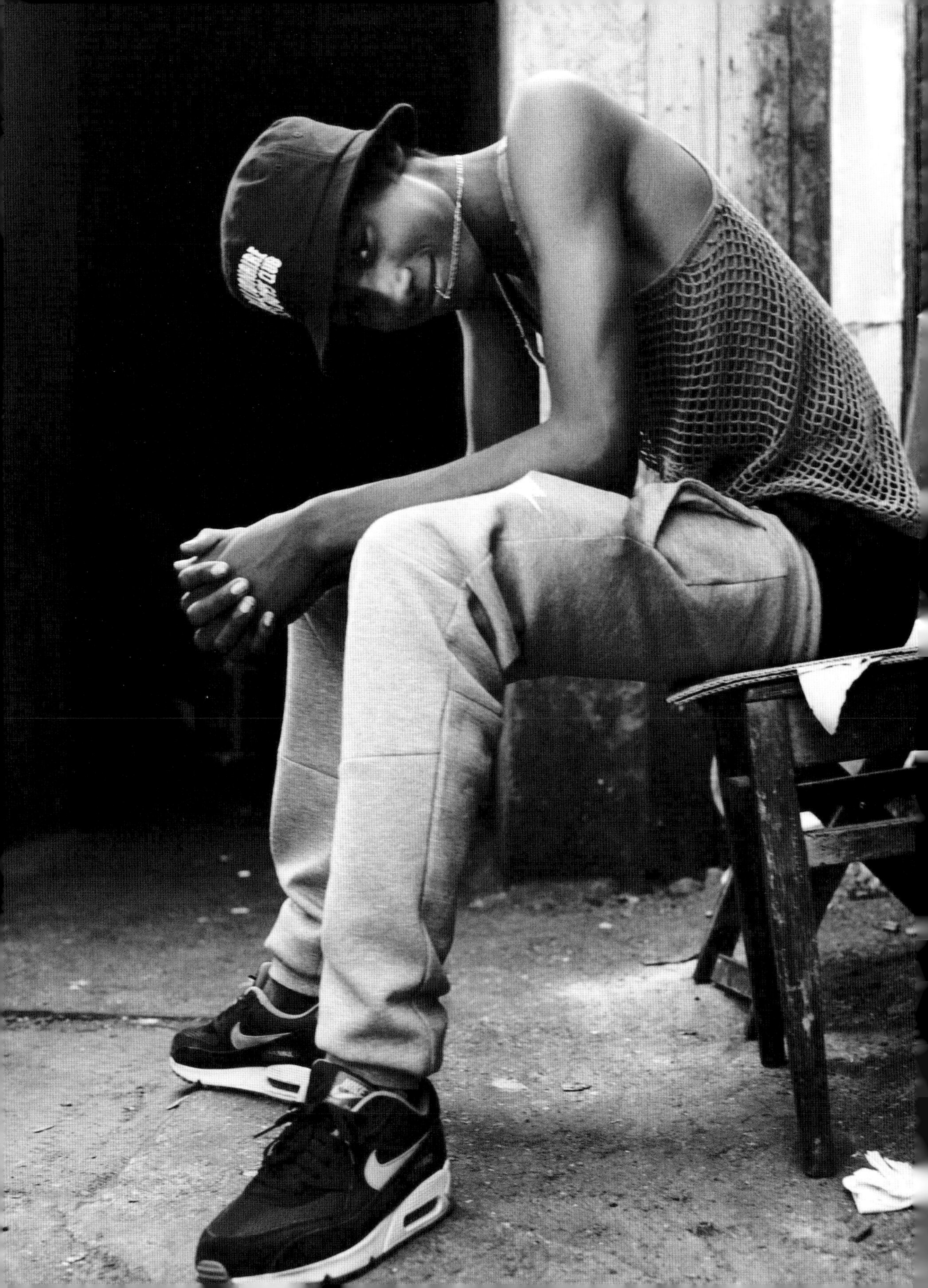

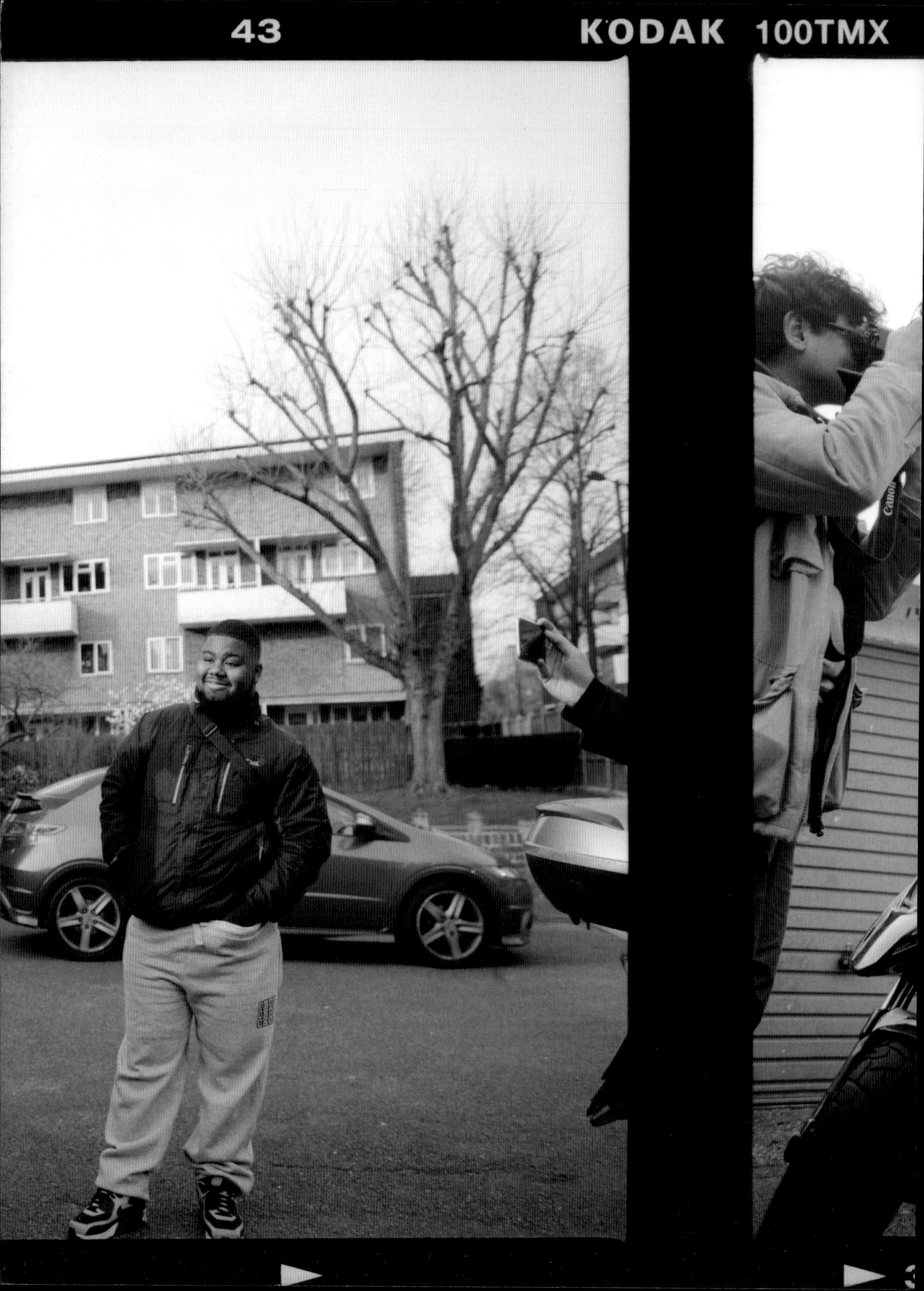
43
KODAK 100TMX

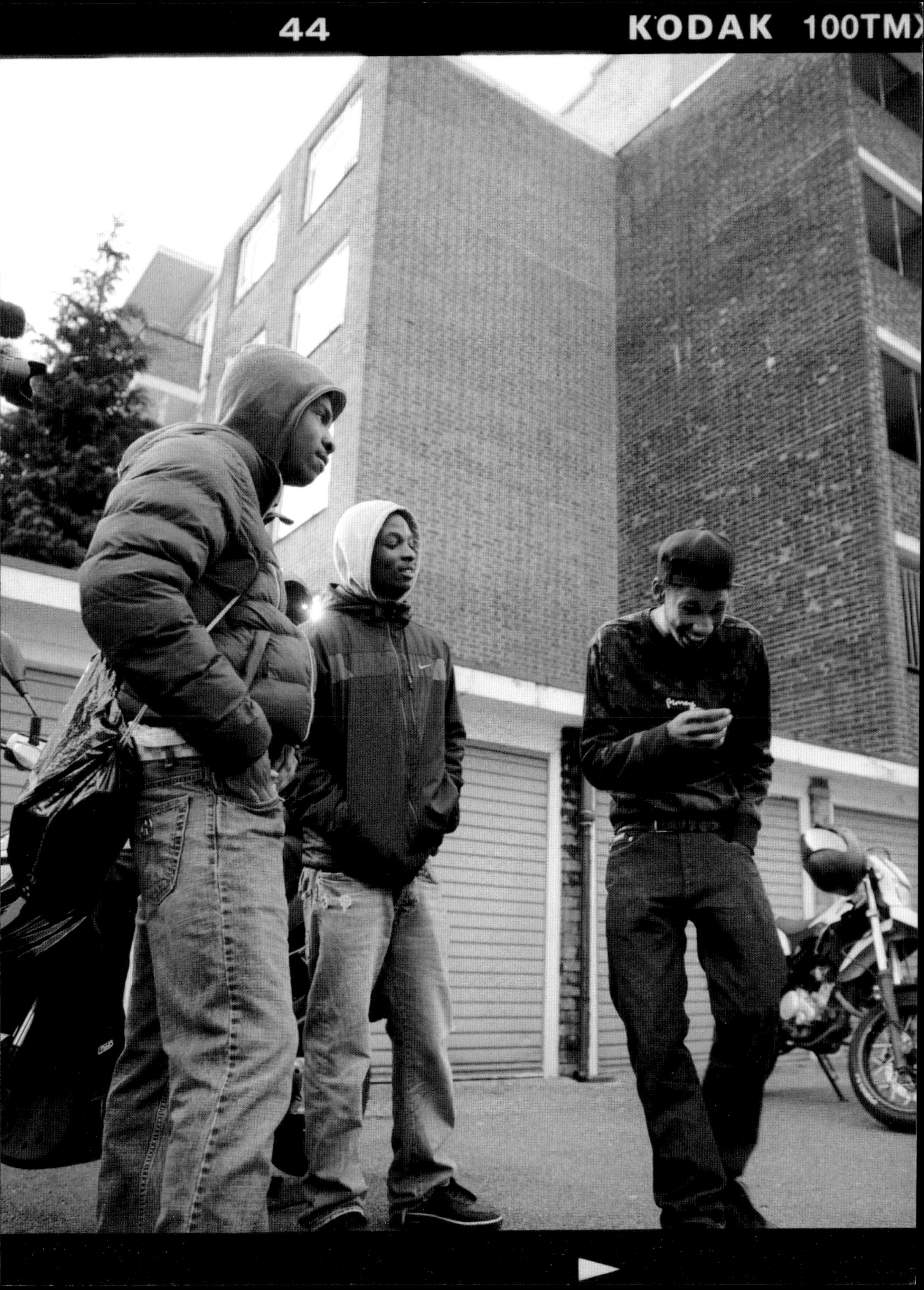
44
KODAK 100TM

Novelist on The Roots

People love to say our culture came from hip-hop but it actually more comes from the Caribbean, ragga scene if anything. You know, actual proper MCing and the only way you can really practise to be like that is on a pirate radio station, because legal radio wants to censor everything so you can't really wile out and just go crazy and do your own thing properly. That's why grime is what it is now. Pirate radio and practising is what made all the MC's how they are, the rhyming schemes and patterns. Because there's rap and there's grime – some people try to rap on grime beats. So what's the difference with someone who's MCing to someone who's rapping? The difference is the approach, the beats and how the beats are played – and pirate is the playground for all of that. It's the playground for understanding.

Man's an MC, man can spit on any tempo, I'm a natural but I'm a natural because I practise. The only way I can flop my bar is if I don't remember a bar, but the actual delivery of it, that all stems from me practising in a way where it's just fluent and that's what pirate radio teaches you to do.

You know what it is? I'm gonna be frank; it's got to a stage where I don't even give a shit to call it grime. I just know the sound so well that I don't even call it grime, because calling it grime, it's gone so many different places that if I speak about 'grime', people are gonna think that I'm talking about what they're talking about. The difference in how I approach something is, I listen to all the sounds in the song, that will let me know what lyric to drop or how to write to a song on a beat to fit to a tempo that works with how I wrote the bar. My thing's more tailored to the actual music. That's what grime is to me. You might even practise the same lyric over different beats and realise that lyric doesn't really sound good on one type of beat. It's like you tailor how you spit to the instrumental. That's not really a thing you do in hip-hop; your lyric's your lyric and again, that goes back to a Caribbean thing. That's when the level of euphoria goes so high that you have to pull it back. Jamaican culture isn't really recognised because people don't like black people as much as they like black culture and if they did, people would be credited for what they do. So, for example, you might see an advert with certain types of music in it, but you won't see a black person in the advert. I'm not really one who has a racial stance on anything, I just know what things are. When you know what things are, you should understand how to manoeuvre and make it work for yourself.

All I done is pirate radio, you get me? I did pirate radio, I really practised, no one was doing it at the time – I don't care what no one says – OK maybe a couple man, but I'm talking my generation, my age, we brought that culture back. I'm talking when I was sixteen, this is before any resurgence. I was really doing it.

Opposite: Novelist chats to an American girl whilst sat on his moped – Brockley, SE4
Next page: Novelist goes for a shape up with friends at Prestige Barbers – Brockley, SE4

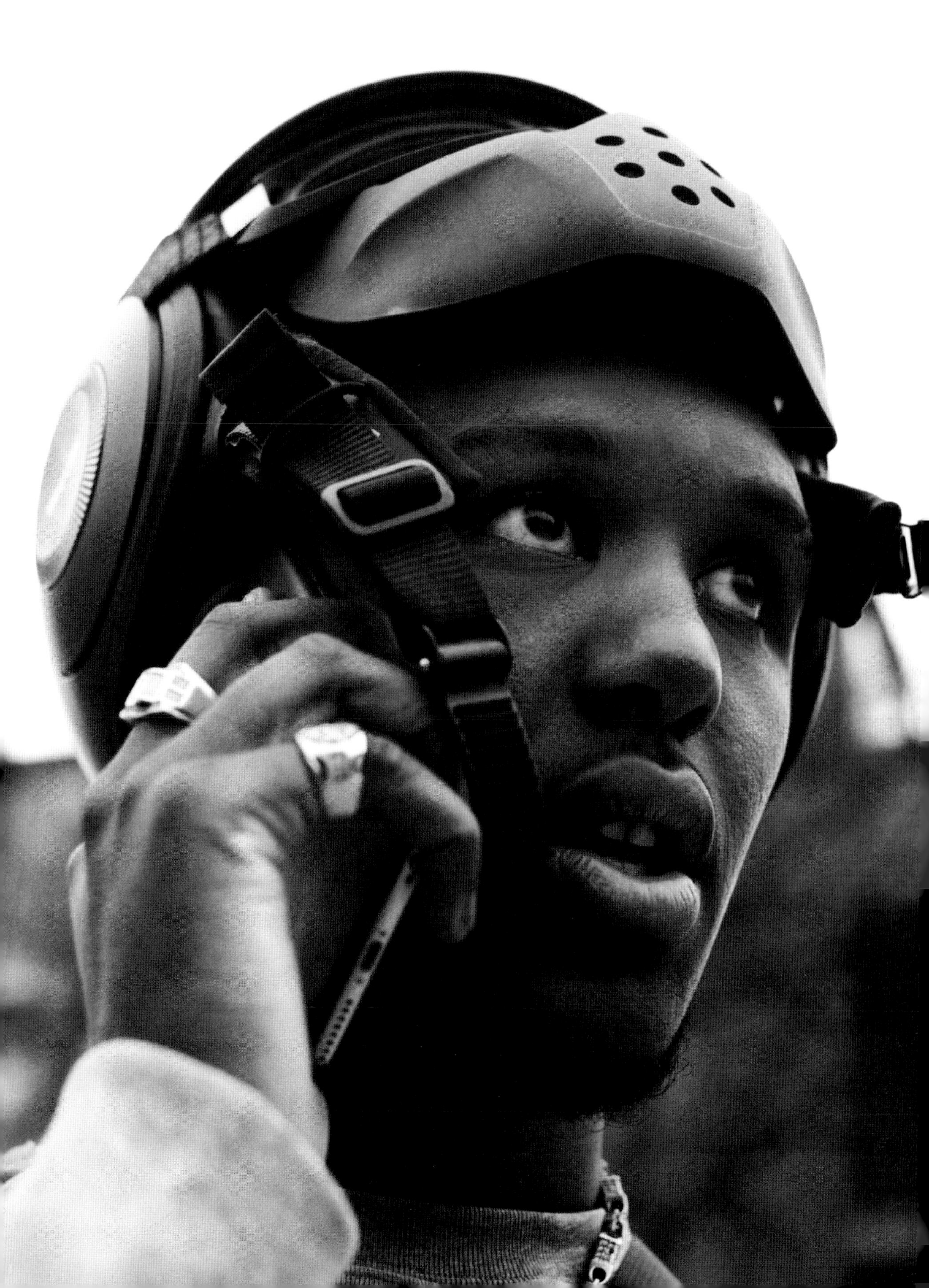

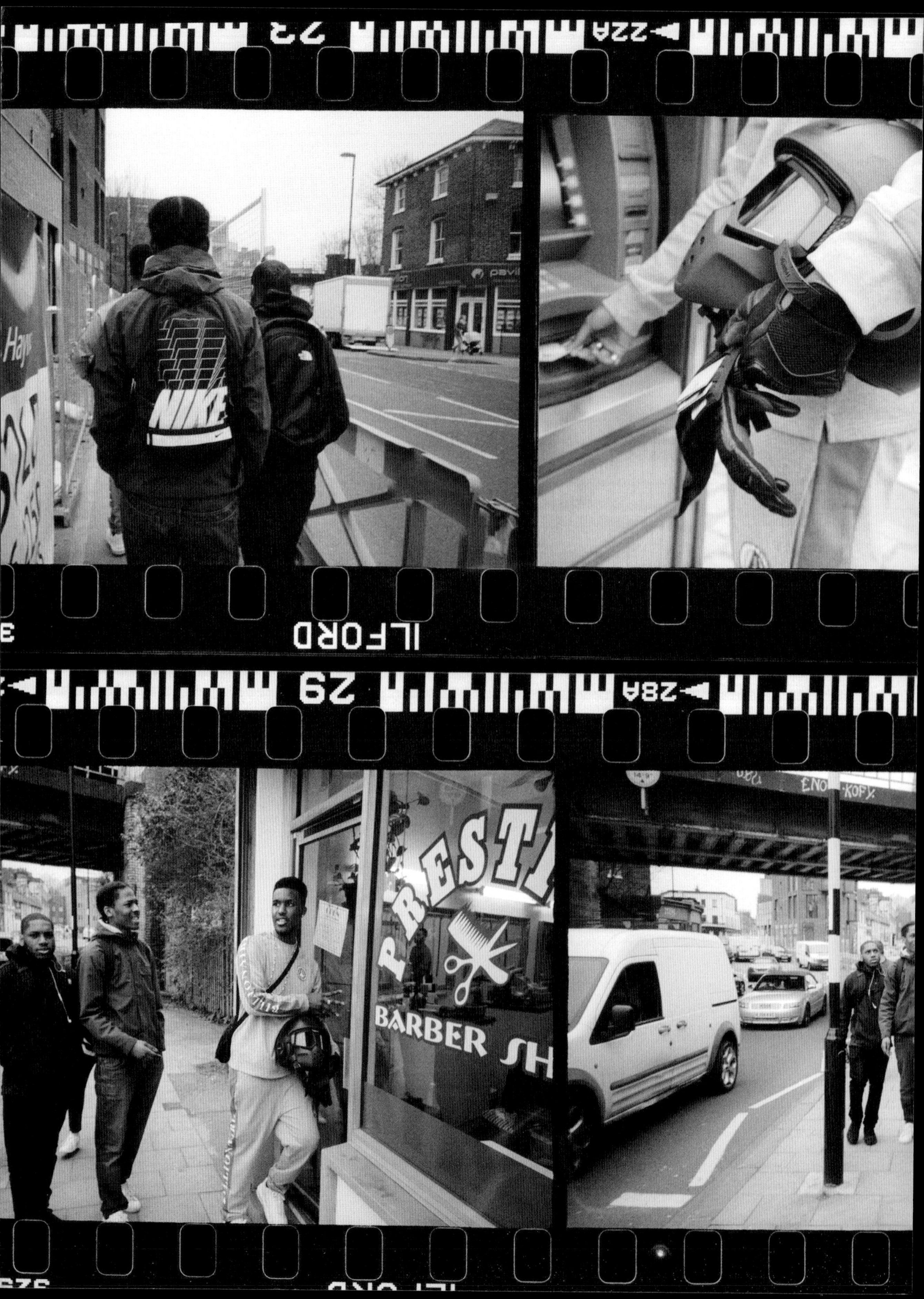

NIKE
ILFORD
29
28A
PRESTI
BARBER SH

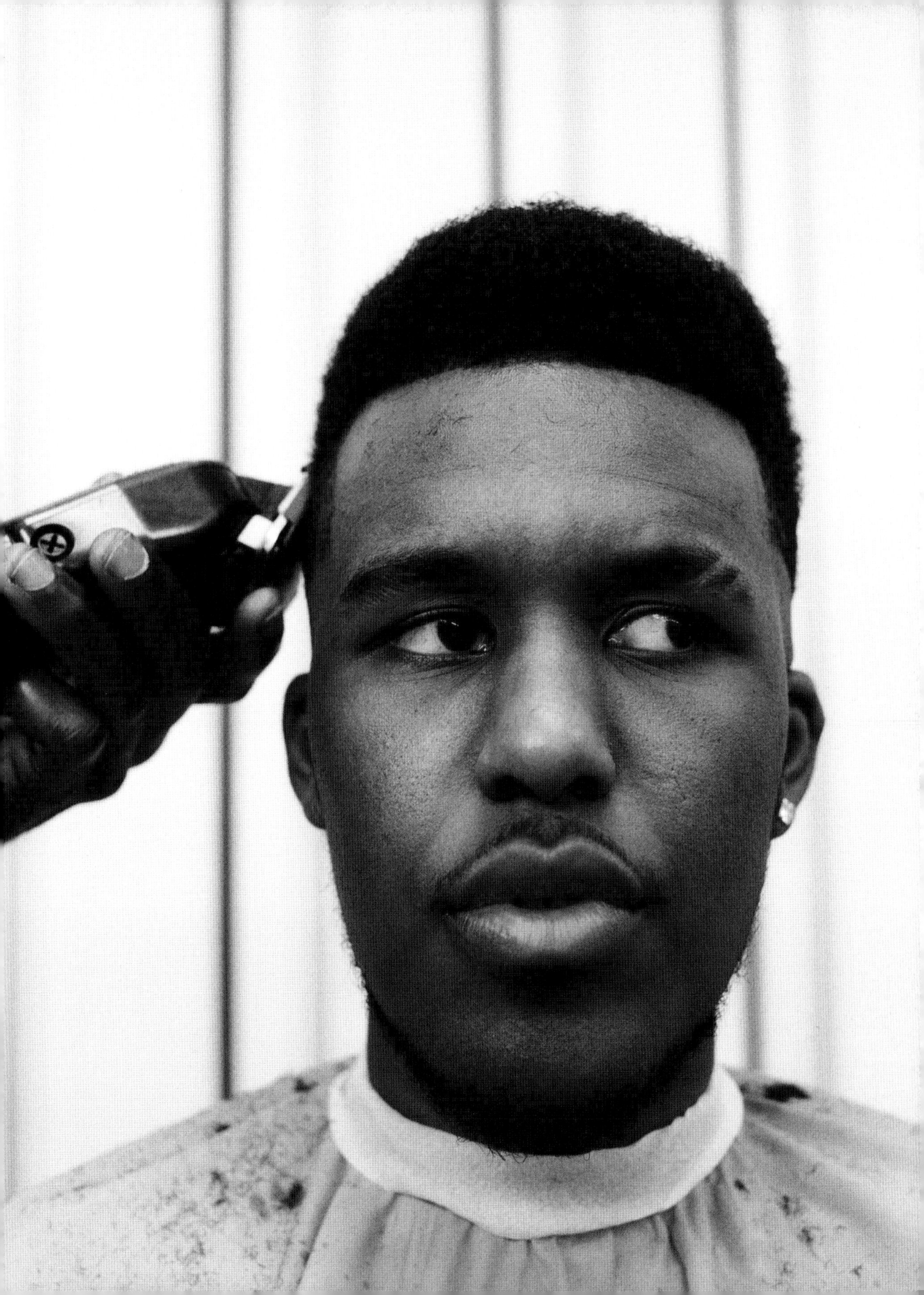

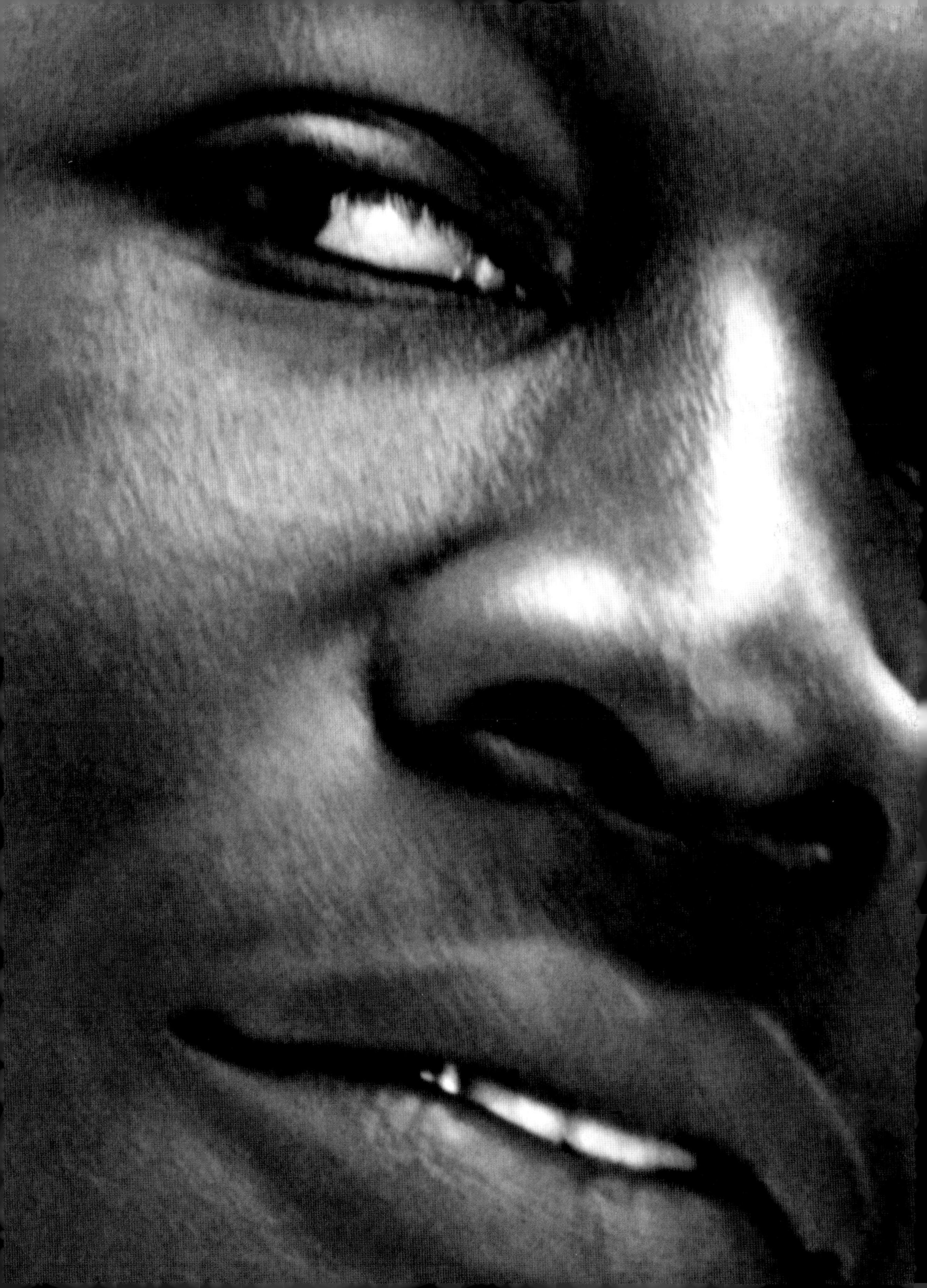

His name is Big Mike, his name is Stiff Chocolate, his name is The Problem...

Crazy Titch Ten years ago me and Wiley used to talk about getting grime in the charts and now ten years later this guy Stormzy has gone and done it with a freestyle. He's just spitting bars on an instrumental and it's in the charts. It's crazy. I was cracking up. I phoned him up laughing. I really can't believe I heard something like that on Radio 1.

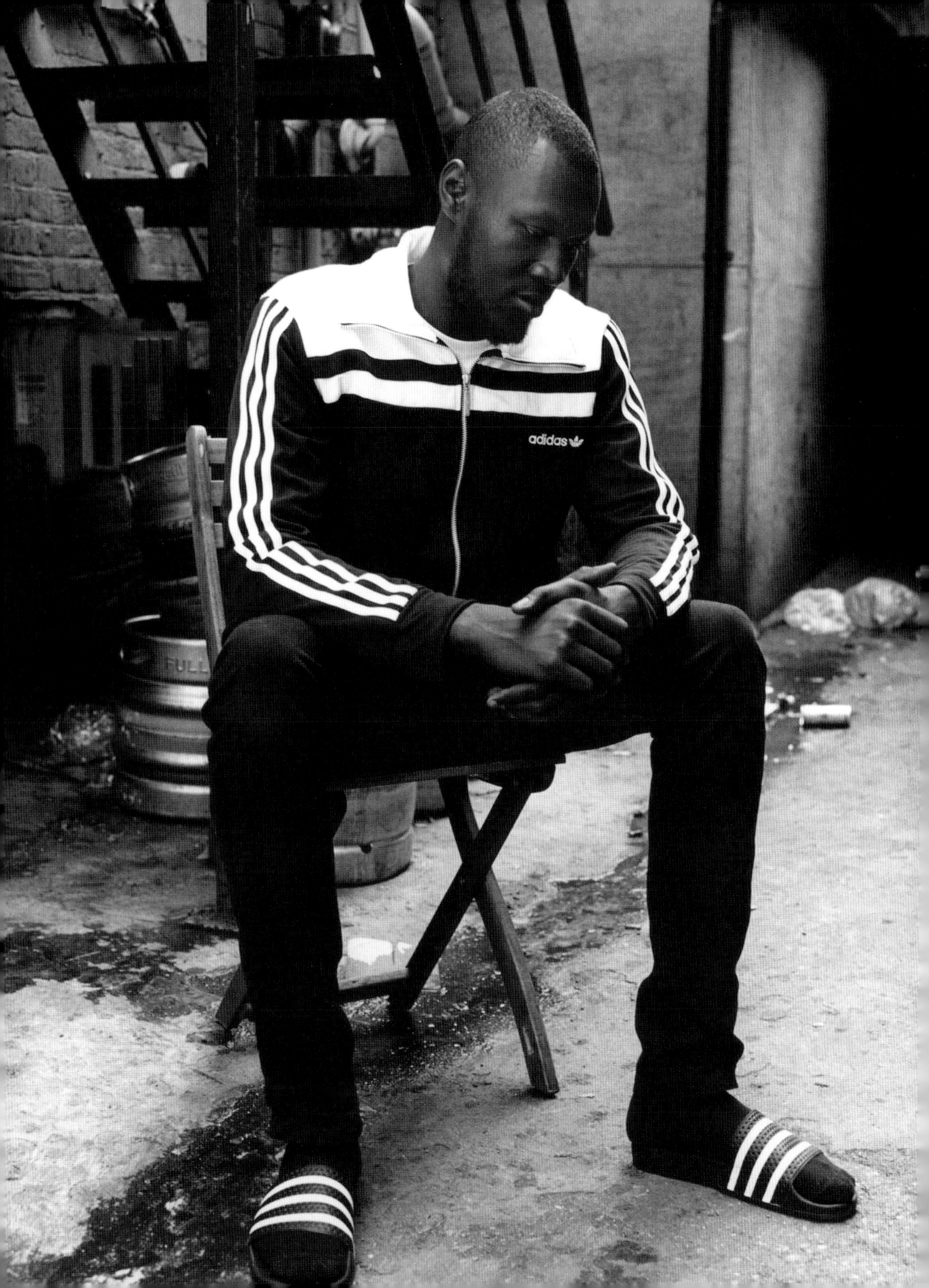
adidas

Bonkaz I'm close with everyone, but I'd say me and Stormzy, we've spent the most time together. He just, like, a weirdo [laughs]. He's always known exactly what he was going to do. It might look effortless and easy, but Stormzy has been planning this carefully, he's worked so hard to make his vision come true.

Tinchy Stryder Stormzy is the man right now. He is killing it and what's so cool about him killing it is that he's killing it with freestyles. He hasn't even got to the song bit yet. He's cool. When he does his thing, everyone knows every single line. In the same way that Skepta's so clear on the mic, so is Stormzy. When someone's doing well you have to applaud. When it's your time, use your time well. And from what I can tell, Stormzy is using it very well.

Crazy Titch Grime is definitely not Section Boyz or Krept and Konan. Grime is Stormzy, Stormzy is grime. I said to him, you're gonna show 'em this grime ting. I can speak to him the way that no-one spoke to me. No-one ever told me it was my time, no one tells you these things. I didn't know.

Miss Abigail Owuo (Stormzy's mum) I call him Stormzy. Sometimes Michael, sometimes Stormzy. Sometimes he phones me and I say, 'Hello Stormzy' and he says, 'Allow it, please mummy [laughs]'.

Stormzy There was a few key moments. I had the #WickedSkengman series and after part 3, Skepta saw it, Wiley, Pro Green, Wretch 32, a lot of the bigger heads. Then there was the MOBOs and then *Jools Holland* was mad. Then the Fire In The Booth cypher was another mad one. It was weird 'cause I had my buzz and then I did the cypher. I was in a room with ten other MCs and I think like people thought, 'OK, he can actually go bar for bar with them.' From there, it's just been mad. So, so mad. I think I came out at the right time, it was the right timing. I didn't plan that obviously, it just happened.

Miss Abigail Owuo I don't see him. If I want to see him, I have to book an appointment! Sometimes I want just for us to have a mother and son talk. Even sometimes when he comes – he loves jollof, 'Stormz I've cooked you jollof,' and he loves okra, so I cook him okra – but now my son doesn't have time to eat it. Because his passion for what he is doing, when he sets his mind on something, he has to do it. I don't distract him at all. I just let him go. I don't worry about him. If I worry, I worry for nothing. With me, all I do is pray for him. I don't have sleepless nights. No, no, no, there's no point. He's caring. He's a good son, oh, my boy is a good son. My son, he's not a bad boy. Right from school, he's top of the class. When I go to all his parent meetings, which I go to, [it's] good comment, good comment, good comment. But yes, then, he's a teenager. When they're out there, you don't know what they're up to. So when they're out, I'll call him and sometimes I said to him, 'When you see a group of children fighting, don't stand there.' I said to him, 'Me, I have eyes all over the place.' Sometimes he'll be standing somewhere and I'll call him and say, 'Move from where you are.' 'Mummy, how do you know…?' 'I told you, I have eyes all over the place.' Oh yes. Yes.

Crazy Titch I heard 'Shut Up' and I was cracking up. I phoned him [Stormzy] up laughing. I really can't believe I heard something like that on Radio 1. I heard that and I thought, 'Fuck that, I want to write a tune.' I put on some instrumentals - I've got some shit old skool instrumentals in here – I said the hook, then I did a 16, then I said the hook, then I said another 16. I had like a 32 in my head, I did another hook and the tune finished. That's after six years of nothing. The last music I wrote was back in 2010.

Miss Abigail Owuo Michael is very intelligent. He is a boy who has always said, 'This is what I want,' and he gets it. Not in a bad way. He was always the leader of his friends. If you follow him, you will fly. And the friends always followed him. By the time they are catching up, he is somewhere else, he is gone.

Stormzy I told her off at the ['Know Me From'] shoot. I had to though man. She kept on getting it wrong. The one that she got right, that was the only time she got it right!

Miss Abigail Owuo You didn't tell me what we were going to do!

Stormzy That's me when I'm in work mode, though.

Miss Abigail Owuo From what I can see today, my son he will go far. He's still so young. I can say when he's thirty, he will be doing so many things, not just music. He went to do an engineering course and he got all distinctions. Yes! All distinctions. Distinction. Distinction, distinction. His sister explained to me he was doing music – I had no clue. No clue! I said, 'This boy, I want this boy to go to Oxford.' He said, 'Mummy, you don't understand what I'm doing!' But then, look, here he is at Oxford! I'm very proud of him. Very proud.

Stormzy I'm just about doing your thing, live and let live. I couldn't care what another MC is saying or doing, I couldn't care about the politics, all that social media stuff, that's all secondary. I'm doing what I'm doing. Go on your journey, I'm trying to make it, and you try and make it as well. I need to make music – I need to be the best and I need to win. For me there's no other option. I've got to make it happen.

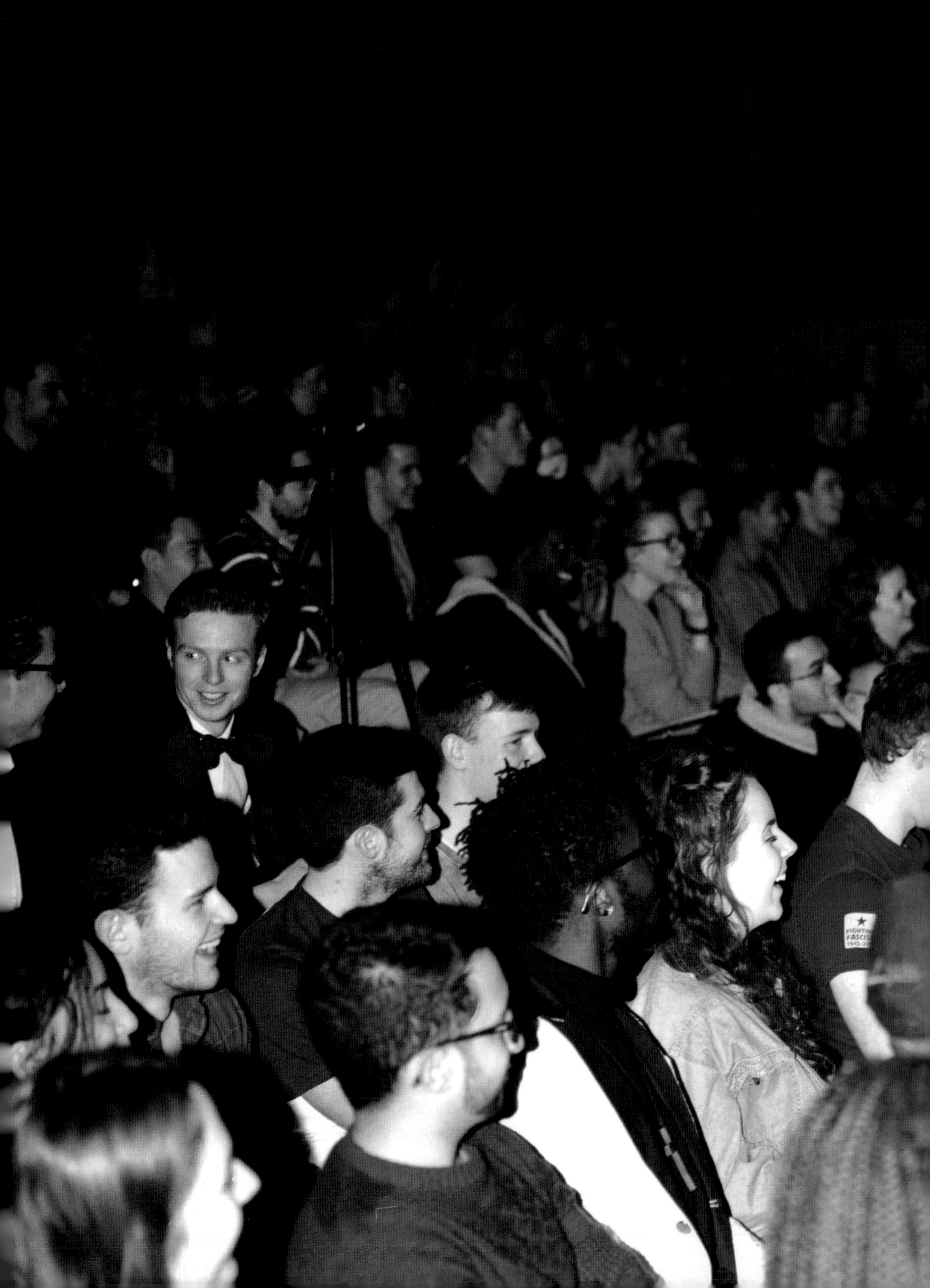

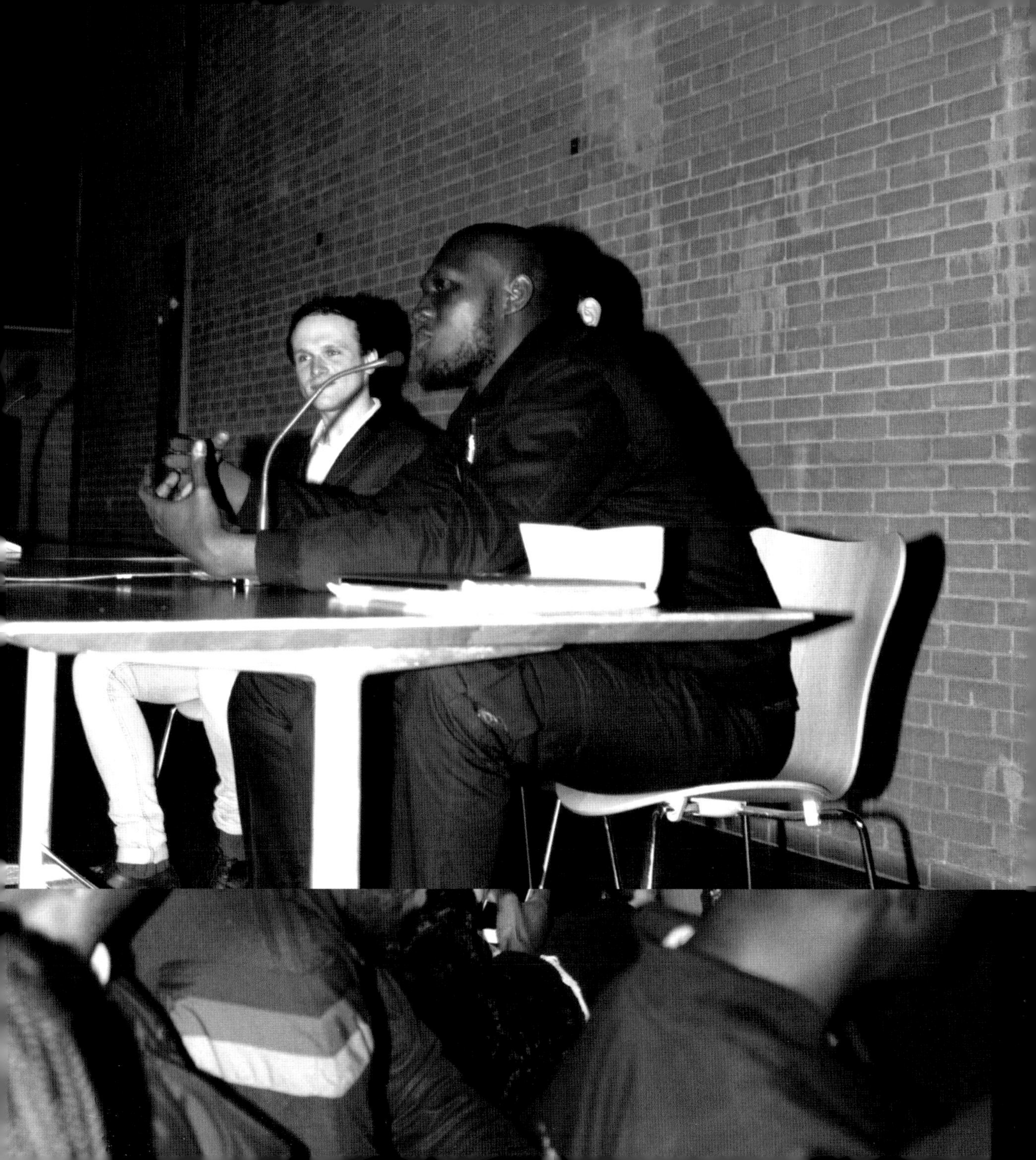

Stormzy on Religion

From young I've been confident in my ability. Growing up, I had an understanding of God. I know a lot of people might not share my views, but this is my views. In term of understanding how God works, that's why I've never, ever, not for one second ever thought this might not work. Never. You hear a lot of musicians who say, 'There was a time when I wanted to quit music.' I've always known God has got me, I'm good, and that's where my confidence comes from. I know I'm here to stay, and that's because I know how God works and I know if I stay close to God, I'm good. No matter what. Even if I decided to quit music today and open a business I know I'm good because of my faith of God. With music, the way that affected my relationship with God and my faith, is a very strange one because with music and the commitment to music and being busy and not even having time to see my mum, that has maybe meant I pray less and I maybe don't speak to God as much as I would like to. But with my journey in music, as much as I've stopped going to church as much, as I've grown I've also realised that it's now more than ever that I need to be closer to God. It's not a case of, 'OK, thanks, I'm good from here.' I know I'm really going to need God now. This is when it gets tough. I'm in that weird limbo stage of what will hopefully be a sky-rocketing career. I understand that I can be gone tomorrow. Not as in dead, but as in my career could be finished. You get so wrapped up in the hype of things, you're on tour, certain tracks are selling this much, the Beats 1 show, this and that achievement, 'Yeah man's a don', but you can be gone just like that. In five years time, you could be like, 'Remember Stormz? Yeah he was alright'. Literally. I understand how fickle things can be and how on point you have to be and so for that reason that's why I'm always like, 'God I need you to hold me down.'

I feel like I've not even got into my stride yet. Sometimes I run before I can walk and God tells me to kick back, he tells me to relax a bit. Sometimes, with, say what happened in Syria, I can use my platform to air my views and be totally uncensored. My heart was in the right place, but my head wasn't. Some people are just here to take care of their family and get out of the ends and that's cool. But for me, because I have my faith in God, that tells me it can't just be the Stormzy show. Anyone that's going to be great in their journey is never going to be just about them. If you look at history, it's people who stand for something that create a legacy. As my platform gets bigger, I'll be in a position where I can make people think; actually, that's fucked up, that's not right. That's what I'm meant to do. Me, Michael, Abigail's son, me with my family and friends, my journey from the get go has always been bigger than myself. I don't want to get too spiritual, but on a destiny one, for me to grow, I have to help other people. And I think that God will help guide me with that.

"Do whatever you like. Do what your heart desires. Don't give a fuck. Don't stress. Make your mum proud, make your friends proud and love unconditionally. And don't give a fuck, again."

STORMZY 7.3.16
#MERKY

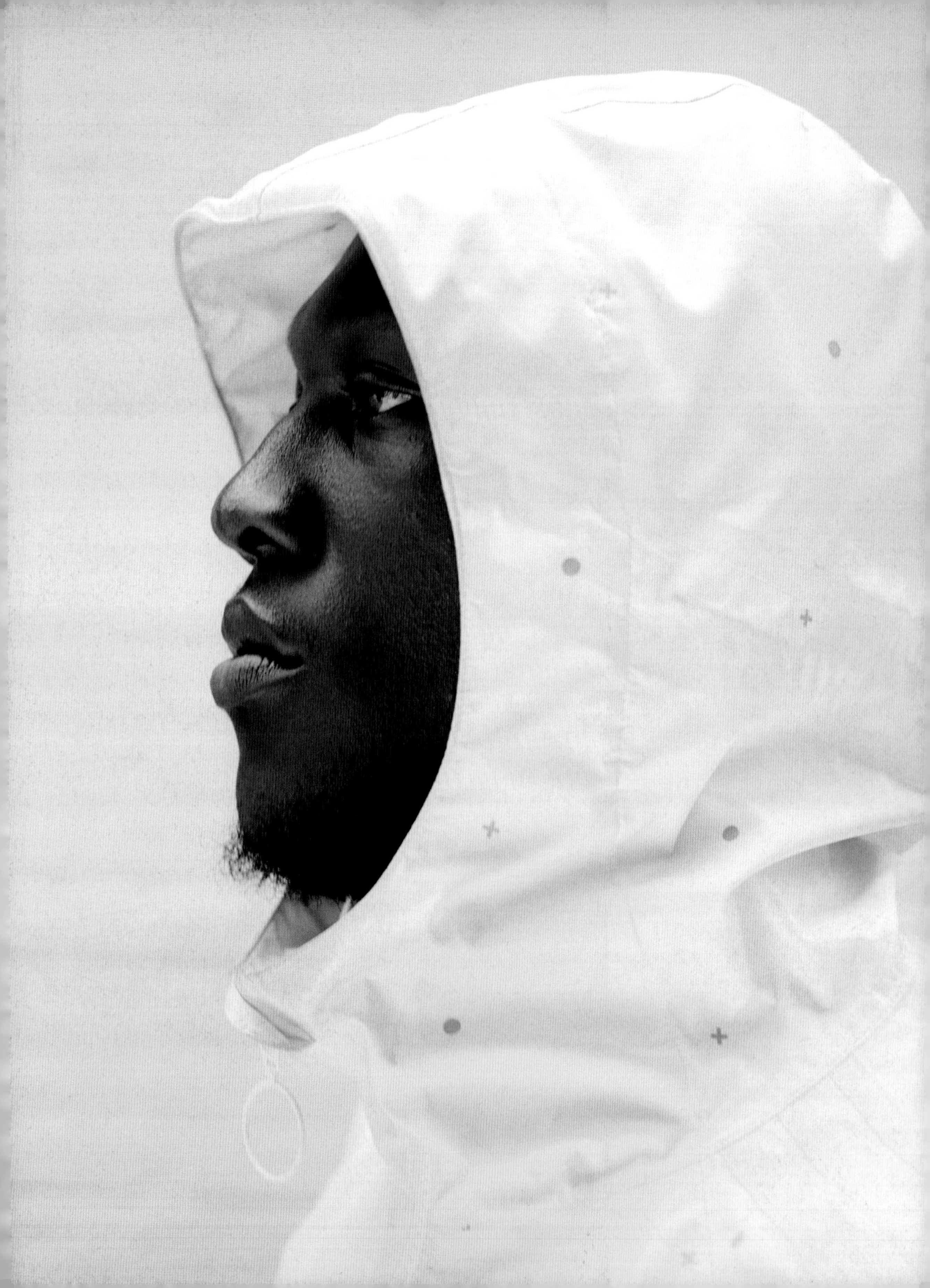

The most important thing is to remain a good person, a good human. Forget music or fame or popularity, just being a good decent human and a polite human is way more important than being the guy. Me being a good brother or a good son or a good friend or a good human means more than being a top MC.
Stormzy

Grime is entering a golden era. Where it will go next is anyone's guess, but it seems certain that the future is so very bright for this scene and its brilliant innovators, creators and music makers...

Elf Kid I think the future of grime for the scene is so amazing right now. People are coming through from my generation. Two years ago, we were dreaming of what we're doing now, dreaming of this. I think there's more of it to come. I definitely know what I'm here to do, I know I'm here to connect with these people. I think keeping things together for my generation, for the next couple of years, is one thing I'm meant to do. Making sure man gets what he deserves, that everything's fair. Making sure that we can do a tour – we can go from that country to that country. All the man dem are headlining and making Ps. I'm here, I'm staying. Elf Kid's just going to do what Elf Kid's meant to do.

Danny Weed There's so much I want to tell younger people. I feel like we didn't pay attention enough to people that came after us. When we were doing grime we didn't pay attention to the influence we might have had on the youngers beneath us. So this new generation needs to not forget the next generation.

Ghetts Do you know why grime's alive and always will be? Because the most successful urban artists from this country are from grime. And no one can argue that point with me. As long as that stays the same, then grime will always be alive because we all wave the flag. We all do.

Donaeo I don't know where it's heading to. I know now we're in the future of it. Grime is gonna last forever now. I think artists like Stormzy and Section Boyz have taken the genre further by being a lot more honest in their lyrics, a lot more descriptive than we were. We were descriptive back then, but these kids? They are telling us about their home life with their mothers and fathers. They're explaining how they felt when they've been on road. We were a bit more boisterous, we weren't really showing that vulnerable side. The kids now are turning more to the artist thing and I think that grime is gonna create more artists, which is gonna create more producers – but what I want it to do is to create more business people. Not every artist is Jay Z, most of us are wild. We don't wanna organise stuff, we wanna make music and go to sleep, or make music and eat food. It's becoming a viable business, it's becoming a worldwide business, people are travelling the world from this little country and that needs managing. That needs organisation.

DJ Semtex I think it's still a baby. When you look at hip-hop, its forty years old. It started in 1973, the first track didn't really come out until six years later and the first proper albums didn't start to emerge until like, nine years later. When you look at the impact it's got now, it took twenty years to establish itself really, from 1973 to 1993. Grime is thirteen years old, there's so much to be done, there's so much to be said, there's so many barriers to be kicked down. I don't even think it's gone a hint of where it could go yet. I think it'll be ten times bigger than what it is and it'll do it naturally. I don't think it's down to a label, I don't think it's down to one individual. I just think it's kids having something to say and experimenting. That's it, it's the UK perspective and it's the UK voice and that's something that's always gonna need to be heard.

Mikey J The thing about grime is, we never had a plan, we were just being us and if it's another vehicle for other people to just be them, then I think it's gonna be around forever.

D Double E I've given grime my life. My contribution has been so dedicated. I've given grime my all. And I've still got more to give. It's just me, it's just me. I'm just naturally fire! I've given them fire. I think it's all to do with the faith, why I've always done well. I've always had faith. I've never had a weak spot or anything that's stopping myself to go forward. I've always known what my music is worth and I'm not stopping until it gets shown in the right light. That keeps me driven.

John McDonnell (Prancehall) I don't think it'll ever go as mainstream as the MCs want it to, to be honest. It is a weird music genre, it's hard and it's harsh, it's not really made for the mainstream so I think it'll probably go underground again. I can't even see Skepta having that massive a career, to be honest; the mainstream isn't ready. I think it's just too fast, too aggressive. He needs to move over to hip-hop if he wants to make money. It's great that Drake's collaborating with him, he'll do well that way, but I don't think he can lift the whole scene into the mainstream. That's the thing, the kids don't want it to change, they listen to it now and don't care about it going into the mainstream. They like it for what it is and if it changes, they'll kill it.

Joseph 'JP' Patterson It's a lot less rough around the edges now – which is both good and bad. Good, because it's less threatening to the people who actually spend money on the music. Bad, because some of that gullyness is missing and that's what attracted us old folk to the scene in the first place. But I've got faith in the new talent like AJ Tracey, Novelist, Big Zuu, Rocks FOE and others to rep that dirt and keep it raw and authentic like how we've always known it to be. Grime is a culture, so it can never die. It's the way we walk, the way we talk, the way we dress; it's deeper than beats at 140.

Terror Danjah When we first come into this we didn't know nothing so we had to have our tumbles and knocks. We've learnt over the years though and in another couple we'll be in an even position. We probably won't be billionaires but we'll be comfortable. We're already powerful in our own right. I've never felt so powerful and comfortable and not in a bad way, because five years ago I didn't feel like this. There wasn't nothing for grime five years ago. The only thing I did five years ago was roll with Elijah and we do the Butterz and Hardrive thing. Everyone called us weird, now look. It's evolving, so don't be a dinosaur, don't be in the cage. Move with the chaos.

Ghetts Grime was a saviour, man, for the fucking kids of the UK. I don't know what I'd fucking do, the thought of what I'd do is frightening. You know what I need to get across clearly? You know what people do? They use success as a perspective. People think 'cause this guy is *there*, we all wannabe that guy. In the natural, human, brain they just think we all want to be a pop star but they don't know most of us count our blessings that we're able to keep the lights on. Man might not have a fucking Ferrari or a mansion, but I've never worked a day in my life. If I only took home £3500 a month, doing what I love, I'm alright fam. I never want to come across like I'm not humble. I don't mind people thinking I'm cocky on the mic, that's cool, I'm meant to be that way 'cause I think I'm whatever on the mic, but not in life with material things. I'd never want to come across like that.

Wiley The future of grime is gonna be sick. It's gonna be all them man; Stormzy, Chip, Elf... The kids who embrace it and love it, they'll go forwards. I'd love to go in there and fuck with them, I'll work with them all day, but I can't be battling no more. Nah, nah, nah. There's things I have to do. I have to be an adult. I'm thirty-seven, I can't be forty years old talking about 'suck ya mudda.' I wish I could, but I've got to be positive. I wish I could chat shit though, I wish I could. But I can't. I think when you're older and the youngers are in here, you have to be as positive as you can and you have to embrace them. 'Cause when I was twenty or twenty-one, it was all about us – Wiley, Slimzee and Dizzee. Grime is a youthful thing. It is. One day I saw KRS-1 trying to war with Nelly. I said, 'Never do that Wiley, don't ever do that.'

Novelist Grime is an unorthodox, rebellious sound that represents madness from the hood, the street. It's like the prototype sound. We've got so many different sounds now. People have their own definitions, so I don't even really wanna define it, but what I do, it *feels* like grime. You see the genre, yeah, people need to just stop trying to change it or it's gonna hit a brick wall.

Skepta I couldn't stop making music, it would be impossible. If I said to myself, 'I'm going to quit, this is my last album', I'd be lying to myself and everyone else. I love music so much, it doesn't let me sleep at night. Every sound I hear, I think, 'How can I sample that?' Every person I see, I think, 'What story can I tell them about my life?' I want to see myself at forty-five, Jay Z's age, that I still need to be rapping. So rather than go for a quick buck now, and kill myself, I'm going to set myself in stone and be like, 'You know what, Skepta's in his own lane. You don't like it, leave him alone. If you do, come party with him [laughs]'. That's it. That's it.

Kano I like to be optimistic and hopeful for the future of young kids. A lot has changed, especially where I've grown up in East London. It's probably harder in some aspects but hopefully in terms of young creative people, hopefully it becomes easier, the more that we can kick doors and break ground and inspire the next generation. We're already seeing the next generation now that we've inspired. The more and more we see that hopefully we've encouraged people to be creative and live through our mistakes and triumphs. Maybe that will be our legacy. We're seeing a generation now that grew up to us and long may that continue.

Wiley It's in the hands of anyone under the age twenty-one, twenty-two, all them kids, it's in their hands, the future. A grime MC's career is limited to some degree and the reason I say that is because it's about MCs shouting and angry and being in pain. The best grime MCs music comes from where she or he was in the most pain. When you were down, when you never had a fiver, that's where the best work come from. So the more money you get that will change and the older you get you shouldn't be shouting anymore. You grow out of grime MC kid and grow into grime MC man, but a grime MC man shouldn't really be shouting. That's for the kids to do. The grime man should be earning his money, have a couple of properties, drinking a cup of coffee, he should be chilled out by now. What is a grime man, thirty-seven, nearly forty, what is he doing still shouting like a nineteen year old? What are you still angry about? It's like football man, you can't play it forever.